OXFORD STUDIES IN EUROPEAN LAW

Series Editors

PAUL CRAIG
Professor of English Law at St John's College, Oxford

GRÁINNE DE BÚRCA
Professor of Law at the European University Institute, and Florence Ellinwood Allen Professor of Law at New York University

When Deportation Fails

OXFORD STUDIES IN EUROPEAN LAW

Series Editors:
Paul Craig, Professor of English Law at St John's College, Oxford and Gráinne de Búrca, Professor of Law at the European University Institute, and Florence Ellinwood Allen Professor of Law at New York University

The aim of this series is to publish important and original research on EU law. The focus is on scholarly monographs, with a particular emphasis on those which are interdisciplinary in nature. Edited collections of essays will also be included where they are appropriate. The series is wide in scope and aims to cover studies of particular areas of substantive and of institutional law, historical works, theoretical studies, and analyses of current debates, as well as questions of perennial interest such as the relationship between national and EU law and the novel forms of governance emerging in and beyond Europe. The fact that many of the works are interdisciplinary will make the series of interest to all those concerned with the governance and operation of the EU.

OTHER TITLES IN THIS SERIES

Legal Mobilization for Migrant Rights
Opportunities and Barriers at the European Court of Justice
Virginia Passalacqua

Saving the European Union from its Illiberal Member States
András Jakab and Lando Kirchmair

Constitutional Disintegration and Disruption
Withdrawal and Opt-Outs from the European Union
Oliver Garner

Business Freedoms and Fundamental Rights in European Union Law
Niall O'Connor

Compliance with European Consumer Law
The Case of E-Commerce
Felix Pflücke

Legislative Authority and Interpretation in the European Union
Martijn van den Brink

Secession and European Union Law
The Deferential Attitude
Núria González Campañá

Fiscal State Aid Law and Harmful Tax Competition in the European Union
Dimitrios Kyriazis

The Abuse of Constitutional Identity in the European Union
Julian Scholtes

Judging European Democracy
The Role and Legitimacy of National Constitutional Courts in the EU
Nik de Boer

EU Values Before the Court of Justice
Foundations, Potential, Risks
Luke Dimitrios Spieker

Postnational Constitutionalism
Europe and the Time of Law
Paul Linden-Retek

The Legislative Priority Rule and the EU Internal Market for Goods
A Constitutional Approach
Eadaoin Ní Chaoimh

The Jurisprudence of Constitutional Conflict in the European Union
Ana Bobić

Reflexive Governance in EU Equality Law
Emma Lantschner

Enhanced Cooperation and European Tax Law
Caroline Heber

When Deportation Fails

Non-Removable Migrants in the European Union

DIEGO GINÉS MARTÍN
Assistant Professor, Universidad Pontificia Comillas

OXFORD
UNIVERSITY PRESS

OXFORD
UNIVERSITY PRESS

Great Clarendon Street, Oxford, OX2 6DP,
United Kingdom

Oxford University Press is a department of the University of Oxford.
It furthers the University's objective of excellence in research, scholarship,
and education by publishing worldwide. Oxford is a registered trade mark of
Oxford University Press in the UK and in certain other countries.

Published in the United States of America by Oxford University Press
198 Madison Avenue, New York, NY 10016, United States of America.

British Library Cataloguing in Publication Data
Data available

Library of Congress Control Number: 2025937115

ISBN 9780198938972

DOI: 10.1093/9780198941231.001.0001

Printed and bound by
CPI Group (UK) Ltd., Croydon, CR0 4YY

MIX
Paper | Supporting
responsible forestry
FSC® C013604
FSC
www.fsc.org

The manufacturer's authorised representative in the EU for product safety is
Oxford University Press España S.A., Parque Empresarial San Fernando de Henares,
Avenida de Castilla, 2 – 28830 Madrid (www.oup.es/en or product.safety@oup.com).
OUP España S.A. also acts as importer into Spain of products made by the manufacturer.

A mis padres

Series Editors' Preface

This book examines the situation of 'non-removable migrants' in the European Union, in other words those migrants who are not entitled to a residence permit but who are nonetheless not being deported from the EU. The number of individuals in this group is sizeable, according to the author, and their situation challenges the binary of legal/illegal migrants in the EU. Indeed, the book argues that the category of non-removable migrants itself is not unitary, but is stratified by EU law into further layers, depending on what the reason or justification for non-removability is. More generally, the author argues that a closer focus on the people who fall into the non-removability limbo, and the reasons for being in that limbo situation, shines light on the failures of deportation policy across the EU, and in particular on the inadequacies of the EU Return Directive.

Various chapters of the book explore the different laws and pressures which produce the situation of non-deportability (but also not lawful residence), including the conflicting standards of the ECtHR and the CJEU on *non-refoulement*, the EU's own ambivalent stance on social membership for non-EU nationals, and the difficulties in implementing deportation policies in practice.

Having explored the broad category of non-removable migrants, the reasons for the existence of this category and the differentiated kinds of status within it, and the patchwork of existing routes to regularization in different states, the author moves on to consider the normative arguments for regularization. He concludes by reflecting on the practices of classification of migrants and where non-removable migrants fit into this classification, and argues for the EU to adopt a holistic response to irregularity and non-removability.

The book should be of interest to EU migration and asylum lawyers in particular, but also to those interested in the ways in which EU law classifies and stratifies different groups, and manages and controls the movement of migrants.

Paul Craig
Gráinne de Búrca

Preface

This book is the result of many years of research, mostly taking shape in the context of my doctoral thesis. I could say that this journey officially started in September 2018, when I began my PhD at the European University Institute (EUI). However, many of the main ideas that gave birth to this book were conceived at an earlier date. I remember discussing the role of human rights law in limiting states' capacities to deport migrants, even when their stay was unauthorized and hence states were, at least in theory, legally compelled to deport those persons under EU law. These discussions took place in a classroom at Bristol University, on a course on migration law and policy taught by Diego Acosta during my LLM studies in 2016–2017. I soon discovered that, year after year, only a tiny fraction of those irregular migrants ordered to leave the European Union (or, for that matter, most states in the Global North) are actually deported. This meant that the resulting situations of precariousness and non-removability were far from an exception, but a daily reality for countless persons in Europe and beyond. I found something intuitively troubling about the realities of so many people who were unable to return to their countries of origin yet denied a right to belong in the places where they inevitably live. These were, after all, people who were being denied their 'right to have rights', in Hannah Arendt's words. I then spent the summer of 2017 writing my LLM thesis on the issue of non-removable migrants, under the supervision of Katie Bales. This book is the result of my research on this topic from that point until today. Unsurprisingly, it looks little like the LLM thesis I submitted in 2017. It is my hope that this book sheds light on such a pressing and often understudied issue, offering some thoughtful reflections on the mechanisms that too often perpetuate these situations of legal limbo for many persons. These situations are, after all, as much a result of the failure of migration control as they are an expression of it.

Writing this book has been both challenging and rewarding. There are countless people who have directly or indirectly inspired me or who have otherwise helped me navigate this process, and without whom this book would not have come to light. Most of this book was written at the EUI, where my PhD research was funded by the Spanish Ministry of Science, Innovation, and Universities with a *Salvador de Madariaga* grant. I would first like to thank my supervisors Claire Kilpatrick and Andrew Geddes for their support throughout this process, for always giving me (the very much needed) confidence about the importance and originality of the topic, and for encouraging me to apply for its publication as a monograph. I would also like to thank the whole academic community at the EUI, where I presented earlier versions of this work in innumerable conferences, seminars, workshops, working groups, and the like. I would also like to thank all my friends there, whose support in Florence was just as important, if not more.

I must also thank the external members of my thesis defence committee, Diego Acosta and Cathryn Costello, for their invaluable comments on my thesis, which have been crucial in turning my doctoral thesis into this book. In particular, I would like to thank Diego for being a source of inspiration and offering me professional guidance since my LLM studies, and Cathryn for hosting me and engaging with my work at the Hertie School in Berlin in 2021.

This book has been written in many places (mainly Florence, Madrid, Vienna, Berlin, and Maastricht), reflecting the privilege of free movement which is often denied to the persons who are at the heart of this book. I would like to thank all the friends and colleagues I met during my research stays at the EU Agency for Fundamental Rights (FRA) in Vienna and at the Hertie School in Berlin, as well as my colleagues at Utrecht University and now at Comillas University in Madrid. All web links referenced in this monograph were last accessed on 10 February 2025.

I would also like to thank the anonymous reviewers at OUP for their feedback, as well as the editorial team, in particular the acquisitions editor, Peter Daniel; the series editors, Gráinne de Búrca and Paul Craig; and the project editor, Paulina dos Santos Major, for her kindness and patience in the process.

Last, but not least, I would like to thank my family and, in particular, my parents, as well as Margarida, whom I met just when this project was starting.

Diego Ginés Martín
Madrid,
30 January 2025

Contents

Figures

Table of Cases

CJEU CASE LAW

EUROPEAN COURT OF HUMAN RIGHTS

UN HUMAN RIGHTS COMMITTEE

UNCAT

CEDAW

CRC

NATIONAL CASE LAW

Spain

United Kingdom

Table of Legislation

EUROPEAN UNION LAW (*IN REVERSE CHRONOLOGICAL ORDER*)

INTERNATIONAL LAW (*IN REVERSE CHRONOLOGICAL ORDER*)

DOMESTIC LEGISLATION

Denmark

The Netherlands

Spain

Abbreviations

AG	Advocate General
CJEU	Court of Justice of the European Union
CoE	Council of Europe
ECHR	European Convention on Human Rights
ECtHR	European Court of Human Rights
EMN	European Migration Network
ESD	Employers' Sanctions Directive
EU	European Union
EURA	European Union Readmission Agreement
FRA	European Union Agency for Fundamental Rights
GAM	Global Approach to Migration
GAMM	Global Approach to Migration and Mobility
IOM	International Organization for Migration
JWF	Joint Way Forward on migration issues between Afghanistan and the EU
LTR	long-term residence
LTRD	Long-Term Residence Directive
MPF	Migration Partnership Framework
QD	Qualification Directive
QR	Qualification Regulation
RD	Return Directive
SOPs	Standard Operating Procedures
RAMM	Regulation on Asylum and Migration Management
TCN	third-country national
TEU	Treaty on European Union
TFEU	Treaty on the Functioning of the European Union
UNCAT	United Nations Convention Against Torture

PART I
INTRODUCTION

1
Introduction
State Sovereignty, Deportation, and Non-Deportability—The Case of the European Union

What shapes migration policies and their outcomes? Do Western states adopt more open migration policies than they openly strive for? Are states really 'sovereign' to decide who comes and stays within their borders? What makes them fail in relation to their alleged goals on border control and deportation? These questions have been central to migration policy theory for decades.

In the context of the European Union, deportation statistics offer perhaps the finest example of the stark contrast between policy discourses and outcomes.[1] Every year, hundreds of thousands of irregular migrants are ordered to leave the EU,[2] yet only a small fraction of them are deported. Return rates, obtained by comparing the number of third-country nationals (TCNs) ordered to leave and those actually returned, remain strikingly low, in a decreasing trend, and always below 50%—falling as low as 19% in 2023 (see Figure 1.1).[3] A significant number of persons fall through the cracks of domestic and EU law and remain in limbo, unable to return to their countries or access a regular status. Throughout this book, these persons will be referred to as *non-removable migrants*. Indeed, while a refugee,

[1] This book will use terms such as 'deportation', 'expulsion', 'return', or 'removal', which may at times be used interchangeably. They however have slightly different meanings. For example, the term 'return' can have a wider meaning that incorporates all expulsion proceedings since a return decision is issued, whereas 'removal' refers to the precise (and forcible) act of physically expelling someone. Moreover, as opposed to 'deportation', 'return' may include both forced and 'voluntary' (albeit mandatory) returns, as well as truly voluntary returns. Being aware that 'return' (EU law's term for deportation) is a rather euphemistic concept that obscures the forcible and many times violent nature of expulsions, the ubiquity of 'return' in EU law would make it difficult to discuss the EU's return *acquis* without using the term. Still, when discussing expulsions beyond EU law, the term 'deportation' will be generally preferred.

[2] Throughout this book, the terms 'illegal migrant' and 'illegal migration' will be avoided due to their demeaning and stigmatizing character, as well as their association with criminal behaviour. By irregular migrants, I refer to non-nationals who do not fulfil, or no longer fulfil, the conditions of entry, stay, or residence in a given state. Being aware of the limitations of binary understandings of migration statuses (see in particular Chapter 5 of this book), and for the sake of clarity, this book relies on the generic definition of irregular migration afforded by EU law in Directive 2008/115 as those who do not fulfil, or no longer fulfil, domestic conditions of entry, stay, or residence.

[3] Eurostat data on the number of third-country nationals (TCNs) ordered to leave and those returned following an order to leave since 2008 are available at: <https://ec.europa.eu/eurostat/statistics-explained/index.php?title=Returns_of_irregular_migrants_-_quarterly_statistics> (last accessed on 04/03/2025). Return rates are, in fact, substantially lower if compared with the estimated irregular migrant population as a whole.

When Deportation Fails. Diego Ginés Martín, Oxford University Press. © Diego Ginés Martín 2025.
DOI: 10.1093/9780198941231.003.0001

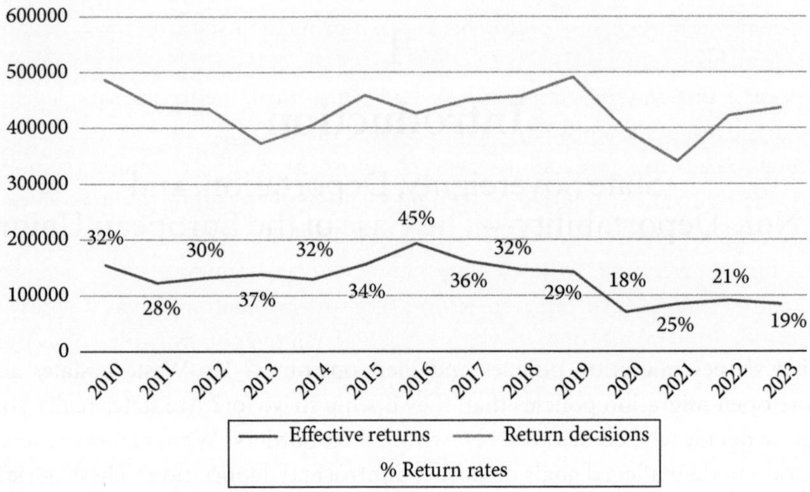

Figure 1.1 Effectiveness of return for EU-27
Source: author's compilation based on Eurostat data.

a long-term resident, or a national of a Member State might be non-deportable, non-removability denotes the concurrence of *both* irregular residence and non-deportability.[4] While this category of persons has also been referred to as 'non-returnable',[5] 'unreturnable',[6] 'unremovable',[7] or 'non-deportable',[8] this book will use the term 'non-removable migrants', as this is also the term more commonly used in EU legal scholarship.[9] This book offers the first comprehensive analysis of this migrant category in Europe, disentangling the mechanisms through which

[4] In contrast, by 'non-removed', I refer to those instances where non-removal ultimately derives from a policy choice of the state, and not from its legal or practical incapacity to do so. While the book focuses mainly on non-removable persons, examples of states' policy choices not to remove will be included sporadically.

[5] Izabella Majcher and Tineke Strik, 'Legislating without Evidence: The Recast of the EU Return Directive' (2021) 23 European Journal of Migration & Law 103.

[6] David James Cantor and others, 'The Emperor's New Clothing: National Responses to "Undesirable and Unreturnable" Aliens under Asylum and Immigration Law' (2017) 36(1) Refugee Survey Quarterly 1.

[7] Jean-Baptiste Farcy, 'Chapter 19. Unremovability under the Return Directive: An Empty Protection?' in Galina Cornelisse and Philippe de Bruycker (eds), *Law and Judicial Dialogue on the Return of Irregular Migrants from the European Union* (Hart 2020).

[8] Sarah Nimführ and Buba Sesay, 'Lost in Limbo? Navigating (Im)Mobilities and Practices of Appropriation of Non-Deportable Refugees in the Mediterranean Area' (2019) 7 Comparative Migration Studies 26; Arjen Leerkes and Marieke Van Houte, 'Beyond the Deportation Regime: Differential State Interests and Capacities in Dealing with (Non-) Deportability in Europe' (2020) 24 Citizenship Studies 319.

[9] Fabian Lutz, 'Non-Removable Returnees under Union Law: Status Quo and Possible Developments' (2018) 20 European Journal of Migration and Law 28; Benedita Menezes Queiroz, 'Non-Removable Migrants in Europe: An Atypical Migration Status?' (2018) 24 European Public Law 29; Katharine T Weatherhead, 'Removing "Non-Removables"' 51 Forced Migration Review 2; Farcy (n 7) 450.

non-removable migrants come to be, and exploring their statuses, rights, and regularization prospects.

Prior to this, the present chapter provides historical, theoretical, and legal context to the rest of the study. It first zooms in on the so-called liberal paradox, which allegedly leads Western democracies to adopt more liberal migration policies than their citizens would seem willing to support.[10] In doing so, it foregrounds the distinction between the *external* and *internal* dimensions of migration control, namely between policies aimed at would-be immigrants (i.e. policies of *non-entrée*) and those directed to the migrant population already within the state—focusing mainly on deportation. Second, it moves on from the policy theory debate to provide an analysis of the EU's legislative and policy framework on return. These foreground the relevance of the topic from the perspective of doctrine, policy, and theory.

1. Setting the scene: State sovereignty, border control, and deportability

The principle of state sovereignty, traditionally understood as the 'supreme' authority within a given territory, stands as the cornerstone of international law, to the extent that the UN System is based on the 'sovereign equality of all its Members'.[11] Responding to the perception that globalization leads to states losing control over a number of policy areas, migration is often projected by governments as the 'last bastion of sovereignty'.[12] Sovereignty, in the field of migration, is widely understood as the prerogative of states to decide who comes and stays within their borders, that is, to exclude and expel non-nationals. While the right to leave one's own country is well established under international law, there is no concomitant right to enter or stay in any specific country, with the exception of one's own country.[13]

In political and legal theory, legitimation for border and migration control has been grounded on popular sovereignty and self-determination. As noted by Benhabib, democratic laws are meant to be binding upon those who have legitimately authorized them, and hence 'require closure precisely because

[10] James Frank Hollifield, Philip L Martin, and Pia M Orrenius, *Controlling Immigration: A Global Perspective* (3rd edn, Stanford University Press 2014); Gary P Freeman, 'Modes of Immigration Politics in Liberal Democratic States' (1995) 29 The International Migration Review 881.

[11] Charter of the United Nations, 24 October 1945, 1 UNTS XVI, art 2(2); Samantha Besson, 'Sovereignty' (April 2011) in Rüdiger Wolfrum (ed), *Max Planck Encyclopedia of Public International Law* (Oxford, online edn).

[12] Catherine Dauvergne, *Making People Illegal: What Globalization Means for Migration and Law* (Cambridge University Press 2008) 2.

[13] International Covenant on Civil and Political Rights, 16 December 1966, 999 UNTS 171 art 12(2).

democratic representation must be accountable to a specific people'.[14] Moreover, the nation-state, or, for the purposes of this book, the European Union,[15] is seen as a territorially and politically bounded community whose right to democratic self-determination includes the right to control the composition of its population.[16] Migration control can thus be seen as *instrumental* to achieve popular sovereignty and self-determination, in what has been labelled as the 'sovereignty nexus'.[17] More broadly, migration control is linked to the notion of sovereignty as the right of states to decide on their internal affairs without external imposition.[18]

But what are the limits of states in defining their rules on entry, stay, and residence, and hence legitimately deciding on the composition of their *demos*? In other words, what are the limits to states' 'supreme' powers of self-governance, both from the perspective of their legitimacy and their capacity? Under modern international law, states are not free to enforce migration control as they please but must keep a balance between territorial sovereignty and international human rights obligations. In 1996, Saskia Sassen famously put forward the claim that states were 'losing control' and that their sovereignty was being transformed in the context of globalization. In the area of migration, the author inquired whether one could still assert that states have exclusive authority over the entry of non-nationals. Answering in the negative, she contended that migration control prerogatives had been altered by globalization as well as by states' participation in human rights regimes, leading to a 'shift to rights of individuals regardless of nationality' and the 'devaluation of citizenship as a condition for access to rights'.[19]

More than twenty-five years have passed since Sassen forecasted the decline of state sovereignty as we knew it, and yet state sovereignty continues reasserting itself *against* human rights, in such a way that the departure from human rights in the name of migration control seems to be on full display now more than ever (see sections 1.1 and 1.2 in this chapter). This reveals not only the failure of legal safeguards and accountability mechanisms, the difficulties that migrants find

[14] Seyla Benhabib, *The Rights of Others: Aliens, Residents and Citizens* (Cambridge University Press 2004) 219.

[15] By introducing the European Union as the unit of analysis of this book, I do not intend to equate the EU to the nation-state (nor to contend that states lose control over migration in favour of the EU). Instead, I merely observe that the abolishing of internal borders means that the logics of migration control are, to a great extent, pushed outwards to the external borders of the EU. As a result, decisions related to the composition of the population of the EU are largely made at the external borders of the Union. Then, the underlying idea is that the dynamics of migration control and enforcement deficits that will be highlighted in this chapter also apply to the EU as a whole.

[16] Linda Bosniak, *The Citizen and the Alien: Dilemmas of Contemporary Membership* (Princeton University Press 2006) 14.

[17] Lukas Schmid, 'Saving Migrants' Basic Human Rights from Sovereign Rule' (2022) 116 American Political Science Review 1.

[18] Jean L Cohen, 'Whose Sovereignty? Empire versus International Law' (2004) 18 Ethics & International Affairs 1.

[19] Saskia Sassen, *Losing Control? Sovereignty in the Age of Globalization* (Columbia University Press 1996) xxv, 64, and 101.

in having access to justice, and the lack of compliance with courts' decisions,[20] but also structural limitations intrinsic to contemporary migration and human rights law.

In this context, legal scholarship is devoting increasing attention to the historical foundations of international migration and human rights law, critically mapping the construction of states' migration control prerogatives. A focus on the historical development of international migration law reveals that, before the statist assumption of sovereign migration control became a core tenet of international law, the prevailing legal doctrine was, for centuries, based on a presumptive right to international mobility—the *ius peregrinandi*.[21] In *The Invention of the Passport*, Torpey identifies different (although internally heterogenous) phases of migration control, which he traces through an analysis of the introduction of identity and nationality documents. He distinguishes between the 'nineteenth-century trend toward freedom of movement' (when European states were more concerned about restricting emigration than immigration), the proliferation of passport and migration control from the late nineteenth century to the First World War,[22] the increasing importance of national (and racial) belonging from the interwar to the post-Second World War era, and the profound changes spurred by the attacks of 11 September 2001, which led to increased securitization and border control.[23] While the establishment of sovereign migration control prerogatives was certainly gradual, it was only with decolonization and the independence of former colonies that the right to deny entry and expel without justification became firmly established as a core prerogative of states, crystallizing into international law the desire to keep the citizens of newly independent states away from former metropoles—but keeping the mobility of citizens from the Global North largely untouched.[24]

[20] Cathryn Costello and Itamar Mann, 'Border Justice: Migration and Accountability for Human Rights Violations' (2020) 21 German Law Journal 311, 312–13; Veronika Fikfak, 'Changing State Behaviour: Damages before the European Court of Human Rights' (2018) 29 European Journal of International Law 1091.

[21] Karin de Vries and Thomas Spijkerboer, 'Race and the Regulation of International Migration. The Ongoing Impact of Colonialism in the Case Law of The European Court of Human Rights' (2021) 39 Netherlands Quarterly of Human Rights 291, 294.

[22] In particular, legal scholars point at the US Supreme Court's rulings in the 'Chinese exclusion cases' as the historical point when an abrupt shift can be observed. In these cases, adopted in the 1890s, the US Supreme Court held that the exclusion of non-nationals was a matter of sovereignty, although this still needed to be grounded on the 'public interests' of the state if the 'non-integration' of foreigners could become 'dangerous to its peace and security' (ibid, 297). There was, however, no 'wrong' or 'right' way to enter the United States and therefore no real dichotomy between regular and irregular migrants (see Aviva Chomsky, *Undocumented: How Immigration Became Illegal* (Beacon Press 2014) 45).

[23] John Torpey, *The Invention of the Passport: Surveillance, Citizenship and the State* (Cambridge University Press 1999) (see Chapters 3, 4, 5, and 6 in particular). See further on the sudden proliferation of passports as a means of migration control, from an international law perspective, Anam Soomro, 'People, Paper and Power: The Birth of the Passport in International Law' (2023) 14 Asian Journal of International Law 1.

[24] De Vries and Spijkerboer (n 21) 293–98; Nandita Rani Sharma, *Home Rule: National Sovereignty and the Separation of Natives and Migrants* (Duke University Press 2020) 27–28. For some decades, however, citizenship and free movement was granted to the inhabitants of former colonies. The UK was

Whereas a deeper analysis of postcolonial studies generally falls beyond the scope of this book,[25] this body of scholarship helps us understand that statist migration control assumptions are not fixed in stone but pertain to a very specific historical context. As noted by Schmid, the notions of popular sovereignty and democratic self-governance used to justify migration control are much older than modern conceptions of state sovereignty and are therefore not intrinsically linked.[26]

The ubiquity of migration control in international law is today accompanied by dichotomous understandings of migration statuses and a growing importance of national citizenship.[27] The sharp distinctions between nationals and foreigners, between refugees and migrants, and between regular and irregular migration, justify and ethically simplify the logics of migration control and establish hierarchies of deservingness among non-nationals. Then, those who lack citizenship or legal status face particular hurdles in navigating the system. Therefore, migration control is exerted not only by means of border control and deportation but also through *classification* (see section 1.2 in this chapter). Again, a historical analysis shows that this was not always the case, as it was not until the 1960s (a while after states had shown efforts to control the movement of people across countries) that states from the Global North deemed it necessary to pre-determine 'right' and 'wrong' ways to migrate and hence make a sharp distinction between 'legal' and 'illegal' residents.[28] This shows that such categorizations are not natural, but rather the result of normative constructs specific to a historical period in which sovereignty narratives have prevailed over free movement.[29]

Statist notions of sovereignty are also deeply entrenched in human rights systems. The UN Convention on the Rights on Migrant Workers, for instance, includes a right for migrants to enter and remain in their country of origin, but acknowledges that the conditions of admission and stay of non-nationals depend on the law and practice of the host state.[30] In the European context, the European Court of Human Rights (ECtHR) has, since the seminal case of *Abdulaziz Cabales and Balkandi*, referred consistently to the 'well-established' principle of international law according to which states are sovereign to decide who comes and

the first of the colonizing powers to undermine such rights within the Commonwealth between 1962 and 1981 through gradual and racially based restrictions on free movement (see Torpey (n 23) 149–51 and de Vries and Spijkerboer (n 21) 298).

[25] See for example E Tendayi Achiume, 'Migration as Decolonization' (2019) 71 Stanford Law Review 1509. On the Eurocentrism of international refugee law, see BS Chimni, 'The Geopolitics of Refugee Studies: A View from the South' (1998) 11 Journal of Refugee Studies 350; Rebecca Hamlin, *Crossing: How We Label and React to People on the Move* (Stanford University Press 2021) 161.

[26] Schmid (n 17) 11.

[27] Torpey (n 23) 151.

[28] Chandran Kukathas, 'Immigration' in *Immigration and Freedom* (Princeton University Press 2021) 13, 17; Chomsky (n 22).

[29] Kukathas (n 28) 13, 17; Soomro (n 23) 7.

[30] International Convention on the Protection of the Rights of All Migrant Workers and Members of their Families, 18 December 1990, 2220 UNTS 3 arts 8(2) and 79.

stays within their borders.[31] One must recall that, although the ECtHR now has an extensive jurisprudence on the human rights of migrants, all the applications lodged by migrants since the 1950s were systematically declared inadmissible until *Abdulaziz* was decided in 1985 (interestingly, a non-violation verdict).[32] Still, its jurisprudence is widely believed to show disproportionate deference to state sovereignty.[33] In fact, in *When Humans Become Migrants*, Dembour famously coined the term 'Strasbourg reversal' to refer to the ECtHR's reasoning in the field of migration, whereby cases begin with statist migration control assumptions and the rights contained in the Convention only take second place.[34] One of the harshest examples of such reversal is provided by the 2020 case of *N.D. and N.T.* (later confirmed in *A.A. and others* and *M.B. and R.A.*), which illustrates Strasbourg's deference to migration control in cases of collective expulsions, and seems to make access to fundamental rights for people who cross irregularly available only in cases where applicants could not have possibly used legal entry points.[35]

In addition, or perhaps as a result of the above, migrants fundamentally struggle to see their human rights protected because dominant narratives on state sovereignty overwhelmingly favour migration control over the protection of human rights, and because state sovereignty is too often exercised in ways that are incompatible with human rights (even when the latter are legally required to prevail).[36] In this context, there seems to be consensus that, particularly after the terrorist attacks of 11 September 2001, states' reluctance to give up their sovereignty in a context of increased securitization of migration has favoured the prevalence of migration enforcement goals over the protection of fundamental rights.[37] This 'migration control impulse' is particularly strong insofar as irregular migration is concerned (which will be the subject of this book).[38]

[31] *Abdulaziz, Cabales and Balkandali v the United Kingdom*, Apps No 9214/80, 9473/81, 9474/81 (ECtHR 28 May 1985) para 67. For an extensive analysis ECtHR jurisprudence on Article 8 ECHR, see Chapter 3 of this book.

[32] Marie-Bénédicte Dembour, 'The Migrant Case Law of the European Court of Human Rights: Critique and Way Forward' in Başak Çalı, Ledi Bianku, and Iulia Motoc (eds), *Migration and the European Convention on Human Rights* (Oxford University Press 2021) 20.

[33] Cathryn Costello, *The Human Rights of Migrants and Refugees in European Law* (Oxford University Press 2015) 316.

[34] Marie-Bénédicte Dembour, *When Humans Become Migrants: Study of the European Court of Human Rights with an Inter-American Counterpoint* (Oxford University Press 2015) (see further in Chapter 3 of this book).

[35] *N.D. and N.T. v Spain* [GC], App No 8675/15 and 8697/15 (ECtHR 13 February 2020); *AA and others v North Macedonia*, Apps No 55798/16 and 4 others (ECtHR 5 April 2022); *M.B. and R.A. v Spain*, App No 20351/17 (ECtHR, Decision of 5 July 2022). See also Sergio Carrera, 'The Strasbourg Court Judgement N.D. and N.T. v. Spain. A Carte Blanche to Push Backs at EU External Borders?' (2020) EUI Working Paper 2020/21; Dana Shmalz, 'Enlarging the Hole in the Fence of Migrants' Rights, A.A. and others v. North Macedonia', *Verfassungsblog*, 6 April 2022, available at: <https://verfassungsblog.de/enlarging-the-hole-in-the-fence-of-migrants-rights/>.

[36] Schmid (n 17) 6.

[37] Diego Acosta Arcarazo, *The National versus the Foreigner in South America* (Cambridge Core 2018) 2; Ruth Rubio-Marín, 'Introduction: Human Rights and the Citizen/Non-Citizen Distinction Revisited' in *Human Rights and Immigration* (Oxford University Press 2014) 2.

[38] Dauvergne (n 12) 169.

In light of the above, it seems reasonable to contend that the role of human rights as a counterweight to state sovereignty might often be overstated. This is due to the discursive prevalence of migration control over fundamental rights and the failure of safeguards and implementation mechanisms in practice, but also because the regimes that are in charge of protecting migrants' rights are characterized by exceptionality and reversal in their reasoning.

For quite some time, however, scholars have inquired into the existing contradictions between formal understandings of sovereignty and 'state capacities', namely the conditions under which state policies (legitimate or not) are more or less likely to be successful in achieving their aims.[39] In the field of migration, scholars have recurrently looked at the gap between migration control narratives and their (lack of) practical implementation across the Global North.[40] The difference between openly stated policy goals and outcomes in the migration field has come to be known as the 'liberal paradox', and the precise mechanisms that make migration policies 'fail' in relation to their stated aims have long been the subject of intense academic debates.[41] But, if migration control prerogatives are at best only partially limited by human rights, what are the processes behind enforcement deficits?

While Sassen might have overemphasized the role of international human rights in undermining migration control, she also stressed the impact of globalization on state sovereignty. In her view, states treat migration as a closed and bounded event resulting from aggregated individual decisions, while it in fact responds to complex patterns which are shaped by systemic economic and social networks, by long-lasting postcolonial relations, and by practical needs for migrant labour in a globalized market.[42]

This 'globalist' approach stands in contrast to the work of other authors who emphasize the influence of 'internal' restrictions on migration control. According to Joppke, external factors linked to globalization dynamics help explain why people seek to move but not why countries in the Global North accept people on the move to a greater extent than they openly strive for.[43] Building on Freeman, he argues that relatively liberal migration policies derive from 'self-limited sovereignty', that is, domestic institutions, rules, and policy processes linked to internal constitutional and rule of law constraints. In his own words, 'accepting unwanted immigration is inherent in the liberalness of liberal states'.[44]

39 Peter B Evans, Dietrich Rueschemeyer and Theda Skocpol (eds), *Bringing the State Back In* (Cambridge University Press 1985).

40 Hollifield, Martin and Orrenius (n 10).

41 Stephen Castles, 'Why Migration Policies Fail' (2004) 27 Ethnic and Racial Studies 205.

42 Sassen (n 19) 80–82.

43 Christian Joppke, 'Immigration Challenges the Nation-State' in *Challenge to the Nation-State* (Oxford University Press 1998) 12.

44 Christian Joppke, 'Why Liberal States Accept Unwanted Immigration' (1998) 50 World Politics 266, 292; Freeman (n 10).

Scholarly focus on the 'liberal paradox' has been rightly criticized as Western-centric, overlooking the fluidity and ambiguity of migration governance, as well as the fact that 'illiberal' migration policies are often adopted in formal democracies and 'liberal' migration policies are also in place beyond Western democracies.[45] Moreover, some scholars argue that migration policies have in fact become more effective and sophisticated,[46] and others suggest that scholarship 'should use *concrete* policies rather public discourses as the evaluate benchmark [of migration policies]'.[47] More fundamentally, debates on migration policy failure (or success) generally lack conceptual clarity as to the meaning attached to the notions of 'effectiveness' and 'failure', as well as a convincing distinction between different types of migration policies or between migration and non-migration policies.[48] As a matter of fact, there are many different types of migration policies with varying degrees of implementation. Moreover, mainstream notions of 'success' and 'failure' many times disregard the fact that policy-makers and the population at large are sometimes well aware of the gap between abstract policy discourses and the complexities of administrative implementation,[49] or the fact that the prevalence of human rights is hardly an example of policy ineffectiveness, but rather the result of the application of norms of a higher hierarchical value.[50] And yet, mainstream scholarship is right in pointing at the evident gap between states' policy discourses seemingly aimed at curtailing immigration, and the everyday realities of migration management.

For now, I will work under the assumption that, while human rights violations in the name of migration control are widespread and well-documented across the Global North, there are also a number of domestic and international norms, social processes, and political dynamics that to a certain extent limit states' prerogatives as to who comes and stays within their borders. In essence, this reveals a conflict between states' 'supreme' authority and 'state capacities'.[51] This study thus assumes that projections of absolute migration control operate at a symbolic level, but also

[45] Katharina Natter, 'Beyond the Dichotomomy of Liberal and Illiberal Migration Governance' in Emma Carmel, Katharina Lenner, and Regine Paul (eds), *Handbook on the Governance and Politics of Migration* (Edward Elgar Publishing 2021) 110.

[46] Francesc Ortega and Giovanni Peri, 'The Effect of Income and Immigration Policies on International Migration' (2013) 1 Migration Studies 47; Jorgen Carling, 'Migration in the Age of Involuntary Immobility: Theoretical Reflections and Cape Verdean Experiences' (2002) 28 Journal of Ethnic and Migration Studies 5; Mathias Czaika and Hein de Haas, 'The Effect of Visa Policies on International Migration Dynamics' (2014) International Migration Institute Working Paper 89.

[47] Mathias Czaika and Hein de Haas, 'The Effectiveness of Immigration Policies: A Conceptual Review of Empirical Evidence' (2011) 33 IMI Working Paper Series 2.

[48] Mathias Czaika and Hein de Haas, 'The Effectiveness of Immigration Policies' (2013) 39 Population and Development Review 487, 489.

[49] Mathias Czaika and Hein de Haas, 'Evaluating Migration Policy Effectiveness' in Alina Triandafyllidou (ed), *Routledge Handbook of Immigration and Refugee Studies* (Routledge 2016) 35–36.

[50] Siyu Luo, 'Human Rights Paradox: Explaining the Undeportability of Irregular Chinese Migrants in the UK' (2024) 29 Theoretical Criminology 25.

[51] Jonathan K Hanson and Rachel Sigman, 'Leviathan's Latent Dimensions: Measuring State Capacity for Comparative Political Research' (2021) 83 The Journal of Politics 1495, 1496.

seeks to contribute to our understanding of why this is the case in the area of deportation in the EU—and what the consequences are for those that subsequently remain in limbo. Before doing so, the following sub-sections distinguish between the *external* (non-entry) and *internal* (deportation) dimensions of sovereignty and the different ways in which migration control prerogatives are expressed, with a particular focus on the EU. As noted above, state sovereignty in the context of migration control is mainly understood as the right to impede entry into one's territory *and* the right to expel once a non-national is present within the boundaries of a state. Taking into account that existing debates on the 'liberal paradox' at times fail to distinguish between both dimensions, non-entry and deportation will be here analysed separately. It is only the *internal* dimension that will be the focus of this book.

1.1 External sovereignty: Building a fortress?

The *external* dimension of sovereignty concerns states' right to control entry into their territory. This is not to be confused with the 'external dimension of migration' or with 'externalization', which generally refer to the development of partnerships with third countries both on non-entry and on the deportation of those already present within a state. Instead, in this chapter, the *external* refers strictly to policies addressed to prevent the entry of would-be migrants that have not yet entered the territory of a state.

For decades, countries in the Global North have developed a series of mechanisms of *non-entrée* with the aim of preventing the arrival of migrants and refugees alike. These are often enforced through pre-border structures that are implemented from abroad, and which are indiscriminate in their application—meaning that around 90% of recognized refugees in Europe arrive through irregular (and unsafe) channels.[52]

Current practices include the use of restrictive visa policies,[53] the securitization of borders and search and rescue operations,[54] the use of illegal pushbacks

[52] Violeta Moreno-Lax, *Accessing Asylum in Europe: Extraterritorial Border Controls and Refugee Rights under EU Law* (Oxford University Press 2017) 2. Hathaway and Gammeltoft-Hansen refer to the 'schizophrenic attitude' of Western states towards international refugee law, according to which they wish to remain formally committed to it but seek to avoid their obligations in practice by denying access routes to refugees (see Thomas Gammeltoft-Hansen and James C Hathaway, 'Non-Refoulement in a World of Cooperative Deterrence' (2015) 53 Columbia Journal of Transnational Law 235, 235).

[53] In the EU context, this takes the form of a common Visa Code (Regulation (EC) 810/2009), external border controls through the Schengen Borders Code (Regulation (EU) 2016/399), and interoperable large-scale information technology systems such as the Visa Information System (VIS), the Schengen Information System (SIS), or the Entry/Exit System (EES).

[54] Daniel Ghezelbash and others, 'Securitization of Search and Rescue at Sea: The Response to Boat Migration in the Mediterranean and Offshore Australia' (2018) 67 International & Comparative Law Quarterly 315.

at both land and sea borders,[55] and various forms of cooperation with third countries, including the set-up of detention centres abroad, the establishment of border controls in countries of transit, or the extraterritorial processing of asylum applications.[56] Between July 2023 and May 2024, the European Commission, alone or jointly with some Member States, concluded soft law agreements aimed at keeping migrants out of Europe with Tunisia, Mauritania, Egypt, and Lebanon.[57] Recent investigations have revealed how EU funds granted in the context of such agreements are used by these countries to round up Sub-Saharan migrants and abandon them in the desert.[58]

The use of these tools, which contribute to the establishment of a 'virtual', 'remote', or 'off-shore' fortress, is coupled with physical fortification. In Europe, the length of border fences and walls at the EU's external borders soared from just 315 kilometres in 2014 to 2,048 kilometres in 2022.[59] This is accompanied

[55] While pushbacks are regularly denied by perpetrating authorities, they are extensively documented by journalists and civil society organizations, as illustrated in the 1,500-page 'Black Book of Pushbacks' produced by the Border Violence Monitoring Network in December 2020 and available at: <https://borderviolence.eu/black-book-of-pushbacks-2020/>. See further: Lighthouse reports, 'Unmasking Europe's Shadow Armies', 6 October 2021, available at: <https://www.lighthousereports.nl/investigation/unmasking-europes-shadow-armies/>.

[56] Nicholas R Micinski, *Delegating Responsibility: International Cooperation on Migration in the European Union* (University of Michigan Press 2022).Whereas countries such as Australia have an institutionalized offshore processing system, in the EU it has so far been based on more informal and sporadic collaboration with third countries, the most well-known case being the processing of asylum claims in Niger with views to future resettlement to the EU in case of a positive decision (Laura Lambert, 'Extraterritorial Asylum Processing: The Libya-Niger Emergency Transit Mechanism' (2021) 68 Forced Migration Review 18). The Italy–Albania Protocol however shows an attempt to transfer asylum seekers from Italy to Albania for the offshore processing of their claims (see Andreina de Leo, 'Managing Migration the Italian Way: The "Innovative" Italy-Albania Deal under Scrutiny', *Verfassungsblog*, 29 October 2024, available at: <https://verfassungsblog.de/managing-migration-the-italian-way/>).

[57] European Commission, 'Memorandum of Understanding on a strategic and global partnership between the European Union and Tunisia', Press Release, 16 July 2023, available at: <https://ec.europa.eu/commission/presscorner/detail/en/ip_23_3887>; European Commission, 'Press statement by President von der Leyen following the meeting with Spanish Prime Minister Sánchez and Mauritanian President Mohamed Ould El-Ghazouani', 8 February 2024, available at: <https://ec.europa.eu/commission/presscorner/detail/en/statement_24_703>; European Commission, 'Press statement by President von der Leyen with Austrian Chancellor Nehammer, Belgian Prime Minister De Croo, Cypriot President Christodoulides, Greek Prime Minister Mitsotakis, Italian Prime Minister Meloni and Egyptian President El-Sisi', 17 March 2024, available at: <https://ec.europa.eu/commission/presscorner/detail/en/STATEMENT_24_1521>; European Commission, 'President von der Leyen reaffirms EU's strong support for Lebanon and its people and announces a €1 billion package of EU funding', 2 May 2024, available at: <https://neighbourhood-enlargement.ec.europa.eu/news/president-von-der-leyen-reaffirms-eus-strong-support-lebanon-and-its-people-and-announces-eu1-2024-05-02_en>.

[58] Lighthouse Reports, 'Desert Dumps', 21 May 2024, available at: <https://www.lighthousereports.com/investigation/desert-dumps/>.

[59] Jennifer Rigby and James Crisp, 'Fortress Europe', *The Telegraph*, 20 December 2021, available at: <https://www.telegraph.co.uk/global-health/fortress-europe-borders-wall-fence-controls-eu-countries-migrants-crisis/>; European Parliament, 'Walls and fences at EU borders', Briefing, 13 December 2022, available at: <https://www.europarl.europa.eu/thinktank/en/document/EPRS_BRI(2022)733692>.

by an ever-increasing role of, and funding for, Frontex, the EU's border control agency.[60]

Taken together, these tools can be seen as relatively successful in achieving their aims. As noted by Dennison and Geddes in relation to the Taliban's seizure of power in Afghanistan in 2021:

> [D]espite these initial and Eurocentric comparisons with Syrian arrivals in 2015, Afghanistan's context and broader changes over the last six years have made a carbon-copy repeat highly unlikely. Greater geographical distance, the end of hostilities in Afghanistan, border closures in Iran and Türkiye's partially EU-funded construction of extensive border walls—motivated by an anti-immigration public backlash following the inflow of over five million Syrians—make just getting to Europe much more difficult.[61]

Increased migration control in the field of border management however comes at the cost of liberal values, human rights, and human lives. According to the International Organisation for Migration (IOM), 2023 was the deadliest year on record for migrants en route worldwide.[62] The practices described above have led to collective expulsions, instances of *refoulement*, or the denial of the right to seek asylum.[63] Moreover, in the EU context, externalization undermines development aid by linking it to migration control,[64] and also challenges the establishment of regional free movement regimes (most notably in Africa) by requiring border controls in countries of origin and transit.[65] It is thus in relation to would-be immigrants that states can more easily avoid accountability and adopt illiberal immigration policies, precisely because it becomes easier to escape jurisdictional links—and their ensuing constitutional, rule of law, and human rights frameworks.

[60] The Agency's budget increased from €6 million in 2005 to €543 million in 2021, with €11 billion expected for the period 2021–27 (European Court of Auditors, 'Frontex, Audit preview', January 2020, available at: <https://www.eca.europa.eu/es/publications?did=52964>).

[61] James Dennison and Andrew Geddes, 'The Fragility of EU Border and Migration Politics', *EUIdeas*, 23 November 2021, available at: <https://euideas.eui.eu/2021/11/23/the-fragility-of-eu-border-and-migration-politics/>.

[62] Internation Organisation for Migration (IOM), Missing Migrants Project, available at: < https://missingmigrants.iom.int/>.

[63] Bill Frelick, Ian M Kysel, and Jennifer Podkul, 'The Impact of Externalization of Migration Controls on the Rights of Asylum Seekers and Other Migrants' (2016) 4 Journal on Migration and Human Security 190. See further the 'Black Book of Pushbacks' (n 55).

[64] European Council on Refugees and Exiles (ECRE), 'Migration Control Conditionality, a Flawed Model', Policy Note, 9 January 2020, available at: <https://ecre.org/ecre-policy-note-migration-control-conditionality-a-flawed-model/>.

[65] In the African context, see Roderick Parkes and Mark McQuay, 'Ending the EU's ambivalence to Free Movement in Africa', *IAI Commentaries*, 13 November 2020, available at: <https://www.iai.it/en/pubblicazioni/ending-eus-ambivalence-free-movement-africa>; Lutz Oette and Mohamed Abdelsalam Babiker, 'Migration Control à La Khartoum: EU External Engagement and Human Rights Protection in the Horn of Africa' (2017) 36 Refugee Survey Quarterly 1, 7.

This is not to say that states' powers remain unchallenged. On the contrary, borders remain relatively porous. This is first because, upon the closing of migration routes, people turn to alternative and more dangerous ones.[66] It is somewhat revealing that, in spite of the previously noted fortification strategies at the EU's disposal, 2023 saw the highest number of irregular border crossings since 2016.[67] In the words of Benhabib:

> [T]he European Union will continue to intercept migrants at sea but unless and until economic dislocations caused by aspects of EU agricultural policy that protect French farmers at the expense of African ones are understood; unless and until state collapse in Libya is handled; unless and until the endemic corruption of some of these regimes that sell their natural resources to international corporations while letting their people starve comes to an end, people from Africa will flock to refugee boats to cross the Mediterranean.[68]

Moreover, while often successful in avoiding jurisdiction, states can occasionally be held accountable for actions conducted beyond or at the edges of their territory, as illustrated by ECtHR jurisprudence in cases of pushbacks at sea and land borders.[69] Lastly, it is remarkable that, despite the spotlight being on irregular crossings, persons who enter regularly with a visa but remain after its expiry ('visa overstayers') account for the majority of irregular migrants in practice, as acknowledged by the European Commission.[70]

Overall, however, one can reasonably conclude that the externalization of migration control is a sphere where projections of control are, to a certain extent, accompanied by state capacities, leading to increasing (and not diminishing) control at the outer boundaries of the state. This comes at the cost of liberal values, as the

[66] Sergio Carrera and Jennifer Allsopp, 'The Irregular Immigration Policy Conundrum: Problematizing "Effectiveness" as a Frame for EU Criminalization and Expulsion Policies' in Ariadna Ripoll Servent and Florian Trauner (eds), *The Routledge Handbook of Justice and Home Affairs Research* (Routledge 2018) 75.

[67] Frontex, 'Significant rise in irregular border crossings in 2023, highest since 2016', News Release, 26 January 2024, available at: <https://www.frontex.europa.eu/media-centre/news/news-release/significant-rise-in-irregular-border-crossings-in-2023-highest-since-2016-C0gGpm>.

[68] Seyla Benhabib, 'The End of the 1951 Refugee Convention? Dilemmas of Sovereignty, Territoriality, and Human Rights' (2020) 2 Jus Cogens 75, 94. Interestingly, part of the scholarship contends that claims about the need to tackle the 'root causes' of migration (mainly poverty) through development aid overlook the fact that, up to a certain threshold, development in poor countries leads to more (and not less) migration to richer countries (see Hein de Haas, *How Migration Really Works: A Factful Guide to the Most Divisive Issue in Politics* (Viking 2023) 78–92). Be that as it may, both strands of the literature agree that migration flows are at best only partially limited by the policies adopted by receiving countries.

[69] *Hirsi Jamaa v Italy* App No 27765/09 (ECtHR 23 February 2012); *MH and others v Croatia* Apps No 15670/18 and 43115/18 (ECtHR 18 November 2021); In the opposite direction, see *N.D. and N.T.* [GC] (n 35).

[70] European Commission, 'Irregular migration and return', available at: <https://home-affairs.ec.europa.eu/policies/migration-and-asylum/irregular-migration-and-return_en>.

'liberalness of liberal states' identified by Joppke is nowhere to be seen in states' external practices. The same logic applies to the European Union, with the exception that internal free movement pushes the outer boundary to the EU external border. It is however in the *internal* dimension of migration control that the so-called liberal paradox becomes more evident.

1.2 Internal sovereignty: The deportation gap

The *internal* dimension of sovereignty, as understood in this chapter, concerns states' right to exert migration control in respect of those already present in their territory, as opposed to the management and exclusion of would-be migrants. By *internal*, I refer to the management of the migrant population already within the territory of a state, notwithstanding the fact that this necessarily needs an external dimension for its effective implementation (e.g. through third country cooperation on readmission).

Particularly after 11 September 2001, scholars have pointed at the increasing use of expulsion in a context of securitization of migration management, in what has been labelled as the 'deportation turn'.[71] This is characterized by a sharp rise in the use of deportation (previously perceived as a secondary tool of migration control), as well as its normalization as *the* tool to manage the presence of irregular migrants—becoming a 'self-evident recourse of statecraft and law-enforcement'.[72]

Lesser attention has been paid to the deportation gap, namely the increasing divergence between 'deportable' persons and those who are effectively expelled. Across countries of the Global North, only a small fraction of irregular migrants who are ordered to leave actually do so, revealing that deportation machineries might not be as effective as is usually assumed.[73] As noted by Paoletti, precisely because deportation is increasingly normalized socially, politically, and legally, states' inability to live up to their projected goals is particularly puzzling.[74] Since this book deals with non-removability as the flip side of deportation, it is situated within this smaller branch of (non-)deportation studies.

Academics have for some time inquired into the mechanisms accounting for the remarkably low deportation rates across countries in the Global North, despite

[71] Matthew J Gibney, 'Asylum and the Expansion of Deportation in the United Kingdom' (2008) 43 Government and Opposition 146, 146–47; Bridget Anderson, Matthew J Gibney and Emanuela Paoletti, 'Citizenship, Deportation and the Boundaries of Belonging' (2011) 15 Citizenship Studies 547, 547.

[72] Nicholas De Genova and Nathalie Mae Peutz, *The Deportation Regime: Sovereignty, Space, and the Freedom of Movement* (Duke University Press 2010) 1.

[73] In the United States, for instance, by 2011, around 86% of its irregular migrant population (estimated at around 11 million) had arrived in 2004 or earlier, and 57% in 1999 or earlier (Hiroshi Motomura, *Immigration Outside the Law* (Oxford University Press 2014) 13).

[74] Emanuela Paoletti, 'Deportation, Non-Deportability and Ideas of Membership' (2010) Refugee Studies Centre Working Paper Series 1, 6, and 15.

deportation being the linchpin of their policies on irregular migration. Some point at the fact that forced returns are socially, morally, and politically controversial; time-consuming; and expensive, resulting in the prioritization of preventative policies of *non-entrée* over the enforcement of deportation.[75] More generally, deportation is legally and factually complicated and constrained by a wide range of norms and operational barriers. It necessarily depends on the agreement and cooperation of countries of origin, and it can also be limited by challenges in the identification and nationality-determination of deportees, as well as by human rights or other norms.[76]

At a deeper level, deportation often does not work for the very same reasons that policies of *non-entrée* do work. Whereas external bordering practices prevent individuals from entering states' jurisdiction, states cannot (or at least not fully) overlook their constitutional, rule of law, and human rights commitments in respect of persons who are already present in their territory. In short, it is still territorial presence that functions as the basis for legal entitlements.[77] This can partially explain why liberal states are comparatively less successful in expelling those already inside than in keeping them outside of their borders. Although human rights may still be characterized by exceptionality in their application and reversal in their reasoning, they become a more tangible reality for those who are physically present. In fact, there are reasonably well-developed norms on the right of irregular migrants to non-removal, be it on grounds of *non-refoulement*, the prohibition of collective expulsion, or family and/or private life (see Chapter 2 and Chapter 3 of this book on the European Convention on Human Rights (ECHR)), whereas the right to enter is either non-existent or framed in (even more) exceptional and vague terms.[78] Even in the context of asylum law, *non-refoulement* obligations are generally triggered only when a person in need of protection enters the jurisdiction of a state,[79]

[75] Gibney (n 71) 147.

[76] Matthew J Gibney and Randall Hansen, 'Deportation and the Liberal State: The Forcible Return of Asylum Seekers and Unlawful Migrants in Canada, Germany and the United Kingdom' (2003) UNHCR, New Issues in Refugee Research, Working Paper No. 77 11.

[77] Benhabib, 'The End of the 1951 Refugee Convention?' (n 68) 78.

[78] *Abdulaziz* (n 31). For current Strasbourg criteria on states' positive obligations to admit persons in the context of family reunification, see *M.A. v Denmark* [GC] App No 6697/18 (ECtHR 9 July 2021).

[79] It is now well established under international human rights law that extraterritorial acts of states, by exercising some form of control, can bring individuals within their jurisdiction and trigger human rights obligations. This is reflected in the ECtHR's jurisprudence on Article 1 ECHR (see, for example, *Loizidou v Turkey* [GC] App No 15318/89 (ECtHR 18 December 1996); *Al-Skeini and others v the United Kingdom* [GC] App No 55721/07 (ECtHR 7 July 2011); *Medvedyev and Others v France* [GC] App No 3394/03 (ECtHR 29 March 2010)). More concretely, the ECtHR found a breach of states' *non-refoulement obligations* in the pushback of people intercepted in international waters by Italian authorities in the landmark case of *Hirsi Jamaa* (n 69). In the EU context, Moreno-Lax and Costello argue that EU law binds EU organs (within their competences) and Member States (when implementing EU law) regardless of territorial notions of jurisdiction. In the case of the protection afforded by the EU Charter of Fundamental Rights, the lack of a jurisdictional threshold becomes rather evident considering the absence of a jurisdictional clause in Article 51 of the Charter (Violeta Moreno-Lax and Cathryn Costello, 'The Extraterritorial Application of the EU Charter of Fundamental Rights: From Territoriality to Facticity, the Effectiveness Model' in Steve Peers and others (eds), *The EU Charter of Fundamental Rights: A Commentary* (Hart Publishing 2014) 1657–83).

but there are no specific and binding obligations towards refugees elsewhere, nor a right to seek refuge in any particular state.[80] Then, policies of *non-entrée* can be completely indiscriminate (and discriminatory) in terms of who is banned from states' territory, while expulsion policies are at least partially limited by the rule of law and judicial oversight. The lack of implementation of the UK–Rwanda deal (aimed at deporting asylum seekers from the UK to Rwanda) offers perhaps one of the clearest examples. By the end of 2023, £240 million had been transferred to Rwanda, and yet not a single person had been sent to Rwanda under the scheme, due to it being halted by both national and supranational courts.[81]

The failure of the literature to inquire into this divergence between *internal* and *external* policies of migration control was expressed as early as 2003 by Gibney and Hansen as follows:

> [A]n entire literature on the relationship between migration and sovereignty—holding globalization and increased immigration undermine the state's capacity to control immigration—has got it backwards. The nation-state has not lost control over entry to its borders; it has rather lost control over movement *within* and *from* its borders . . . Putting it another way, the restrictiveness of the liberal state's policy towards asylum seekers can be seen as flowing from the liberalism (intentional or otherwise) of its policy towards foreigners inside the state.[82]

Their claim that countries in the Global North adopt 'liberal' policies towards migrants within their borders is highly questionable. One could argue that deportation policies are still effective, if not at deportation *per se*, at keeping irregular migrants excluded from basic rights and under a prolonged threat of deportation, in what De Genova conceptualizes as *deportability*.[83] As noted by Kukathas:

> In the popular imagination, immigration control is border control . . . Yet further reflection suggests that immigration control begins not at the border, or even beyond the borders (where it extends, as we shall see) but with the definitions of immigration an immigrant—and so, by implication, of the notions of native and national. The first step in the exercise of control is to determine who is to be subject to control . . . establishing through definition the number and type of people who need no permission to travel or to enter a territory or to exercise a variety of rights that are denied to others. Immigration control begins not with walls or

[80] According to Moreno-Lax, among others, states are also responsible and should be held accountable for the admission of protection-seekers at the pre-entry stage (Moreno-Lax (n 52) 4).

[81] *N.S.K. v. the United Kingdom*, App No 28774/22 (ECtHR (Interim Measures) 14 June 2022); *R (on the application of AAA (Syria) and others)* [2023] UKSC 42.

[82] Gibney and Hansen (n 76) 14.

[83] Nicholas P De Genova, 'Migrant "Illegality" and Deportability in Everyday Life' (2002) 31 Annual Review of Anthropology 419, 438.

> fences but with *classification* ... That this is so is especially evident in discussions of 'illegal immigration'.[84]

The production and perpetuation of 'illegality' is to be understood not as a natural phenomenon but as a legally produced one.[85] Thus, *internal* migration control can be simultaneously ineffective at deporting irregular residents, while fully effective at keeping them outside of membership and without access to rights.[86] Deportable or not, the 'illegalization' of people (be it through restrictive visa conditions, low asylum recognition rates, or the lack of regularization opportunities) and the infliction of limbo-like statuses of non-removability are also tools of migration control—giving rise to the category of migrants studied in this book. Indeed, the presence of non-removable migrants reflects conflicting trends intrinsic to migration policies, unable to exert full exclusion via deportation, but unwilling to let go of its migration control impulses. And yet, Gibney and Hansen were right in pointing out the divergence between *external* and *internal* policies of migration control and the different logics and principles underpinning them. The laws and policies applicable to those already within the state seem to be at least *more* liberal and open than those applicable to would-be migrants and refugees. They are also time-dependent, so that the longer individuals remain in a given place, the more difficult it will be to deport them.[87] It also remains true that the enforcement gap becomes more obvious in the management of migration within the state (particularly in the sphere of deportation) and that, while examples of 'illiberal' migration policies adopted in the name of migration control are manifold, non-deportability can also respond to the application of liberal norms.

For the purposes of this study, I do not seek to debate extensively whether states have generally 'lost control' over their irregular migrant population, but rather to systematically analyse how and why deportation is not implemented in a specific institutional setting (the European Union), as well as to elaborate the consequences that irregularity and non-deportability have for those who remain on the EU's territory without a valid residence permit. Prior to outlining the general structure of the book, the following section examines the applicable legal framework in the EU.

[84] Kukathas (n 28) 10–11.

[85] Vicky Squire, 'The Construction and Contestation of Illegality' in Emma Carmel, Katharina Lenner, and Regine Paul (eds), *Handbook on the Governance and Politics of Migration* (Edward Elgar Publishing 2021) 138.

[86] Bendixsen and Näre introduce the concept of 'welfare state bordering' to refer to the use of welfare policies by states as a means to control access to rights based on residence, migrancy, and/or citizenship, and therefore as a tool of migration control (see Synnøve Bendixsen and Lena Näre, 'Welfare State Bordering as a Form of Mobility and Migration Control' (2024) 50 Journal of Ethnic and Migration Studies 2689, 2693).

[87] Gibney and Hansen (n 76) 13. Başak Çalı, 'All You Need Is Time? Discrepancies between the European Court of Human Rights Case Law and Liberal Normative Theory on Long-Term Migrants' (2017) 50 Israel Law Review 447.

2. Deportation in the European Union: The Return Directive and non-removable migrants

Since the transfer of the area of immigration to shared competence between the EU and its Member States in the Treaty of Amsterdam, there has been an impressive and ever-growing body of EU law in the fields of migration and asylum, with the aim of furthering an 'area of freedom, security and justice'. EU asylum law now covers all aspects of Member States' asylum systems (from qualification to reception conditions, asylum procedures, and state responsibility for asylum applications) and features legislation on both regular and irregular migration. The New Pact on Migration and Asylum, adopted in May 2024, has led to several regulations and one directive, which are either entirely new or revamped versions of prior legislation. These instruments are to be applied from 1 July 2026 onwards.[88]

2.1 The EU's framework on irregular migration: The Return Directive

Since the very beginning, the establishment of a coherent and comprehensive policy that manages migration 'in all its aspects'[89] has been framed as a *sine qua non* for the smooth functioning of internal open borders within the EU.[90]

With free movement within the EU being linked to security threats and irregular migration, EU policies have stressed the need for 'flanking' measures that address the stay of irregular migrants, 'protect' the Schengen area, and compensate for free movement within the EU.[91] There is, in this context, a binary distinction that guides European policy-making in this area between 'legal migrants', to whom the EU owes 'fair treatment', and 'the prevention of, and enhanced measures to combat, illegal immigration'.[92] Legislation in the area of irregular migration covers,

[88] The New Pact repeals Directives 2011/95 and 2013/32 on qualification for international protection and asylum procedures respectively, which are replaced by two regulations (2024/1347 and 2024/1348 respectively). Further to this, the new Regulation on Asylum and Migration Management (2024/1351) replaces the Dublin III Regulation (604/2013), and a new Directive on the reception of applicants for international protection (2024/1346) repeals the previous Directive on the matter (2013/33). Regulation 2024/1358 on the establishment of 'Eurodac' repeals Regulation 603/2013. The Pact also includes entirely new legislation on the screening of TCNs at the external borders (2024/1356), on addressing situations of crisis and force majeure (2024/1359), on establishing a return border procedure (2024/1349), and on the establishment of a Union Resettlement and Humanitarian Admission Framework (2024/1350). All the instruments are available at: <https://eur-lex.europa.eu/>. For further information on the New Pact, see European Commission, 'Pact on Migration and Asylum', 21 May 2024, available at: <https://home-affairs.ec.europa.eu/policies/migration-and-asylum/pact-migration-and-asylum_en>.

[89] European Commission, 'Communication on Managing Migration in All Its Aspects: Progress Under the European Agenda on Migration', COM(2018) 798 Final, 4 December 2018.

[90] European Council (Tampere), Presidency Conclusions, 15 and 16 October 1999 para 3.

[91] Carrera and Allsopp (n 66) 71.

[92] Consolidated version of the Treaty on the Functioning of the European Union (TFEU), [2012] OJ C 326 art 79. The terms 'combat' or 'fight' have been used consistently in policy and legislative documents on irregular migration since the early 2000s (Kevin Fredy Hinterberger, *Regularisations*

among other topics, the definition of the facilitation of unauthorized entry, transit, and residence (Directive 2002/90); the strengthening of the legal framework to prevent (Council Framework Decision 2002/946); and the minimum sanctions and measures applicable against employers of irregular migrants (Directive 2009/52). With the New Pact on Migration and Asylum, EU law now also regulates the screening of persons who do not fulfil entry conditions or who, having been apprehended within a Member State, have not been subjected to control at the external borders (and their subsequent referral to either asylum or return procedures).[93] More importantly, EU law regulates the expulsion of irregular migrants in Directive 2008/115 (hereinafter Return Directive or simply RD).[94] While domestic policies on irregular migration 'combat' irregular migration using both deportation *and* regularization, EU law presents an asymmetric framework that rules on the former but not on the latter. Thus, despite claims for a holistic approach to migration, the sphere of regularization remains, as of today, a core prerogative of the Member States.[95]

Under the Return Directive, EU Member States *shall* issue a return decision to any TCN who is staying irregularly in the territory of a Member State, taking 'all necessary measures' to (forcibly) enforce the return decision if the obligation to return has not been complied with 'voluntarily'.[96] In this regard, the Court of Justice of the European Union (CJEU) has clarified that the Directive's main goal is the establishment of an 'effective' removal policy,[97] and this must take place 'as soon as possible'.[98] Measures other than expulsion, including criminal law sanctions for irregular residence, are permitted by the CJEU so long as they do not run against the Directive's effectiveness (that is, to return more and faster).[99]

of Irregularly Staying Migrants in the EU: A Comparative Legal Analysis of Austria, Germany and Spain (Nomos 2023) 91).

[93] Regulation (EU) 2024/1356 introducing the screening of third-country nationals at the external borders [2024] OJ L.

[94] The recast Return Directive was left out in the negotiations leading to the New Pact on Migration and Asylum, and no advances have been made since the 2018 proposal drafted by the European Commission.

[95] An exception is provided by the temporary residence permit granted to victims of trafficking who cooperate with authorities during domestic proceedings as stipulated in Directive 2004/81.

[96] Directive 2008/115/EC on common standards and procedures in Member States for returning illegally staying third-country nationals [2008] OJ L348/98 (Return Directive) arts 6(1) and 8(1). The use of the concept of 'voluntary' return in the context of the Directive is purely euphemistic and does not refer to truly voluntary departure, but rather to compulsory return during a period where the state must refrain from resorting to the use of force to carry out the removal (see 'period for voluntary departure' in Article 7 of the Directive).

[97] Case C-38/14, *Subdelegación del Gobierno en Gipuzkoa v Zaizoune* [2015] EU:C:2015:260 para 30.

[98] Case C-329/11, *Alexandre Achughbabian v Préfet du Val-de-Marne* [2011] EU:C:2011:807 para 45; Case C-430/11, *Md Sagor* [2012] EU:C:2012:777 para 43; *Zaizoune* (n 97) para 34.

[99] Case C-61/11 PPU, *Hassen El Dridi, alias Karim Soufi* [2011] EU:C:2011:268 para 59; *Achughbabian* (n 98) para 33.

Even if the Return Directive's goal is to provide 'first of all, principally, for an obligation for Member States to issue a return decision against any TCN staying illegally on their territory',[100] Article 6(4) notes that Member States *may*, alternatively, afford irregular migrants a residence permit under domestic law at any time due to 'compassionate, humanitarian, or other reasons'.[101] In the course of the Directive's negotiations, the possibility to issue administrative fines or other lighter measures as an alternative to expulsion was considered but finally discarded and is therefore not foreseen in the final text.[102] The Directive is thus based on a seemingly straightforward approach according to which Member States must either return or regularize undocumented migrants. According to the Commission, this is supposed to provide greater certainty, as Member States are 'obliged to say either "A" (grant a permit or a legal right to stay) or "B" (carry out return procedures) . . . reducing grey areas and improving legal certainty for all involved'.[103] As noted by Lutz, this novel approach whereby Member States are compelled to deport irregular migrants (unless they opt for regularisation following Article 6(4)) means that they are no longer free to simply 'tolerate' them without taking further action, as the Directive aims for the 'termination of illegal stay'.[104]

For these reasons, the Court of Justice ruled in *Zaizoune* that a Spanish norm which (according to the referring judge) penalized irregular residence with *either* an administrative fine *or* removal depending on the individual circumstances of the case was incompatible with the Return Directive.[105] Interestingly, while the legal principles affirmed by the CJEU in *Zaizoune* (i.e. 'return or regularize') seem to remain valid, the CJEU recently ruled that the very same norm under scrutiny in *Zaizoune* is in conformity with the Return Directive, because in Spain the pecuniary fine for irregular residence comes with an obligation to leave attached (amounting to a period for 'voluntary' departure), and state authorities can *subsequently* proceed to forced removal.[106] In this recent ruling, the CJEU endorses the 'return or regularize' principle by accepting the extension of the period for

[100] *El Dridi* (n 99) para 35.

[101] Return Directive (n 96) arts 6(4) and 8(1).

[102] Fabian Lutz, *The Negotiations on the Return Directive: Comments and Materials* (WLP 2010) 42.

[103] European Commission, 'Commission Recommendation (EU) 2017/2338 of 16 November 2017 Establishing a Common "Return Handbook" to be used by Member States' Competent Authorities when Carrying out Return-Related Tasks' [2017] OJ L 339 (Return Handbook) 20.

[104] Lutz (n 102) 42; Hinterberger (n 92) 79; Alan Desmond, 'The Return Directive: Clarifying the Scope and Substance of the Rights of Migrants Facing Expulsion from the EU' in Russell King and Katie Kuschminder (eds), *Handbook of Return Migration* (Edward Elgar Publishing 2022) 146.

[105] *Zaizoune* (n 97) paras 40 and 41. In a subsequent case the CJEU stressed that Spanish authorities could not directly apply the Directive to the detriment of the third-country national, since it is a matter of well-established EU law that directives are not directly applicable against individuals without adequate transposition from Member States (see Case C-568/19, *MO v Subdelegación del Gobierno en Toledo* [2020] EU:C:2020:907).

[106] Case C-409/20, *UN v Subdelegación del Gobierno en Pontevedra* [2022] EU:C:2022:148. The case was based upon further clarifications on Spanish law by the referring court which contradicted the version of the referring judge in *Zaizoune* (n 97) (see para 29 of the judgment).

voluntary departure foreseen in the Return Directive if there are regularization procedures in place—although these remain a Member State prerogative. Be that as it may, in *TQ* the CJEU clarified that the 'return or regularize' rule also applies to children, in such a way that Member States cannot keep migrant children in limbo until they become adults, but must instead proceed with return procedures or alternatively offer them lawful residence under national law.[107]

2.2 The politics of expulsion in the EU: In search of 'effectiveness'

Even though the management of irregular migration is meant to be based on a 'return or regularize' logic, policy discourses have followed a unidirectional approach according to which a fully 'effective' return policy requires that *every* irregular migrant should leave.[108]

Increasing the number of deportations has long been a priority for EU institutions and Member States. As early as 1992, the Member States of the then European Communities sought to harmonize the treatment of failed asylum seekers, including the set-up of readmission agreements and the use of pre-removal detention, with a view to increasing the 'speed, efficiency, effectiveness and economy' of expulsions.[109] In the years prior to the adoption of the Return Directive, the EU adopted further measures in this field, including standardized travel documents, recommendations on concerted action and cooperation in expulsion proceedings, a Commission green paper on expulsion, the 2004 Council Decision (1004/573) on the organization of joint removal flights, and the Regulation (2007/2004) establishing Frontex.[110] Moreover, although the Return Directive is an EU-internal tool of migration control, deportation demands the participation and collaboration of third countries. Thus, EU Readmission Agreements (or other informal readmission tools) form the external side of return and have, for decades, attempted at bringing third countries in line with the EU's (internal) return goals. The Union's readmission policies, and their implementation gaps, are discussed at length in Chapter 5 of this book.

After the Return Directive's adoption, and particularly following the 2015 refugee (protection) crisis, such discourses have only intensified, putting forward

[107] Case C-441/19, *TQ v Staatssecretaris van Justitie en Veiligheid* [2021] EU:C:2021:9 paras 81 and 82.

[108] European Commission, '2021 State of the Union Address by President von der Leyen', 15 September 2021, available at: <https://state-of-the-union.ec.europa.eu/state-union-2021_en>.

[109] Draft Recommendation regarding practices followed by Member States on expulsion by the Ministers of the Member States of the European Communities responsible for Immigration, London, 30 November and 1 December 1992, available at: <https://www.statewatch.org/media/documents/e-library/trevi-asylum-19immres.pdf>.

[110] Statewatch, 'Deportation Union: Rights, accountability and the EU's push to increase forced removals', 19 August 2020 5, available at: <https://www.statewatch.org/deportation-union-rights-accountability-and-the-eu-s-push-to-increase-forced-removals/>.

the view that an 'ineffective' return apparatus (i.e. one with unimpressive deportation numbers) acts as an incentive for irregular migrants to come to Europe.[111] The concept of effectiveness is here a purely quantitative one which disregards the potential impact of expulsion on fundamental rights and the sustainability of returns.[112] The reasoning goes that a sharp increase in deportation should (and can) be achieved through increased cooperation on readmission with third countries and speedy and integrated return procedures. This narrative can be found across Commission Communications,[113] but also in the Commission's 'Return Handbook' (the Directive's main interpretative tool), the proposed recast of the Return Directive, and the freshly adopted Pact on Migration and Asylum, among other documents. To increase deportation numbers, these soft law tools and legislative proposals rely, among other things, on more frequent and lengthier pre-removal detention,[114] reduced periods for 'voluntary' departure,[115] the linking of asylum and return procedures,[116] and the limitation of the suspensive effect of appeals and access to legal remedies.[117] In the meantime, the common approach towards irregular residents is one of social and legal exclusion so that they are disincentivized to stay and instead leave by their own means.[118]

The calls for higher return rates have for some time been coupled with anti-regularisation dynamics. Prior to 2008, regularizations were frequently considered as legitimate tools to fight exploitation, address labour market needs, and avoid the marginalization of migrant communities,[119] be it via regularization 'programmes' (one-off, time-limited schemes generally involving a large number of applicants) or 'mechanisms' (structural, open-ended procedures to regularize individuals upon the fulfilment of legally defined conditions).[120] Between 1996 and 2008, more than five million people were regularized through regularization programmes in the

[111] European Commission, 'Communication on a European Agenda on Migration', COM(2015) 240 Final, 13 May 2015 9.

[112] Carrera and Allsopp (n 66) 76. According to the authors, for returns to be sustainable they need to take into account the livelihood options for returned persons as well as the ability of the country of origin to absorb and reintegrate them.

[113] European Commission, 'Communication on a More Effective Return Policy in the European Union', COM(2017) 200 Final, 2 March 2017.

[114] European Commission, 'Proposal for a Directive of the European Parliament and the Council on common standards and procedures in Member States for returning illegally staying third-country nationals (recast)', COM(2018) 634 final (Recast Return Directive) art 18.

[115] Recast Return Directive (n 114) Article 9; Return Handbook (n 103) 36–42.

[116] Regulation (EU) 2024/1356 (n 93); Recast Return Directive (n 114) art 8(6).

[117] Recast Return Directive (n 114) art 16(3).

[118] Nicola Delvino, 'European Cities and Migrants with Irregular Status: Municipal Initiatives for the Inclusion of Irregular Migrants in the Provision of Services' (2017) COMPAS—University of Oxford 3. Chapter 5 of this book provides an analysis of the rights of irregular migrants under EU law (zooming in on non-removable migrants in particular).

[119] European Commission, 'Communication on Immigration, Integration and Employment', COM(2003) 336 Final, 3 June 2003 26; European Commission 'Communication on the Links between Legal and Illegal Immigration', COM(2004) 412 Final, 4 June 2004 9–10.

[120] Martin Baldwin-Edwards and Albert Kraler (eds), *REGINE—Regularisations in Europe* (Amsterdam University Press 2009) 10. These are analysed extensively in Chapter 6.

EU (3 million in Spain, Portugal, Italy, and Greece alone).[121] With the adoption of the 2008 European Pact on Immigration and Asylum, however, EU Member States committed, very much against the opinion of Mediterranean Member States, to use only case-by-case regularization.[122] Even if the Pact did not result in binding obligations but merely in political guidelines, the strong message sent by the Pact permeated the Commission's position,[123] and led Member States to refrain from conducting large-scale regularization programmes in the decade that followed—although national developments during and in the aftermath of Covid-19 seem to question the extent to which this policy taboo remains.[124]

2.3 EU law versus reality: Return rates and the manufacturing of non-removable migrants

Almost fifteen years have passed since the Return Directive was adopted and there is no evidence that either the current framework or the new (but very similar) recast proposal has led, or will lead, to greater return rates.[125] Indeed, despite ever-increasing attention and resources devoted to return and readmission, return rates hit record lows year after year (see Figure 1.1). To put it in numbers, in 2023, out of 1,265,350 irregular migrants found to be present in the EU, 435,860 were ordered to leave, and 84,580 were deported. Equally important is that deportation gaps can accumulate over the years. While statistics on irregular migration populations are inherently limited and vary from year to year, estimates in Europe have generally ranged from 2 to 5 million residents over the past decades.[126] This means that, if one compares the number of effective returns with the (estimated) total population of irregular migrants in Europe, return rates would in fact be much lower.

Whereas the fate of those who are not returned is not recorded in official statistics, it can be assumed that some of them accounted for unrecorded voluntary

[121] Kate Brick, 'Regularizations in the European Union: The Contentious Policy Tool', *Migration Policy Institute Insight*, December 2011 5, available at: <https://www.migrationpolicy.org/pubs/EURegularization-Insight.pdf>.

[122] Council of the European Union, 'European Pact on Immigration and Asylum', 13440/08, 24 September 2008 7.

[123] Costello (n 33) 100.

[124] Regularisation practices by the Member States are dealt with separately in Chapter 6.

[125] European Parliament, 'The Proposed Return Directive (Recast) Substitute Impact Assessment', 12 February 2019, 9, available at: <https://www.europarl.europa.eu/thinktank/en/document.html?reference=EPRS_STU(2019)631727>.

[126] By 2008, the most comprehensive study on the issue to date, conducted by the CLANDESTINO project, estimated an irregular migrant population of 1.9 to 3.8 million people (Dita Vogel, Vesela Kovacheva, and Hannah Prescott, 'The Size of the Irregular Migrant Population in the European Union—Counting the Uncountable?' (2011) 49(5) International Migration 78). According to the Pew Research Centre, by 2017, there were between 3.9 and 4.8 million irregular residents (Phillip Connor and Jeffrey S Passel, 'Europe's Unauthorized Immigrant Population Peaks in 2016, Then Levels Off', *Pew Research Centre*, 13 November 2019, available at: <https://www.pewresearch.org/global/2019/11/13/europes-unauthorized-immigrant-population-peaks-in-2016-then-levels-off/>).

departures, while some others were granted a residence permit. There are also instances of irregular migrants being subjected to more than one return decision. There are, however, a substantial number that remain within the EU's territory in a situation of protracted irregularity.

Non-removable migrants are a group of persons that, following the Return Directive's 'return or regularize' logic, should not exist, but whose realities are well documented. As acknowledged by the Commission, although the EU framework is aimed at avoiding these situations, reality is far more complex, and this approach may in fact increase the number of persons who are issued unenforceable return decisions.[127]

Yet there is no obligation for Member States to regularize undocumented migrants (non-removable or otherwise) at any stage, as the Return Directive does not include a maximum time limit after which a residence permit should be issued following failed deportation attempts. The European Parliament has, however, suggested that Member States expand the use of the 'may' clause of Article 6(4) RD to regularize when return proves to be impossible.[128]

Nevertheless, the Court of Justice has made clear that there is no such an obligation under EU law. In *Mahdi*, one of several CJEU cases involving non-removable migrants,[129] the applicant could not be returned to Sudan because the country was only willing to readmit voluntary returnees, refusing the issuance of travel documents for the purposes of forcible removal.[130] In this context, the referring court inquired about whether the Return Directive, interpreted in light of the need to respect fundamental rights, the dignity of the person, and the principle of proportionality, was to be interpreted as granting a temporary residence permit in a situation in which a person who does not receive identity documents from the country of origin, has exhausted the maximum period of pre-removal detention, and still has no 'reasonable prospect' of being removed.[131] While the ruling was quite protective in a number of areas, including pre-removal detention, the conceptualization of returnee cooperation or the access to written notification of non-removability, the Court remained on the safe side as regards regularization, holding that the Return Directive contains no binding obligations to issue a residence permit.[132] Then, EU law, as it stands, does not provide a way out of

[127] Return Handbook (n 103) 74.

[128] European Parliament, 'Report on the Implementation of the Return Directive', 2019/2208(INI), 17 December 2020 para 23, available at: <https://www.europarl.europa.eu/doceo/document/A-9-2020-0238_EN.html>.

[129] See further Case C-357/09, *Said Shamilovich Kadzoev* [2009] EU:C:2009:741; Case C-562/13, *Centre public d'action sociale d'Ottignies-Louvain-la-Neuve v Abdida* [2014] EU:C:2014:2453.

[130] Case C-146/14 PPU, *Bashir Mohamed Ali Mahdi* [2014] EU:C:2014:1320 para 21.

[131] Ibid, para 86.

[132] Ibid, paras 74, 85, and 89. TCNs might regularize their stay under EU law as family members of both static and mobile EU citizens (see Case C-34/09, *Gerardo Ruiz Zambrano v Office national de l'emploi (ONEm)* [2011] EU:C:2011:124; Case C-127/08, *Metock and others v Minister for Justice, Equality and Law Reform* [2008] EU:C:2008:449). In these cases, however, the right to regularize

irregularity for non-removable migrants.[133] Still, and even though their situation is only marginally addressed in the Return Directive,[134] the CJEU has produced several rulings which are relevant for at least some non-removable migrants in a number of areas, including detention, criminalization, access to safeguards, and access to written confirmation of their situation. These will be addressed at length in Chapter 5 of this book.

But how do non-removable migrants come to be in the first place, and to what extent is this phenomenon problematic? The creation of non-removability is a two-way process. First, it begins with persons' classification as irregular, that is, by placing them outside of legality. This is to be determined by domestic law and as such generally falls beyond the scope of EU law, which merely defines 'illegally-staying third-country nationals' as those 'who do not or who no longer fulfil the [domestic] conditions for entry, stay or residence in a Member State'.[135] While EU law is also partially responsible for the illegalization of people, for example, via narrow interpretations of EU asylum law (see Chapter 2 of this book on subsidiary protection), as well as by endorsing binary understandings of migration status, the processes through which TCNs fall into irregularity occur *mainly* at the national level, and as such fall largely beyond the scope of this study. Second, and most importantly for our purposes, non-removability materializes when there are reasons precluding the deportation of an irregular migrant. The difficulties encountered by Member States relate to various and complex factors, many of which are beyond the control of both the Member State and the migrant.

The EU Agency for Fundamental Rights (FRA) distinguishes between three types of causes precluding removal in the EU, namely: (1) 'Human rights law and humanitarian considerations' (legal barriers to expulsion);[136] (2) 'Practical circumstances and technical reasons'; and (3) 'Policy choices' not to remove.[137] These obstacles show that the 'return or regularize' binary is based on a flawed premise, namely that every migrant that is not in possession of a residence permit can be deported. This book will look precisely at the processes that generate non-removability at the EU level, putting forward the claim that the EU, alone or in

derives from a primary right of EU citizens to be accompanied by their family members, be it under Directive 2004/38 or directly by the treaties.

[133] This has been confirmed in *X*, where the referring court had inquired about the obligation to regularize seriously ill persons whose removal would be contrary to Article 19(2) of the EU Charter of Fundamental Rights. The CJEU answered again in the negative (see Case C-69/21, *X v Staatssecretaris van Justitie en Veiligheid* [2022] EU:C:2022:913 paras 83--87).

[134] See mainly Recital 12, Article 9, and Article 14 of the Return Directive.

[135] Return Directive (n 96) Recital 5.

[136] In this book, purely 'humanitarian' cases where there is no legal obligation for the state to refrain from expulsion will be considered as a 'policy choice' rather than a legal obstacle to deportation.

[137] European Agency for Fundamental Rights (FRA), 'Fundamental Rights of Migrants in an Irregular Situation in the European Union', 21 November 2011 30–32, available at: <https://fra.europa.eu/en/publication/2012/fundamental-rights-migrants-irregular-situation-european-union>.

interaction with European human rights law, has not only been unable to reduce grey areas in this field but actively participates in the creation of non-removability. Leaving aside theoretical discussions on whether states or the EU have generally 'lost control' over the migrant population, I will zoom in on the mechanisms that lead to irregular migrants remaining on EU territory without a permit (Chapters 2, 3, and 4), as well as on the legal framework applicable to non-removable migrants under EU law (Chapter 5) and their regularization prospects (Chapter 6). In some cases, non-removability derives from the clash between sovereign state prerogatives and norms of a higher hierarchical value, be it in the form of states' *non-refoulement* obligations or migrants' membership claims—leading to the creation of 'legal non-removables'. In other cases, however, irregular migrants do not hold a subjective right not to be removed, but expulsion fails due to many other reasons related to identity-determination challenges and the lack of documents, inter-state diplomatic hurdles, migrant agency, or statelessness—leading to 'practical non-removables'.[138] Lastly, states may decide not to expel an irregular migrant merely as a result of a policy choice not to do so—leading to 'non-removed' rather than 'non-removable' migrants. This can be, among other reasons, as a response to anti-deportation campaigns, due to the excessive cost attached to deportation, or because forced removal may at times simply prove pointless for the host state. This book will deal primarily with 'legal' and 'practical' non-removables, although situations of non-removed persons due to states' policy choices will be incorporated sporadically.

Yet, why is the study of non-removable migrants relevant for EU law scholarship? After all, the impossibility to expel individuals might derive from the 'liberality' of state practice. Migrants make their cases for non-removal before national and supranational courts on human rights grounds and, as such, non-removal is a victory for migrants' rights. Moreover, concerning the readmission of so-called 'economic migrants', the position of non-cooperative countries of origin might be seen as challenging statist migration control assumptions and correcting for historical injustices tied to colonialism.[139] Non-deportability, *per se*, can be considered as a positive feature of liberal democracies which, due to a variety of reasons, cannot (and should not) expel every person that does not have lawful administrative status. Yet there seems to be something particularly troubling about keeping people stuck between a country in which they live, but are not allowed to, and a country to which they should go back, but cannot.[140]

[138] Even though, under national law, statelessness might offer legal safeguards to deportation, or a residence permit, there is no legal obligation under EU law to do so. Thus, it is common that states seek to deport stateless migrants but are subsequently unable to find third countries willing to readmit them. Therefore, statelessness is addressed in this book as a 'practical' obstacle to deportation even if, under national law, it might also be a legal 'obstacle' to return.

[139] Achiume (n 25) 1517.

[140] Maaike Vanderbruggen and others, 'Point of No Return: The Futile Detention of Unreturnable Migrants', *Detention Action*, 7 January 2014, available at: <https://ecre.org/point-of-no-return-the-futile-detention-of-unreturnable-migrants>.

First, non-removability poses a conceptual and normative challenge. At a conceptual level, non-removable migrants challenge existing migrant categorizations due to the chronic *liminality* of their stay.[141] EU migration laws are grounded not only on the legal fiction that regular and irregular migration are perfectly distinguishable categories,[142] but also on the idea that irregularity is a short-term and purely transitional phase, a relatively unproblematic prelude to full exclusion (via deportation) or inclusion (via regularization). Irregularity is then, by definition, a temporary status, as it is based on the prognosis that irregular migrants will soon transition out of irregularity. The situation of non-removable migrants illustrates the *chronification* of irregularity,[143] challenging predominant notions of irregularity as an inherently provisional (non)status. Normatively, non-removable migrants acquire moral claims to membership with the passage of time. In short, the social membership argument goes that irregular residents should be granted a right to belong to the societies in which they live on the basis of the personal, social, and familial links they develop therein. There seems to be consensus among theorists working on immigration that physical presence in a state for a considerable period of time creates at least a strong presumption for formal inclusion.[144] Scholarly consensus in this area shows that it is not necessary to go as far as asserting a universal human right to migrate,[145] nor to advocate for open borders,[146] to unveil the

[141] The notion of liminality was first introduced in anthropology studies in Turner's analysis of communal social rituals to refer to transitional and ambiguous periods of 'statuslessness' taking place during tribal *rites de passage* from lower to higher social categories (Victor W (Victor Witter) Turner, 'Liminality and Communitas' in *The Ritual Process: Structure and Anti-structure* (Aldine de Gruyter 1995) 94–129) (although the term was originally coined by Arnold van Gennep in 1909 (see Arnold van Gennep, *Les rites de passage* (A et J Picard 1981)). Liminal statuses are thereby understood as temporary and transitional phases of 'limbo' that take place between different statuses and finalize when individuals are re-incorporated into society and 'revitalized', acquiring a new status with clearly defined rights and obligations (Turner 95). The related concept of legal liminality was later introduced by sociologists studying immigration in the US. In 2005, Cecilia Menjívar famously applied the concept to refer to spaces between conventional legal categories in the context of Salvadoran immigrants in the US. The 'legal non-existence', uncertainty, ambiguity, and precariousness (ie the *liminality*) of their status was however not a transitory and empowering phase, as described by Turner, but instead an indefinite and long-lasting position of many undocumented migrants in the US, who were often protected from expulsion but unable to access lawful and stable residence (Cecilia Menjívar, 'Liminal Legality: Salvadoran and Guatemalan Immigrants' Lives in the United States' (2006) 111 American Journal of Sociology 999, 999, 1001, 1008, 1015).

[142] Anna Triandafyllidou, *Irregular Migration in Europe: Myths and Realities* (Ashgate Pub 2010) 8–9. As this book partially illustrates, non-removable migrants at times challenge binary understandings of migrant (il)legality (see Chapter 5).

[143] By *chronification*, I refer both to a time dimension (namely the continuation of irregularity over time) and to the fact that, just like a chronic health condition, it has persistent effects which make it incompatible with leading an ordinary life.

[144] David Miller, *Strangers in Our Midst: The Political Philosophy of Immigration* (Harvard University Press 2016) 121, 127; See further Ayelet Shachar, *The Birthright Lottery: Citizenship and Global Inequality* (Harvard University Press 2009) 184–88; Thomas Nagel, 'The Problem of Global Justice' (2005) 33 Philosophy & Public Affairs 113, 133; Joseph H Carens, *The Ethics of Immigration* (Oxford University Press 2013) 151.

[145] Kieran Oberman, 'Immigration as a Human Right' in Sarah Fine and Lea Ypi (eds), *Migration in Political Theory: The Ethics of Movement and Membership* (Oxford University Press 2016).

[146] Joseph H Carens, 'Aliens and Citizens: The Case for Open Borders' (1987) 49 The Review of Politics 251.

morally troubling nature of long-term irregular migrant populations. Moreover, the *sui generis* situation of non-removable migrants makes their case particularly problematic if compared with other irregular residents. This is the case first because their moral claims cannot be said to compete against migration control prerogatives—due to the state's incapacity to realistically enforce the latter. Second, non-removability often reveals a situation of *de facto statelessness*, denying non-removable migrants the 'right to have rights' (be it in the host or home country), in an Arendtian sense.[147] The extent to which such claims might be legally recognized under European law is analysed in Chapters 3 and 6 of this book. For now, it suffices to note that neither EU law nor the ECHR set a time limit beyond which a residence permit should be issued to irregular migrants, no matter the time spent in the country nor the reason preventing removal.

Second, non-removability undermines the rights of migrants. Non-removability effectively solves the potential human rights violations that might occur in the countries of origin upon removal (and as such is generally preferable to deportation) but raises new fundamental rights issues in the host country. Despite universalist aspirations of human rights frameworks, it is common knowledge that irregular migrants are not only entitled to fewer rights than citizens and lawful residents, but also struggle to have access to the rights to which they are entitled in practice.[148] Migrants' categorization as regular or irregular is key for them to have access to basic rights, and also make their exclusion legally justified and ethically acceptable to the public. As a result, irregular migrants live in a situation of vulnerability which puts them at increased risk of human rights violations, including labour exploitation as well as lack of access to housing, healthcare, or education for children, among others.[149] This remains true for non-removable migrants, although an in-depth examination of the rights to which non-removable migrants, as a *sui generis* migrant category, are entitled under EU law is conducted in Chapter 5.

Third, non-removability poses a challenge to the effectiveness of EU law. In the EU context, deportation can no longer be seen as a sovereign prerogative of states but rather as a 'sovereign obligation', as states are obliged to carry out return decisions, and to do so efficiently and as soon as possible.[150] As explained in section 2.1 of this chapter, while the Return Directive is, primarily, a tool for expulsion, the rationale of the Directive, as interpreted by the CJEU, is that Member States should either return or regularize so as to reduce grey areas. As seen above, the CJEU has clarified that measures other than enforcing the return decision or regularization

[147] Noora Lori, 'Statelessness, "In-Between" Statuses, and Precarious Citizenship', *The Oxford Handbook of Citizenship* (Oxford University Press 2017) 755.

[148] Colm O'Cinneide, 'The Human Rights of Migrants with Irregular Status: Giving Substance to Aspirations of Universalism' in Sarah Spencer and Anna Triandafyllidou (eds), *Migrants with Irregular Status in Europe: Evolving Conceptual and Policy Challenges* (Springer International Publishing 2020).

[149] European Agency for Fundamental Rights (FRA) (n 137) 3.

[150] *El Dridi* (n 99); *Achughbabian* (n 98).

are not allowed by EU law. Then, non-removable migrants are a category of people that, from the viewpoint of EU law, 'should not exist' because their presence runs directly against the Return Directive's objectives.[151] Precisely because the logic is that persons should be either expelled or granted a permit, little is foreseen for those who are neither expelled nor regularized, as their very existence is a challenge to EU legality.

Fourth, at a more general level, and although the EU has very limited powers as regards social policies, the phenomenon of non-removable migrants is against EU policies in the social domain, which are aimed at reducing poverty, homelessness, destitution, and social exclusion.[152] Also, non-removability runs contrary to the EU's goal to reduce informal labour. Unable to access lawful employment, long-term irregular migrants necessarily resort to irregular work, in contrast with the Union's goal to 'fight illegal employment' through employers' sanctions.[153] This shows the irrationality of not letting long-term residents contribute to the societies in which they necessarily live. Moreover, EU institutions have expressed the view that the issue of non-removable migrants, in the absence of comprehensive and harmonized rules on their treatment, constitutes an incentive for 'secondary movements', as these persons might simply move to countries where the conditions of stay are comparatively better.[154] Indeed, for protection-seekers who do not qualify for subsidiary protection, refugee status, or temporary protection under EU law, there are more than sixty non-EU harmonized statuses of protection across EU Member States.[155] Moreover, for those who do not qualify for asylum under domestic or EU law, Member States also foresee a wide range of sub-statuses, and access to rights varies greatly.[156]

Paradoxically, non-removability is a phenomenon that challenges EU law but that also proliferates as a result of the workings of EU laws and policies.

[151] Mathilde Heegaard Bausager, Johanne Köpfli Moller, and Solon Ardittis, 'Study on the Situation of Third-Country Nationals Pending Return/Removal in the EU Member States and the Schengen Associated Countries', Ramboll and Eurasylum—European Commission, 11 March 2013 4, available at: <11032013_sudy_report_on_immigration_return-removal_en.pdf>.

[152] Nicola Delvino, 'The European Union and Migrants with Irregular Status: Opportunities and Limitations in EU Law and Policy for European Local Authorities Providing Assistance to Irregular Migrants' (2018) COMPAS—University of Oxford 25–28.

[153] Directive 2009/52/EC providing for minimum standards on sanctions and measures against employers of illegally staying third-country nationals [2009] OJ L 168 Recital 1.

[154] European Commission, 'Fitness Check on EU Legislation on Legal Migration', SWD(2019) 1055 Final, 29 March 2019 51; Council of the European Union, 'Presidency paper on addressing challenges relating to migrants in a situation of prolonged illegal stay', 7560/20, 27 April 2020.

[155] European Migration Network (EMN), 'The Different National Practices Concerning Granting of Non-EU Harmonised Protection Statuses', December 2010 105, available at: <https://emn.ie/publications/the-different-national-practices-concerning-granting-of-non-eu-harmonised-protection-statuses-emn-synthesis-report-2/>.

[156] European Migration Network (EMN), 'Responses to long-term irregularly staying migrants: practices and challenges in the EU and Norway', July 2021, available at: <https://www.emnspain.gob.es/en/-/responses-to-long-term-irregular-staying-migrants-practices-and-challenges-in-the-eu-and-norway>.

Non-removability derives from challenges to deportation and state sovereignty from *outside* but also from *within* EU law. As shown in Chapters 3 and 4, non-removability remains a challenge to EU law that can be simultaneously the result of EU (fundamental rights) law in action. As a matter of fact, the Return Directive, once perceived as a 'Directive of shame', has gradually constitutionalized a number of guarantees for irregular migrants and led to an increase in judicial review and accountability.[157] Thus, non-removability is not (or at least not always) an unfortunate anomaly resulting from inadequate transposition or implementation of EU law, but can rather result from the application of European norms of a higher hierarchical value. Thus, EU law may co-create and reproduce (but not solve) some of the very issues it aims to confront.

3. Aims, arguments, and structure

As explained in this chapter, non-removability embodies the ambiguities of a migration framework that is often incapable of meeting its own deportation aims, but that is simultaneously unwilling to let go of its migration control tendencies. On the basis of the foregoing, the first aim of the book (Part I—Chapters 2, 3, and 4) is to offer a critical diagnosis of non-removability at the EU level, rather than a solution to it. Building on the previously discussed theoretical scholarship on whether and why migration policies generally 'fail' (if at all), this book sheds light on the legal and policy processes that help explain why, despite decades of return-oriented policies, the EU's return *acquis* seems to be structurally ineffective in relation to its stated aims. In doing so, it puts forward the argument that EU law, alone or in interaction with European human rights, has not only been unable to reduce grey areas in this field, but also participates in the creation of limbo spaces of non-removability. The book provides, for the first time, a systematic and critical account of the legal, practical, and policy processes that often render deportation attempts futile across the EU. This book's second aim (Part II—Chapters 5 and 6) is closely related to the first. It is to showcase the legal implications of such a gap and suggest adequate solutions to it. What are the consequences for those who stay without a valid residence permit in Europe? What are the legal (sub)statuses and rights available to non-removable migrants under EU law? What are their possible regularization prospects? In answering these questions, the book is structured as follows.

[157] Madalina Moraru, Galina Cornelisse, and Philippe de Bruycker, *Law and Judicial Dialogue on the Return of Irregular Migrants from the European Union* (Hart 2020); Violeta Moreno-Lax and others, 'The EU Approach on Migration in the Mediterranean' European Parliament, Study requested by the LIBE Committee, June 2021 47, available at: <https://www.europarl.europa.eu/thinktank/en/document/IPOL_STU(2021)694413>.

Chapters 2 and 3 expose the legal processes that, at the European level, manufacture situations of non-removability. Chapter 2 exposes the gaps that exist between EU asylum law and European human rights law. In doing so, it explores the possibility that states' *non-refoulement* obligations under Article 3 ECHR, as interpreted by the ECtHR, are not followed by the award of refugee status or subsidiary protection under EU asylum law, as interpreted by the CJEU. First, this can take place because, for subsidiary protection, the CJEU has interpreted the concept of 'torture or inhuman or degrading treatment' in a narrower manner than the ECtHR. This has so far been the case in situations of illness, where the CJEU demands the existence of 'intentional deprivation' of treatment by the country of origin for subsidiary protection to apply—in contrast with Strasbourg's absolute and non-derogable *non-refoulement* obligations. Second, non-removability takes place where refugees or beneficiaries of subsidiary protection are excluded from such status, or this is withdrawn, ended, or not renewed, normally in the context of criminal convictions. Again, applicants remained protected from deportation by absolute and non-derogable obligations under the ECHR.

Chapter 3 zooms in on membership-based challenges to deportation, analysing three legal manifestations of belonging in European law, namely family and private life under Article 8 ECHR, and long-term residence and EU citizenship under EU law. In the context of the ECHR, the right to have respect for one's private and family life, though offering shallow and unpredictable levels of protection, functions as a legal safeguard against expulsion (often without offering legal status). Chapter 3 also shows that precarious residence and non-removability can affect even the most privileged categories of non-nationals. For TCNs and EU citizens, long-term residence under Directive 2003/109 and EU citizenship under Directive 2004/38 offer the most notable recognitions of civic membership under EU law—particularly in the case of EU citizens. Yet, as this chapter illustrates, even in these cases, EU law does not fully shield foreigners from precarity and non-deportability.

Chapter 4 focuses on 'practical' obstacles to deportation, that is, those that arise when migrants do not have a subjective right to remain in the host state. Aware that the main obstacles undermining the EU's deportation agenda are found in the lack of readmission cooperation from third countries and the difficulties in identifying and documenting returnees, the response of the EU has been to develop a common readmission policy with countries of origin and transit. Chapter 4 maps these policies and focuses on their operability gaps, pointing at the lack of coherence between the Union's internal policy aims and their external implementation.

Chapter 5 inquires into the ambiguous legal statuses that result from non-removability under the Return Directive. In a context of binary understandings of migration statuses, non-removable migrants are often subsumed within the irregular migrant population, being therefore targeted by laws and policies of exclusion. Chapter 5 however brings to light the subtle yet far-reaching role of EU law in regulating their status and rights. It identifies narrow but clearly identifiable spaces of inclusion and exclusion, and puts forward the argument that the Return Directive, as interpreted by the CJEU, stratifies non-removable migrants into different sub-categories, depending on their actual or perceived behaviour and on how 'justified' their reasons for non-return are perceived by the EU legislator.

Considering the precarious situation of those who inevitably remain in Europe, Chapter 6 looks into their possible avenues for regularization. In doing so, it looks into the scant EU framework on regularization and its relationship with the EU return *acquis*, and it proposes normative claims for the regularization of non-removable migrants. Moreover, it looks into domestic regularization practices, which are systematized based on their methods of implementation and their underlying purposes. Lastly, Chapter 6 hints at possible regularization avenues under European law.

PART II

MANUFACTURING NON-REMOVABILITY IN THE EUROPEAN UNION

2

Human Rights, *Non-Refoulement*, and Non-Removability—The Mismatch Between Asylum and Human Rights in the EU

How do non-removable migrants come to be and what is the role of EU law in the creation of their liminal spaces? As anticipated in Chapter 1, the impossibility to deport irregular migrants can result from legal reasons, practical obstacles, or states' policy choices not to deport. This chapter deals with legally produced situations of non-removability that arise when persons who hold human rights claims to non-removal under Article 3 of the European Convention on Human Rights (ECHR) are not recognized (or lose their status) as refugees or beneficiaries of subsidiary protection under EU law. These are, in short, situations where deportation is prohibited because there are substantial grounds for believing that the person would be at risk of suffering irreparable harm upon return, but that nevertheless fall beyond the reach of EU asylum law. The non-removability gap as a result of this cannot be underestimated, as research shows that the countries of origin of non-removable migrants and asylum-seekers often coincide.[1]

Section 1 opens with a review of the European Court of Human Rights' (ECtHR) jurisprudence on Article 3 ECHR as a *non-refoulement* obligation, emphasizing the Court's jurisprudence in purely situational cases (i.e. those where the country of origin bears no direct responsibility on the potentially inflicted harm), and in particular its 2016 Grand Chamber ruling in *Paposhvili*.

Section 2 then compares the scope of Article 3 ECHR with the protection afforded under Article 15 of Directive 2011/95/EU (hereinafter 'Qualification Directive' or simply QD).[2] In doing so, it zooms in on Article 15(b) QD, whose

[1] Sergio Carrera and Massimo Merlino, 'Assessing EU Policy on Irregular Immigration Under the Stockholm Programme', Centre for European Policy Studies (CEPS), 14 October 2010, 33. Eurostat statistics on asylum applications are available at: <https://ec.europa.eu/eurostat/statistics-explained/index.php?title=Asylum_applications_-_monthly_statistics>, while the number of orders to leave and return rates disaggregated by countries of origin is available at the European Commission's Knowledge Centre on Migration and Demography (KCMD) Data Portal (available at: <https://migration-demography-tools.jrc.ec.europa.eu/dashboards/eu-migration-return-msc-and-sacs-perspective>).

[2] Following the adoption of the 2024 Pact on Migration and Asylum, the Qualification Directive will be repealed by the Qualification Regulation (2024/1347), which is meant to increase the degree of harmonization in this area and will enter into force in 2026. The rules discussed in this chapter remain largely unaffected by legislative change. However, the Regulation will be discussed where it introduces changes to the norms established under the Directive.

When Deportation Fails. Diego Ginés Martín, Oxford University Press. © Diego Ginés Martín 2025.
DOI: 10.1093/9780198941231.003.0002

wording and risk-assessment criteria (i.e. the existence of *substantial grounds* to believe that there is a *real risk* of *torture or inhuman or degrading treatment or punishment* upon removal) mirror those of Article 3 ECHR in an attempt to narrow the gap between *non-refoulement* and asylum law. Based on an analysis of the jurisprudence of the Court of Justice of the EU (CJEU), I find that, contrary to the ECtHR, the CJEU has been unwilling to engage in a dialogue with the Strasbourg Court, holding that both provisions do not necessarily go hand in hand, while attaching a narrower scope to the very same concept (so far in cases of illness). Acknowledging the legal arguments against a coherent interpretation of both provisions, I contend that the Qualification Directive allows for a different interpretation of subsidiary protection that captures the latest developments of the principle of *non-refoulement* and avoids non-removability.

In section 3, I shift the focus to situations where non-removability does not derive from differing interpretations as to what amounts to 'torture or inhuman or degrading treatment', but rather from the exclusion from or withdrawal of international protection. This will normally take place in the context of criminal behaviour, where exclusion or withdrawal from asylum takes place in a context where persons remain protected from expulsion under absolute and non-derogable obligations.

1. Article 3 ECHR and *non-refoulement*

1.1 *Soering* and beyond: Absolute and non-derogable protection under the ECHR

The principle of *non-refoulement*, first envisaged in the 1951 Convention Relating to the Status of Refugees (hereinafter Refugee Convention or Geneva Convention),[3] has been expanded by different instruments under international human rights law. In the European context, the ECtHR has consistently interpreted Article 3 ECHR as a non-removal clause since the seminal case of *Soering* in 1989.[4] Despite the fact that this provision simply states that 'no one shall be subject to inhuman or degrading treatment or punishment' and does not make an explicit reference to the prohibition of *refoulement*, the ECtHR ruled that the extradition of the applicant to face the death row in the United States would be 'contrary to the spirit and intendment of the Article'. As a result, Article 3 included an obligation not to extradite if there were *substantial grounds* to believe that there was a *real risk*

[3] The Refugee Convention states that '[n]o Contracting State shall expel or return ('refouler') a refugee in any manner whatsoever to the frontiers of territories where his life or freedom would be threatened on account of his race, religion, nationality, membership of a particular social group or political opinion' (Convention Relating to the Status of Refugees, 28 July 1951, 189 UNTS 137 art 33(1)).

[4] *Soering v the United Kingdom*, App No 1/1989/161/217 (ECtHR 7 July 1989).

that treatment proscribed by Article 3 would have followed upon the applicant's removal.[5] In other words, Article 3 ECHR not only prohibits torture or inhuman or degrading treatment within Convention countries, but also prohibits extradition to countries where applicants would face such treatment.

Since *Soering*, the ECtHR has maintained that the principles and reasoning there articulated apply not only to cases of extradition but to any form of expulsion,[6] underscoring the absolute and non-derogable nature of states' *non-refoulement* obligations. As a result, the ECtHR has granted protection from removal to former refugees whose legal residence was withdrawn due to criminal convictions,[7] or international criminals accused of terrorist acts, irrespective of the applicant's conduct and offence committed,[8] among other persons.

It is also due to the absolute nature of *non-refoulement* that the ECtHR decided to abandon the idea that state actors must be the source of the alleged risk in *H.L.R* and subsequent jurisprudence.[9] In these cases, the Court positioned itself with the so-called protection view (as opposed to the 'accountability view'), according to which the accountability of a state is not a necessary condition to grant international protection.[10]

As regards the substantive conceptualization of torture or inhuman or degrading treatment or punishment, the ECtHR has extended its scope to the death penalty, situations of indiscriminate violence, and medical cases.

Concerning the death penalty, the Court made explicit in *Al-Saadoon* that a real risk of execution amounts to inhuman or degrading treatment, and therefore that the transfer of the applicants to Iraqi authorities to face a *real risk* of being condemned to the death penalty and executed had violated their rights under Article 3 ECHR.[11] Whereas in *Soering* the source of inhuman or degrading treatment was not the death penalty itself but the 'death-row phenomenon', in *Al-Saadoon* the Court found that consistent state practice among Council of Europe States had led to the complete abolition of the death penalty, and hence that a real risk of being sentenced to death and executed, regardless of its materialization in practice, was enough to trigger Article 3 ECHR.[12]

The Court has also observed a violation of Article 3 ECHR in the return of third-country nationals (TCNs) to situations of indiscriminate violence in the country of

[5] Ibid, para 91.

[6] *Cruz Varas and Others v Sweden*, App No 15576/89 (ECtHR 20 March 1991) paras 69–70.

[7] *Ahmed v Austria*, App No 71/1995/577/663 (ECtHR 17 December 1996).

[8] *Saadi v Italy*, App No 37201/06 (ECtHR 28 February 2008).

[9] *H.L.R. v France*, App No 24573/95 (ECtHR 29 April 1997). In the same line, see: *Salah Sheekh v the Netherlands*, App No 1948/04 (ECtHR 11 January 2007) para 163; *Sufi and Elmi v the United Kingdom*, App No 8319/07 and 11449/07 (ECtHR 28 June 2011) para 213.

[10] Ben Vermeulen and others, 'Persecution by Third Parties' (1998) 75 Nijmegen University Centre for Migration Law 10–17; Catherine Phuong, 'Persecution by Third Parties and European Harmonization of Asylum Policies' (2001) 16 Georgetown Immigration Law Journal 81, 81.

[11] *Al-Saadoon and Mufdhi v the United Kingdom*, App No 61498/08 (ECtHR 2 March 2010) para 144.

[12] Ibid, para 116.

origin. In *N.A.*, the Court stressed that it had never excluded the possibility that a situation of generalized violence in a country of destination reached such a level of intensity as to entail that any removal to that country or region would necessarily be in breach of Article 3 of the Convention,[13] but it did not provide any further guidance and it finally decided the case based on a series of individual risk factors. It was in *Sufi and Elmi* that the ECtHR found that the situation of indiscriminate violence in Somalia was of such intensity that persons returned to Mogadishu and relocated to the region in question would be at risk of suffering inhuman or degrading treatment solely on account of their presence there.[14] Interestingly, both applicants had been convicted for crimes committed in the United Kingdom (and their humanitarian protection had been withdrawn as a result), giving the ECtHR another opportunity to highlight the absolute and non-derogable character of states' obligations under Article 3 ECHR regardless of the applicants' behaviour.[15] More recently, in *Liu*, the ECtHR concluded that China's refusal to let independent monitoring mechanisms access their detention centres, together with independent reports from UN bodies and NGOs suggesting that torture and other forms of ill-treatment are regularly used in Chinese detention facilities, could be 'equated to a general situation of violence'.[16] This exempted the Taiwanese applicant, charged with a vast telecommunications fraud, from having to show 'specific personal grounds of fear, it being enough that it is established that, upon extradition, he will be placed in a [Chinese] detention centre or penitentiary'.[17]

1.2 From inflicted to situational risks: Cases of illness and *non-refoulement*

In addition to the case law described above, the Court has ruled that Article 3 ECHR can prevent removal in cases of illness. As early as 1997, the ECtHR had stressed in *D* that it could examine claims in medical cases where the risk stemmed from factors that did not directly or indirectly engage the responsibility of state (or non-state) actors in the country of origin.[18] However, the Court adopted a very restrictive approach, to the extent that some authors questioned the absolute nature of Article 3 ECHR in this field.[19] In *N*, the Court, arguably concerned about the budgetary burden that an expansive interpretation would place upon states,[20]

[13] *NA v the United Kingdom*, App No 25904/07 (ECtHR 17 July 2008) para 115.
[14] *N.D. and N.T. v Spain* [GC], App No 8675/15 and 8697/15 (ECtHR 13 February 2020).
[15] Ibid, para 212.
[16] *Liu v Poland*, App No 37610/18 (ECtHR 6 October 2022) paras 81–83.
[17] Ibid, para 83.
[18] *D v the United Kingdom*, App No 146/1996/767/964 (ECtHR 2 May 1997) para 115.
[19] Celine Bauloz, 'Foreigners: Wanted Dead or Alive: Medical Cases before European Courts and the Need for an Integrated Approach to Non-Refoulement' (2016) 18 European Journal of Migration and Law 409.
[20] *N v the United Kingdom*, App No 26565/05 (ECtHR 27 May 2008) para 44.

and probably reluctant to offer generous protection in cases involving purely situational risks with no specific actors involved in the causing of the harm,[21] denied protection to the applicant and reiterated that Article 3 ECHR only precluded removal in cases of illness under very exceptional circumstances. Although the applicant was suffering from an advanced state of AIDS which decreased her life expectancy from decades to less than a year if deported,[22] the Court determined that the applicant was 'stable' and 'fit to travel', and authorized her expulsion to Uganda, where she died a few months later.[23] The Court's strict interpretation in *N* was heavily criticized by the joint dissenting opinion,[24] since applicants had to be on their deathbed, as in *D*,[25] in order to be protected from expulsion under Article 3 ECHR. Then, despite the Court's claim that medical cases involving situational risks were included under the umbrella of the ECHR due to the absolute nature of *non-refoulement*, these were *de facto* excluded, tacitly concurring with the theory that those risks that do not stem from the acts of states or non-state actors are not worthy of protection.[26] In practice, this insurmountable threshold meant that every case that had sought to rely on this provision in cases of illness was rejected by the Court—until *Paposhvili*.

The case law changed drastically in 2016 under the Grand Chamber judgment of *Paposhvili*, where the threshold of severity needed to trigger Article 3 ECHR was significantly lowered. Under *Paposhvili*, the deportation of a seriously ill person will be contrary to Article 3 if there are substantial grounds to believe that the applicant, 'although not at imminent risk of dying, would face a real risk, on account of the absence of appropriate treatment in the receiving country or the lack of access to such treatment, of being exposed to a serious, rapid and irreversible decline in his or her state of health resulting in intense suffering or to a significant reduction in life expectancy'.[27] As a result, if states find that this lowered (yet still high)[28] standard of ill-treatment could be reached upon removal, they are now obliged not to deport the TCN concerned even if there is no imminent risk of death.

Paposhvili can thus be seen as the logical consequence of the ECtHR's 'protection view', which now finally recognizes the absolute nature of *non-refoulement*

[21] Bauloz (n 19) 414.

[22] *N v the United Kingdom* (n 20) paras 12 and 17.

[23] Ibid, para 47.

[24] Ibid. See Joint Dissenting Opinion of Judges Tulkens, Bonello and Spielmann in page 20.

[25] *D* (n 18). In *D*, as opposed to *N*, the applicant was critically ill, appeared to be close to death, and could not be guaranteed any basic nursing, medical care, food, or shelter in his country of origin.

[26] Kathryn Greenman, 'A Castle Built on Sand: Article 3 ECHR and the Source of Risk in Non-Refoulement Obligations in International Law' (2015) 27 International Journal of Refugee Law 264, 266.

[27] *Paposhvili v Belgium* [GC], App No 41738/10 (ECtHR 13 December 2016) para 183.

[28] In the recent Grand Chamber ruling in *Savran*, Judge Serghides contended that the standards of 'serious', 'rapid', and 'irreversible' decline, as interpreted by the Court, were 'overly restrictive and not compatible with the absolute character of the right under Article 3' (see *Savran v Denmark* [GC], App No 57467/15 (ECtHR 7 December 2021), partly concurring and partly dissenting opinion of Judge Serghides, para 21).

regardless of the source of ill-treatment. The Court's approach under *N* in which ill migrants were sent to perhaps not immediate, but certain, death was surely difficult to reconcile with its commitment to absolute and non-derogable protection. The *de facto* non-application of this general principle in cases of illness is thus to be considered as an anomaly which was finally addressed in *Pasposhvili*. And yet, protection from expulsion might simply mark the beginning of precarity and fundamental rights violations *within* the host country.

1.3 What next? *Non-refoulement* and non-removability

The ECtHR has consistently noted, first, that the obligations enshrined in the ECHR do not contain a right to asylum,[29] and second, that protection against deportation does not provide the necessary legal basis for any type of residence permit. This could already be observed in *Ahmed v Austria*, where the ECtHR protected the applicant against expulsion but noted that his status as a refugee (withdrawn due to criminal convictions) fell beyond the Court's jurisdiction.[30] Moreover, the Court stressed in *S.J.* that the fact that a TCN with a return decision is non-removable does not mean that he or she can claim entitlements to medical, social, or other forms of assistance in the host state.[31] Even in *Paposhvili*, hailed for increasing safeguards against deportation, the ECtHR framed *non-refoulement* strictly as a negative obligation of host states, disregarding their responsibility to actively protect individuals, *inter alia*, by guaranteeing access to medical care.[32]

There is, in this context, a clear gap between refugee protection as defined in the Geneva Convention, which is subject to derogations and requires the persecution of the applicant to be based on Convention grounds for refugee law to apply,[33] and the situations covered under Article 3 ECHR, which 'only' require evidence of a *real risk* of torture or inhuman or degrading treatment upon removal. The ECtHR, along with other international and regional human rights courts and bodies,[34]

[29] *M.S.S. v Belgium and Greece*, App No 30696/09 (ECtHR 21 January 2011) para 286. See also *Ahmed* (n 7) para 38.

[30] *Ahmed* (n 7) paras 35–38. For more recent cases of refugees that had their status removed but remained non-removable, see: *S v France*, App No 18207/21 (ECtHR 6 October 2022); *KI v France*, App No 5560/19 (ECtHR 15 April 2021).

[31] *SJ v Belgium*, App No 70055/10 (ECtHR 15 March 2015). The case was later referred to the Grand Chamber, which avoided ruling on the merits of the case due to a friendly settlement between the government of Belgium and the applicant.

[32] Vladislava Stoyanova, 'How Exceptional Must "Very Exceptional" Be? Non-Refoulement, Socio-Economic Deprivation, and Paposhvili v Belgium' (2017) 29 International Journal of Refugee Law 580, 586–92.

[33] Under Article 1(A)(2) of the Refugee Convention, these are 'race, religion, nationality, membership of a particular social group or political opinion'.

[34] Due to the book's geographic scope and its emphasis on legally binding standards, this chapter will focus on ECtHR jurisprudence on the issue of *non-refoulement*. It will therefore not elaborate on the jurisprudence of other international and regional human rights courts and bodies—even if these might, at times, offer protection over and above the standards set by the ECtHR. Still, it is worth noting

has expanded the scope of *non-refoulement* obligations well beyond the Refugee Convention's original intention and, as mentioned above, has offered protection from expulsion not only to (narrowly defined) refugees but also to applicants facing the death penalty, former refugees whose status had been revoked, and seriously ill people, among others. Therefore, the situations falling under the ECHR's umbrella, but outside the Refugee Convention, are manifold. This asymmetrical interaction between different supranational legal systems effectively addresses the human rights concerns in the country of origin, while giving rise to a new set of human rights issues in the host country resulting from irregular residence and destitution.[35]

It is precisely due to the Geneva Convention's incapacity to provide a comprehensive and up-to-date response to contemporary patterns of forced migration that this gap was filled (as this chapter argues, only partially) by the EU through the Qualification Directive. Under the Qualification Directive, subsidiary protection aims at complementing the narrow refugee definition by granting asylum not only to refugees *stricto sensu* but also to other persons 'genuinely in need of international protection'.[36]

that the principle of *non-refoulement* is widely regarded as a norm of customary international law, and that it can be found, explicitly or implicitly, in many international human rights treaties (where non-removal is also detached from asylum). In the UN Human Rights System, *non-refoulement* is explicitly included in Article 3 of the UN Convention Against Torture (UNCAT), and in Article 16 of the International Convention for the Protection of All Persons from Enforced Disappearance (ICPPED). Moreover, in a similar manner to the ECtHR, other UN Human Rights Treaty Bodies (UNTBs) have interpreted provisions of, *inter alia*, the International Covenant on Civil and Political Rights (ICCPR), the Convention on the Rights of the Child (CRC), and the Convention on the Elimination of All Forms of Discrimination Against Women (CEDAW), as prohibiting expulsion to third countries where some of their protected rights would be violated upon return. For recent case law, see: *Elezjana Elezaj v Denmark*, C/137/D/2858/2016 (CCPR 16 June 2023); *Tahereh Mohammdi Bandboni et al v Switzerland*, C/85/D/173/2021 (CEDAW 6 June 2023); *H.K. and S.K. v Denmark*, CRC/C/90/D/99/2019 (CRC 28 October 2022); *F.M.A. and H.K.A. v Denmark*, CRC/93/D/140/2021 (CRC 9 June 2023); *Kibrom Berhane v Switzerland*, CAT/C/76/D/983/2020 (CAT 18 July 2023).

[35] In fact, the ECtHR ruled in *M.S.S.* that migrants' situations of destitution in the host country can amount to inhuman or degrading treatment in breach of Article 3 ECHR (see *M.S.S.* (n 29)). For further insight on how the vulnerability deriving from irregularity can itself amount to inhuman or degrading treatment, see Diego Acosta Arcarazo, 'The Charter, Detention and Possible Regularization of Migrants in an Irregular Situation under the Returns Directive: Mahdi' (2015) 52 Common Market Law Review 1361.

[36] Directive 2011/95/EU on standards for the qualification of third-country nationals or stateless persons as beneficiaries of international protection, for a uniform status for refugees or for persons eligible for subsidiary protection, and for the content of the protection granted [2011] OJ L 337 (Qualification Directive) Recital 12. The same provision is now mirrored in Recital 7 of Regulation (EU) 2024/1347 on standards for the qualification of third-country nationals or stateless persons as beneficiaries of international protection, for a uniform status for refugees or for persons eligible for subsidiary protection and for the content of the protection granted [2024] OJ L 2024/1347 (Qualification Regulation).

2. Subsidiary protection in EU law: Judicial dialogue and non-removability

There is, from the EU legislator, a declared intention to complement and add to the Refugee Convention.[37][38] According to Article 2(f) QD (Article 3(6) of the Qualification Regulation (QR)), a TCN, or stateless person, will be eligible for subsidiary protection if there are *substantial grounds* to believe that, upon return to the country of origin (former country of residence if stateless), he or she would face a *real risk* of suffering *serious harm*.[39] Article 15 defines serious harm as consisting of: '(a) the death penalty or execution; or: (b) torture or inhuman or degrading treatment or punishment of an applicant in the country of origin; or: (c) serious and individual threat to a civilian's life or person by reason of indiscriminate violence in situations of international or internal armed conflict.'[40]

Therefore, in Articles 2(f) and 15 QD (3(6) and 15 QR respectively) the legislator adopts, for subsidiary protection, Strasbourg's risk-assessment criteria for non-removal cases,[41] namely the existence of *substantial grounds* to believe that there is a *real risk* of suffering *serious harm* upon removal. Article 15 QD criteria as to what a *serious harm* is also correspond, in essence, to those enshrined in ECtHR jurisprudence. Indeed, the latter now adopts a wide concept of 'torture or inhuman or degrading treatment or punishment' that includes not only Article 15(b) of the Directive but also the death penalty (*Al-Saadoon*) and situations of generalized violence in the country of origin (*Sufi and Elmi*).

The Qualification Directive was praised by the literature as the first supranational instrument harmonizing international protection beyond the Refugee Convention,[42] as well as a remarkable effort to afford status to many migrants in need of international protection which would otherwise become non-removable.[43] Indeed, the Directive, although less ambitious than the original proposal,[44] still provided a human rights–refugee law nexus. Along these lines, Recital 34 QD

[37] Part of this section is based on material that I previously published in the following article: Diego Ginés Martín, 'In Limbo: Divergent Conceptualisations of Ill-Treatment by European Courts and the Creation of Non-Removable Migrants' (2021) 6 European Papers—A Journal on Law and Integration 1173.

[38] Qualification Directive (n 36) Recital 33; Qualification Regulation (n 36) Recital 48.

[39] Qualification Directive (n 36) art 2(f); Qualification Regulation (n 36) art 3(6).

[40] Qualification Directive (n 36) art 15; Qualification Regulation (n 36) art 15.

[41] UNHCR, 'Statement on Subsidiary Protection Under the EC Qualification Directive for People Threatened by Indiscriminate Violence', January 2018 15, available at: <https://www.unhcr.org/protection/operations/479df9532/unhcr-statement-subsidiary-protection-under-ec-qualification-directive.html>.

[42] Jane McAdam, 'The European Union Qualification Directive: The Creation of a Subsidiary Protection Regime' (2005) 17 International Journal of Refugee Law 461.

[43] Cathryn Costello, *The Human Rights of Migrants and Refugees in European Law* (Oxford University Press 2015) 139.

[44] Gregor Noll, 'Fixed Definitions or Framework Legislation? The Delimitation of Subsidiary Protection Ratione Personae' (2002) 55 UNHCR New Issues in Refugee Research, Working Paper 10.

highlights that the criteria to determine an applicant's eligibility for subsidiary protection should be drawn from international obligations under human rights instruments.[45] More specifically, Recital 48 suggests that the Directive's implementation should be evaluated regularly considering the evolution of states' obligations regarding *non-refoulement*.[46] This, together with the fact that the Directive borrows the notion of *serious harm* and the risk-assessment criteria from the ECtHR, suggests that the legislator aimed at a coherent interpretation of both provisions, particularly as to what amounts to a *real risk* of suffering *torture or inhuman or degrading treatment*, in order to fill the gap of those potentially left in a legal limbo under Strasbourg's non-removal case law. As this chapter shows, however, CJEU jurisprudence indicates that this may not always be the case.[47]

Before the Directive's adoption, non-removal under Article 3 ECHR did not guarantee any legal status. Thus, in the absence of domestic forms of protection,[48] it would merely classify a person as non-removable. Under the current framework, however, non-removability will depend on whether Article 15 QD (from 2026 Article 15 QR) has a wider, narrower, or equivalent scope to that of Strasbourg's jurisprudence on Article 3 ECHR. Non-removability may thus derive from the interaction between EU asylum law and European Human Rights Law only insofar as the scope of subsidiary protection becomes narrower than that of Article 3 ECHR.

The following sub-sections will determine the extent to which this is legally possible by analysing the scope of application of subsidiary protection in paragraphs a, b, and c of Article 15, which will then be compared with ECtHR's non-removal case law. I will argue that, even if Articles 15 (a) and (c) can potentially be interpreted differently to Article 3 ECHR due to the principle of autonomy of EU law, it is the difference between Luxembourg's and Strasbourg's understandings as to what amounts to a *real risk* of suffering *torture or inhuman or degrading treatment* (Article 15 (b)) that most endangers a harmonized interpretation of EU asylum law and European human rights law.

2.1 Subsidiary protection under Articles 15(a) and 15(c) QD

The situations covered by Articles 15(a) and 15(c) QD, which provide subsidiary protection in cases of death penalty and situations of indiscriminate violence

[45] Qualification Directive (n 36) Recital 34. This is maintained in Recital 49 QR.

[46] A similar provision is included in Recital 49 QR.

[47] Since the Qualification Regulation maintains the Directive's rules on qualification, the case law discussed in this chapter remains relevant.

[48] For an overview of domestic forms of protection, see European Migration Network (EMN), 'The Different National Practices Concerning Granting of Non-EU Harmonised Protection Statuses', December 2010, available at: <https://emn.ie/publications/the-different-national-practices-concerning-granting-of-non-eu-harmonised-protection-statuses-emn-synthesis-report-2/>.

respectively, are also covered by Article 3 ECHR following *Al-Saadoon* and *Sufi and Elmi* (see section 1.1). The inclusion of paragraphs (a) and (c) originally aimed to go beyond ECHR obligations, as they were first introduced by the 2004 Qualification Directive,[49] when Strasbourg's jurisprudence did not cover the death penalty and situations of indiscriminate violence, *per se*, within the scope of Article 3 ECHR.[50] The maintenance of these provisions in the Directive's 2011 recast instead of their subsumption within Article 15(b) denotes the will of the legislator to stress the autonomy of EU law by not making it permeable to the evolutionary interpretation coming from Strasbourg, but casts doubt on their added value today.

In the case of Article 15(a), even if there is no CJEU jurisprudence to date, the fact that states are compelled to grant subsidiary protection to those facing a risk of being subjected to the death penalty upon removal does not seem to leave much scope for divergent interpretations stemming from Luxembourg and Strasbourg as to what the death penalty actually means.

As regards Article 15(c), the CJEU ruled on it for the first time in *Elgafaji*.[51] The CJEU was asked whether the provision, which prohibits expulsion to situations of 'indiscriminate violence' leading to a 'serious and individual threat to a civilian's life', should be interpreted as offering equal or wider protection than Article 3 ECHR and, if protection went beyond the Convention, what were the criteria determining its specific scope.[52] First, the Court reaffirmed the autonomy of EU law by arguing that the content of the provision in question is different to that of Article 3 ECHR and that its interpretation must be carried out independently. In doing so, the Court did not actively engage with the ECHR to formulate its view, despite the fact that, after *N.A.*, the ECtHR had already considered situations of indiscriminate violence as potentially falling within the scope of Article 3. Instead, it merely noted that 'it is . . . Article 15(b) of the Directive which corresponds, in essence, to Article 3 ECHR'.[53] Whether this assertion is coherent with the Court's subsequent jurisprudence will be addressed in section 2.3.

Second, the CJEU argued that Article 15(c) covers a more general risk of harm than paragraphs (a) and (b), and thus that a lesser degree of individualization needs to be shown by the applicants.[54] Where no individual risk is shown, the

[49] Council Directive 2004/83/EC of 29 April 2004 on minimum standards for the qualification and status of third country nationals or stateless persons as refugees or as persons who otherwise need international protection and the content of the protection granted [2004] OJ L 304 arts 15(a) and 15(c).

[50] By 2004, the ECtHR was of the view that a situation of general instability would not give rise to a breach of Article 3 ECHR unless applicants showed a stronger level of individuality by demonstrating that their personal situation was worse than that of other members of their social group (see *Vilvarajah and others v the United Kingdom*, Apps No 13163/87; 13164/87; 13165/87; 13447/87; 13448/87 (ECtHR 30 October 1991).

[51] For an in-depth analysis of the case, see R Errera, 'The CJEU and Subsidiary Protection: Reflections on Elgafaji—and After' (2011) 23 International Journal of Refugee Law 93.

[52] Case C-465/07, *Elgafaji* [2009] EU:C:2009:94 para 26.

[53] Ibid, para 28.

[54] Ibid, para 33.

CJEU did not rule out the capacity of a situation of indiscriminate violence, *per se*, to trigger subsidiary protection, but it argued that the more the applicants are able to show that they are individually affected by the threat, the lower the level of indiscriminate violence shall be required, and vice versa.[55] This approach, known as the 'sliding scale' test, sought to reconcile the *prima facie* irreconcilable tension between indiscriminate violence and the existence of an individualized threat which is by definition required in asylum cases.[56]

It was only after *Elgafaji* that the ECtHR afforded equivalent protection against expulsion. In *Sufi and Elmi*, the Strasbourg Court explicitly engaged with EU law and CJEU jurisprudence to inform and update its jurisprudence on *non-refoulement*. After conducting a thorough analysis of Article 15(c) QD,[57] the ECtHR stated that, even though it was commonly assumed that the Directive offered greater protection than the ECHR in situations of indiscriminate violence, it was not persuaded that Article 3 ECHR failed to offer protection comparable to that of the Directive. In particular, it noted that both Article 3 ECHR and 15(c) QD may be triggered in a situation of general violence where the sole presence of the applicants, regardless of their individual circumstances, would contravene both the ECHR and the QD.[58]

As occurred with Article 15(a), we find a situation in which EU asylum law once offered greater protection but where the ECtHR has willingly caught up, in this case explicitly incorporating references to EU law in its *non-refoulement* case law. Although the added value of Articles 15(c) and 15(a) is now unclear,[59] the emergence of situations of non-removability beyond those resulting from withdrawal and exclusion from subsidiary protection (see section 3 in this chapter) does not seem likely in the near future.

[55] Ibid, para 39. In *CF and DN*, the CJEU made clear that such a situation of indiscriminate violence cannot be determined exclusively on the basis of a quantitative assessment of the number of civilian casualties in a given area (Case C-901/19, *CF and* DN [2021] EU:C:2021:472 paras 21–37). Moreover, in *X, Y*, the Court ruled that national authorities *must* assess all factors related to the applicants' personal circumstances *and* the general situation in the country of origin, before assessing which type of serious harm affects an applicant (Case C-125/22, *X, Y, their six minor children v Staatssecretaris van Justitie en Veiligheid* [2023] EU:C:2023:843 para 55).

[56] Lilian Tsourdi, 'What Protection for Persons Fleeing Indiscriminate Violence? The Impact of the European Courts on the EU Subsidiary Protection Regime' in David Cantor and Jean-François Durieux (eds), *Refuge from Inhumanity? War Refugees and International Humanitarian Law* (Brill Nijhoff 2014) 277. This is not the only jurisprudential strand where the CJEU has accepted the possibility of asylum being granted without an individual assessment of applications. In October 2024, the CJEU held that Afghan women can qualify for refugee status under Article 9 QD only on the basis of gender and nationality (Joined Cases C-608/22 and C-609/22, *AH and FN* [2024] EU:C:2024:828).

[57] *Sufi and Elmi* (n 9) paras 220–26. There is, in the judgment, a full sub-section of three pages entitled 'The relationship between Article 3 of the Convention and Article 15(c) of the Qualification Directive', where the Strasbourg Court explains in detail the relationship between both provisions.

[58] Ibid, para 226.

[59] Tsourdi (n 56) 279. The author wonders: 'Is it still the case that Article 15(b) of the Directive cannot offer this kind of protection that the CJEU in *Elgafaji* has read into Article 15(c)?'

2.2 Subsidiary protection under Article 15(b) QD

Despite the fact that both the death penalty and situations of indiscriminate violence are now brought within Article 3 ECHR, it is Article 15(b) that fundamentally mirrors Article 3 of the Convention. According to Article 15(b), *serious harm* consists of 'torture or inhuman or degrading treatment *in the country of origin*' (emphasis added). However, the text of the Directive becomes ambiguous in at least two of its provisions, namely Article 15(b) itself and Article 6.[60] The wording of these articles arguably endangers the reconciliation between subsidiary protection and *non-refoulement* and can partially shed light on the restrictive understanding of subsidiary protection provided by the Court of Justice in *M'Bodj* and *MP*, according to which the Directive does not necessarily grant subsidiary protection to those protected from expulsion under Article 3 ECHR.

2.2.1 Torture or inhuman or degrading treatment in the country of origin

In the Commission's initial proposal for a Qualification Directive, Article 15(a) (now 15(b)) defined *serious harm* as 'torture or inhuman or degrading treatment or punishment',[61] mirroring the wording of Article 3 ECHR. The final version slightly departed from it and was reworded in order to include the addition 'in the country of origin', casting doubts on its scope of application.

According to McAdam, the words 'in the country of origin' might indicate the legislator's intention to obviate claims of asylum-seekers who would face ill-treatment in a third country to which return may be considered.[62] Such an interpretation would mean that those TCNs sent back to a country other than their own would still be protected from *refoulement* under the ECHR—but would be left unprotected by the Directive.

Conversely, Battjes argues that the reference to the country of origin was not added with the intention to restrict the geographical reach of subsidiary protection, but rather its substantive scope, in order to leave humanitarian cases beyond the reach of Article 15(b). According to him, a twofold distinction should be drawn in *non-refoulement* cases: on the one hand, 'classic' asylum cases in which the applicant fears torture or inhuman or degrading treatment in the country of origin; on the other hand, humanitarian cases, where it is the withdrawal of medical treatment and the act of expulsion that triggers state liability under Article 3 ECHR. The latter cases would thus be excluded for lack of serious harm in the country of origin, with the harm being caused by the deporting state.[63] If one looks at the

[60] The norms included in Articles 6 and 15 QD are kept in Articles 6 and 15 QR.

[61] European Commission, 'Proposal for a Council Directive on minimum standards for the qualification and status of third country nationals and stateless persons as refugees or as persons who otherwise need international protection', COM(2001) 510 final art 15(a).

[62] McAdam (n 42) 478.

[63] Hemme Battjes, *European Asylum Law and International Law* (Brill Nijhoff 2006) 236.

micro-history of the negotiations of the Directive, the Danish Council Presidency seemed to support this approach in a note sent to the Strategic Committee on Immigration, Frontiers and Asylum:

> Sub-paragraph (b), which is generally supported by Member States, is based on the obligations of Member States laid down in Article 3 of the ECHR and the jurisprudence of the ECtHR. However, if sub-paragraph (b) was to fully include the jurisprudence of ECtHR relating to Article 3 of ECHR, cases based purely on compassionate grounds as was the case in D versus UK (1997), also known as the Stt. Kitt's case, would have to be included. In the Stt. Kitts case, although the lack of access to a developed health system as well as lack of a social network in itself was not considered as torture or inhuman or degrading treatment, the expulsion to this situation, which would have been life threatening to the concerned person, was described as such.[64]

Similarly, Recital 15 QD establishes that TCNs who are allowed to remain in the territory of a Member State 'for reasons not due to a need for international protection but on a discretionary basis on compassionate or humanitarian grounds' fall beyond the scope of the Directive.[65] Whether this fallacious dichotomy between international protection and discretionary non-removal (which disregards states' non-removal obligations under Article 3 and 8 ECHR) is conceptually and legally sound is another matter—and will be analysed in turn.

In the meantime, the CJEU has not so far clarified the meaning of the 'in the country of origin' addition. However, the fact that it endorsed a narrow interpretation of subsidiary protection in *M'Bodj* on the basis that 'its scope does not extend to persons granted leave to reside in the territories of the Member States for other reasons, that is, on a discretionary basis on compassionate or humanitarian grounds'[66] suggests that the Court has aligned itself with this approach. Yet, by failing to clarify what 'in the country of origin' actually means, if anything at all, the Court has maintained the provision's ambiguity. In this regard, it is revealing that by 2016 (two years after *M'Bodj*) 17 out of 27 Member States bound by the Directive had not transposed the 'country of origin' limitation into domestic legislation.[67] Moreover, it is my view that the Directive allows for a different interpretation in light of recent developments in European human rights law.

[64] Council of the European Union, 'Presidency Note to Strategic Committee on Immigration, Frontiers and Asylum', 12148/02, 20 September 2002 5-6.

[65] In the Qualification Regulation, this is incorporated into the operative part of the regulation, with its Article 2(2), on the material scope of the Regulation, stating as follows 'This Regulation does not apply to national humanitarian statuses granted by Member States to third country nationals and stateless persons who do not fall under the scope of this Regulation. National humanitarian statuses, where granted, shall not entail a risk of confusion with international protection'.

[66] Case C-542/13, *M'Bodj v État Belge* [2014] EU:C:2014:2452 para 37.

[67] Bauloz (n 19) 437.

First, a literal interpretation of the words 'in the country of origin' does not seem to endorse the above-mentioned interpretation. Even if, in medical cases, ill-treatment is performed in two acts (the withdrawal of treatment in the host country and the conditions faced upon return), this only materializes in the country of origin, as it results from the combination of individual circumstances and country (of origin) conditions. Then, the removal will merely be the triggering factor of a risk to suffer an Article 3 ECHR violation, the effects of which will be felt in the country of origin after removal.[68] This becomes even clearer after *Paposhvili*, given that ill persons no longer have to be facing immediate death to be afforded protection against deportation, but 'only' must be in a situation where expulsion would trigger a real risk of 'rapid and irreversible decline in his or her state of health resulting in intense suffering or . . . a significant reduction in life expectancy'.[69] Therefore, the proscribed ill-treatment will take place mostly, if not completely, *in* the country of origin and not immediately following the withdrawal of protection in the host state.

Second, the distinction between 'classic' *non-refoulement* obligations and purely humanitarian cases no longer holds after *Paposhvili*, if it ever did. Under *D* and *N* the protection against expulsion in cases of illness was rather exceptional and limited to cases of 'compelling humanitarian grounds'.[70] The medical cases now covered under the jurisprudence of the ECtHR are wider in scope and by no means restricted to people who remain 'on a discretionary basis on compassionate or humanitarian grounds', but rather remain owing to a full-fledged *non-refoulement* obligation under the ECHR. One wonders, however, whether medical cases were ever out of the reach of the Directive on this basis, given that, even before *Paposhvili*, applicants protected under Article 3 ECHR did not remain in the territory of the host state on a discretionary basis, but owing to a legal right to stay under the ECHR—falling somewhere in between international protection and discretionary non-removal. In this line, the reasoning followed by the Court in *M'Bodj* that the applicant did not fall under the Directive because he remained in the host country 'on a discretionary basis on compassionate or humanitarian grounds' is valid so long as it refers to the granting of a discretionary domestic status of protection (in *M'Bodj*, indefinite leave to remain on medical grounds under Belgian law), but it is invalidated from the moment that the state recognizes that the applicant also has protection from expulsion under Article 3 ECHR.

2.2.2 Serious harm and situational risks

The second challenge comes from Article 6 QD, on actors of persecution or serious harm. This provision reads: 'Actors of persecution or serious harm include: (a) the

[68] Ibid, 425–26 and 431–32.
[69] *Paposvhili* [GC] (n 27) para 183.
[70] *D* (n 18) para 54.

State; (b) parties or organisations controlling the State or a substantial part of the territory of the State; (c) non-State actors . . .'[71]

In *M'Bodj*, the CJEU noted that Article 6 QD offers a list of those deemed responsible for inflicting the harm, supporting the view that it must necessarily derive from the conduct of an actor rather than simply resulting from general shortcomings in the health system of the country of origin.[72] According to the Court, it follows that the deterioration of the state of health of an applicant due to the absence of treatment in the country of origin will not be worthy of subsidiary protection unless he or she is 'intentionally deprived' of medical care.[73] The notion of intentional deprivation had already been introduced by Advocate General (AG) Bot, who, in his Opinion, expressed that inherent to the concept of serious harm is a 'deliberate intention on the part of the perpetrator to inflict particularly intense physical or mental suffering'.[74] In other words, it is not sufficient for applicants to prove the existence a real risk of suffering inhuman or degrading treatment; they must also prove that this would be the result of a deliberate and intentional act.

The interpretation of this provision can however vary greatly if analysed in view of asylum law and the principle of *non-refoulement*. First, the wording of Article 6 QD does not preclude the application of subsidiary protection to cases of illness where the risks are situational rather than coming from an identifiable actor. The list provided under this provision is merely indicative as it establishes that actors of persecution or serious harm 'include' states, non-state actors, and so on. Article 7 QD on actors of protection, conversely, clearly mandates that '[p]rotection against persecution or serious harm *can only be provided by* . . . the State; or . . . parties or organisations' (emphasis added).[75] As it was highlighted by the Commission in its proposal for the 2011 recast of the Directive, '[w]here the Directive establishes indicative lists, it uses terms such as "include" or "inter alia"; therefore, the absence of such terms in Article 7 is already an indication of the exhaustive character of the list'.[76] Hence, the Directive offers an exhaustive list of actors of protection, but not of actors of persecution or serious harm. Neither does it mention that the risk needs to be posed by an actor at all.[77]

[71] Qualification Directive (n 36) art 6. The wording of Article 6 QR, instead, will rule that '[a]ctors of persecution *can be*: (a) the state . . .' (emphasis added).

[72] *M'Bodj* (n 66) para 35.

[73] Ibid, para 36.

[74] Ibid, Opinion of AG Bot, para 99.

[75] Qualification Directive (n 36) art 7. Similarly (yet with a different wording), Article 7 of the Qualification Regulation states that '[o]nly the following actors can provide protection against persecution or serious harm ... (a) the State; (b) stable, established non-State authorities, including international organisations, which control the State or a substantial part of the territory of the State'.

[76] European Commission, 'Proposal for a Directive of the European Parliament and of the Council on minimum standards for the qualification and status of third country nationals or stateless persons as beneficiaries of international protection and the content of the protection granted', COM(2009) 551 Final 7.

[77] The same applies to the Qualification Regulation which, despite its changed wording, establishes in its Articles 6 and 7 that actors of persecution *can be* state or non-state actors, while actors of protection *can only be* state and established non-state actors.

Moreover, if analysed in the context of its adoption, the purpose of Article 6 was precisely to expand subsidiary protection and avoid that states opt for an 'accountability' notion of asylum. As explained above, the Directive was adopted in the context of an intense debate between protective and accountability-based notions of asylum (see section 1.1). Prior to the adoption of the Directive, many civil law jurisdictions, including France and Germany, opted for the 'accountability theory', according to which asylum was only granted when the state of origin was directly responsible for the risk of harm.[78] The inclusion of Article 6 QD indicates the preponderance of the so-called protection approach in EU law, in line with the Refugee Convention and Article 3 ECHR, and contrary to other instruments such as the UN Convention Against Torture (UNCAT).[79]

By requiring intentionality as a necessary component of *serious harm*, *M'Bodj* is arguably reminiscent of the accountability theory, as it emphasizes the unwillingness of states to protect while leaving aside their inability to do so.[80] Conversely, the principle of *non-refoulement* in the ECHR, on which Article 15(b) QD is based, prohibits expulsion regardless of the source of the risk. Making protection dependent on the subjective element of state intentionality misunderstands the essence of the *non-refoulement* principle, which is based on risk assessment and absolute protection.[81] More importantly, by claiming that seriously ill applicants who are non-removable under Article 3 ECHR are not necessarily granted residence by way of subsidiary protection,[82] the CJEU creates a group of people who might simply be left statusless.

Lastly, the Court's argument that Recital 35 of the Directive supports its *intentional deprivation* threshold rests on poor reasoning.[83] First, because the provision notes that the general risks to which the population of a country is exposed will not 'normally' qualify as *serious harm*, evidently allowing for exceptions, as it was already clarified by the CJEU in *Elgafaji*. Second, the presence of Recital 35 in the Directive responds to the inclusion of situations of generalized violence in the country of origin in line with *Elgafaji* and *Sufi and Elmi* (Article 15(c) QD) and was not included with medical cases in mind. Third and most importantly, the serious harm in medical cases like *M'Bodj* does not respond to general risks to which the population of a country are exposed, but rather to a combination of these and the personal circumstances deriving from the illness of the applicant.

[78] James C Hathaway and Michelle Foster, *The Law of Refugee Status* (Cambridge Core 2014) 303.

[79] Convention against Torture and Other Cruel, Inhuman or Degrading Treatment or Punishment, 10 December 1984, 1465 UNTS art 1.

[80] Tristan Wibault, 'Is There a Space for Humanitarian Protection within Subsidiary Protection? A Reading of M'Bodj', *European Database of Asylum Law*, 5 February 2015, available at: <https://www.asylumlawdatabase.eu/en/journal/there-space-humanitarian-protection-within-subsidiary-protection-reading-m%E2%80%99bodj>.

[81] Bauloz (n 19) 427.

[82] *M'Bodj* (n 66) para 40.

[83] Ibid, para. 36. It should be noted that this provision is absent in the new Qualification Regulation.

Even though the ECtHR had always left the door open to find a breach of Article 3 ECHR in purely situational cases,[84] the fact that it *de facto* kept these out of its reach meant that the difference in scope between both provisions was of little relevance in practice. It must be borne in mind that *M'Bodj* came about two years before *Paposhvili*, at a time when Strasbourg's protection from expulsion was only available for dying applicants. Nevertheless, by setting a higher standard of protection in *Paposhvili*, Strasbourg's revisiting of its non-removal case law offers the dual outcome of setting a higher standard of protection against human rights violations in the country of origin, while bringing to the surface a new series of challenges for those who might simply become non-removable in the host country. This is analysed in relation to the case of *MP* next.

2.3 Interpreting subsidiary protection after *Paposhvili*: *MP*, judicial dialogue, and non-removability

2.3.1 MP v Secretary of State for the Home Department: A missed opportunity for the CJEU

The above-mentioned limitations in the CJEU's reasoning were tested in *MP*, where the Court had its first (and so far only) opportunity to revisit its jurisprudence after *Paposhvili*. In *MP*, the applicant was a Sri Lankan national of Tamil origin who, after obtaining various permits in the UK, applied for asylum on the grounds that he had been, and would again be subjected to torture if returned to Sri Lanka. This was rejected on the grounds that he was no longer of interest to Sri Lankan authorities and was therefore not at risk of suffering torture.[85]

Following rejection, the applicant brought an action before the Upper Tribunal, submitting medical evidence that, as a torture victim, he was suffering post-traumatic stress disorder, severe depression, and suicidal tendencies which would likely materialize if returned to Sri Lanka.[86] The Upper Tribunal (and later the Court of Appeal) gave credibility to the applicant's testimony and ruled that, considering the lack of available treatment in Sri Lanka, his deportation would be in breach of Article 3 ECHR. Nevertheless, the Court of Appeal found, in line with *M'Bodj*, that the Qualification Directive was not intended to cover medical cases where the risk was to health or suicide rather than one of persecution. This left the applicant in a situation of non-removability—as he was unable to obtain a residence permit under domestic legislation.[87] Upon appeal, and considering the

[84] *D* (n 18) para 49.
[85] Case C-353/16, *MP v Secretary of State for the Home Department* [2018] EU:C:2018:276 paras 16–18.
[86] Ibid, para 19.
[87] Ibid, paras 21–22.

unique factual circumstances of the case (that involved a torture victim no longer at risk of being tortured, but whose rights under Article 3 ECHR precluded deportation), the Supreme Court inquired whether Articles 2(f) and 15(b) of the Directive offered asylum in cases such as that of MP.[88]

The CJEU first built on *M'Bodj* to affirm that the fact that Article 3 ECHR precludes the removal of TCNs suffering from a serious illness does not mean that they should be granted subsidiary protection under EU law.[89] On the contrary, there needs to be a real risk of being 'intentionally deprived' of appropriate health care treatment by the country of origin.[90] Whereas this reasoning might have led to the dismissal of the claims of the applicant, as AG Bot suggested,[91] the Court decided otherwise by making explicit reference to the UNCAT. According to the Court, in cases of (previous) torture, victims should be considered intentionally deprived of treatment if they are 'at risk of committing suicide because of the trauma resulting from the torture he was subjected to by the authorities of his country of origin, [and] it is clear that those authorities, notwithstanding their obligation under Article 14 of the Convention against Torture, are not prepared to provide for his rehabilitation'.[92] In short, the CJEU extends subsidiary protection not only to those cases in which the (torturer) state of origin is unwilling to provide for rehabilitation, but also to those where it is unable to do so.

MP is greatly relevant for the study of non-removability through the lens of EU asylum law. First because, unlike *M'Bodj*, where the applicant had already been granted indefinite leave to remain in Belgium on account of his state of health, *MP* concerned a non-removable migrant, whose non-removability precisely derived from the asymmetrical interaction between the ECHR and EU asylum law. It is thus a paradigmatic example of how non-removability may occur; second, because *MP* has been the first judgment adopted by the CJEU on the scope of subsidiary protection after *Paposhvili*, offering a unique opportunity for the Court to reassess its approach in light of recent development of the principle of *non-refoulement*; third, because the CJEU has expanded the scope of subsidiary protection, which now must be granted to torture victims if medical care would be unavailable in the country of origin responsible for their torture. This applies both when the state is unwilling or unable to provide such treatment, protecting the applicant in the main proceedings. Even though the CJEU has made clear that non-removal under Article 3 ECHR does not necessarily lead to subsidiary protection, it has narrowed the gap between the interpretation of both provisions by offering a lower threshold of *intentional deprivation* in cases of torture. It is because of this that the judgment was celebrated for 'ensuring greater protection . . . for the most

[88] Ibid, para 26.
[89] Ibid, para 101.
[90] Ibid, paras 51–52.
[91] Ibid, Opinion of AG Bot.
[92] Ibid, para 57.

vulnerable migrants: torture victims and the terminally ill'.[93] Fourth, because the CJEU upholds the standard of *intentional deprivation* and openly interprets subsidiary protection in a narrower manner than Article 3 ECHR, despite the fact that the QD stresses the need to revisit the scope of subsidiary protection in light of the evolution of states' *non-refoulement* obligations.[94]

2.3.2 *Judicial dialogue and non-removable migrants*

The response of the Court in *MP* can be better understood if analysed in light of the ambivalent approach of the CJEU towards the ECHR, where the specific position and normative value of the ECHR remain ambiguous.[95] Indeed, the Court of Justice has long combined judgments which emphasized the relevance of the ECHR as interpreted by the Strasbourg Court[96] with others that stressed that it is not formally bound by it, or simply ignored the role of the Convention.[97] At present, the relationship between both Courts is heavily marked by the legal bindingness of the EU Charter of Fundamental Rights (the Charter) post-Lisbon and by Opinion 2/13, where the Court of Justice held that the draft agreement for the EU's accession to the ECHR was incompatible with Article 6(2) of the Treaty on European Union (TEU).[98] In this context, and despite the mutual influence of both courts, it has been argued that the Strasbourg Court might have seen the Charter as a way to show consensus and modernize the ECHR, whereas the CJEU has rather used it as a tool to legitimize its status and the autonomy of EU law.[99]

In the asylum field, and particularly after the Charter came into effect, the CJEU has been eager to stress the autonomy of EU law while seeking to avoid norm conflicts and reflect on the jurisprudence of the ECtHR. In *N.S*, the CJEU relied on the landmark case of *M.S.S.* in finding that Article 4 of the Charter (equivalent to Article 3 ECHR) precludes the establishment of a conclusive presumption that the responsible Member State in a Dublin transfer observes the fundamental rights of the applicant.[100] And yet, the CJEU's standard of proof was established autonomously and circumscribed to those situations where the requesting state

[93] Steve Peers, 'Torture Victims and EU Law', *EU Law Analysis*, 28 April 2018, available at: <http://eulawanalysis.blogspot.com/2018/04/torture-victims-and-eu-law.htm>.

[94] Qualification Directive (n 36) Recital 48.

[95] Francesca Ippolito and Samantha Velluti, 'The Relationship between the ECJ and the ECtHR: The Case of Asylum' in Kanstantsin Dzehtsiarou and others (eds), *Human Rights Law in Europe: The Influence, Overlaps and Contradictions of the EU and ECHR* (Routledge 2014) 165–66.

[96] See among others Case C-94/00, *Roquette Frères* [2002] EU:C:2002:603; Case C-400/10 *J McB* [2010] EU:C:2010:582; Case C-404/15, *Aranyosi and Căldăraru* [2016] EU:C:2016:198.

[97] Case C-46/87, *Hoechst v Commission* [1989] EU:C:1989:337; Case C-571/11, *Kamberaj* [2012] EU:C:2012:233.

[98] Opinion 2/13 *Accession of the European Union to the ECHR* [2014] EU:C:2014:2475.

[99] Dean Spielman, 'The Judicial Dialogue between the European Court of Justice and the European Court of Human Rights or How to Remain Good Neighbours after the Opinion 2/13', 27 March 2017 11, available at: <ECHRCJUEdialog.BRUSSELS.final_.pdf>.

[100] Case C-411/10, *NS and others* [2011] EU:C:2011:865 paras 88–92.

'cannot be unaware' of the systemic deficiencies in the requested state—in contrast with Strasbourg's reference to a 'shared burden of proof'.[101] In *Puid*, which again scrutinized mutual trust in the context of Dublin, the Court seemed rather concerned about the consequences of an overly wide application of the *N.S.* exception, stressed the need for 'systemic deficiencies' in the asylum system of the requested state, and did not include any references to the Strasbourg Court or the Convention.[102] This contrasts with Strasbourg's judgment in *Tarakhel* where the ECtHR broke free from the 'systemic deficiencies' approach and required the requesting state to undertake a thorough and individualized examination of the circumstances the applicants would face upon their transfer to Italy—where the situation could 'in no way be compared to the situation in Greece at the time of the *M.S.S.*'.[103]

Going back to Article 15 QD, *Elgafaji* (see section 2.1) again represents the tension between the autonomy of EU law and respect for the ECHR. In *Elgafaji*, however, the CJEU manifested that its interpretation was not only fully compatible with that of the ECtHR at the time, but even went beyond it.[104] Conversely, in *M'Bodj* and (more significantly) in *MP*, the CJEU fails to meet ECHR standards.

Whereas the ECtHR had entered an explicit and thorough dialogue with the CJEU in *Sufi and Elmi*, to the extent that it justified its evolutionary interpretation of Article 3 almost exclusively on the CJEU's interpretation of the QD in *Elgafaji*, no equivalent exercise was made by the CJEU when EU law fell short of protection *vis-à-vis* ECHR standards. Far from it: the Court made clear in *MP* that Article 15(b) QD does not go hand in hand with Article 3 ECHR. Interestingly, when the CJEU refers to *Paposhvili* to support the need for states' intentional deprivation of treatment to access subsidiary protection, it does so distorting the content of the ruling. According to the CJEU, '[i]t follows from the case-law of the European Court of Human Rights relating to Article 3 of the ECHR that the suffering caused by a naturally occurring illness, whether physical or mental, may be covered by that article if it is, or risks being, exacerbated by treatment, whether resulting from conditions of detention, removal or other measures, for which the authorities can be held responsible'.[105] The Court of Justice however omits that, within the very same paragraph quoted by the CJEU, the ECtHR noted that '[the Court] is not

[101] Sonia Morano-Foadi, Lucy Vickers, and Samantha Velluti (eds), 'Who Has the Right to Have Rights?' in *Fundamental Rights in the EU: A Matter for Two Courts* (Hart Publishing 2015).

[102] Case C-4/11, *Puid* [2013] EU:C:2013:740. See further Case C-394/12, *Abdullahi* [2013] EU:C:2013:813. In *Abdullahi*, the CJEU clarified that the only way in which an asylum applicant can contest a Dublin transfer is by pleading systemic deficiencies in the asylum system of the requested Member State, in a judgment with no references to the ECHR. In *X*, the CJEU applied the 'Dublin exception' to prevent transfers to a Member State where applicants would face a real risk of being subjected to pushbacks, if these are deemed contrary to Article 4 of the Charter (Case C-392/22, *X v Staatssecretaris van Justitie en Veiligheid* [2024] EU:C:2024:195 para 65).

[103] *Tarakhel v Switzerland* [GC] App No 29217/12 (ECtHR 4 November 2014) para 114.

[104] *Elgafaji* (n 52) para 44.

[105] *MP* (n 85) para 38.

prevented from scrutinising an applicant's claim under Article 3 where the source of the risk of proscribed treatment in the receiving country stems from factors which cannot engage either directly or indirectly the responsibility of the public authorities of that country'.[106]

It is not my contention that the CJEU has erred in its interpretation of Article 15(b) by ruling *contra legem*. Indeed, Article 52(3) of the Charter, which establishes that the meaning and scope of the Charter rights which are also included in the ECHR must have at least the meaning and scope guaranteed by the latter, would only bind the CJEU in its interpretation of Article 4 of the Charter—and not of Article 15(b) QD. In its latest medical case, the CJEU built on *Paposhvili* to interpret Directive 2008/115 (Return Directive) in light of the Charter, establishing that no return decision can be issued to irregular migrants suffering from serious illnesses, 'where there are substantial grounds for believing that the person concerned would be exposed, in the third-country to which he or she would be removed, to a real risk of a significant, permanent and rapid increase in his or her pain, if he or she were returned, on account of the only effective analgesic treatment being prohibited in that country'.[107] In doing so, the CJEU noted that (by virtue of Article 52(3)) the severity threshold needed to apply Article 4 of the Charter is equivalent to that of Article 3 ECHR.[108] While this case can help avoid states issuing non-enforceable return decisions, it also confirms the lack of positive obligations to issue residence permits, be it by means of asylum or migration law.[109] In other words, while the CJEU has been willing to incorporate ECtHR jurisprudence to strengthen states' (negative) *non-refoulement* obligations under the Return Directive, it has refused to interpret EU asylum law in a way that closes the non-removability gap arising from conflicting interpretations of human rights and asylum law provisions. It is my view that this need not be the case.

As argued above, the fact that the wording and risk-assessment criteria used by the Directive in Articles 15(b) and 2(e) respectively are borrowed from Strasbourg's jurisprudence on Article 3 ECHR, together with the obligation to derive the scope of subsidiary protection from human rights law under Recital 34 QD, indicates a strong nexus between ECHR *non-refoulement* case law and subsidiary protection. I have argued that the wording of the Qualification Directive in Articles 6 and 15(b) does not necessarily put this view into question.

Even if one accepts AG Maduro's reasoning in *Elgafaji* that a completely coherent interpretation of subsidiary protection with Article 3 ECHR is not feasible due to the non-linear, dynamic interpretation of this provision coming from

[106] *Paposhvili* (n 27) para 175.
[107] Case C-69/21, *X v Staatssecretaris van Justitie en Veiligheid* [2022] EU:C:2022:913 para 76.
[108] Ibid, para 65.
[109] Ibid, paras 22 and 84–87.

Strasbourg,[110] the CJEU has unnecessarily departed from Strasbourg's criteria by adopting a threshold (*intentional deprivation*) that was strongly rejected by the ECtHR already in 1997.[111] It must also be borne in mind that Recital 48 mandates that the implementation of the Qualification Directive be re-assessed at regular intervals taking into consideration Member States' *non-refoulement* obligations.

This discrepancy becomes particularly relevant after *Paposhvili*, given that states' *non-refoulement* obligations in medical cases are now significantly widened, making non-removability a more likely outcome. The CJEU's attempt to justify its *intentional deprivation* threshold by referring to the ECtHR remains particularly puzzling considering the latter Court's outright rejection of the very same standard. It is thus my view that the CJEU missed an opportunity to extend its 'unwilling or unable' criteria used with victims of torture to its wider case law on subsidiary protection. This would have been consistent with the absolute nature of the *non-refoulement* principle (now an integral part of EU law under the EU Charter of Fundamental Rights), upon which Article 15(b) QD is based. The fact that the Court applied Article 15(b) QD to a purely situational risk in *MP* also confirms that a different interpretation of Article 6 QD is not a no-go.

As noted by Costello, the main significance of Article 15(b) QD is precisely found in 'according a status, rather than simply rendering non-removable, persons in these [Article 3 ECHR] circumstances'.[112] The threshold of the ECtHR, significantly lowered in *Paposhvili*, requires the applicant to prove a risk of being exposed to a 'serious, rapid, and irreversible decline in his or her state of health resulting in intense suffering or to a significant reduction in life expectancy',[113] yet no reference can be found as to the unwillingness of the state to provide for treatment. It is thus the potential violation as such, and not the (lack of) intentionality of the state of origin, that matters. The CJEU, by adding intentionality as a necessary subjective element, compromises the scope of subsidiary protection, departs from the foundations of the *non-refoulement* principle, and allows non-removability inasmuch as it permits Member States to simultaneously observe that there is a real risk of inhuman or degrading treatment upon removal and that there is no such risk, within the very same case.

Interestingly, the CJEU has so far been able to adopt a legal approach that gives rise to situations of non-removability, yet it has managed to sidestep the practical consequences of its own approach. In *M'Bodj*, the applicant already had access to indefinite leave to remain in Belgium on account of his state of health. This status, although affording a narrower set of rights than subsidiary protection, did not

[110] See Opinion of AG Maduro in *Elgafaji* (n 52) para 20. On the contrary, AG Trstenjak argued in *N.S* that the reference to the ECHR in Article 52(3) is to be understood as a dynamic reference which covers the jurisprudence of the European Court.

[111] *D v the United Kingdom* (n 18) para 49.

[112] Costello (n 43) 217.

[113] *Paposhvili v Belgium* [GC] (n 27) para 183.

leave him in a situation of irregularity and destitution. In *MP*, the interpretation of the CJEU seems to grant subsidiary protection to Mr MP, but only because of his status as a torture victim. Nevertheless, torture victims aside, it is now clear that, in medical cases, protection from expulsion comes with a legal vacuum and, in the absence of a domestic status of protection, with rightlessness and destitution. More generally, this approach can potentially apply to any form of torture or inhuman or degrading treatment beyond medical cases, as the CJEU notes that Article 3 ECHR and 15(b) QD do not necessarily go hand in hand.[114] By upholding the international deprivation threshold, the CJEU undermines one of the main achievements of the Directive, namely closing the gap between *non-refoulement* obligations and asylum law by offering a status to those who would otherwise remain in limbo.

3. 'Undesirable and unreturnable': Exclusion and withdrawal of international protection

Non-removability due to states' *non-refoulement* obligations may also emerge when people are excluded from refugee status or subsidiary protection, or if their protection is withdrawn, ended, or not renewed, normally in the context of criminal convictions. In these cases, non-removability does not derive from a judicial mismatch in the interpretation of a provision, but rather owes to the explicit will of the EU legislator to exclude the 'undeserving' from international protection. As noted by the CJEU in *Ahmed*, the purpose is precisely 'to exclude . . . persons who are deemed to be undeserving of the protection which that status entails and to maintain the credibility of the Common European Asylum System'.[115]

The exclusion of the 'undeserving' is not unique to the EU *acquis* but a longstanding (and increasingly used) feature of refugee law.[116] Indeed, the Geneva Convention establishes under Article 1(F) that refugee protection shall not apply if there are serious reasons to consider that the applicant has committed crimes against peace, war crimes, or crimes against humanity; if he or she has committed a 'serious non-political crime outside the country of refuge prior to his admission to that country as a refugee'; or if he or she 'has been guilty of acts contrary to the purposes and principles of the United Nations'.[117] Moreover, Article 33(2) foresees a derogation from *non-refoulement* obligations if an applicant is regarded as a

[114] Costello (n 43) 217.
[115] Case C-369/17, *Ahmed* [2018] EU:C:2018:713 para 51.
[116] Cathryn Costello, 'On Refugeehood and Citizenship' in Ayelet Shachar and others (eds), *The Oxford Handbook of Citizenship* (Oxford University Press 2017) 725; Júlia Zomignani Barboza, 'International Protection for Criminals: To Grant or Not to Grant? Lessons from Australia, Belgium, and Canada' (2024) 36 International Journal of Refugee Law 223.
[117] Refugee Convention (n 3) art 1(F).

'danger to the security of the country in which he is, or... having been convicted by a final judgment of a particularly serious crime, constitutes a danger to the community of that country'.[118]

3.1 Exclusion and withdrawal of refugee status

Building on the Refugee Convention, the Qualification Directive mirrors Article 1(F)'s refugee exclusion grounds in its Article 12(2).[119] Moreover, the Qualification Regulation will introduce a new paragraph according to which exclusion must take place 'without performing a proportionality assessment linked to the fear of being persecuted'.[120] This addition merely codifies the jurisprudence of the CJEU in *B and D*, where the Court excluded the proportionality test at this stage precisely because the withdrawal of refugee status does not authorize removal—and therefore the risk upon removal should be taken into consideration at a later stage, when dealing with the separate issue of whether the person in question should be deported.[121] In addition, Recital 46 will give effect to *Lounani*,[122] establishing that, for those who are members of the leadership of a terrorist group, there shall be no requirement as to their instigation or involvement in any specific terrorist acts.[123]

Moreover, Article 14 QD establishes that Member States may revoke, end, or refuse to renew refugee status when applicants are considered a danger to the security of the Member State, or when 'he or she, having been convicted by a final judgment of a particularly serious crime, constitutes a danger to the community of that Member State'.[124] Interestingly, this provision reproduces the wording of Article 33(2) of the Geneva Convention, yet this time enshrining not a *non-refoulement* derogation but the grounds for the revocation of refugee status.[125] As noted by the

[118] Ibid, art 33(2).

[119] Qualification Directive (n 36) art 12(2). The same exclusion grounds are included under Article 12(2) QR.

[120] Qualification Regulation (n 36) art 12(4).

[121] Case C-57/09, *B and D* [2010] EU:C:2010:661 paras 110 -111. This finding was contrary to the view of UNHCR (See UNHCR, 'UNHCR public statement in relation to cases Bundesrepublik Deutschland v. B and D pending before the Court of Justice of the European Union', July 2009, available at: <https://www.refworld.org/type,AMICUS,UNHCR,4a5de2992,0.html>).

[122] Case C-573/14, *Commissaire général aux réfugiés et aux apatrides v Mostafa Lounani* [2017] EU:C:2017:71.

[123] Qualification Regulation (n 36) Recital 46.

[124] Ibid, art 14(4). The CJEU has confirmed that the requirements of Article 14(4)(b) are cumulative, ie that its application requires *both* a criminal conviction for a particularly serious crime *and* the determination that a person constitutes a danger to the community of that state—precluding domestic legislation which automatically presumes the existence of a danger to the community of the state from the commission of certain crimes (Case C-8/22, *XXX v Commissaire général aux réfugiés et aux apatrides* [2023] EU:C:2023:542 paras 27–45).

[125] Since these grounds for revocation are not enshrined in the Geneva Convention, the compatibility of this Article with the Convention was contested in *M*. The CJEU however held, even if a person no longer resides lawfully under the Directive and does not have 'refugee status', those persons can still

CJEU, this means that EU law offers greater protection than the Geneva Convention, since the grounds listed lead to the revocation of refugeehood but do not make the person returnable.[126] While the substantive provisions of Article 14 QD again make it almost entirely into the new Regulation, the withdrawal of refugee status becomes mandatory (shifting from a *may* clause to a *must*) if there are reasonable grounds for regarding the applicant as a 'danger to the security of the Member State', and if the applicant 'is convicted by a final judgment of a particularly serious crime and constitutes a danger to the community of the Member State'.[127]

3.2 Exclusion and withdrawal of subsidiary protection

For beneficiaries of subsidiary protection, the grounds for exclusion are listed in Article 17 QD, which reproduces some of the exclusion grounds applicable to refugees. In this case, the commission of a 'serious non-political crime outside the country of refuge prior to his or her admission as a refugee' is substituted by the commission of a 'serious crime'.[128] In the Qualification Regulation, this exclusion will affect those who commit 'a serious crime prior to arriving on the territory of the Member State or [have] been convicted for a serious crime after arrival'.[129] As with refugee status, the Qualification Regulation now includes a provision confirming that no proportionality assessment connected to the risk of serious harm upon removal shall take place when excluding an applicant from subsidiary protection status.[130] Contrary to refugees, beneficiaries of subsidiary protection can also be excluded due to the commission of less serious crimes if the applicant left the country to avoid the sanctions resulting from those crimes.[131] Moreover, an applicant shall be excluded from subsidiary protection if he or she 'constitutes a danger to the community or to the security of the Member State in which he or she is present'.[132]

While the CJEU has expressed that the EU legislature's intention was to introduce exclusion and withdrawal grounds from subsidiary protection 'similar' to those from refugee status,[133] there is no doubt that the Directive adopts broader exclusion grounds from subsidiary protection, as the concept of 'serious crimes' includes both political and non-political crimes, those committed in the country

be refugees for the purposes of Article 1(A) of the Geneva Convention and be protected as such (see Case C-391/16, *M* [2019] EU:C:2019:403 paras 98–100).

126 Case C-663/21, *Bundesamt für Fremdenwesen und Asyl v AA* [2023] EU:C:2023:540 para 38.
127 Qualification Regulation (n 36) art 14.
128 Qualification Directive (n 36) art 17(1).
129 Qualification Regulation (n 36) art 17(1)(b).
130 Ibid, art 17(4).
131 Qualification Directive (n 36) art 17. This provision is maintained in Article 17(3) QR.
132 Ibid, art 17(1)(d). In the Qualification Regulation, exclusion takes place if the person 'constitutes a danger to the community or to national security'.
133 *Ahmed* (n 115) para 45.

of origin and in the host country, as well as those committed before and after the admission to the country of refuge. Some of the changes introduced by the Qualification Regulation will reduce this gap by offering less protection to refugees, incorporating a greater number of mandatory grounds for withdrawal under Article 14 QR.[134] Then, the protection offered by subsidiary protection, and, to a lesser extent, refugee status, are limited by the existence of clauses which either require or allow Member States to exclude persons who would otherwise be beneficiaries of international protection.

3.3 Life after exclusion: Statusless and non-removable

The withdrawal and exclusion grounds outlined in this section say little about the (non-)removability of the persons involved. In its case law on the exclusion and withdrawal of international protection, the CJEU has made clear that withdrawal and exclusion are legally detached from deportation, these being two distinct administrative procedures with different legal frameworks.[135] While the former is regulated under EU asylum law, the latter must be adopted following a return decision under the Return Directive, in full observance of states' *non-refoulement* obligations—which remain absolute, non-derogable, and immune to the criminal behaviour of applicants. In fact, the CJEU has made clear that, in such cases, states are not only unable to enforce return decisions, but must refrain from issuing return decisions in the first place.[136] In sum, states' negative obligations not to deport under Article 3 ECHR and Article 4 of the Charter go well beyond their positive obligations to grant asylum. This is yet another way through which the gap between human rights and asylum law may lead to situations of non-removability.

Considering this asymmetrical framework, it is unsurprising that the ECtHR's non-removal case law is replete with cases of 'undesirable and unreturnable' refugees.[137] In *Ahmed*, the ECtHR halted the deportation of a former refugee whose status was withdrawn due to criminal convictions, while at the same time noting its lack of jurisdiction over his migration or asylum status. The applicant became a non-removable migrant, resulting in a situation of destitution that led to him committing suicide some months later.[138] Similarly, in *Saadi* the Court protected a

[134] Qualification Regulation (n 36) art 14(1).

[135] *AA* (n 126) paras 26-43; *B and D* (n 121) paras 110–11.

[136] *AA* (n 126) paras 44–52. In *AA*, the CJEU, in essence, reproduces the findings of the Court in *X* (n 107), where the CJEU established that no return decision can be adopted if return would be contrary to Article 4 of the Charter.

[137] By 'undesirable and unreturnable' I refer to those who are criminally convicted but cannot be deported (see David James Cantor and others, 'The Emperor's New Clothing: National Responses to "Undesirable and Unreturnable" Aliens under Asylum and Immigration Law' (2017) 36(1) Refugee Survey Quarterly 1).

[138] Nuala Mole, *Asylum and the European Convention on Human Rights* (Revised edition, Council of Europe Publishing 2010) 193.

refugee from expulsion, in a context in which he was residing irregularly for being considered a danger to national security.[139] In *Sufi and Elmi* one of the applicants was a former refugee whose status was withdrawn and who was issued a deportation order based on the fact that he was considered 'a danger to the community'. The answer of the ECtHR was, again, to protect the applicant under Article 3 ECHR while noting the lack of jurisdiction on his status as a refugee.[140] More recently, in *KI*, the ECtHR found that the deportation of the applicant, a Chechen refugee whose status under the Qualification Directive was revoked on grounds of terrorism, would violate Article 3 ECHR.[141] In all cases, we find non-removable persons whose only legal avenue to a residence permit could be found in asylum law, a status no longer available to them.

This widespread practice of asylum withdrawal and the resulting situation of destitution for these 'undesirable and unreturnable' persons has been repeatedly challenged before the ECtHR on Article 3 ECHR grounds.[142] In *When Humans Become Migrants*, Dembour maps a series of largely overlooked inadmissibility decisions where the ECtHR has systematically rejected these claims.[143] The first case, *Bonger*, concerned an Ethiopian national who, according to the Dutch government, fell within the scope of Article 1(F) of the Geneva Convention (and hence was also excluded from refugee status under EU law), but remained protected under Article 3 ECHR. The applicant, who had been residing for more than ten years in the Netherlands, claimed that, although not at risk of being expelled to Ethiopia, the open-ended rejection to issue a residence permit was in itself a violation of Article 3 ECHR, making it impossible for him to become a member of Dutch society and live in dignity. The decision, which took place only a few months after the Court had found a violation of Article 8 ECHR in the denial of a residence permit in *Sisojeva* (see Chapter 3 of this book),[144] declared the application inadmissible since 'neither Article 3 nor any other provision of the Convention and its Protocols guarantees, as such, a right to a residence permit'.[145]

The position adopted by the ECtHR in *Bonger* was confirmed in subsequent inadmissibility decisions.[146] Remarkably, these decisions took place after the

[139] *Saadi* (n 8) paras 32 and 35.

[140] *Sufi and Elmi* (n 9) paras 22 and 212.

[141] *KI* (n 30).

[142] Their situation has also been challenged under Article 8 ECHR. This case law is analysed in Chapter 3 of this book.

[143] Marie-Bénédicte Dembour, 'The Darkest Case Law: Condoning Rightlessness (Bonger et Alia)' in *When Humans Become Migrants: Study of the European Court of Human Rights with an Inter-American Counterpoint* (Oxford University Press 2015).

[144] *Sisojeva and others v Latvia*, App No 60654/00 (ECtHR 16 June 2005).

[145] *Teshome Goraga Bonger v the Netherlands*, App No 10154/04 (ECtHR, Decision of 15 September 2005).

[146] *I v the Netherlands*, App No 24147/11 (ECtHR, Decision of 10 July 2012); *K v the Netherlands*, App No 33403/11 (ECtHR, Decision of 25 September 2012); *Mohammad Rafiq Naibzay v the Netherlands*, App No 68564/12 (ECtHR, Decision of 25 October 2012).

ECtHR's landmark judgment in *M.S.S.* In this case, the Court had ruled that the situation of destitution and extreme poverty of an asylum seeker amounted to inhuman or degrading treatment proscribed by Article 3 ECHR, taking into account '[state authorities'] inaction . . . . the prolonged uncertainty in which he has remained and the total *lack of any prospects of his situation improving*' (emphasis added).[147]

Since Article 3 ECHR is an absolute and non-derogable provision, the applicant's status as an asylum seeker (*M.S.S*) or as a (criminally convicted) non-removable migrant (*Bonger*) should be irrelevant so long as the severity of ill-treatment necessary to find a violation is reached. Thus, the reasoning articulated in *M.S.S.* could well apply to the factual circumstances of non-removable migrants excluded from refugee status or subsidiary protection—or to any non-removable migrant in a situation of rightlessness and destitution with no reasonable prospect of deportation. However, the ECtHR has so far been unwilling to do this. This leaves non-removable migrants in a situation of *de facto* statelessness which Dembour describes as a 'Kafkaesque stalemate',[148] unable to return to their countries of origin without putting their lives at risk, and unable to become members of the societies in which they inevitably live.

4. Conclusions

The ECtHR grants protection from expulsion under Articles 3 and 8 ECHR. This chapter has analysed the existing gap between Article 3 ECHR non-removal jurisprudence and EU asylum law to analyse the extent to which it is legally possible to be protected from expulsion on the basis of human rights, while not being granted asylum.

To do so, I have first analysed Strasbourg's jurisprudence on Article 3 ECHR, emphasising the protection afforded by the ECtHR in *Paposhvili*, which now covers 'purely situational' cases of illness—that is, those with no identifiable actor to blame for the inhuman or degrading treatment following upon expulsion. This has been compared with Article 15 QD, as interpreted by the CJEU. In its medical cases,[149] the CJEU has interpreted the notion of torture or inhuman or degrading treatment or punishment in a narrower manner than the ECtHR, adopting a threshold (*international deprivation* of treatment) which was discarded by the ECtHR already in the 1990s. This leads to a situation where those TCNs who are granted protection against expulsion on account of their state of health, but who would not be intentionally deprived of treatment in the country of origin are left in a legal

[147] *M.S.S.* (n 29) para 263.
[148] Dembour (n 143) 448.
[149] To date, these are the only cases dealt with by the CJEU under Article 15(b) QD.

limbo, with the exception of torture victims covered under the narrow factual circumstances concurring in *MP*. In doing so, the CJEU undermines one of the main achievements of EU asylum law, namely closing the existing gap between human rights and asylum law by granting protection to those who would otherwise fall in a legal limbo. This is particularly striking considering that Article 15(b) QD borrows its language from Article 3 ECHR, that Article 2(f) QD adopts the risk-assessment tests used by the ECtHR, that Recital 34 QD explicitly mentions the need to draw the eligibility criteria for subsidiary protection from human rights law, and that Recital 48 QD stresses the need to revisit the Directive considering the evolution of states' *non-refoulement* obligations. Both the text of the Directive and the generally ambivalent attitude of the CJEU towards the ECHR can partially account for the approach of the Court of Justice. In practice, this gap is substantially widened after *Paposhvili*, when the ECtHR lowered the severity of ill-treatment required to protect seriously ill people from expulsion. The *Paposhvili* criteria therefore offer the dual outcome of granting TCNs greater human rights protection against expulsion while potentially leading to further situations of non-removability, generating a whole new set of human rights issues in the host country. This chapter has argued that, despite the arguments put forward by the CJEU, the Qualification Directive (and, after it, the Qualification Regulation) allows for a different interpretation in conformity with the basic pillars of *non-refoulement*.

Lastly, non-removability can also derive from the application of withdrawal and exclusion clauses that apply to both refugee status and subsidiary protection. In this case, non-removability does not derive from a restrictive judicial interpretation of an ambiguous provision, but from the evident will of the legislator to exclude the 'undeserving' from refugee status and subsidiary protection—while keeping them protected from expulsion. This has been analysed, again, in light of ECtHR jurisprudence and its reluctance to secure residence permits to these people under Article 3 ECHR. In this legal context, the rather unsurprising result is that the jurisprudence of both courts is rife with cases involving excluded refugees who, following criminal behaviour, experience a double penalty: criminal punishment for their actions, and a life in limbo.

3

Membership Claims, Expulsion, and Non-Removability in the EU

Human rights can (and often do) protect irregular migrants who would otherwise be compelled to leave the territory of the EU. Though often presented as legal 'obstacles' to removal that render return policies 'ineffective',[1] these derive from the effective application of norms of a greater value. As seen in Chapter 2, human rights safeguards against expulsion can derive from absolute and non-derogable obligations under the principle of *non-refoulement*—which, in certain respects, has a wider reach than EU asylum law. But these are not the only human rights claims that can be invoked to challenge deportation.

Social membership theories argue that long-term residence and participation in society creates strong claims of belonging by foreigners.[2] These links are recognized, to varying degrees, by national and supranational legal frameworks. This chapter examines membership-based challenges to deportation, with a particular emphasis on situations where claims to social membership are enough to resist expulsion but not to secure lawful residence. Contrary to Chapter 2, the cases analysed here are not grounded on the existence of a risk of ill-treatment after removal, but rather on the links that already connect the applicants with the host society. In particular, it analyses supranational manifestations of belonging under European law, and the ways in which these manifest tensions between expulsion, residence rights, and non-removability.

Sections 1–3 examine the jurisprudence of the European Court of Human Rights (ECtHR) on Article 8 of the European Convention on Human Rights (ECHR). This provision, which protects the right to respect for family and private life, is analysed in the context of non-removal cases. This is framed as a subsidiary (and unpredictable) system of protection to resort to when residence rights and non-removal are unavailable under domestic or EU legislation. Nevertheless,

[1] European Council, Conclusions, EUCO 25/24, 17 October 2024 9; European Commission, 'Communication on Enhancing Cooperation on Return and Readmission as Part of a Fair, Effective and Comprehensive EU Migration Policy', COM(2021) 56 Final, 10 February 2021, 2 and 10.

[2] Joseph H Carens, *The Ethics of Immigration* (Oxford University Press 2013); Joseph H Carens, 'Aliens and Citizens: The Case for Open Borders' (1987) 49 The Review of Politics 251; Ayelet Shachar, *The Birthright Lottery: Citizenship and Global Inequality* (Harvard University Press 2009); Thomas Nagel, 'The Problem of Global Justice' (2005) 33 Philosophy & Public Affairs 113.

When Deportation Fails. Diego Ginés Martín, Oxford University Press.
DOI: 10.1093/9780198941231.003.0003

the analysis of Article 8 ECHR is of particular importance for the purposes of this book: first, because the social and family ties developed in the host country can be used to challenge deportation, turning deportable migrants into non-removable ones; second, because, for those who are already non-removable, Article 8 ECHR can exceptionally provide a human rights-based entitlement to a residence permit in the host state (as developed in Chapter 6 of this book). It is precisely in the in-between of both strands of jurisprudence that non-removability emerges.

Considering the subsidiary, incomplete, and unpredictable protection offered by the ECHR, EU law appears to offer greater protection to non-nationals in terms of legal statuses and access to rights. However, this chapter shows that, even for those whose residence seems firmly secured under EU law, their vulnerability *vis-à-vis* nationals becomes manifest upon the materialization of diverse life events, namely a criminal conviction, the loss of a job, descent into poverty, and the like. Then, precarious residence and non-removability might affect even the most privileged categories of non-nationals.

Section 4 examines regimes of social membership for foreigners under EU law. First, it zooms in on the residence rights and protection against expulsion of long-term residents under Directive 2003/109 (hereinafter Long-term residence Directive or simply LTRD). This is the EU legal instrument that more clearly recognizes the social links that third-country nationals (TCNs) acquire through the passage of time. And yet, this chapter exposes its protective gaps, such as the lack of recognition of informal residence and the conditions under which long-term residence (LTR) can be lost—while maintaining protection against deportation. Second, it focuses on EU citizenship. While the book concentrates on the situation of TCNs, this section briefly examines how even EU citizenship (arguably the most privileged form of post-national membership) allows for a strong national–non-national divide in the context of poverty and criminality, leading to precarious residence. First, for those (poor and economically inactive) who do not fulfil residence conditions, lack of access to social benefits, precarious residence, and non-removability are a possible outcome between lawful residence and expulsion. This results from an ambiguous EU citizenship framework that struggles to accommodate diverging dynamics of opening and closure and, in some cases, facilitates the emergence of precarious residence and non-removal. In the context of criminality, however, the expulsion of EU citizens ceases to be a latent threat and becomes an actual practice of Member States—and one that is generally validated by the Court of Justice of the European Union (CJEU).

1. Article 8 ECHR: General features in migration case law

Unlike Article 3 ECHR, Article 8 ECHR is not an absolute right, but a qualified one. This means that, whenever there is an interference with applicants' right to respect for their family and/or private life, the ECtHR follows a three-pronged approach to determine whether there is a violation of Article 8 ECHR. First, it must rule whether state action is in accordance with the law. Second, it must determine whether the alleged aim pursued with such action is a legitimate one as foreseen in Article 8(2). Third, it must determine whether the interference with the applicant's right is 'necessary in a democratic society', namely, if it is proportionate to the legitimate aim pursued.[3]

In these cases, Strasbourg's balancing exercise reflects an uneasy conflict, not embodied explicitly in Article 8(2) ECHR, between acknowledging migrants' rights and states' migration control prerogatives (see Chapter 1 of this book). This tension can be seen in Strasbourg's very first migration case, *Abdulaziz, Cabales and Balkandali*,[4] which did not address a claim against expulsion, but one to family reunification. Interestingly, the ECtHR did not seek to refute that Article 8 ECHR rights were affected or that family reunification did not fall under the umbrella of Article 8. Instead, it noted that 'as a matter of well-established international law . . . a State has the right to control the entry of non-nationals into its territory'.[5] Then, in migration cases, assessing whether an interference with one's family or private life amounts to a violation of Article 8 ECHR requires balancing this right both against Article 8(2) ECHR considerations *and* against the state's 'wide margin of appreciation' in controlling the entry, stay, or residence of non-nationals.[6]

Since *Abdulaziz*, the 'well established principle of international law' has been repeated as a mantra in Strasbourg's migration cases, both in violation and non-violation verdicts. The 'statist immigration control assumption', as Costello puts it,[7] plays a central role in Strasbourg's balancing of interests. As anticipated in Chapter 1, Dembour even speaks of the 'Strasbourg reversal' to refer to the argumentative priority of state sovereignty over human rights in migration cases:

> This is so much so that one can talk of a human rights reversal. In a human rights reasoning one would expect human rights to come first, so that what is checked is that states are exercising their functions in a way which respects these rights. Instead, the fact that the Strasbourg reversal has in effect given the state power to exclude aliens is generally considered as the master principle in the Strasbourg migrant case law; inevitably, then, human rights appear merely as exceptions which, if they are persuasive enough, manage to curtail the state not quite

[3] European Court of Human Rights, 'Guide on Article 8 of the European Convention on Human Rights', 31 August 2021, available at: <https://www.echr.coe.int/documents/guide_art_8_eng.pdf>.
[4] *Abdulaziz, Cabales and Balkandali v the United Kingdom*, Apps No 9214/80, 9473/81, 9474/81 (ECtHR 28 May 1985).
[5] Ibid, para 67.
[6] Ibid.
[7] Cathryn Costello, *The Human Rights of Migrants and Refugees in European Law* (Oxford University Press 2015) 56.

completely unfettered power to act as it wishes. The default position is however state sovereignty.[8]

In rejecting the applicants' claim in *Abdulaziz,* the ECtHR established another key principle of Strasbourg's migration case law, that is, requiring applicants to demonstrate obstacles to exercising their rights elsewhere.[9] In *Gül,* the Court rejected the applicants' claims, noting that there were 'strictly speaking, no obstacles preventing them from developing family life in Turkey'.[10] Such logic is arguably pushed to the extreme in *Joseph William Kwakye-Nti and Akua Dufie*, where the ECtHR declared the application inadmissible despite the fact that the applicants, who were seeking to bring their children from Ghana, were Dutch nationals who had lost their Ghanaian citizenship. The reasoning was, again, based on the claim that nothing prevented them from continuing their family life in Ghana,[11] in what seems to be the ECtHR's very particular interpretation of Arendt's 'right to have rights'.

These features anticipate that an interference with migrants' rights to respect for their family and private life will not very often entail a violation of Article 8 ECHR. However, Strasbourg's statist assumptions do not imply that the human rights reversal cannot be reversed. For example, exclusion from the territory (or, exceptionally, from residence) can be in breach of Article 8 ECHR, as states must strike a 'fair balance' between the interests of the migrant and those of the state. For the purposes of this chapter, namely to elucidate how non-removable migrants come to be, the following section will analyse Article 8 ECHR case law in deportation cases. This illustrates the thin line between violation and non-violation verdicts—which can be, in short, a thin line between deportation and non-removability in the host state.

2. Article 8 ECHR as a right to stay

This section analyses Strasbourg's non-removal case law under Article 8 ECHR. Given the extensive and complex body of jurisprudence since the ECtHR first found a breach of Article 8 ECHR in *Berrehab,* this section is structured in two

[8] Marie-Bénédicte Dembour, *When Humans Become Migrants: Study of the European Court of Human Rights with an Inter-American Counterpoint* (Oxford University Press 2015) 127–28.

[9] *Abdulaziz* (n 4) para 68. See further *Gül v Turkey*, App No 22676/93 (ECtHR 14 December 2000) para 42; Nuala Mole, *Asylum and the European Convention on Human Rights* (Revised edition, Council of Europe Publishing 2010) 184.

[10] *Gül v Turkey* (n 9) para 42.

[11] *Joseph William Kwakye-Nti and Akua Dufie v the Netherlands*, App No 31519/96 (ECtHR, Decision of 7 November 2000) 6. As of today, the ECtHR maintains a very high threshold in family reunification cases. For example, see recent non-violation verdicts in: *D.H. and others v Sweden*, App No 34210/19 (ECtHR 25 July 2024); *Okubamichael Debru v Sweden*, App No 49755/18 (ECtHR 25 July 2024).

parts. The first focuses on the Court's 'criminal conviction case law', which involves persons described as 'long-term migrants',[12] 'second-generation migrants',[13] 'settled migrants',[14] or 'quasi-nationals',[15] who face expulsion following a criminal offence. This is the most numerous, discussed, and controversial branch of the ECtHR's jurisprudence. Second, it goes on to analyse Strasbourg's non-removal jurisprudence beyond criminality.

2.1 Long-term migrants, criminality, and non-removal

It has long been a common practice to expel migrants when they engage in criminal behaviour, in substitution of prison sentences or in addition to them. Prisons in Europe are not only about punishment, deterrence, and rehabilitation, but also a tool to identify and expel offenders.[16] These practices have been consistently challenged by long-term migrants. Many of these individuals, who are not foreigners in a human or sociological sense, argue that expulsion measures would violate their rights under Article 8 ECHR. Although the Council of Europe's (CoE) Parliamentary Assembly, as early as 2001, called for the non-expulsion of long-term migrants in its Recommendation 1504,[17] and despite the fact that some CoE States already forbid their expulsion,[18] the ECtHR has been unwilling to infer such a comprehensive obligation from the ECHR.

2.1.1 ECtHR's early case law (1990s)

Strasbourg's seminal case on this issue was delivered in *Moustaquim*. The applicant was a Moroccan national born in 1963 who had been living in Belgium since 1965. He had been, together with his parents and seven brothers and sisters (some of whom were Belgian nationals), a legal resident there until he was deported in 1984 due to repeated charges of robbery and theft committed during adolescence.[19]

[12] Council of Europe Parliamentary Assembly (PACE), 'Recommendation 1504: Non-Expulsion of Long-Term Immigrants', 14 March 2001.

[13] Ryszard Cholewinski, 'Strasbourg's Hidden Agenda: The Protection of Second-Generation Migrants from Expulsion under Article 8 of the European Convention on Human Rights Part A' (1994) 12 Netherlands Quarterly of Human Rights 287.

[14] European Court of Human Rights, 'Guide on the Case Law of the European Convention on Human Rights: Immigration', 31 December 2021, 21, available at: <https://first.vaks.gov.ua/wp-content/uploads/sites/2/2022/02/Guide_Art_8_ENG.pdf>.

[15] Dembour (n 8) 20.

[16] Patricia Faraldo-Cabana, 'One Step Forward, Two Steps Back? Social Rehabilitation of Foreign Offenders under Framework Decisions 2008/909/JHA and 2008/947/JHA' (2019) 10 New Journal of European Criminal Law 151, 166.

[17] Parliamentary Assembly of the Council of Europe (PACE) (n 12). In this document, the PACE even advocated for a Protocol to the ECtHR enshrining their protection against removal.

[18] European Court of Human Rights, 'Guide on Article 8 of the European Convention on Human Rights' (n 3) 71.

[19] *Moustaquim v Belgium*, App No 12313/86 (ECtHR 18 February 1991) paras 9–10.

Even though the ECtHR began by referring to Belgium's sovereign migration control prerogatives, it went on to scrutinize whether deportation was 'necessary in a democratic society'.[20] To do so, it balanced the state's claim that the large number of criminal offences and the risk of reoffending 'made his presence on Belgian territory unacceptable to the community' with the applicant's claims, namely: that his alleged offences all went back to the applicants adolescence and were committed within a short period of time and long before the deportation order; all his close relatives had lived in Liège for a long time; he was less than 2 years old when he arrived in Belgium and had lived there for about twenty years with his family; he had returned to Morocco twice in his life; and all his schooling was in French.[21] In light of this, the Court ruled that deportation did not strike a fair balance between the interests at stake and was disproportionate with the legitimate aim pursued, therefore violating Article 8 ECHR.[22]

Yet, after *Moustaquim*, the Court struggled to find a consistent balance between the competing interests at stake, leading to an erratic jurisprudence that was from the very beginning criticized for its unpredictability.[23] In the decade that followed *Moustaquim*, the ECtHR accumulated violation and non-violation verdicts (mostly directed against France), some of which unfolded as follows:

In *Beldjoudi*, decided a year after *Moustaquim*, the ECtHR found again a violation of Article 8 in the applicant's deportation. Mr. Beldjoudi was an Algerian national born in France in 1950, when Algeria was still a French colony, and had lost his French nationality as he had never made a declaration recognizing it.[24] The applicant was convicted due to serious criminal offences, and was issued a deportation order on the grounds that he was a threat to public order.[25] Despite the seriousness of the criminal offences (i.e. assault, robbery, aggravated theft, and possession of weapons) and the fact that these were substantially worse than in *Moustaquim*,[26] the Court ruled that his deportation would violate the ECHR in light of the fact that the applicant was a 'quasi-Frenchman'.[27]

[20] Ibid, para 43.

[21] Ibid, paras 42–45.

[22] Ibid, para 46.

[23] Ann Sherlock, 'Deportation of Aliens and Article 8 ECHR' (1998) 23 European Law Review 62; Colin Warbrick, 'The Structure of Article 8' (1998) 1 European Human Rights Law Review 32; Aileen McHarg, 'Reconciling Human Rights and the Public Interest: Conceptual Problems and Doctrinal Uncertainty in the Jurisprudence of the European Court of Human Rights' (1999) 62 The Modern Law Review 671, 694–95; Colin Harvey, 'Promoting Insecurity: Public Order, Expulsion and the European Convention on Human Rights' in Elspeth Guild and Paul Minderbound (eds), *Security of Residence and Expulsion: Protection of Aliens in Europe* (Kluwer Law International 2001) 42.

[24] *Beldjoudi v France*, App No 12083/86 (ECtHR 26 March 1992) para 9.

[25] Ibid, para 15.

[26] Ibid, paras 12 and 75.

[27] In particular, the Court made reference to the fact that the applicant was born in France, was a minor at the time when he had the opportunity to re-nationalize, spent all his life there, and was married to a French woman. This was criticized in the Dissenting Opinion of Judge Pettiti, who noted that 'the majority of the Court also considered that Mr Beldjoudi was a quasi-Frenchman, a concept which is unknown in international law'.

In 1995, the Court gave another violation verdict in *Nasri*. In this case, despite the gravity of the offences committed by the migrant (gang rape, theft with violence, and assaulting a public official), the 'well-established principle of international law' and the 'public safety' interests of the state gave way to the applicant's right to respect for his family life, given that he had arrived to France in 1965 (aged 5) and was a deaf-mute person who would only be able to achieve a minimum psychological and social equilibrium within his family members, most of whom were French nationals with no ties to Algeria.[28]

In *Boujlifa*, the applicant had entered France, again, at the age of 5. The facts of the case are briefly summarized in the Dissenting Opinion of Judge Morenilla in the following terms:

> Mr Boujlifa—like Mr Nasri—is the son of an immigrant and came to France from Morocco in 1967 at the age of 5 under a family-reunion procedure. His whole family lives in France and three of his brothers have French nationality on account of their birth in French territory. He has never returned to Morocco, whose language he says he does not know, and he has been living since 1991 with a French national who will not follow him to Morocco.[29]

In this case, the crimes committed by Mr Boujlifa were limited to one conviction for robbery and another one for armed robbery, both committed in 1985 and not followed by further criminal conduct until the issuance of the expulsion decision in 1991.[30] Despite the fact that, as put forward by Judges Baka and Van Dijk in their Joint Dissent Opinion, the crimes were less numerous and serious than in *Moustaquim*, *Beldjoudi*, and *Nasri*,[31] the Court surprisingly ruled that deportation was not contrary to Article 8 ECHR, signalling the beginning of a highly erratic strand of jurisprudence.

Boujlifa was followed by another non-violation verdict in *Bouchelkia* (where the applicant, convicted for aggravated rape, had entered France at the age of 2, and had lived there for more than twenty years, got married, and formed a family there);[32] by a violation verdict in *Mehemi* (concerning, again, an Algerian national who was born and raised in France, had formed a family there, and was issued a deportation decision after being convicted for drug trafficking);[33] and, again, by a

[28] *Nasri v France*, App No 19465/92 (ECtHR 13 July 1995) paras 12 and 46.

[29] Dissenting Opinion of Judge Morenilla in *Boujlifa v France*, App No 122/1996/741/940 (ECtHR 21 October 1997).

[30] Ibid, paras 8–10.

[31] Joint Dissenting Opinion of Judges Baka and Van Dijk in *Boujlifa v France* (n 29).

[32] *Bouchelkia v France*, App No 23078/93 (ECtHR 29 January 1997) paras 45–53. It is remarkable that, in balancing the applicant's rights and state interests, the Court gave particular importance to the fact that the child he had with his wife in France had been born after the deportation order had been officially filed (see para 52 of the judgment).

[33] *Mehemi v France*, App No 85/1996/704/896 (ECtHR 26 September 1997).

non-violation judgment in *Dalia*, where the fact that the applicant lived in France since 1976 and was the single mother of a French child did not persuade the Court to find a violation of Article 8 ECHR in a case of expulsion on the basis of drug trafficking.[34]

2.1.2 The ECtHR attempts to systematize its case law: Boultif and Üner

In response to the concerns about the lottery-like character of its jurisprudence, which also responded to a stark division within the ECtHR itself,[35] the Court attempted to systematize its jurisprudence. In *Boultif*, the ECtHR not only ruled, unanimously, that there had been a breach of Article 8, but also provided a set of criteria 'to establish guiding principles in order to examine whether the measure in question was necessary in a democratic society'.[36] Interestingly, Mr Boultif was not a 'quasi-national', but an Algerian national who entered Switzerland in 1992 (aged 25), married a Swiss national, and was subsequently convicted for possession of weapons, robbery, and damage to property.[37] In establishing whether the measure was 'necessary in a democratic society', the Court established the following principles, commonly referred to as the 'Boultif criteria':

> In assessing the relevant criteria in such a case, the Court will consider [1] the nature and seriousness of the offence committed by the applicant; [2] the duration of the applicant's stay in the country from which he is going to be expelled; [3] the time which has elapsed since the commission of the offence and the applicant's conduct during that period; [4] the nationalities of the various persons concerned; [5] the applicant's family situation, such as the length of the marriage; [6] other factors revealing whether the couple lead a real and genuine family life; [7] whether the spouse knew about the offence at the time when he or she entered into a family relationship; [8] and whether there are children in the marriage and, if so, their age. Not least, the Court will also consider [9] the seriousness of the difficulties which the spouse would be likely to encounter in the applicant's country of origin, although the mere fact that a person might face certain difficulties in accompanying her or his spouse cannot in itself preclude expulsion.[38]

If one looks closely into the facts of the case, it would seem that *Boultif* not only systematized Article 8 balancing criteria, but also adopted a far more protective approach. As seen above, the Court had given non-violation verdicts in cases

34 *Dalia v France*, App No 154/1996/773/974 (ECtHR 19 February 1998).

35 With the exception of the violation verdicts in *Mehemi* and *Nasri*, there was always a divided Court as to the final verdict. This led to strong criticisms from within dissenting opinions, particularly in non-violation verdicts. See in this sense the dissenting opinions in *Boujlifa*, *Bouchelkia*, and *Dalia*.

36 *Boultif v Switzerland*, App No 54273/00 (ECtHR 2 August 2001) para 48.

37 Ibid, paras 7–9.

38 Ibid, para 48.

where the applicants were born and raised, married, and/or had children in the host country. In *Boultif*, even though the applicant had arrived in Switzerland as an adult and there was a possibility to enjoy family life elsewhere, the fact that the (European) wife would have had difficulties in moving to Algeria because she had never lived there and did not speak Arabic was key in finding a breach of Article 8 ECHR. In *Boujlifa*, where the applicant had committed similar crimes to the ones in *Boultif*, it was not enough that the applicant himself had never been to his country of nationality and did not speak the language, whereas in *Boultif* the risk that the applicant's partner would face difficulties adapting to Algeria was deemed sufficient to trigger Article 8 ECHR. As we will see, however, *Boultif* cannot be viewed as a game-changing judgment in terms of the protection offered by the Court, but as a one-off case whose underlying motivations are difficult to identify.[39]

In *Üner*, the applicant was a Turkish national who moved to the Netherlands in 1981 at the age of 12, accompanying his parents and brothers.[40] By the time he was convicted for manslaughter and assault in 1993, he already had a permanent residence permit, had entered a relationship with a Dutch national, and had a son with her.[41] While in prison, he took several courses and qualified as a sports instructor; he had regular visits from his family, partner, and child; and a second child was born to the applicant and his partner in 1996. Despite the fact that his children and partner were Dutch and did not speak any Turkish, the Court found no violation in the applicant's deportation and ten-year entry ban.[42]

The Court's judgment in *Üner* is very relevant on various fronts. First, it was the first case of its kind that was referred to the Grand Chamber, undertaking a more detailed account of expulsion's impact on the migrant's family and private life than its predecessors.[43] Following *Slivenko* (see section 2.2.1), it was one of the first cases in which the Court acknowledged the possibility for private (and not family) life to preclude deportation. The concept of private life was held to be formed by the 'totality of social ties between settled migrants and the community in which they are living'.[44] In addition, *Üner* made clear that the ECtHR was not willing to afford a qualitatively greater deal of protection to those born and raised in the host country. In other words, the ECtHR does not afford independent normative value to the passage of time in the country, but this is merely one of multiple normative

[39] Dembour, for example, points to the fact that the wife of the applicant was a white European woman who would have found it difficult to settle in Mr Boultif's country of origin (see Dembour (n 8) 182).

[40] *Üner v the Netherlands* [GC], App No 46410/99 (ECtHR 18 October 2006) paras 12–13.

[41] Ibid, paras 13–15.

[42] Ibid, paras 19–20.

[43] See C Steinorth, 'Uner v The Netherlands: Expulsion of Long-Term Immigrants and the Right to Respect for Private and Family Life' (2008) 8 Human Rights Law Review 185.

[44] *Üner* [GC] (n 40) para 59.

considerations in the balance of interests at stake.[45] Even though this could be inferred from its previous jurisprudence, the Court made it explicit that the principle first established in *Abdulaziz*, namely states' powers to control entry, stay, or residence of aliens, applied 'regardless of whether an alien entered the host country as an adult or at a very young age, or was perhaps even born there'.[46] Lastly, the ECtHR acknowledged the added value of *Boultif* in providing guiding criteria, and provided two more, namely: '[10] the best interests and well-being of the children, in particular the seriousness of the difficulties which any children of the applicant are likely to encounter in the country to which the applicant is to be expelled; and [11] the solidity of social, cultural and family ties with the host country and with the country of destination'.[47]

2.1.3 The Court's jurisprudence post-Üner: Towards a more coherent case law?

After *Üner*, however, the jurisprudence has continued to develop in an irregular manner. The fact that there is no identifiable 'core content' to Article 8 ECHR rights,[48] but rather 11 guiding criteria with uncertain relative weight, has given way, again, to a seemingly arbitrary combination of violation and non-violation verdicts.

In *Kaya*, the ECtHR found no violation in a case where the applicant was born and lived his entire life in Germany with his family. Mr. Kaya was deported following criminal convictions for which the sentences amounted to only three years and four months in prison.[49] Interestingly, the German government and the ECtHR agreed that the applicant was not fully 'integrated' in Germany.[50] One wonders whether Mr Kaya was more integrated in Turkey, which he had visited twice in his lifetime for holidays and where he had no direct family links.[51] In the following year the ECtHR found a violation in *Maslov*, where the applicant had moved to Austria at the age of 6, had returned to Bulgaria twice in his life, and was convicted for aggravated gang burglary, extortion, assault, and unauthorized use of a vehicle.[52] Interestingly, *Maslov* is the first of the cases analysed in this chapter that concerns an Article 8 ECHR violation for the expulsion of an EU national. Whether

[45] Başak Çalı, 'All You Need Is Time? Discrepancies between the European Court of Human Rights Case Law and Liberal Normative Theory on Long-Term Migrants' (2017) 50 Israel Law Review 447, 447.

[46] *Üner* [GC] (n 40) para 55.

[47] Ibid, para 58.

[48] Anuscheh Farahat, 'The Exclusiveness of Inclusion: On the Boundaries of Human Rights in Protecting Transnational and Second Generation Migrants Special Issue: The European Court of Human Rights and Immigration: Limits and Possibilities' (2009) 11 European Journal of Migration and Law 253.

[49] *Kaya v Germany*, App No 31753/02 (ECtHR 28 June 2007).

[50] Ibid, para 47.

[51] This shows, again, a very simplistic notion of integration according to which the behaviour of 'bad' citizens will always be the responsibility of the state of origin, despite the fact that Mr Kaya was entirely socialized in Germany.

[52] *Maslov v Austria* [GC], App No 1638/03 (ECtHR 23 June 2008).

the applicant's status as an EU national played a role in the ECtHR finding a violation is impossible to know, although the ECtHR does mention Directive 2004/38 in passing.[53] In *A.W. Khan*, decided in 2010, the Court precluded again the deportation of an applicant, in this case an Afghan national residing in the UK since he was 3 years old. Despite the gravity of the crimes (which included the importation of large amounts of heroin), and the facts that family life could be conducted elsewhere and that the UK government had conducted an Article 8 assessment balancing the gravity of the offence with the applicant's rights, the Court found deportation to be contrary to Article 8 ECHR.[54]

The more recent cases of *Ndidi* and *Saber and Boughassal* illustrate Strasbourg's inconsistency, giving a non-violation and a violation verdict respectively despite the seemingly similar circumstances.[55] In *Ndidi,* the applicant was a Nigerian national who had entered the United Kingdom in 1989, when he was 2 years old. He committed various crimes between 2004 and 2008, including robbery, assault, and drug supply. The applicant was sentenced to seven years of imprisonment, replaced by detention in a young offenders' institution. Upon release in 2011, he was issued a deportation order.[56] Despite the fact that his parents, brothers, partner, and son were all living in the UK, the gravity of the offences was in this case sufficient for deportation to be considered proportionate under Article 8 ECHR.[57] *Saber and Boughassal* concerns two applicants born in Morocco in 1985 and 1987 who entered Spain on an unknown date, but received their schooling there at least since 1998, and subsequently obtained long-term residence. The first applicant resided with his mother and five brothers and sisters in Spain, whereas the second one married a Moroccan national who moved to Spain, where his parents and brothers also resided. They were both convicted of drug trafficking and ordered to leave on the basis of their criminal convictions.[58] Even though the ECtHR noted that the links that the applicants had with their families in Spain could not qualify as family life,[59] the interference with their right to private life was considered disproportionate, not 'necessary in a democratic society', and therefore the expulsion order amounted to a violation of Article 8 ECHR.[60]

Other recent cases include *Noorzae* and *Sharifi*. In both cases, the applicants were Afghan nationals who had lived in Denmark for most of their lives (arriving at the age of 5 and 9 respectively) and faced deportation following convictions for

[53] Ibid, paras 41 and 82. For an analysis of EU citizenship and its protective gaps in the context of poverty and criminality, see section 5 in this chapter.

[54] *A.W. Khan v the United Kingdom*, App No 47486/06 (ECtHR 12 January 2010) paras 5–8.

[55] This inconsistency can be partially explained by the Court's procedural turn (see section 2.3) and the fact that domestic authorities had conducted a balancing exercise in *Ndidi* but not in *Saber.*

[56] *Ndidi v the United Kingdom*, App No 41215/14 (ECtHR 14 September 2017) paras 5–20.

[57] Ibid, para 80.

[58] *Saber and Boughassal v Spain*, Apps No 76550/13 and 45938/14 (ECtHR 18 December 2018) paras 1–5.

[59] Ibid, para 43.

[60] Ibid, paras 51–52.

drug-related offences (*Noorzae*) and possession of firearms (*Sharifi*). The ECtHR found violations of Article 8 ECHR in both cases, emphasizing that, despite the gravity of the crimes, Danish authorities had failed to sufficiently account for their long-term residence and the strength of their ties to Denmark.[61]

In sum, the ECtHR has made several attempts to systematize its case law (most notably in *Boultif* and *Üner*). Whereas the gravity of the crime and having strong family links seem to be key factors, the right to respect for family and private life still lacks an identifiable 'core content'. This undermines the legal certainty needed for individuals and domestic authorities to reasonably foresee the outcome of specific cases. But European states do not only deport 'misbehaving' migrants. Despite the fact that the majority of the criteria listed in *Boultif* and *Üner* primarily apply to long-term migrants who have committed criminal offences, Article 8 ECHR expulsion cases are not restricted to them. The following section elaborates on this jurisprudence.

2.2 Non-removal case law beyond criminality

2.2.1 Berrehab *and subsequent case law*

Berrehab, decided almost three years before *Moustaquim*, was the first case concerning the removal of a migrant under Article 8 ECHR. By 1986 (two years before *Berrehab*) the then Commission of Human Rights had already dealt with around ninety cases challenging the expulsion of migrants under Article 8 ECHR.[62] The majority of these cases concerned expulsion following criminal convictions, and they were consistently declared inadmissible on the basis that an expulsion due to criminal behaviour would always be justified, under Article 8(2) ECHR, as 'necessary in a democratic society'.[63]

In admitting the application and finding an Article 8 ECHR violation in *Berrehab*, the Commission and the Court might have found it easier to step in, as the applicant was not a criminal but a law-abiding father who simply lost his residence permit after a divorce.[64] Mr Berrehab was a Moroccan national who obtained a residence permit in the Netherlands in 1978, aged 26, after marrying a Dutch national.[65] He divorced in 1979, right before his daughter was born, and maintained regular contact with her. However, upon the expiry of his residence

[61] *Noorzae v Denmark*, App No 44810/20 (ECtHR 5 September 2023); *Sharifi v Denmark*, App No 31434/21 (ECtHR 5 September 2023).

[62] Mark E. Villiger, 'Expulsion and the Right to Respect for Private and Family Life (Article 8 of the Convention)—An Introduction to the Commission's Case Law' in Franz Matscher and Herbert Petzold (eds), *Protecting Human Rights: The European Dimension* (Heymans 1988).

[63] Ibid, 660–61.

[64] Dembour (n 8) 162.

[65] *Berrehab v the Netherlands*, App No 10730/84 (ECtHR 21 June 1988) paras 7–8.

permit, he was denied its renewal and deported.[66] The Court acknowledged, for the first time, that the applicant's expulsion was in violation of Article 8 ECHR. In doing so, it referred to his lawful residence, noted that he had a home and a job there, and stressed that the government did not have any complaints about his behaviour and, most importantly, that he had family ties in the host country.[67] Interestingly, in *Berrehab* we cannot find a reference to the 'well-established principle of international law' to control entry, stay, and residence.

The case of *Berrehab* triggered the beginning of a very rich jurisprudence in the 1990s, mainly concerning second-generation migrants with deportation orders following criminal convictions, as seen in the previous section (2.1). Yet, what are the balancing criteria for *Berrehab*-like cases? The essential difference is that, in these cases, applicants are not necessarily 'quasi-nationals' (although they can be), nor have they been criminally convicted. Even though the balancing exercise to be done is essentially the same, many of the *Boultif/Üner* criteria do not apply, as these require weighting, among others, the nature and seriousness of the criminal offence, the time elapsed since its commission, the person's subsequent conduct, and whether the spouse knew about the offence when entering the family relationship.[68] In addition, for those who did not have family links in Europe, the question arose: was there a right to contest expulsion on the basis of private life alone? Out of the nine criteria listed by the ECtHR in *Boultif*, three made reference to the applicant's criminal record, and five to family links.[69] By the beginning of the 2000s, such a question had not yet been addressed by the ECtHR. It took a fairly extreme case for the Court to step in, but it answered in the positive in *Slivenko*.

The case of *Slivenko* concerned one of the so-called erased people who emerged in Latvia and Slovenia upon the breakup of the Soviet Union.[70] It concerned two applicants: Mrs Slivenko (ethnically Russian, from Estonia), who had arrived in Latvia in 1959 when she was 1 month old, and her daughter. Both became stateless in 1991 after the Soviet Union's collapse; they were refused entry into the register of Latvian residents as 'ex-USSR citizens', and were deported in 1999.[71] Despite the fact that they had established family life in Latvia, this could also be developed elsewhere, as it was demonstrated by the fact that they moved to Russia, where her husband was, and adopted Russian citizenship.[72] As a result, and in the absence

[66] Ibid, para 12.

[67] Ibid, para 29.

[68] *Boultif* (n 36) para 48.

[69] Ibid. These referred to the nationality of the persons, the family situation, the existence of genuine family links, the existence of children, and the difficulties for the spouse to leave the host state. Only one criterion seemed to fit the concept of private life, this being 'the duration of the applicant's stay in the country from which he is going to be expelled'.

[70] Sanja Vrbek, 'Reasons for EU Double Standards: Comparative Overview of the Cases of the Erased and the Non-Citizens' (2015) 43 Nationalities Papers 302. For further details on this phenomenon, see Nida M Gelazis, 'The European Union and the Statelessness Problem in the Baltic States' (2004) 6 European Journal of Migration and Law 225.

[71] *Slivenko v Latvia*, App No 48321/99 (ECtHR 9 October 2003) paras 14–17, 31, and 114.

[72] Ibid, para 46.

of strong legal claims under the heading of 'family life', the ECtHR proceeded to evaluate the extent to which 'private life' was disrupted. In doing so, the Court found that deportation had disproportionately affected 'the network of personal, social and economic relations that make up the private life of every human being'.[73]

It is therefore on the basis of private life alone that the ECtHR found a violation of Article 8 ECHR in *Slivenko*. Even though the Court has generally shown greater sympathy for those who have formed a family in the host state, the inclusion of private life (no doubt a more encompassing concept than family life) was fundamental in enlarging human rights-based protection against expulsion—but potentially opens yet another door for precarious residence and non-removability, as section 3 illustrates. In *Üner*, adopted two years after *Slivenko*, the Court again highlighted the relevance of private life, and added the criterion that, in an expulsion decision, 'the solidity of social, cultural and family ties with the host country and with the country of destination' should also be taken into account.[74]

In *Omoregie*, the applicant married a Norwegian national while his asylum claim was pending and had a daughter with her. He was ordered to leave the country after his asylum claim was rejected, but remained, working irregularly, for a year. The Court did not find a breach of Article 8 ECHR, considering the links that he maintained with his country of origin (*Üner* criterion) and the fact that he had formed his family after the issuance of the return decision—thus being aware that his migration status would be precarious from the outset.[75]

In *Nunez*, however, the ECtHR ruled that an applicant who had resided in Norway for only a few years and had two daughters there had a right to remain under Article 8 ECHR, even though her whole stay in the country had been unauthorized. It decided so in light of what the Court considered to be 'exceptional' circumstances, primarily stemming from best interests of the child considerations.[76]

In *Antwi*, on the expulsion of an irregular migrant living in Norway, the applicant was also married (in this case to a Norwegian national) and had a Norwegian daughter. Strikingly, the ECtHR noted that the exceptional circumstances found in *Nunez* did not apply, given the special links of the applicant and his wife to Ghana (even though the Norwegian child had never been there).[77]

In sum, when long-term residence and criminal convictions are removed from the equation, migrants still have to ground their Article 8 ECHR claims on the remaining *Boultif* and *Üner* criteria, together with those added in subsequent cases like *Omoregie*, *Antwi* or *Nunez*. Still, no core content of the right can be observed, and therefore the case law remains highly unpredictable.

[73] Ibid, para 96.
[74] *Üner* [GC] (n 40) para 58.
[75] *Omoregie and others v Norway*, App No 265/07 (ECtHR 31 July 2008) para 57.
[76] *Nunez v Norway*, App No 55597/09 (ECtHR 28 June 2011) para 84.
[77] *Antwi and others v Norway*, App No 26940/10 (ECtHR 14 February 2012) paras 98 and 103.

2.2.2 Ill-treatment below Article 3 as a barrier to deportation

Lastly, in *Paposhvili* (see Chapter 2 of this book) the ECtHR held that, for seriously ill migrants, states should evaluate whether, regardless of Article 3 ECHR claims, the applicants depend on their family as a result of the deterioration of their state of health.[78] This is, even if the threshold of 'inhuman or degrading treatment' is not reached upon expulsion, Article 8 ECHR might be triggered.[79] This is confirmed in *I.M.*, where the applicant had an 80% physical disability and was dependent on his children. The Court observed a violation of Article 8 ECHR because the Swiss government had not considered the applicant's dependency on his children and lacked a proportionality test.[80]

These recent judgments, in addition to corroborating the procedural turn of the ECtHR,[81] seem to confirm Mole's intuition that Article 8 ECHR can preclude ill-treatment that has adverse effects to one's 'physical and moral integrity' when this does not reach the threshold of severity needed for Article 3 ECHR to be triggered,[82] opening yet another door for non-removability.

2.3 Putting method to the madness? Implementing Article 8 ECHR at the national level

One immediate question that arises after analysing Article 8 ECHR case law concerns its domestic implementation. Beyond the lucky ones that make it to Strasbourg, what is the use of Article 8 ECHR in expulsion cases? If the ECtHR does not provide consistently applicable criteria, cannot public administrations simply remove by default, hoping that the case does not make it to Strasbourg and that, if it does, the state ends up on the lucky side? State practice shows that this is not necessarily the case.

First, there might be (limited) guidance for domestic courts in their balancing of the interests at stake. Searching for consistency, some authors have pointed at possible underlying patterns in the ECtHR's jurisprudence. According to Costello, the case law suggests that the gravity of the crime might be a decisive criterion, capable of justifying deportation even for the most settled migrants.[83] Whereas the seriousness of the crime is certainly a crucial (if not the most important) factor in cases of criminally convicted deportees, this explanation can be at odds with the approach followed in cases such as *Boujlifa, Nasri, Mehemi* or *A.W. Khan* (see sections 2.1

[78] *Paposhvili v Belgium* [GC], App No 41738/10 (ECtHR 13 December 2016) para 223.
[79] Ibid, paras 225–26.
[80] *I.M. v Switzerland*, App No 23887/16 (ECtHR 9 April 2019).
[81] Thomas Kleinlein, 'The Procedural Approach of the European Court of Human Rights: Between Subsidiarity and Dynamic Evolution' (2019) 68 International and Comparative Law Quarterly 91.
[82] Mole (n 9) 100.
[83] Costello (n 7) 116.

and 2.2). According to Çalı and Cunningham, the passage of time seems to matter more for those who arrived in the host country and/or committed the crime as children. However, the authors acknowledge that these predictors are still rebuttable and sometimes inconsistent with existing case law— again leaving considerable leeway for states to find otherwise.[84] Lastly, recent jurisprudence might be partially explained in light of the Court's 'procedural turn', that is, the fact that the ECtHR seems to increasingly scrutinize procedural diligence at the domestic level (i.e. whether a reasonable 'balancing exercise' is performed by the state), while following a practice of (partial or total) deference towards domestic courts insofar as the normative assessment of the merits is concerned.[85] This could help explain the violation verdicts of the Court in cases such as *Saber* (where Spanish law only looked into the gravity of the offences without requiring an individualized proportionality assessment—see section 2.1.3), or more recently in *Abdi* (where Denmark deported a Somali citizen without looking into his family ties under Article 8),[86] as well as the non-violation verdict in *Ndidi*,[87] or more recently in cases such as *Khan*, *Munir Johanna*, or *Ngumbu Kikoso*.[88] Even though it indeed seems like the ECtHR often preaches a balancing exercise while exercising deference to domestic courts, explanations based exclusively on the Court's procedural turn fail to explain the result of other judgments (including recent ones) where the ECtHR has actually replaced the balancing exercise of domestic courts with its own.[89]

Then, it is clear that the Strasbourg Court maintains at least a role as a 'regulatory watchdog' which monitors the quality of decision making at the national level.[90] Regardless of the conclusion reached, states still need to show that they

[84] Başak Çalı and Stewart Cunningham, 'The European Court of Human Rights and Removal of Long-Term Migrants: Entrenched Statism with a Human Voice?' in Başak Çalı, Ledi Bianku, and Iulia Motoc (eds), *Migration and the European Convention on Human Rights* (Oxford University Press 2021) 169–70.

[85] Kleinlein (n 81); Oddný Mjöll Arnardóttir, 'The "Procedural Turn" under the European Convention on Human Rights and Presumptions of Convention Compliance' (2017) 15 International Journal of Constitutional Law 9.

[86] *Abdi v Denmark*, App No 41643/19 (ECtHR 14 September 2021).

[87] In *Ndidi*, the Court emphasized that, where domestic Courts have examined the facts, applied the ECtHR case law, and balanced the interests of the applicant and those of the state, it is not for the Court to substitute the state's assessment of the merits with its own (see *Ndidi* (n 56) para 76).

[88] *Khan v Denmark*, App No 26957/19 (ECtHR 31 May 2021); *Munir Johana v Denmark*, App 56803/18 (ECtHR 12 April 2021); *Ngumbu Kikoso v France*, App No 21643/19 (ECtHR, Decision of 21 October 2021). In all these cases, the Court showed high deference to states' reasoning. In *Khan* and *Munir Johanna*, the applicants were convicted to less than one year in prison and they were either born in the host state or moved there at the age of four. However, the fact that Denmark conducted the assessment and that 'very serious reasons' were adduced by Danish authorities was deemed enough to find that the authorities had struck a 'fair balance'. In *Ngumbu Kikoso*, where the applicant had lived for more than twenty years and was convicted to six months in prison for falsification of documents, the case was not even found admissible because expulsion was justified by French authorities in light of proportionality considerations.

[89] *A.W. Khan* (n 54); *Noorzae* (n 61); *Sharifi* (n 61) .

[90] Patricia Popelier, 'The Court as Regulatory Watchdog: The Procedural Approach in the Case Law of the European Court of Human Rights' in Patricia Popelier, Armen Mazmanyan and Werner Vandenbruwaene (eds), *The Role of Constitutional Courts in Multilevel Governance* (Intersentia 2012).

have observed the applicable criteria in each specific case. This includes an assessment of whether family or private life can be conducted elsewhere,[91] the best interests of the child,[92] applicants' knowledge and expectations over their migration status,[93] the existence of migration law breaches,[94] the length of residence in the host state and the links with the country of origin,[95] their cohabitation with family members,[96] and so on. Even if the ECtHR does not provide truly authoritative guidance, it is clear that proportionality considerations and the fair balance between the interests at stake in expulsion cases cannot be done solely through law, but require an administrative and judicial balancing exercise for each and every case of expulsion.

This does not mean, of course, that jurisprudential inconsistency does not lead to a high degree of legal uncertainty for both individuals and CoE States. But comparative analysis shows that, in general, neither administrative nor judicial authorities behave as if Article 8 ECHR was non-existent. For example, in the Netherlands, the Foreigners Decree was modified so that expulsion after a criminal conviction may only take place if balanced with the person's rights under Article 8 ECHR.[97] It is reported that the Dutch Council of State generally follows the guiding principles established by the ECtHR in order to establish whether the administration and the lower courts have taken all the relevant elements into consideration.[98] Similarly, UK immigration laws were amended in 2012 to reflect factors that can weigh for and against an Article 8 ECHR claim according to ECtHR jurisprudence, and include a compulsory proportionality assessment by domestic courts.[99] It is also reassuring to see the formulation of the balancing exercise performed by Lord Wilson in finding a violation of Article 8 ECHR in an expulsion case in the following terms:

> The burden of proof is upon the Secretary of State to establish that the interference with the rights of the applicants under Article 8 . . . was justified under paragraph 2 . . . [The interference] was 'in accordance with the law.' But was it 'necessary in a democratic society'? . . . [I]n such a context, four questions generally arise, namely: a) is the legislative objective sufficiently important to justify limiting a fundamental right?; b) are the measures which have been designed to meet it rationally connected to it? c) are they no more than are necessary to accomplish

[91] *Abdulaziz* (n 4).
[92] *Nunez* (n 76).
[93] *Jeunesse v the Netherlands* [GC], App No 12738/10 (ECtHR 3 October 2014).
[94] *Omoregie* (n 75).
[95] *Üner* [GC] (n 40).
[96] *Berrehab* (n 65).
[97] See Article 3(86) of the 2000 Foreigners Decree (Netherlands).
[98] Mark Klaassen, 'Between Facts and Norms: Testing Compliance with Article 8 ECHR in Immigration Cases' (2019) 37 Netherlands Quarterly of Human Rights 157, 171.
[99] Ibid, 173.

it?; d) do they strike a fair balance between the rights of the individual and the interests of the community?[100]

In Spain, the government reached a friendly settlement with the applicant in *G.V.A.*, with the government acknowledging the violation of Article 8 ECHR posed by the automatic expulsion of foreigners following convictions of certain gravity,[101] and committing to interpret its legislation on expulsion following an individualized assessment on the basis of Article 8 ECHR criteria (as it had already been mandated by the Spanish Constitutional Court).[102]

The above-mentioned examples do not naturally imply that the balance will be the same as that of the ECtHR, but rather that domestic tribunals are the ones that must ensure that Article 8 ECHR translates into an effective legal tool for protecting migrants against expulsion.

3. Article 8 ECHR and non-removable migrants

3.1 Protection from expulsion and non-removable migrants

Does a human right not to be deported under Article 8 ECHR entail a right to a (any) residence permit? Similarly to litigation under Article 3 ECHR, the ECtHR has made clear that successfully challenging deportation does not come with lawful residence attached (as will be developed in section 3.2). The very fact that migrants are issued (unenforceable) return decisions indicates that they do not meet domestic conditions for a residence permit—and their presence is often perceived as a challenge to state sovereignty. If expulsion is contrary to Article 8 ECHR and migrants do not leave voluntarily, one might believe that forcing them into situations of rightlessness and destitution will encourage self-deportation, sending the message that irregular stay, even if prolonged enough to preclude deportation, will not lead to lawful residence. In this vein, it is commonplace for the EU and its Member

[100] *R (on the application of Quila and another) (FC) (Respondents) v Secretary of State for the Home Department (Appellant)* [2011] UKSC 45 paras 44–45.

[101] *G.V.A. v Spain*, App No 35765/14 (ECtHR, Decision of 17 March 2015). The provision challenged was the same as in *López Pastuzano* (Case C-636, *Wilber López Pastuzano v Delegación del Gobierno en Navarra* [2017] EU:C:2017:949) and *Saber and Boughassal* (n 58).

[102] Constitutional Court of Spain, STC 186/2013, 4 November 2013 ES:TC:2013:186 FJ 7. Paradoxically, the right to family life as enshrined in the ECHR, is present in a provision of the Spanish Constitution (Article 39) which is not subject to constitutional appeal after the passing of the Law 6/2007 on the Spanish Constitutional Court (aimed at alleviating the burden of cases for the Constitutional Court). The jurisprudence of the ECtHR on Article 8 thus has to be followed by the administration and through ordinary judicial practice, but these cannot be reviewed in constitutional appeal. These cases can therefore make it to Strasbourg without being reviewed by the Spanish Constitutional Court.

States to assert that rewarding irregular stay with legal residence constitutes a pull factor for irregular migration.[103]

Moreover, there are few legal obligations towards Article 8 ECHR non-removable migrants under the EU *acquis*, as Member States are not obliged to postpone their removal and give them additional rights under Articles 9 and 14 Directive 2008/115 (Return Directive)—contrary to non-removables under Article 3 ECHR (see Chapter 5 of this book for a detailed account of their legal status).[104]

Policy choices across Member States of course vary substantially. In some Member States, national legislation explicitly incorporates references to Article 8 ECHR and even includes a right to regularize their stay, whereas in other states this will lead to a 'toleration status', and in some they will remain fully clandestinely.[105] Be that as it may, it is not uncommon for state authorities to halt return due to family and/or private ties, while still refusing to grant a residence permit on the grounds that it is not required by the law.[106]

In this context, it can be the case that a migrant chooses to contest, under Article 8 ECHR, both deportation and the lack of a residence permit. For those who are already non-removable (due to *non-refoulement*, family and/or private life, or other reasons), the right to respect for family and private life has also been used to contest irregularity and non-removability. The ECtHR's overarching logic has been that physical presence (regardless of lawful residence) in a CoE country will be sufficient to maintain one's family and/or private links in full respect of the ECHR. This is made clear in the *Mehemi* saga, where the same applicant reached the ECtHR in 1996 and 1999 to claim non-removal and a residence permit respectively. Whereas in *Mehemi (No1)*, as analysed above, the ECtHR established that

[103] Martin Baldwin-Edwards and Albert Kraler (eds), *REGINE—Regularisations in Europe* (Amsterdam University Press 2009) 50 and 65; European Commission, 'Communication on a European Agenda on Migration', COM(2015) 240 Final, 13 May 2015, 9.

[104] Directive 2008/115/EC on common standards and procedures in Member States for returning illegally staying third-country nationals [2008] OJ L348/98 (Return Directive) arts 9 and 14. However, the CJEU has ruled that Member States may not adopt a return decision without taking into account the family life of the person concerned (see Case C-82/16, *K.A. and Others v Belgische Staat* [2018] EU:C:2018:308 para 104; Case C-482/22, *Bundesrepublik Deutschland v GS* [2023] EU:C:2023:122 para 25; Case C-392/22, *X v Staatssecretaris van Justitie en Veiligheid* [2024] EU:C:2024:195 para 91).

[105] European Agency for Fundamental Rights (FRA), 'Fundamental Rights of Migrants in an Irregular Situation in the European Union', 21 November 2011, 30, available at: <https://fra.europa.eu/en/publication/2012/fundamental-rights-migrants-irregular-situation-european-union>; European Migration Network (EMN), 'Responses to Long-Term Irregularly Staying Migrants: Practices and Challenges in the EU and Norway', 30 July 2021, 14, available at: <https://www.emnspain.gob.es/en/-/responses-to-long-term-irregular-staying-migrants-practices-and-challenges-in-the-eu-and-norway>; European Migration Network (EMN), 'The Different National Practices Concerning Granting of Non-EU Harmonised Protection Statuses', December 2010, available at: <https://emn.ie/publications/the-different-national-practices-concerning-granting-of-non-eu-harmonised-protection-statuses-emn-synthesis-report-2/>.

[106] For real-life examples, see Maaike Vanderbruggen and others, 'Point of No Return: The Futile Detention of Unreturnable Migrants', *Detention Action*, January 2014, 5, 31, and 41–43, available at: <https://ecre.org/point-of-no-return-the-futile-detention-of-unreturnable-migrants>.

deportation would breach Article 8 ECHR, in *Mehemi (No2)*, where the applicant claimed a residence permit, the Court did not find such a violation. In doing so, it noted that he was no longer obliged to live in a country with which he had no links other than nationality, he was able to maintain his family ties, and he was under no risk of imminent deportation.[107] As the next section (3.2) shows, it is not by chance that the ECtHR grants greater protection against expulsion than against statuslessness and destitution, as the latter requires positive obligations from states.

3.2 Article 8 ECHR as a right to regularize? Cases of failure

The ECtHR has acknowledged that, even though Article 8 ECHR does not generally require states to grant migrants a certain status or documentation, under exceptional circumstances there might be a positive obligation to regularize.[108] This has led some scholars to claim that the ECtHR now grants autonomous human rights protection to long-term residents, including an eventual obligation for CoE States to grant residence permits to otherwise irregular migrants.[109] However, given that access to a residence permit on the basis of Article 8 ECHR remains exceptionally difficult to obtain, the remainder of this chapter will not focus on the stories of success (see Chapter 6 of this book on regularization) but rather on those of failure, which are far more numerous in practice and have received significantly less attention in the literature.

First, it must be noted that, in the same way that *Berrehab* emerged after decades of inadmissibility decisions, claims for a residence permit were already being filed in Strasbourg in the 1990s. In a separate opinion to the Commission's report in *H.L.R v France*, decided in 1995, Mr Cabral Barreto, later judge of the ECtHR, noted that in a case where expulsion was already precluded under Article 3 ECHR, some sort of residence permit that allowed the applicant to access employment and social benefits should be afforded if a breach of Article 8 ECHR was to be avoided.[110] Three years later, the applicant in *B.B. v France* claimed that '[o]nly a residence permit, even if only temporary, would give him full rights under the social welfare system'.[111] Given that the applicant was no longer under a risk of deportation, the Court decided to strike the case out of the list.[112] In *Dremlyuga*, where the applicant had claimed an Article 8 violation on the basis of the problems created by his irregular status in Latvia, the ECtHR declared the application

[107] *Mehemi v France (No2)*, App No 53470/99 (ECtHR 10 April 2003) para 54.
[108] See *Rodrigues da Silva and Hoogkamer v the Netherlands*, App No 50435/99 (ECtHR 31 January 2006); *Jeunesse* (n 93); *Hoti v Croatia*, App No 63311/14 (ECtHR 26 April 2018).
[109] Daniel Thym, 'Respect for Private and Family Life under Article 8 ECHR in Immigration Cases: A Human Right to Regularize Illegal Stay?' (2008) 57 International and Comparative Law Quarterly 87.
[110] Mole (n 9) 193.
[111] *BB v France*, App No 30930/96 (ECtHR 7 September 1998) para 35.
[112] Ibid, para 40.

inadmissible, noting that the Convention does not grant a right to a particular type of residence permit (temporary, permanent, or other) as long as the solution proposed by states allows migrants to have their family life respected.[113]

In 2005 and 2006, however, the ECtHR gave its first violation verdicts in *Sisojeva* (which concerned the residence permit of yet another stateless person in Latvia),[114] *Mendizabal* (concerning the residence permit of an EU national),[115] and *Rodrigues da Silva* (on the residence permit granted to an irregular migrant, mother of a Dutch child).[116] As noted by the Court in *Ejimson*, the applicable principles are similar in respect of positive and negative obligations under Article 8 ECHR. In both cases, a 'fair balance' must be made between the competing interests of the migrant and the community as a whole.[117] The Court has not made clear, so far, how much higher the threshold is in residence permit cases in comparison with non-removal ones, but it has noted that, only in exceptional circumstances, the lack of a residence permit will impede the exercise of Article 8 rights. While the Court has recently shown promising signs by referring to a 'neutral starting point' in the assessment of residence permit cases—as opposed to the principle of exceptionality,[118] it remains the case that non-removal under Article 8 ECHR does not normally go as far as affording a residence permit, and therefore the non-removability gap remains.

In *Nunez*, where the applicant contested both the expulsion and the lack of a residence permit, the ECtHR established that deportation would violate Article 8 ECHR, but also that the applicant could not have any legitimate expectations regarding the granting of a residence permit, due to the fact that she had been aware of her irregular residence and her prohibition to re-enter Norway all along.[119] In *Ejimson*, regarding a Nigerian national living in Germany, father to a German national, and convicted of drug trafficking, the applicant did not contest the expulsion decision but the lack of access to a residence permit. The ECtHR suggested that deportation would be contrary to Article 8 ECHR:

> [T]here would have been a significant lapse of time between the final decision denying him a residence permit on 16 February 2012 and the actual deportation, allowing the Court to have regard to the developments during that time . . . He would not, in such circumstances, be prevented from arguing that his deportation

[113] *Dremlyuga v Latvia*, App No 66729/01 (ECtHR, Decision of 29 April 2003).

[114] *Sisojeva and others v Latvia*, App No 60654/00 (ECtHR 16 June 2005). The case was struck out in a Grand Chamber judgment in 2007 because the regularization options granted by the Latvian Government were considered to be sufficient to comply with Article 8 ECHR (*Sisojeva and others v Latvia* [GC], App No 60654/00 (ECtHR 15 January 2007)).

[115] *Aristimuño Mendizabal v France*, App No 51431/99 (ECtHR 17 January 2006).

[116] *Rodrigues da Silva and Hoogkamer* (n 108).

[117] *Ejimson v Germany*, App No 58681/12 (ECtHR 1 March 2018) para 56.

[118] *Pormes v the Netherlands*, App No 25402/14 (ECtHR 14 December 2020) para 61. See further in Chapter 6.

[119] *Nunez* (n 76) para 42.

has now become impossible for reasons of law, notably his rights under Article 8 of the Convention.[120]

The Court, however, did not rule on the deportation's legality since it had not been contested by the applicant, who still had domestic remedies available for it. Despite suggesting that deportation would entail a violation of Article 8 ECHR, the Court did not find such a violation in the denial of a residence permit.[121] Even in *Pormes*, where the Court introduced the notion of a 'neutral starting point' in residence permit cases, it noted that, for settled migrants, 'very serious reasons' are required to justify deportation, but not for withdrawing a residence permit—thus finding no violation in the denial of a residence permit of a non-removable migrant who moved to the host country at the age of 4.[122]

3.3 The case of 'undesirable and unreturnable' migrants under Article 3 ECHR

Lastly, this section focuses on 'undesirable and unreturnable' migrants, that is, those who have committed or are suspected of having committed 'serious crimes' (and hence are excluded from international protection), but who still cannot be deported in accordance with states' absolute and non-derogable *non-refoulement* obligations (as discussed in Chapter 2). These persons are often subjected to protracted periods of limbo, lacking a defined legal status and access to basic rights in the host state.[123] It is in these situations that many applicants have contested their migration status under Articles 3 (see Chapter 2) and 8 ECHR, so far leading to inadmissibility decisions.

In the inadmissibility decisions following *Bonger*, the ECtHR has repeatedly rejected the applicants' claims to regularization under Articles 3 and 8 ECHR. As seen in Chapter 2, the applicant in *Bonger* contended that the rejection of a residence permit and the resulting situation of rightlessness and destitution was in itself a violation of Article 3 ECHR because it made it impossible for him to become a member of Dutch society. The Court rejected the complaint as manifestly ill-founded given that neither Article 3 nor any other provision of the ECHR afforded, as such, a right to a residence permit.[124] One wonders, however, whether it would have been more appropriate for the applicant to claim a residence permit under

[120] *Ejimson* (n 117) paras 61–63.
[121] Ibid, para 65.
[122] *Pormes* (n 118) para 49.
[123] David James Cantor and others, 'The Emperor's New Clothing: National Responses to "Undesirable and Unreturnable" Aliens under Asylum and Immigration Law' (2017) 36(1) Refugee Survey Quarterly 1.
[124] *Teshome Goraga Bonger v the Netherlands*, App No 10154/04 (ECtHR, Decision of 15 September 2005).

Article 8 of the Convention: first, because the Chamber judgment in *Sisojeva* had been decided three months earlier, finding for the first time a positive obligation for the state to provide a residence permit to the applicant; second, because the applicant's main argument in *Bonger* (i.e. that he was not allowed to become a member of Dutch society) was essentially a claim to social membership that would fit better within Article 8 than under Article 3 ECHR. Still, the inadmissibility decisions that have followed *Bonger* over the years show that the outcome would have likely been the same.

In *I*, the applicant, his spouse, and his children applied for refugee status, which was granted to all the family except for Mr I, to whom the exclusion from refugee status under Article 1(F) of the Geneva Convention applied.[125] In this case, the applicant claimed that the denial of a residence permit violated his rights not only under Article 3, but also under Article 8 ECHR.[126] The Court decided to adjourn the examination of the application concerning family life, and one year later decided that, whereas the Convention might demand positive obligations from the state (in the form of a residence permit or others), the fact that he resided irregularly (as if he had a choice) and was not able to work and make a living led to the conclusion that the application was manifestly ill-founded and did not raise any issues under Article 8 ECHR.[127]

The Court used the same reasoning to file inadmissibility decisions in *H* and *K*.[128] In the latter case, the applicant was excluded from international protection because, in the Netherlands, every Afghan national who had held a rank of lieutenant or higher during the communist regime was automatically excluded from international protection. In the meantime, he resided irregularly for almost fifteen years in the Netherlands, despite the fact that he enjoyed absolute and non-derogable protection from expulsion under Article 3 ECHR and his spouse and children had residence permits there.[129] Again, the application was considered inadmissible since the applicant was under no real threat of being deported and separated from his family. The same rationale was applied to find the complaint inadmissible in *A. v the Netherlands*, where the applicant, suspected of terrorism, was non-removable under Article 3 ECHR, had been residing irregularly for more than fifteen years, and claimed a residence permit based on both family and private life.[130]

In sum, the ECHR (as interpreted in Strasbourg) offers a shallow and incomplete protection. It is also highly unpredictable. As noted by Dembour, 'neither the

[125] *I v the Netherlands*, App No 24147/11 (ECtHR, Decision of 18 October 2011) paras 3–4.
[126] Ibid, para 35.
[127] *I* (n 125) paras 48–49.
[128] *H v the Netherlands*, App No 37833/10 (ECtHR, Decision of 19 June 2012); *K v the Netherlands*, App No 33403/11 (ECtHR, Decision of 25 September 2012).
[129] *K* (n 128) para 5.
[130] *A v the Netherlands*, App No 60538/13 (ECtHR, Decision of 12 November 2013).

facts of the cases, nor the composition of the relevant judicial panels, nor an evolution in the overall political climate explain in themselves the inconsistency in the case law'.[131] Even in cases of protection, this is often incomplete, as non-removal does not come with residence attached. Considering these features, the protection under Article 8 ECHR must be regarded as a subsidiary system of membership when the protection offered by other (national or supranational) legal frameworks is out of reach. The following section focuses on systems of social membership under EU law. Unlike the ECtHR, which offers an uncertain, case-by-case assessment of non-removal or residence rights, EU law *entitles* certain non-nationals to become members of the host society upon the fulfilment of certain conditions. I will zoom in on the most advanced supranational forms of membership under EU law, namely long-term residence (for third-country nationals) and EU citizenship (for EU citizens). Yet, even in these cases, residence rights can prove fragile and lead to non-removability, particularly in the context of poverty and criminality.

4. Membership claims, exclusion, and non-removability in EU law: Long-term residence and EU citizenship

In parallel to the ECHR system, the CJEU has incorporated the jurisprudence of the ECtHR in its case law on the Return Directive. This means that, when implementing the Directive, Member States must take into account Article 7 of the EU Charter of Fundamental Rights (the Charter).[132] Article 7 of the Charter corresponds to Article 8 ECHR and, following Article 52(3) of the Charter, its meaning and scope must be at least the same as that of Article 8 ECHR.[133] However, in recognizing non-nationals' right to belong, EU law goes well beyond mirroring ECtHR jurisprudence concerning non-removal. The clearest recognition of the membership of non-nationals can be found in long-term residence and EU citizenship. The remaining part of this chapter elaborates on these systems and how their protection gaps can lead to precarious residence and non-removability.

4.1 The Long-term Residence Directive, membership, and exclusion

The strongest manifestation of the civic membership of TCNs in the EU can be found in the Long-term Residence Directive. The acquisition of LTR, the rights attached to it,[134] and the conditions for its loss are all governed under EU law and

[131] Marie-Benedicte Dembour, 'Human Rights Law and National Sovereignty in Collusion: The Plight of Quasi-Nationals at Strasbourg' (2003) 21 Netherlands Quarterly of Human Rights 63.

[132] *K.A. and Others* (n 104) para 104; *GS* (n 104) para 25; *X* (n 104) para 91.

[133] *X* (n 104) para 60.

[134] These are primarily (some) security of residence, equal treatment, and family reunification.

therefore fall beyond the sovereignty of states, which cannot freely deny access nor withdraw the residence permit of long-term residents.[135] As a result, some have come to describe long-term residence as a 'subsidiary form of EU citizenship'.[136] It is not the purpose of this section to analyse the Directive, its interpretation, and its implementation extensively, but rather to revisit some of its key provisions and point to their grey areas.

The objective of the LTRD is to grant a permanent residence permit to those TCNs who have legally and continuously resided in the territory of a Member State for five years, granting them 'rights which are as near as possible to those enjoyed by citizens of the European Union'.[137] The LTRD therefore confers legal recognition to the social links developed by TCNs over the time spent in the host country. In this line, the Commission mentioned in 2000 the need for the recognition of membership in the form of 'civic citizenship', comprising a common set of core rights and obligations for third-country nationals.[138] Three years later, in the context of the Directive's adoption, the Commission again highlighted that its adoption was an expression of states' 'long tradition' that the extent of migrants' rights is linked to their length of residence, and that it was meant to create 'a sense of belonging and being part of a community and of society in general'.[139]

As noted by Acosta, LTR is remarkable as a post-national form of membership because, unlike other residence permits issued to TCNs, the rights granted by it 'are not stratified, do not vary cross-nationally and do not depend, except in the case of students, upon entry category or functional sector since any TCN having regularly and continuously resided in a Member State for five years has the right to long-term residence'.[140]

Yet, unlike EU citizenship, which comes automatically with the nationality of an EU Member State, LTR is a privilege that must be 'earned' and that can also be lost.[141] Under Article 4 LTRD, TCNs *shall* be granted LTR after having resided legally and continuously for five years in the host state immediately prior to the submission of the application. The requirement for lawful residence contrasts with Article 8 ECHR cases before the ECtHR where legal residence is only one of many

[135] However, the Directive allows Member States to issue national long-term residence permits in parallel to the permits under the Directive (see Council Directive 2003/109/EC of 25 November 2003 concerning the status of third-country nationals who are long-term residents [2003] OJ L 16 (Long-Term Residence Directive) art 13).

[136] Diego Acosta Arcarazo, *The Long-Term Residence Status as a Subsidiary Form of EU Citizenship: An Analysis of Directive 2003/109* (Brill Nijhoff 2011).

[137] Long-Term Residence Directive (n 135) Recital 2 and art 4(1).

[138] European Commission, 'Communication on a Community Immigration Policy', COM(2000) 757 Final 19 and 22.

[139] European Commission, 'Communication on Immigration, Integration and Employment', COM(2003) 336 Final, 3 June 2003 5 and 21.

[140] Diego Acosta Arcarazo, 'Civic Citizenship Reintroduced: The Long-Term Residence Directive as a Post-National Form of Membership' (2015) 21 European Law Journal 200, 207.

[141] It must be noted that, whereas EU citizenship itself is not conditional, the enjoyment of its rights is subject to the limitations enumerated in section 4.2 of this chapter.

elements to be balanced in establishing a right to stay or regularize. Second, Article 5 LTRD rules that Member States *shall* require TCNs to prove that they have 'stable and regular resources' to maintain themselves and their families, as well as sickness insurance,[142] and that they *may* require integration conditions for TCNs to acquire LTR. Unlike for EU citizens, integration is not only a goal to be achieved through the conferral of rights, but can also be a precondition to have access to them.

Once acquired, the Directive foresees the conditions for the withdrawal of residence permits and the expulsion of long-term residents. Article 12 LTRD, on protection against expulsion, establishes that Member States can deport long-term residents solely when they constitute an 'actual and sufficiently serious threat to public policy or public security'.[143] Before taking such a decision, Article 12(3) LTRD establishes, in line with Article 8 ECHR, that states must have regard to the length of residence, age, and personal and family consequences of expulsion, as well as to the links with the host country and the country of origin.[144] The CJEU interpreted Article 12 LTRD in *López Pastuzano*, ruling that Spanish legislation, which automatically excluded long-term residents who had been sentenced to a term of imprisonment of more than one year, violated the Directive.[145]

Moreover, Article 9 LTRD rules on the withdrawal of LTR. Strikingly, Article 9(3) establishes that 'Member States may provide that the long-term resident shall no longer be entitled to maintain his/her long-term resident status in cases where he/she constitutes a threat to public policy, in consideration of the seriousness of the offences he/she committed, but such threat is not a reason for expulsion within the meaning of Article 12'.[146] With this provision, the Directive explicitly acknowledges the existence of a gap between the maintenance of LTR and deportability, opening the door to the creation of a category of people who are unworthy of lawful residence, but not of protection from deportation. According to the Commission, as of 2019, twelve Member States were making use of this clause to withdraw residence permits while refraining from expulsion.[147]

Equally draconian is the possibility of losing LTR if the person spends more than twelve consecutive months outside of the Union under Article 9(1)(c), making it possible that a person who has lived for thirty years in the EU may be stripped of LTR because of this.[148] While the CJEU has recently ruled that physical presence

[142] Note here the difference with the *sufficient resources* criterion required for EU nationals under Directive 2004/38.

[143] Long-Term Residence Directive (n 135) art 12(1).

[144] Ibid, art 12(3).

[145] *López Pastuzano* (n 101) paras 27–29. This was confirmed in Case C-448/19, *Subdelegación del Gobierno en Guadalajara* [2020] EU:C:2020:467. As seen in section 2.1.3, the application of the same Spanish provision was found to be in breach of Article 8 of the ECHR in the case of *Saber*.

[146] Long-Term Residence Directive (n 135) art 9(3).

[147] European Commission, 'Report on the Implementation of Directive 2003/109/EC Concerning the Status of Third-country Nationals Who Are Long-term Residents', 29 March 2019, COM(2019) 161 final 5.

[148] Damian Chalmers, Gareth Davies, and Giorgio Monti, *European Union Law: Cases and Materials* (Cambridge University Press 2010) 514.

for just a few days is enough to prevent the loss of the LTR permit,[149] the provision does not make any reference to proportionality considerations or the need to take family and/or private life criteria into account, opening yet another door for non-removability to arise whenever social and family links are strong enough to prevent deportation under Article 8 ECHR. Moreover, LTR might be lost in the context of intra-EU mobility, if the person loses LTR following absences of more than six years without acquiring LTR in another Member State.[150]

In sum, LTR is limited by conditionality in its acquisition and derogation from its rights. TCNs must prove five years of legal and continuous residence, and often integration measures, to qualify for LTR. The Directive does not recognize the links with the host society forged through informal residence, or the links of those who happened to be absent from the host state for twelve consecutive months, however long their previous stays. Also, there is no context in which the passage of time alone can provide for absolute protection against expulsion or precarious residence. For those who are not (or are no longer) protected by the Directive, Article 8 ECHR may grant a right to stay and even a right to regularize in the host state. It is then unsurprising to find, in the jurisprudence of the ECtHR, multiple cases of long-term residents who, unable to obtain any status under EU or domestic law, were found to be non-removable due to their existing links to the host societies in which they live (see sections 1–3).

4.2 A (not so) fundamental status? Expulsion and precariousness in the context of EU citizenship

Political membership has traditionally been regulated by means of one core category: national citizenship.[151][152] Yet, by creating a form of belonging that shifts away from state-centred notions of citizenship and minimizes the distinction between nationals and (some) foreigners, EU citizenship is widely regarded as the most advanced form of post-national membership.[153] Quite naturally, it has always

[149] Case C-432/20, *ZK v Landeshauptmann von Wien* [2022] EU:C:2022:39.

[150] Long-Term Residence Directive (n 135) art 9(4)(2). Here, too, the CJEU has expressed that 'any physical presence' in the six-year period is enough to interrupt and re-start a new six-year period in the first Member State (Joined Cases C-829/21 and C-129/22, *TE and RU v Stadt Frankfurt am Main* [2023] EU:C:2023:525 para 66).

[151] Part of this section is based on material that I previously published in the following article, which contains a more comprehensive analysis of this issue: Diego Ginés Martín, 'Citizens or Migrants? Precarious Residence in the Context of EU Citizenship' (2021) 25 Revista de Derecho Comunitario Europeo 653.

[152] Seyla Benhabib, 'The Rights of Others: Aliens, Residents, and Citizens' (*Cambridge Core*, November 2004) 1.

[153] Ibid, 'Transformations of Citizenship: the European Union'. See also Yasemin Nuhoğlu Soysal, *Limits of Citizenship: Migrants and Postnational Membership in Europe* (University of Chicago 1994); Patricia Mindus, 'The Status of European Citizenship: An Overview' in Patricia Mindus (ed), *European Citizenship after Brexit: Freedom of Movement and Rights of Residence* (Springer International Publishing 2017).

been presumed in the literature that EU citizenship goes well beyond Member States' international obligations, it being only for TCNs that Article 8 ECHR can provide additional protection against expulsion and potentially a right to a residence permit.[154] It is because of these reasons that the study of EU citizenship would, *prima facie*, appear irrelevant for the study of precarious forms of residence, let alone irregularity and non-removability.

However, the development of Union citizenship, far from being a linear progression, constitutes a 'hesitant process of polity building' beyond the state,[155] with room for diverse processes of 'othering' involving EU nationals. This section focuses on the existing restrictions on residence rights under Directive 2004/38 (Citizens' Rights Directive or simply CRD), emphasizing the grey areas of liminality that may result from the setup of EU citizenship law as interpreted by the CJEU.

4.2.1 Citizenship conditionality and security of residence

Directive 2004/38 distinguishes between three types of residence available for mobile EU nationals: short-term residence (up to three months, generally unconditional, and lacking entitlement to welfare); medium-term residence (from three months to five years, subject to conditionality, and including equal treatment); and permanent residence, which is conditional on having resided legally for five years in the host state and grants full equal treatment.[156] Article 7 CRD, on the right of residence for more than three months, makes lawful residence conditional on being economically active (as workers or self-employed) or, alternatively, having comprehensive sickness insurance and sufficient resources 'not to become a burden on the social assistance system of the host Member State'.[157] This provision offers one of the most controversial and widely discussed elements of EU citizenship law. It is also one in which the distinctions between the EU citizen and the migrant, and between regular and irregular residence, may have become particularly hazy and at times unable to encompass the experiences of an important number of mobile EU citizens.

While the literature has analysed the jurisprudence of the CJEU in this field extensively (generally distinguishing between two clearly demarcated jurisprudential phases before and after the *Dano* case), this section zooms in on the ambiguous legal statuses that may follow for citizens that do not fulfil residence conditions.

[154] Cathryn Costello, 'Metock: Free Movement and "Normal Family Life" in the Union' (2009) 46(2) Common Market Law Review 587, 590.

[155] Jo Shaw, 'EU Citizenship: Still a Fundamental Status?' in Rainer Bauböck (ed), *Debating European Citizenship* (Springer, 2019) 5.

[156] Directive 2004/38 of the European Parliament and of the Council of 29 April 2004 on the rights of citizens of the Union and their family members to move and reside freely within the territory of the Member States [2004] OJ L 158 (Citizens' Rights Directive) Chapters III–V.

[157] Ibid, art 7(1)(b).

4.2.1.1 CJEU jurisprudence: From citizenship expansion to citizenship contraction

The CJEU's foundational stage of citizenship law was marked by *Martínez Sala*, where the Court inferred equal treatment from the applicant's lawful residence, regardless of the fact that the applicant did not seem to formally comply with residence conditions.[158] Subsequent cases seemed to confirm that EU citizenship was not a trivial membership but the 'fundamental status' of nationals of the Member States.[159] In this context, the CJEU relied on primary law and the principle of proportionality to interpret residence conditions leniently,[160] precisely because the objective of EU citizenship law was to 'facilitate' free movement and residence.[161] Moreover, it acknowledged that lawful residence triggered equal treatment, regardless of whether the permit stemmed from EU, national, regional, or municipal law—and irrespective of whether residence conditions were actually being fulfilled.[162]

In these cases, it could already be observed that citizenship litigation was, at least theoretically, not only about access to welfare, but also about residence rights and expulsion. The conditionality of residence was repeatedly brought up by the CJEU, which in *Brey* and *Trojani* recognized the possibility to expel EU nationals if they became an 'unreasonable burden' on the social assistance system of the host Member State.[163] Yet these claims were very distant from the Court's practice, where the boundaries between equal treatment, residence, and expulsion became rather blurred. In the cases analysed above, the CJEU not only made Article 7 CRD 'virtually meaningless as a Member State instrument for deportation',[164] but was also reluctant to make it a source of inequality and irregular residence. In doing so, however, it sometimes relied on citizenship in an unclear manner that did not clarify in which cases EU citizens could face unequal treatment, irregularity, or expulsion on economic grounds (if at all). Citizenship litigation therefore seemed to be about ensuring access to social benefits for mobile EU nationals, who always happened to be on the winning side. In doing so, the CJEU mitigated the effects that a literal interpretation of Article 7(1)(b) would have had on the enjoyment of citizenship rights.

Nevertheless, the widely praised jurisprudence of the Court in the citizenship field was fragile on at least two fronts. First, as noted by O'Leary shortly after *Martínez Sala*, by deriving equal treatment automatically from lawful residence,

[158] Case C-85/96, *Martínez Sala* [1998] EU:C:1998:217 paras 14–16.

[159] Case C-184/99, *Grzelczyk* [2001] EU:C:2001:458 para 31.

[160] Case C-413/99, *Baumbast* [2002] EU:C:2002:403; Case C-140/12, *Brey* [2013] EU:C:2013:565 paras 16–17.

[161] *Brey* (n 160) para 71.

[162] *Martínez Sala* (n 158) paras 47 and 53; Case C-456/02, *Trojani* [2004] EU:C:2004:488 paras 37,40,43, and 46; Case C-209/03, *Bidar* [2005] EU:C:2005:169.

[163] *Brey* (n 160) paras 69 and 72; *Trojani* (n 162) para 45.

[164] Niamh Nic Shuibhne, 'Derogating from the Free Movement of Persons: When Can EU Citizens Be Deported?' (2006) 8 Cambridge Yearbook of European Legal Studies 187, 210.

the CJEU gave incentives for Member States to inquire as to who was within their borders and whether they fulfilled residence conditions in the first place (although the principle of proportionality still provided backup protection for EU citizens not fulfilling residence conditions entirely).[165] Second, precisely because landmark cases turned out to have a positive outcome for the applicant, little attention was paid to the legal situation of those EU citizens who did not meet residence conditions, as the applicants seemed to always obtain the whole 'citizenship pack'. This approach not only postponed a decision that the CJEU would eventually need to make (namely finding that a mobile EU citizen did not fulfil residence conditions), but also lacked guidance as to what were the rights, legal status, and protection against expulsion of those who did not fulfil residence conditions.

The CJEU's long-standing claim that economically inactive EU citizens did not have unconditional access to welfare benefits in the host Member State finally materialized in *Dano*. This ruling not only evidenced that Article 7 CRD conditions were there for a reason, but is also widely viewed as a shift towards doctrinal conservatism in the field of EU citizenship that departs from previous case law.[166] In *Dano*, where the applicant was an economically inactive (and poor) Romanian citizen living in Germany, the CJEU turned to a literal interpretation of the Directive, ignoring the principle of proportionality and primary law—to conclude that she did not have a right to reside in Germany.[167] *Alimanovic* and *García Nieto* later confirmed the CJEU's conservative turn, establishing that individual proportionality assessments were not necessary if objective residence conditions were not met.[168] Moreover, these cases establish the automatic acquisition and loss of free movement rights. In *Dano*, the applicant held a valid permit for EU nationals,[169] but this was not an obstacle for the CJEU to find that she was not a lawful resident and was therefore not entitled to social assistance.[170] In *Commission v UK*, two years after *Dano*, the CJEU endorsed the UK's 'right to reside test', according to which the fulfilment of residence conditions was monitored every time that an EU citizen applied for certain benefits.[171] This turn increases the uncertainty surrounding residence rights for poorer (and economically inactive) EU citizens,

[165] Siofra O'Leary, 'Putting Flesh on the Bones of European Union Citizenship' (1999) 24 European Law Review 68.

[166] Daniel Thym, 'When Union Citizens Turn into Illegal Migrants: The Dano Case' (2015) 40 European Law Review 249. Explanations can be found in Member States' concerns about 'welfare tourism' in pre-Brexit UK and in the context of the post-2008 financial crisis. Part of the CJEU's shift can also be explained due to the changing nature of the profile of the litigants (see Gareth Davies, 'Has the Court Changed, or Have the Cases? The Deservingness of Litigants as an Element in Court of Justice Citizenship Adjudication' (2018) 25 Journal of European Public Policy 1442).

[167] Case C-333/13, *Dano* [2014] EU:C:2014:2358 paras 74 and 78.

[168] Case C-67/14, *Alimanovic* [2015] EU:C:2015:597; Case C-299/14, *García-Nieto* [2016] EU:C:2016:114.

[169] *Dano* (n 167) para 36.

[170] A similar reasoning could already be observed in *Dias* (Case C-325/09, *Dias* [2011] EU:C:2011:498 para 54).

[171] Case C-308/14, *Commission v UK* [2016] EU:C:2016:436.

given that it is not only difficult to ascertain whether one is lawfully residing in another EU country, but also the loss of residence follows automatically once the conditions of residence stop being fulfilled, regardless of whether the EU citizen in question held a valid permit, registration certificate, or otherwise.[172] Lastly, this jurisprudence points at the end of domestic residence permits as a valid source of citizenship rights—contradicting earlier cases such as *Martínez Sala* and *Trojani*. In the words of the Court, '[t]o accept that persons who do not have a right of residence *under Directive 2004/38* [emphasis added] may claim entitlement to social benefits under the same conditions as those applicable to nationals of the host Member State would run counter to an objective of the directive'.[173] This seemed to rule out equal treatment when the lawful residence of an EU citizen stems from domestic law alone,[174] as was recently confirmed in *CG*.[175]

4.2.1.2 What next? Legal ambiguities and Member State practice

The CJEU's shifting jurisprudence exposes the ambiguities of an EU framework that seeks to reconcile both 'the logic of closure which underpins national dispositions and practices of social sharing, and the logic of opening which typically inspires the European integration project'.[176] Certainly, the development of European citizenship is marked by a fragile balance between the Directive's commitment to facilitating the exercise of the fundamental right to free movement, while reassuring Member States that EU citizens will not become a financial burden on their welfare systems. At the legal level, however, the tension between these different dynamics is buried under a seamless link between residence rights and equal treatment.

The jurisprudential turn in *Dano* has generally made it easier for states to find that mobile EU citizens do not satisfy residence conditions. But, if the 'Danos' are no longer residing legally under EU law, one wonders: What is their status in the host country? Are they irregular migrants? Can they be expelled solely on the basis of their lack of sufficient resources? Are they deported in practice? It is no longer feasible to postpone answering these questions.

In this context, it must be noted that becoming an 'unreasonable burden' is directly related to becoming an unlawfully staying citizen,[177] and so EU Member States are legally entitled to expel EU citizens who do not fulfil residence conditions—yet

[172] Daniel Thym, 'The Elusive Limits of Solidarity: Residence Rights of and Social Benefits for Economically Inactive Union Citizens' (2015) 52 Common Market Law Review 17, 41.

[173] *Dano* (n 167) para 74. The same wording was repeated in *Alimanovic* (n 168) para 50.

[174] Niamh Nic Shuibhne, 'Limits Rising, Duties Ascending: The Changing Legal Shape of Union Citizenship' (2015) 52 Common Market Law Review 889, 931–32.

[175] Case C-709/20, *CG v The Department for Communities in Northern Ireland* [2021] EU:C:2021:515 para 93.

[176] Maurizio Ferrera, *The Boundaries of Welfare: European Integration and the New Spatial Politics of Social Protection* (Oxford University Press 2005) 252.

[177] Benedita Menezes Queiroz, *Illegally Staying in the EU: An Analysis of Illegality in EU Migration Law* (Bloomsbury 2018) 54.

this is far from being a common practice of Member States. Notwithstanding the seemingly unequivocal outcome in *Dano* (that poor and economically inactive citizens are not legal residents under Directive 2004/38), the status of these citizens remains unclear in practice.

First, it must be highlighted that neither the Directive nor the Commission Communication on the Directive's transposition foresee a procedure for the expulsion of EU citizens on the basis of a lack of sufficient resources or comprehensive sickness insurance.[178] Moreover, Article 15 CRD prohibits the issuing of entry bans if residence is lost 'on grounds other than public policy, public security or public health'.[179] This would mean that, if expelled, the 'Danos' could simply go back to the host state, showing the paradox of applying the concepts of illegality and expulsion to EU citizens in the context of European integration and internal open borders. This was partially challenged in *FS*, concerning a Polish national who, having left the territory of the Netherlands following a expulsion decision on grounds of his lack of resources, returned to the Netherlands soon after.[180] The CJEU clarified that an expulsion decision on Article 7 CRD grounds is not complied simply with the physical departure from the Member State, but must be accompanied by a 'genuine and effective' termination of the residence in the territory. If this is not the case, Member States will be able to rely on prior expulsion orders as the persons will not be considered to have actually interrupted their residence.[181] And yet, the Court also acknowledged that Member States cannot limit EU citizens' right to re-enter their territory under Article 5 CRD (even if this is not accompanied by a right to reside), and that, if the persons show that they now fulfil residence conditions, this will deprive the expulsion decision of all its effects.[182]

Thus, following the logics of opening, citizenship rights, when lost, can be reactivated by leaving and re-entering the host Member State, offering citizens another opportunity to justify their free movement rights or simply go unnoticed by state authorities—despite recent contestation by Member State practice and the CJEU. As a result, states' prerogatives to deport poor EU citizens are deeply constrained by an institutional framework that is not built to do so (except in cases of public policy, public security, and public health derogations—see section 4.2.2), inasmuch as it is not accompanied by the competence to regulate and control entry. It then comes as no surprise that little evidence of expulsion taking place in these

[178] European Commission, 'Communication on Guidance for Better Transposition and Application of Directive 2004/38/EC on the Right of Citizens of the Union and Their Family Members to Move and Reside Freely within the Territory of the Member States', COM(2009) 313 Final 38. In fact, the Communication uses the word expulsion eight times, and always in the context of public policy and public security derogations (see section 4.2.2)

[179] Citizens' Rights Directive (n 156) arts 15(1) and 15(3).

[180] Case C-719/19, *FS v Staatssecretaris van Justitie en Veiligheid* [2021] EU:C:2021:506 paras 35–36.

[181] Ibid, para 81.

[182] Ibid, paras 101 and 95.

cases can be found across Member States.[183] This does not mean that Member States do not have recourse to expulsion at all. In fact, the lack of clarity of an EU framework that neither prohibits expulsion, nor offers clear rules on the procedures leading to the expulsion of EU citizens, facilitates selective and discriminatory deportation.[184]

Despite these practices, deportation is not necessarily *the* tool for states to manage the issue of irregular EU nationals. In practice, it might be easier for states to follow a 'starve them out' strategy,[185] denying access to social benefits or residence, or issuing unenforceable deportation orders hoping that people leave by their own means. With *Dano*, the CJEU facilitates such an interpretation of EU law, as it makes it easier for states to find that an EU citizen ought to leave, yet in a legal setting that, unlike the migration *acquis*, does not enable Member States to realistically expel as a norm. Again, deportation is simply too expensive (and time-consuming) a venture for a state with no power to decide over the re-entry of deportees. This interpretation can create an underclass of EU citizens who are simply 'present' until or unless they are issued a residence permit or actually removed.

Belgium offers perhaps the clearest example of such policies,[186] using cross-checks between welfare and immigration databases to withdraw permits when EU citizens are deemed to have become an 'unreasonable burden' on the Belgian welfare state.[187] Although deportation orders are issued on purely economic grounds,[188] these are largely symbolic, with deportation being a theoretical possibility which does not materialise in practice.[189] In the meantime, their irregular stay is characterized by lack of access to rights, the removal of their data from

[183] Jo Shaw and Niamh Nic Shuibhne, 'General Report: Union Citizenship: Development, Impact and Challenges' in Ulla Neergaard, Catherine Jacqueson and Nina Holst-Christensen (eds), *Union Citizenship: Development, Impact and Challenges* (DJØF Publishing 2014) 93. By the time that this report was written, there was no evidence that expulsion on purely economic grounds was taking place in Austria, Bulgaria, Croatia, Estonia, Greece, Hungary, Italy, Malta, Poland, Portugal, Slovenia, Spain, or Sweden.

[184] This seems to be the case with homeless and Roma people. See Marie-Laure Basilien-Gainche, 'European States Returning European Citizens: France and the Roma Populations' in Elspeth Guild, Paul Minderhoud, and Sandra Mantu (eds), *EU Citizenship and Free Movement Rights Taking Supranational Citizenship Seriously* (Brill 2020) 268; Owen Parker, 'Roma and the Politics of EU Citizenship in France: Everyday Security and Resistance' (2012) 50 JCMS: Journal of Common Market Studies 475; Mathew Evans, 'Abusing or Misusing the Right of Free Movement? The UK's Policy towards EU Nationals Sleeping Rough' in Elspeth Guild, Paul Minderhoud and Sandra Mantu (eds), *EU Citizenship and Free Movement Rights Taking Supranational Citizenship Seriously* (Brill 2020).

[185] Nic Shuibhne, 'Limits Rising, Duties Ascending' (n 174) 933; Thym, 'When Union Citizens Turn into Illegal Migrants' (n 166) 260.

[186] For further examples see Ginés Martín (n 151) 667–70.

[187] Jean-Michel Lafleur and Elsa Mescoli, 'Creating Undocumented EU Migrants through Welfare: A Conceptualization of Undeserving and Precarious Citizenship' (2018) 52 Sociology 480, 484.

[188] Between 2012 and 2018, deportation orders on these grounds ranged from 1,350 to 2,712 per year (Anthony Valcke, 'Expulsion from the "Heart of Europe": The Belgian Law and Practice Relating to the Termination of EU Residence Rights' in Elspeth Guild, Paul Minderhoud and Sandra Mantu (eds), *EU Citizenship and Free Movement Rights Taking Supranational Citizenship Seriously* (Brill 2020) 184).

[189] Ibid, 184; Lafleur and Mescoli (n 187) 484.

residence registries, personal intimidation in bureaucratic interactions, and a threat of being deported.[190]

These EU citizens have become, *de facto*, non-removable migrants, staying irregularly and under the threat of deportation, but never actually deported. In is not my contention that this is *the* way through which the Member States generally deal with economically vulnerable citizens, but rather that, when these situations occur, they can be understood as a by-product of EU law. In *Dano*, the CJEU facilitates the withdrawal of residence rights by bringing to life the dynamics of closure embedded in the Citizens' Rights Directive. According to this interpretation, EU citizens can only ask for social benefits if they are legal residents, but asking for social benefits may reveal a lack of resources and make them automatically lose social benefits, legal residence, and protection from expulsion altogether—without an individualized proportionality assessment. Nevertheless, the dynamics of opening and free movement which are (too) rooted in the Directive severely limit states' capacity to deport in practice. Thus, while citizens remain *de facto* non-removed due to a state's policy choice not to enforce removal, this decision is deeply constrained by an EU citizenship framework that is not designed to deport EU citizens.

Some solutions to precarious residence and non-removability can be found within EU law. For example, Spaventa has advocated for an interpretation of *Dano* according to which legal residence and access to full equal treatment do not necessarily go hand in hand. Then, if an EU citizen does not have access to the host state's welfare system, it is hard to envisage how this person would become an 'unreasonable burden' that would justify the loss of residence rights.[191] This would satisfy states' concerns about 'welfare tourism' while maintaining a reasonably meaningful (though incomplete) status for EU citizens, avoiding irregular residence, institutionalized bullying, and threat of expulsion solely on the basis of economic considerations. While the separation of legal residence from equal treatment rests on shaky legal grounds,[192] recent CJEU jurisprudence seems to partially support this view. In *Bajratari*, concerning the right of residence of a child whose resources derived from the unlawful employment of his father (an irregular migrant from Albania), the CJEU protected the right to reside of the EU citizen and his father. More importantly, it did so in light of primary law and an individualised proportionality assessment, carefully examining the applicant's situation and highlighting that the purpose of the Citizens' Rights Directive is precisely to 'facilitate' the fundamental right to free movement.[193]

[190] Lafleur and Mescoli (n 187) 487–88.

[191] Eleanor Spaventa, 'Once a Foreigner, Always a Foreigner: Who Does Not Belong Here Anymore? Expulsion Measures' in Hendrik Verschueren (ed), *Residence, Employment and Social Rights of Mobile Persons* (Intersentia 2016) 98.

[192] Offering lawful residence under the Citizens' Rights Directive without granting equal treatment in cases not explicitly provided for by EU law appears to be contrary to Article 24(1) of the Directive, Article 34 of the Charter, and Article 18 TFEU.

[193] Case C-93/18, *Bajratari* [2019] EU:C:2019:809 paras 35 and 47.

Is the CJEU now, through a chamber judgment, overturning its own shift in *Dano* and *Alimanovic* and going back to *Baumbast* and *Brey*? It seems highly unlikely. It must be recalled that, in *Bajratari*, not only there is no access to social benefits involved, but the fact that the no one in the family had never asked for them weighted in favour of their status as lawful residents.[194] Instead, *Bajratari* supports the claim that the CJEU might have *de facto* adopted different standards depending on whether the case is about residence only, or whether it also includes social assistance claims. It thus seems easier for litigants to obtain a positive outcome from Luxembourg if social benefits are out of the equation. This would probably be the only way to make sense of the CJEU's leap from *Brey* to *Dano*, and back to individualized proportionality in *Bajratari*, and one that might address the issue of precarious residence for some non-removed EU citizens. However, as soon as a dispute over social benefits comes into play, the legal link between residence rights and equal treatment drags the CJEU into adopting an 'open-open' or 'closed-closed' solution, despite the fact that, in the real world, both elements are affected by ongoing (and sometimes differing) dynamics of opening and closure.[195]

Be that as it may, the situation of precariousness of irregular EU citizens is in many ways difficult to compare with that of TCNs. This is the case first, because the CJEU has created an autonomous (and broad) concept of worker under EU law.[196] Employment is considered 'genuine' even if brief and minor,[197] part-time (e.g. 3–14 hours per week),[198] or an internship .[199] Thus, from a litigant's perspective, it might be desirable to undertake any economic activity so as to be regarded as a worker under EU law and hence enjoy full equal treatment, or alternatively register as a first-time jobseeker with no access to benefits other than those intended to facilitate access to the labour market. Second, upon the loss of residence rights, EU citizens may alternatively opt to leave and re-enter the country in other to reactivate their citizenship rights. Even if, according to recent CJEU jurisprudence,

[194] Ibid, paras 44–45.

[195] Nevertheless, some Member States, such as Spain, Italy, Germany, and, to a lesser extent, Austria, do separate their policies as regards residence and equal treatment (see Roberto Valina Hoset and Carmen Roman Vaca, 'Obstacles to the Right of Free Movement and Residence for EU Citizens and their Families: Country Report for Spain', European Parliament, Study requested by the LIBE and PETI Committees, December 2016, available at: <https://op.europa.eu/en/publication-detail/-/publication/fc3b3d49-9a84-11e6-9bca-01aa75ed71a1>; Silvia Brunello and Anna Perego, 'Obstacles to the Right of Free Movement and Residence for EU Citizens and their Families: Country Report for Italy', European Parliament, Study requested by the LIBE and PETI Committees, June 2016, available at: <https://www.europarl.europa.eu/thinktank/sl/document/IPOL_STU(2016)556970>; Anita Heindlmaier and Michael Blauberger, 'Enter at Your Own Risk: Free Movement of EU Citizens in Practice' (2017) 40 West European Politics 1198.

[196] Case C-66/85, *Lawrie-Blum* [1986] EU:C:1986:284; Case C-53/81, *Levin* [1982] EU:C:1982:105; Case C-14/09, *Genc* [2010] EU:C:2010:57. More recently, on the retention of the status as a self-employed person, see Case C-442/16, *Florea Gusa* [2017] EU:C:2017:1004.

[197] Case C-22/08, *Vatsouras and Kouparantze* [2009] EU:C:2009:344 para 25.

[198] Case C-213/05, *Geven* [2007] EU:C:2007:438 para 30.

[199] Case C-109/04, *Kranemann* [2005] EU:C:2005:187 para 13; Case C-229/14, *Balkaba* [2015] EU:C:2015:445 para 52.

deported EU citizens (or those who return 'voluntarily' following an order to leave) need to 'genuinely and effectively' terminate their residence, they are still allowed to enter the territory of the host state under Article 5 CRD for purposes other than residence. While these persons can no longer reside under Article 6 CRD upon re-entry, they have another opportunity to show that they now fulfil Article 7 CRD conditions. If this is the case, the expulsion order will no longer be valid and citizenship rights will be re-activated.[200] Then, unlike for third-country nationals, the loss of residence rights is not necessarily game over for EU citizens.

However, even though EU citizenship is arguably intended to go well beyond states' obligations under Article 8 ECHR, violations of their rights under the Convention cannot be ruled out. In *Dano*, the CJEU did not require German authorities to assess the number and length of the applicant's previous stays in the country, her private and family ties with both the host country and the country of origin, or the fact that her son was born in the host state. The lack of a proportionality assessment and a balancing exercise may end up in an Article 8 ECHR violation, making human rights litigation a fruitful route to explore for EU citizens.

4.2.2 Citizenship derogation and expulsion of EU nationals

If for poor EU citizens expulsion only emerges in the context of welfare access and mostly as a lurking threat which is not enforced in practice, EU Member States do expel a considerable amount of EU citizens in the context of public policy, public health, and public security derogations.

Articles 27 and 28 CRD provide an ascending scale of protection whereby the length of residence in the host state determines the degree of protection against removal. Firstly, citizens who have resided for less than five years in the host Member State can see their right to free movement restricted on grounds of public policy, public security, or public health.[201] After five years, permanent residents can only be deported in the case of 'serious grounds of public policy or public security'.[202] Lastly, the Directive provides additional protection against expulsion for minors and for those who have resided in the host Member State for the previous ten years, who can only be expelled on 'imperative grounds of public security'.[203]

The Directive includes several veiled references to Article 8 of the ECHR, noting that 'the greater the degree of integration of Union citizens and their family members in the host Member State, the greater the degree of protection against expulsion should be'.[204] It also dictates that, in expelling EU citizens, states must take due consideration of their length of residence, age, state of health, family links, integration, links to the state of origin, and so on.[205] This requires a balancing of

[200] *FS* (n 180).
[201] Citizens' Rights Directive (n 156) art 27(1).
[202] Ibid, art 28(2).
[203] Ibid, art 28(3).
[204] Ibid, Recital 24.
[205] Ibid, Recital 23.

interests that resembles that of the ECtHR on Article 8 ECHR cases (see sections 1–3 in this chapter). For all EU citizens, but in particular for those with permanent residence and enhanced protection against expulsion under Article 28 CRD, one would expect the protection offered by the Directive to go well beyond Article 8 ECHR. Nevertheless, the interpretation of these provisions by the CJEU has watered down this protection in the context of criminality.

This is the case first, because the CJEU has interpreted eligibility for permanent residence (five years) and enhanced protection against expulsion (ten years) very strictly. The jurisprudence of the CJEU shows a vast divergence between actual residence and residence *in accordance with EU law*, making it exceptionally challenging to benefit from enhanced protection against expulsion.[206]

Second, because the CJEU has interpreted the derogations of free movement rights in a very broad manner. In *Tsakouridis* and *P.I.*, the CJEU considered that drug trafficking and a case of rape in the family context could both lead to deportation on the basis of 'imperative grounds of public security'.[207] In these cases, the CJEU focused on the seriousness and reprehensibility of the crime and the criminal, and not on the threat posed by the conduct, blurring the distinction between public policy and public security derogations.[208] In *K*, the CJEU even accepted the deportation of EU citizens based on 'imperative grounds of public security' for criminal convictions prior to residence in the host Member State, regardless of the possibility of reoffending, and without the existence of a present threat to the security of the state.[209]

In these judgments the CJEU risks treating 'bad' EU citizens as perpetual outsiders, even if they were born, raised, and spent all of their life in the host state.[210] This is a simplistic notion of belonging and integration (according to which

[206] Case C-378/12, *Onuekwere* [2014] EU:C:2014:13 paras 24, 27, and 32; Case C-400/12, *MG* [2014] EU:C:2014:9 paras 28 and 38; Case C-316/16, *B* [2018] EU:C:2018:256 paras 83 and 65. The CJEU's interpretation of the Directive is particularly draconian in *MG*, where it ruled that the ten-year period must be counted back from the date of the expulsion order, rendering the enhanced protection of Article 28(3) CRD virtually meaningless. For critical scholarship on this, see Stefano Montaldo, 'Offenders' Rehabilitation: Towards a New Paradigm for EU Criminal Law?' (2018) 8 European Criminal Law Review 223; E Spaventa, 'Striving for Equality: Who "Deserves" to Be a Union Citizen?' in *Scritti in onore di Giuseppe Tesauro*, vol 3 (Editoriale Scientifica 2014).

[207] Case C-145/09, *Tsakouridis* [2010] EU:C:2010:708; Case C-348/09, *P.I.* [2012] EU:C:2012:300.

[208] Dimitry Kochenov and Benedikt Pirker, 'Deporting the Citizens within the European Union: A Counter-Intuitive Trend in Case C-348/09, P.I. v. Overbürgemeisterin Der Stadt Remscheid' (2013) 19 Columbia Journal of European Law 381; Loïc Azoulai and Stephen Coutts, 'Restricting Union Citizens' Residence Rights on Grounds of Public Security. Where Union Citizenship and the AFSJ Meet: P.I.' (2013) 50 Common Market Law Review 553, 561.

[209] Case C-331/16, *K* [2018] EU:C:2018:296 para 56; Stephen Coutts, 'A Contingent Citizenship—Union Citizenship and Expulsion' in Elspeth Guild, Paul Minderhoud, and Sandra Mantu (eds), *EU Citizenship and Free Movement Rights Taking Supranational Citizenship Seriously* (Brill 2020) 250.

[210] Recital 24 of the Directive, for example, does not rule out deportation of EU citizens even when they have spent most of their lives or are even born and raised in the host Member State. In *P.I.*, the offender, aged 47, had been living in Germany since the age of 22 (*P.I.* (n 207) para 9).

'integrated' citizens do not commit crimes),[211] which reaffirms the Union citizen as a non-national and undermines the Directive's objective of dismantling the difference between nationals and EU citizens through a regime of permanent residence.[212] Indeed, the idea behind ascending levels of protection is that one gradually becomes a member of the host society to the extent that if he or she misbehaves, the host state becomes increasingly responsible for it.[213]

Then, what is left of protection against expulsion in the context of criminality for EU nationals is limited to the vague references to Article 8 ECHR in the Directive and CJEU jurisprudence,[214] as well as the obligation that expulsion cannot be the automatic consequence of a criminal conviction,[215] as was already obvious from the text of the Directive. Moreover, the CJEU has so far been unwilling to interpret Article 7 of the Charter in the cases,[216] and therefore it must be assumed that the protection for EU nationals under Article 7 of the Charter is just as unpredictable as that afforded by Article 8 ECHR. Thus, it is no surprise that, at least by 2014, countries such as Austria, Cyprus, Finland, France, and Italy considered expulsion claims of EU nationals almost exclusively in relation to Article 8 ECHR.[217] As seen in sections 1–3, protection under Article 8 of the ECHR is neither high nor consistent, and it does not generally lead to a residence permit.[218]

5. Conclusions

Many rights that were once only accessible to nationals have now become available to foreigners, but some are still core to national citizenship. One of them is the absolute and unconditional right to reside and be protected from expulsion in one's country of nationality. Whereas the great majority of liberal and even communitarian political theorists, from Carens to Miller or Walzer, have widely endorsed the moral significance of the passage of time in generating a right to belong

[211] Uladzislau Belavusau and Dimitry Kochenov, 'Kirchberg Dispensing the Punishment: Inflicting "Civil Death" on Prisoners in Onuekwere (C-378/12) and MG (C-400/12)' (2016) 41 European Law Review 557, 24–26.

[212] Azoulai and Coutts (n 208) 568.

[213] For a more theoretical take on this debate, read: Rainer Bauböck, 'Whose Bad Guys Are Terrorists?' in Rainer Bauböck (ed), *Debating Transformations of National Citizenship* (Springer International Publishing 2018).

[214] See Citizens' Rights Directive (n 156) Recital 24 and art 28; *Tsakouridis* (n 207) paras 17,50, and 53; *P.I.* (n 207) paras 32 and 34.

[215] Case C-50/06, *Commission v the Netherlands* [2007] EU:C:2007:325.

[216] Eleanor Spaventa, 'What Role for Fundamental Rights in Expulsion Cases?' in Sandra Mantu (ed), *Expulsion and EU Citizenship* (Nijmegen Migration Law Working Paper Series, 2017).

[217] Shaw and Nic Shuibhne (n 183) 135.

[218] Moreover, Chapter VI of the Directive has been, since its adoption, consistently reported as the one in which the lack of transposition has been more blatant (see European Commission, 'Communication on Guidance for Better Transposition' (n 178) 2). This means that EU citizens are often deported for minor offences in violation of the Directive (and perhaps of Article 8 ECHR) (see Shaw and Nic Shuibhne (n 183) 126–29).

regardless of their support to open or closed borders,[219] the EU legislator and the ECtHR have been unwilling to give the passage of time an independent normative value to prevent expulsion, let alone to regularize.

This chapter has sought to illustrate the uneasy relationship between membership claims, non-removal and residence rights. The three legal instruments analysed above expose that foreigners seem to never become full members of the host society (unless they do naturalize).[220] Non-national membership is, in the best scenario, a strong legal presumption of belonging to the host community, which can always be rebutted. In this context, this chapter has shed light on the dual role of European law in acknowledging migrants' membership while simultaneously holding a key role in the manufacturing of precarious residence and non-removability. To do so, I have focused on three different European systems of belonging, namely: family and private life; long-term residence; and EU citizenship. Whereas EU citizenship comes automatically with domestic (EU) citizenship, third-country nationals *acquire* membership by gradually sliding into it. This chapter has mainly focused on situations where the protection offered by these systems is either missing or, more interestingly for the purposes of this book, where it is only partial—that is, offering protection from expulsion but not stable and regular residence. Indeed, successfully resisting expulsion, although a partial victory for EU citizens or TCNs, can also put them one step closer to precarious residence and non-removability in the host state. Non-removability, as analysed in this chapter, can be caused by EU law or the ECHR, alone or combined.

First, Article 8 ECHR does not include a general (or legally certain) right to either stay or residence. There is, in Article 8 ECHR, no core content but rather a number of interests that have been balanced by the Strasbourg Court in an unclear manner, making it difficult to predict whether a given situation will end up in expulsion, non-removal, or regularization. However, for the 'lucky' ones who have their non-removal claims accepted under Article 8 ECHR, or for those who are already non-removable, protection from expulsion comes with no additional rights attached. For these people, Article 8 ECHR can also be a way out of irregularity. Strasbourg's non-removal and residence permit case law are ultimately two sides of the same coin, as the ECtHR has acknowledged that the principles to be balanced are the same in cases involving negative and positive obligations from states, the difference being that a higher threshold is needed to obtain a residence permit. In these cases, the ECtHR faces a trilemma between expulsion, non-removal, and regularization. As it currently stands, Strasbourg's balancing of interests means that a migrant's mere physical (regular or irregular) presence in a state will most

[219] See 'The Theory of Social Membership' in Carens, *The Ethics of Immigration* (n 2) 158; Joseph H Carens, *Immigrants and the Right to Stay* (MIT Press 2010); David Miller, 'Immigrants, Nations, and Citizenship' (2008) 16 Journal of Political Philosophy 371; Michael Walzer, *Spheres of Justice: A Defense of Pluralism and Equality* (Basic Books 1983) 52.

[220] Even in cases of naturalization, criminality may lead to citizenship stripping and deportation.

likely be considered enough to allow migrants to have their family and private life respected.

Second, membership claims under long-term residence and EU citizenship are meant to offer a much higher degree of protection than the ECHR. This chapter has however focused on their protection gaps, normally arising in the context of poverty and criminality. It is precisely in those grey areas falling beyond the reach of EU law that Article 8 ECHR can come back into play, both as a barrier to expulsion or as a right to regularize. Given that the purpose of this chapter has been to describe the manufacturing of situations of non-removability, I have primarily focused on those cases where the claims to a residence permit under Article 8 ECHR have been unsuccessful, since it is in these situations that non-removability emerges. The cases of success will be elaborated in Chapter 6 of this book, precisely because they offer not an explanation of how non-removability occurs, but a way out of it.

4
EU Readmission Policies, Practical Obstacles to Deportation, and Non-Removability

As seen in Chapter 1 of this book, EU return policies rest on the assumption that every third-country national (TCN) without a valid permit can (and should) be deported, but return rates are strikingly low and continue to decline.[1] This book has already dealt with the legal provisions that protect irregular migrants from deportation, primarily as a result of Member States' human rights obligations. Yet it remains the case that, according to the Commission, '[t]he main reasons for non-return relate to practical problems in the identification of returnees and in obtaining the necessary documentation from non-EU authorities'.[2] This chapter deals with practical obstacles to the deportation of TCNs. Even if the processes precluding removal that will be analysed in this chapter are often deeply political, they are referred to as 'practical' obstacles because returnees do not hold a subjective right not to be deported. Instead, their presence in EU territory responds to the host Member State's incapacity to do so. Thus, contrary to the cases previously examined, non-deportability will result in a situation of practical (and not legal) non-removability. This will have an impact on the rights available to non-removable migrants (as elaborated upon in Chapter 5).

At the crossroads between the EU's internal policy aims and external relations, the response to overcome these obstacles has been to develop a common readmission policy. Indeed, it is only normal that the EU looks outwards for the effective implementation of its deportation agenda, as readmission is a two-way process that necessarily requires the cooperation of countries of origin (or transit). Whereas Member States maintain their competences to conclude bilateral readmission agreements, the EU seeks to 'develop a fully coordinated approach for acting in unity and speaking to third countries with one voice'.[3] Adopted in May 2024, the

[1] Eurostat data on TCNs ordered to leave and those returned following an order to leave since 2008 are available at: <https://ec.europa.eu/eurostat/databrowser/view/migr_eiord/default/table?lang=en> and: <https://ec.europa.eu/eurostat/databrowser/view/migr_eirtn/default/table?lang=en>.

[2] European Commission, 'Communication on EU Return Policy', COM(2014) 199 Final, 28 March 2014, 30.

[3] European Commission, 'Communication on Enhancing Cooperation on Return and Readmission as Part of a Fair, Effective and Comprehensive EU Migration Policy', COM(2021) 56 Final, 10 February 2021, 11.

When Deportation Fails. Diego Ginés Martín, Oxford University Press. © Diego Ginés Martín 2025.
DOI: 10.1093/9780198941231.003.0004

Pact on Migration and Asylum,[4] though framed as a 'fresh start', reiterates, in the field of readmission, the existing *status quo* of developing a common and 'comprehensive' approach based on 'mutually beneficial partnerships' on migration management and readmission with key countries of origin and transit.[5]

This chapter first maps EU readmission policies and then points at ways in which these fail to overcome different barriers to the deportation of TCNs. Whereas the external dimension of the EU's return policies has been analysed extensively from a fundamental rights and rule of law perspective, little research has been conducted on their operability gaps and the consequences for migrants' legal status.[6] The main aim of this chapter is thus to point at various gaps faced by Member States when implementing readmission in collaboration with third countries, and to link these to an EU readmission system that too often fails to live up to its stated aims. These implementation gaps are framed as the consequence of a mismatch between the boundaries of EU law and politics *vis-à-vis* the external realities that the EU encounters in the implementation of its agenda jointly with third countries. Concerning internal EU law, the controversies over the different legislative instruments in the Pact illustrate the difficulties in reaching EU-wide consensus on migration management and responsibility sharing within the EU.[7] This stands in stark contrast to the EU-wide consensus as regards the external dimension of migration, including the externalization of borders and cooperation with third countries on readmission.[8] To put it simply, it remains easier to agree on what third countries could and should do than to agree on what EU Member States

[4] Although labelled as a 'Pact', this in fact consists of a legislative package. See European Commission, 'Pact on Migration and Asylum', 21 May 2024, available at: <https://home-affairs.ec.europa.eu/policies/migration-and-asylum/pact-migration-and-asylum_en>.

[5] European Commission, 'Communication on a New Pact on Migration and Asylum', COM(2020) 609 Final, 23 September 2020, 1–2.

[6] On the implementation challenges of EU Readmission Agreements, see Sergio Carrera, *Implementation of EU Readmission Agreements: Identity Determination Dilemmas and the Blurring of Rights* (Springer International Publishing 2016).

[7] The Regulation on Asylum and Migration Management (2024/1351) largely keeps pre-existing rules on the responsibility for asylum applications, but introduces interstate solidarity mechanisms to compensate for the outcomes of standard rules (via relocation, financial contributions, or operational assistance—see art 56(2)). The Pact does include other important legal reforms, most notably the Regulation on the screening of third-country nationals at the external borders (2024/1356), and the Regulation on a return border procedure (2024/1349). It also includes a new Regulation on addressing situations of crisis and force majeure (2024/1359). These norms do not however demand important commitments from Member States, but rather a contraction in the rights of migrants and refugees. The Pact also shows a shift from the usage of Directives to Regulations in an attempt to further harmonize the migration and asylum *acquis* (though many of its norms remains largely unaltered).

[8] Externalization practices, broadly understood, include partnerships with third countries for the purposes of *non-entrée* and deportation. Policies of *non-entrée* include restrictive visa policies, the securitization of borders and search and rescue operations, the use of pushbacks at borders, and the setup of border controls, migration detention, and asylum processing centres abroad (see section 1.1 in Chapter 1 of this book). Instead, this chapter focuses on the external dimension of deportation policies, i.e. on readmission cooperation for the expulsion of those already present in Europe.

owe to each other internally. As a result, the key issue is not whether EU Member States agree on a common agenda on readmission, but rather how to bring third countries on board. The resulting picture is one in which, as opposed to internal migration laws and policies, the (internal and external) boundaries of law and politics do not always coincide, as EU law does not necessarily possess transformative power over the international environment that surrounds it. Under this framework, this chapter is structured as follows.

Section 1 begins by mapping the EU's common readmission policy from the 1999 Tampere European Council to the 2024 Pact on Migration and Asylum. It highlights that, albeit subject to changes, the Union's current approach reflects continuity rather than rupture. It further analyses the available tools used by the EU for readmission purposes, namely EU Readmission Agreements (EURAs), soft law arrangements, and hybrid 'quasi-instruments' of EU law.

In section 2 I examine the different ways in which readmission policies fail in achieving their stated objectives, yet bearing in mind that the systematic lack of access to information surrounding the implementation of many of the Union's readmission tools renders its evaluation limited from a quantitative perspective. I scrutinize the difficulties that the EU faces in bringing third countries on board with cooperative readmission frameworks. By prioritizing the EU's own interests, supposedly 'comprehensive' solutions are based on narrow views of global affairs which overlook that the boundaries of EU law and politics do not necessarily align with the complexities of (EU) international relations. Moreover, regardless of the existence of cooperative frameworks, there are a number of specific obstacles that further complicate readmission. These may again derive from a misunderstanding of the reach of EU law in shaping real-world diplomacy, but also from identity determination challenges, statelessness, different understandings of existing norms (by the EU and third countries), and other implementation challenges.

After an analysis of how and why EU readmission policies 'fail' to achieve their stated outcomes, section 3 contends that this is a policy failure that matters. Whereas the overambitious goals set by the EU in terms of return and readmission can be understood to operate at a symbolic level, its consequences for those persons who cannot be deported are very real.

1. The EU's common policy from Tampere to the 2024 Pact on Asylum and Migration: Of agreements and arrangements

Increasing the rate of 'effective' returns has been a long-standing concern for the EU and its Member States and, in seeking to do so, readmission has always been high on the agenda. However, the readmission mantra has never been as prevalent in the Union's policy discourse as it is today, it being regularly framed as *the* instrument for achieving more effective and operational returns—in particular since 2015. In the words of the Commission, 'the need for the EU to cooperate with other countries in the management of migratory flows has grown steadily in recent years, putting migration at the top of the EU's external relations agenda with key countries of origin and transit'.[9] By way of example, in its 2015 Action Plan on return, the Commission stressed the importance of enhanced cooperation on readmission with third countries, putting a particular emphasis on African countries (whose return rate was then below 30%).[10] Also, at the peak of the refugee crisis, the European Council demanded to mobilize 'all tools' to promote the readmission of irregular migrants to the countries of origin and transit.[11] In the same vein, the Commission's proposal for a New Pact on Migration and Asylum called for more effective cooperation with third countries on return and readmission, based on '[c]omprehensive, balanced and tailor-made partnerships, [which] can deliver mutual benefits'.[12]

In order to understand the evolution of this policy field, this section briefly maps its key policy developments from Tampere to the 2024 Pact, as well as the available toolbox for the EU to increase return rates through readmission. Section 2 will focus instead on the operational effectiveness of the EU's readmission system, evaluating whether or not, to what extent, and why the available tools have or have not contributed to surmounting the practical obstacles precluding the deportation of irregular migrants in Europe.

1.1 Mapping a common readmission policy: from Tampere to the New Pact on Migration and Asylum

Whereas the 2015 refugee crisis has sparked renewed academic interest in the external dimension of EU migration policies, this practice can be understood as a policy continuation rather than as a new phenomenon. As noted by Lavenex in 2006, the Union's 'shift outwards' could then be interpreted as an approach that sought to benefit from Europeanization (i.e. making use of the negotiating weight of the Union) while avoiding the institutional constraints deriving from both domestic and EU law. The author further pointed at the conclusion of intergovernmental readmission agreements under the political sponsorship of the European

[9] European Commission, 'Fitness Check on EU Legislation on Legal Migration', SWD (1019) 1055 Final, 29 March 2019, 4.

[10] European Commission, 'Communication on an EU Action Plan on Return', COM(2015) 453 Final, 9 September 2015, 10. See also European Commission, 'Communication on a European Agenda on Migration', COM(2015) 240 Final, 13 May 2015, 9.

[11] European Council, Conclusions, 25 June 2015, 3.

[12] European Commission, 'Communication on a New Pact on Migration and Asylum' (n 5) 21.

Council as early as the early 1990s, the first such case being the 1991 readmission agreement between the Schengen States and Poland.[13]

The external dimension of EU asylum and migration policies was however officially embraced at the 1999 European Council Conclusions in Tampere—shortly after the EU obtained competences in immigration—and it has been of increasing relevance ever since. The Tampere Conclusions called for a comprehensive migration approach based on 'greater coherence of internal and external policies', partnerships with third countries, and 'addressing political, human rights and development issues in countries and regions of origin and transit'.[14] Despite the focus on the external dimension of migration already in 1999, each migration 'crisis' has pushed towards the contention of migration flows and an increased relevance of readmission.[15]

Following increased arrivals to the Canary Islands and Lampedusa in 2005, the European Council launched the Global Approach to Migration (GAM), highlighting the need for a more 'balanced, global and coherent approach' to 'combat illegal immigration' in cooperation with third countries.[16] In 2009, the Stockholm Programme emphasized the need to strengthen the GAM, consolidating a comprehensive approach towards return and readmission by stepping up cooperation with countries of origin and transit.[17]

The GAM was evaluated and renamed in November 2011, giving rise to the Global Approach to Migration and Mobility (GAMM), aimed at ensuring that the EU's external migration policy is embedded in its overall foreign policy.[18] Whereas the GAMM manifests the drive for return by linking visa facilitation agreements to third countries' cooperation on readmission, it also attempts to offer an overarching framework for cooperation with third countries. The GAMM is composed of four pillars: legal migration and mobility; fighting irregular migration and trafficking in human beings and ensuring return; international protection and asylum policy; and maximizing the development impact of migration and mobility in the countries of origin.[19] The most visible outputs of the GAMM are Mobility Partnerships which, built around the four pillars of the GAMM, are meant to offer a comprehensive framework for migration cooperation, normally including, but not limited to, the conclusion of readmission agreements.[20]

[13] Sandra Lavenex, 'Shifting Up and Out: The Foreign Policy of European Immigration Control' (2006) 29 West European Politics 329, 334.

[14] European Council (Tampere), Presidency Conclusions, 15–16 October 1999 para 11.

[15] Paula García Andrade, 'EU External Competences in the Field of Migration: How to Act Externally When Thinking Internally' (2018) 55 Common Market Law Review 157.

[16] European Council, Presidency Conclusions, 15–16 December 2005, 3.

[17] European Council, 'The Stockholm Programme: An Open and Secure Europe Serving and Protecting Citizens' [2010] OJ C 115, 31.

[18] European Commission, 'Communication on a Global Approach to Migration and Mobility', COM(2011) 743 Final, 18 November 2011, 22.

[19] Ibid, 6 and 16.

[20] Ibid, 10.

It was with the adoption of the Migration Partnership Framework (MPF) in 2016 that the Commission, at the height of the refugee crisis and building on the 2015 Valletta Summit on Migration, focused even more clearly (and almost exclusively) on readmission. Under the MPF, the overall relationship between the EU and third countries should be guided by the capacity and readiness of these countries to effectively cooperate on migration management.[21] In the words of the Commission, '[t]he EU's goal should now be specific and measurable increases in the number and rate of return and readmissions. Therefore, the essential part of any compact will be joint efforts to make returns and readmission work.'[22] With the adoption of the MPF and subsequent instruments, the EU externalizes its internal obsession with return, turning the relationship with target countries into a combination of positive and negative incentives on the basis of their (un)willingness to cooperate in the implementation of the EU migration agenda.

The 2024 Pact on Migration and Asylum, despite claiming to offer a 'fresh start',[23] does not seem to deliver significant changes in the field. The Regulation on Asylum and Migration Management (RAMM) rules that the Member States shall 'promote and build tailor made and mutually beneficial partnerships . . . [to] enhance effective return, readmission and reintegration'.[24] Aside from the fact that readmission is now formally incorporated into secondary legislation (although with broad obligations that are not easy to enforce),[25] the substance of the approach is essentially identical to the 'global', 'balanced', or 'comprehensive' approaches based on 'mutually beneficial partnerships' which have become a commonplace since Tampere. As noted by García Andrade shortly after the announcement of the Pact, neither the goal of mainstreaming migration into the overall external action of the EU, nor the conditionality between mobility opportunities and cooperation on migration control, nor the overall political emphasis on the need to make third countries cooperate on return and readmission are new to the Pact.[26] Similarly, the relationship between the lack of cooperation on readmission and the denial of Schengen visas was already established through the 2019 Visa Code reform.[27]

[21] European Commission, 'Communication on Establishing a New Partnership Framework with Third Countries under the European Agenda on Migration', COM(2016) 385 Final, 7 June 2016, 6.

[22] Ibid.

[23] European Commission, 'Communication on a New Pact on Migration and Asylum' (n 5) 1.

[24] Regulation (EU) 2024/1351 on asylum and migration management [2024] OJ L 2024/1351 art 5(e).

[25] Paula Garcia Andrade, 'Cooperation with Third Countries within the EU Legislative Reform on Migration and Asylum', *EU Immigration and Asylum Law and Policy*, 09 September 2024, available at: <https://eumigrationlawblog.eu/cooperation-with-third-countries-within-the-eu-legislative-reform-on-migration-and-asylum/>.

[26] Paula García Andrade, 'EU Cooperation on Migration with Partner Countries within the New Pact: New Instruments for a New Paradigm?' *Immigration and Asylum Law and Policy*, 8 December 2020, available at: <https://eumigrationlawblog.eu/eu-cooperation-on-migration-with-partner-countries-within-the-new-pact-new-instruments-for-a-new-paradigm/>.

[27] Regulation (EU) 2019/1155 establishing a Community Code on Visas [2019] OJ L 188 (Visa Code) art 25(a).

In sum, the long-lasting tension between the commitment to mutually beneficial partnerships and the persistent emphasis on readmission being at the centre of the Union's relations with partner countries remains unsolved—and so do the difficulties in bringing third countries on board.

1.2 The EU's readmission toolbox

In September 2020, the Commission reported that the EU had twenty-four agreements and arrangements on readmission with third countries. By 'agreements and arrangements' the Commission refers to the adoption of EURAs, as well as other soft law instruments concluded with third countries.[28] These do not include other types of (broader) association agreements, which may include, among many other topics, readmission clauses.

1.2.1 EU Readmission Agreements (EURAs)

EURAs, as their domestic counterparts, are international agreements that impose reciprocal obligations (or rather stress existing obligations under international law) on the parties to readmit their own nationals[29] and, under certain conditions, third-country nationals and stateless people. EURAs are considered as one of the main tools for a comprehensive EU return policy,[30] and are institutionally viewed as a central concern for the EU in its relationship with third countries, as well as the basis for an efficient return policy in facilitating the swift return of irregular migrants.[31] As of December 2024, the EU has concluded eighteen EURAs with third countries.[32]

[28] European Commission, 'Communication on a New Pact on Migration and Asylum' (n 5) 21.

[29] The existence of such an obligation under international law is in itself contentious. In 1999, the Council Legal Service argued that, if the returnee does not want to return to his/her country of origin, it was 'doubtful that . . . a general principle of international law exists which would oblige those states to readmit their own nationals' (Council of the European Union, 'Standard Readmission Agreement between the Member States of the EU, of the One Part, and a Third Country, of the Other Part—Impact of the Entry into Force of the Treaty of Amsterdam', 10 March 1999 para 6). However, for purposes of clarity and considering that there seems to a wide degree of consensus among policy-makers and academics, it will be assumed that such a norm of customary international law exists. See, in this regard: Kai Hailbronner, 'Readmission Agreements and the Obligation of States under Public International Law to Readmit Their Own and Foreign Nationals' (1997) 57 Zeitschrift für ausländisches öffentliches Recht und Völkerrecht; Marion Panizzon, 'Readmission Agreements of EU Member States: A Case for EU Subsidiarity or Dualism?' (2012) 31 Refugee Survey Quarterly; Nils Philip Coleman, *European Readmission Policy: Third Country Interests and Refugee Rights* (Brill Nijhoff 2008) 28.

[30] Katharina Eisele, 'The EU's Readmission Policy: Of Agreements and Arrangements' in Sergio Carrera, Juan Santos Vara, and Tineke Strik (eds), *Constitutionalising the External Dimensions of EU Migration Policies in Times of Crisis: Legality, Rule of Law and Fundamental Rights Reconsidered* (Edward Elgar Publishing 2019) 136.

[31] Council of the European Union, Press Release 10011/11, 12 May 2011, 9, available at: < https://www.consilium.europa.eu/uedocs/cms_data/docs/pressdata/en/jha/121967.pdf>.

[32] According to the website of the European Commission, these are (by date of entry into force): Hong Kong, Macao, Sri Lanka, Albania, Russia, Ukraine, North Macedonia, Bosnia, Montenegro, Serbia, Moldova, Pakistan, Georgia, Armenia, Azerbaijan, Turkey, Cape Verde, and Belarus (list available

Once the subject of heated debates between the Commission, the Council, and Member States,[33] the Union's competence to conclude readmission agreements can now be found in Article 79(3) of the Treaty on the Functioning of the European Union (TFEU). Member States can reach bilateral readmission agreements with third countries, but theylose their competence to do so as soon as the EU establishes a mandate for the negotiation an EURA with a given country.[34]

The objectives of EURAs are not restricted to facilitating the return of irregular migrants to countries of origin and transit; they also include migration control by partner states, stimulating the negotiation of readmission agreements between third countries, and inciting third countries to intercept transiting migrants, among other goals.[35] Moreover, EURAs have certainly become a *sine qua non* for discussions on regular migration with some non-EU countries (see, for example, section 1.2.3 on visa facilitation).[36]

1.2.2 Soft law instruments

The Union's return policy is not only externalized but also increasingly *informalized*. Internally, this is exemplified by the Commission's Return Handbook.[37] However, the most significant developments occur externally, through the proliferation of informal arrangements with third countries. These include informal arrangements focusing exclusively on readmission, as well as broader migration cooperation frameworks that incorporate readmission obligations. They may also be concluded directly by the EU, or have the EU involved in an unclear manner, as in the EU–Turkey Statement.

The shift towards soft law cooperation with third countries has been extensively covered by the literature, particularly insofar as these arrangements have circumvented EU legality (by escaping the decision-making procedures and the institutional balance foreseen in the treaties) or undermined the rule of law or

at: <https://eur-lex.europa.eu/EN/legal-content/summary/readmission-agreements-between-the-eu-and-certain-non-eu-countries.html>). Belarus however suspended its readmission agreement in 2021. For an overview of the common structure of EURAs and standardized obligations, see: Jean-Pierre Cassarino, 'Readmission Policy in the European Union', Study for the LIBE Committee, September 2010, 14–16, available at: <https://www.europarl.europa.eu/RegData/etudes/etudes/join/2010/425632/IPOL-LIBE_ET%282010%29425632_EN.pdf>.

[33] Steve Peers and others (eds), *EU Immigration and Asylum Law (Text and Commentary): Second Revised Edition: Volume 2: EU Immigration Law* (Brill Nijhoff 2012) 553.

[34] Francesca Ippolito and Seline Trevisanut (eds), *Migration in the Mediterranean: Mechanisms of International Cooperation* (Cambridge University Press 2016) 287. In practice, Member States sometimes ratify bilateral readmission agreements with countries with which the EU already has a negotiating mandate (see Paula García Andrade, 'The External Dimension of the EU Immigration and Asylum Policies Before the Court of Justice' (2022) 7 European Papers 113).

[35] Coleman (n 29) 64.

[36] Paul James Cardwell, 'New Modes of Governance in the External Dimension of EU Migration Policy' (2013) 51 International Migration 54, 57.

[37] Peter Slominski and Florian Trauner, 'Reforming Me Softly—How Soft Law Has Changed EU Return Policy since the Migration Crisis' (2021) 44 West European Politics 93.

the fundamental rights of individuals.[38] Whereas the EU's escape from the treaty framework for the sake of effectiveness seems evident and well documented in the literature, my aim is to briefly outline these practices to subsequently analyse whether they have meaningfully contributed to an increase in deportations, and to what extent.

Even if migration cooperation through soft law is far from new, the expansion of its use since 2015 is certainly unprecedented.[39] According to the EU Commission, there were, as of May 2021, six arrangements with third countries on readmission.[40] Considering the lack of success of formal cooperation on return, and following the logic of increasing return rates, the EU has favoured the use of soft law instruments whenever third countries are unwilling to conclude formal EURAs. Authorities in third countries are unenthusiastic about concluding legally binding (and publicly visible) readmission agreements with the EU due to their lack of popularity.[41] In this context, the use of joint declarations, memoranda of understanding, codes of conduct, migration dialogues, and the like, aims to achieve equivalent results to those of EURAs, but without the need to go through the lengthy and technical procedures internally,[42] and seeking to secure cooperation from partner countries

[38] See, among others: Sergio Carrera, Juan Santos Vara, and Tineke Strik, *Constitutionalising the External Dimensions of EU Migration Policies in Times of Crisis: Legality, Rule of Law and Fundamental Rights Reconsidered* (Edward Elgar Publishing 2019); Andrea Ott, 'Informalization of EU Bilateral Instruments: Categorization, Contestation, and Challenges' (2020) 39 Yearbook of European Law 569; Jorrit J Rijpma, 'External Migration and Asylum Management: Accountability for Executive Action Outside EU-Territory' (2017) 2 European Papers; Paula García Andrade, 'The Distribution of Powers between EU Institutions for Conducting External Affairs through Non-Binding Instruments' (2016) 1 European Papers; Paula García Andrade, 'The Role of the European Parliament in the Adoption of Non-Legally Binding Agreements with Third Countries' in Juan Santos Vara and Sánchez-Tabernero Soledad R (eds), *The Democratization of EU International Relations Through EU Law* (Routledge 2018); Andrade, 'EU External Competences in the Field of Migration' (n 15); Sara Poli, 'The Integration of Migration Concerns into EU External Policies: Instruments, Techniques and Legal Problems' (2020) 5 European Papers; Tineke Strik, 'The Global Approach to Migration and Mobility' (2017) 5 Groningen Journal of International Law 310; Eleonora Frasca and Emanuela Roman, 'The Informalisation of EU Readmission Policy: Eclipsing Human Rights Protection Under the Shadow of Informality and Conditionality' (2023) 8 European Papers—A Journal on Law and Integration 931.

[39] Juan Santos Vara, 'Soft International Agreements on Migration Cooperation with Third Countries: A Challenge to Democratic and Judicial Controls in the EU' in Sergio Carrera, Juan Santos Vara, and Tineke Strik, *Constitutionalising the External Dimensions of EU Migration Policies in Times of Crisis: Legality, Rule of Law and Fundamental Rights Reconsidered* (Edward Elgar Publishing 2019) 24.

[40] European Commission, 'Communication on Enhancing Cooperation on Return and Readmission' (n 3) 6. These were Afghanistan (2016 and 2021), The Gambia (2017), Guinea (2017), Bangladesh (2017), Ethiopia (2018), and Ivory Coast (2019). The list excludes Mobility Partnerships, as these are comprehensive frameworks on migration and mobility which may or may not include the conclusion of readmission instruments. It also excludes other instruments such as the EU–Turkey statement, as the Commission does not consider this an EU instrument, but one concluded separately by the members of the European Council.

[41] Carrera (n 6) 45.

[42] European Commission, 'Communication on the First Progress Report on the Partnership Framework with Third Countries under the European Agenda on Migration', COM(2016) 700 Final, 18 October 2016, 3.

externally. Then, the rationale is that non-binding and many times secretive arrangements might prove more adequate to secure cooperation considering the politically sensitive nature of the topic.

Whereas the GAMM already relied on the conclusion of Mobility Partnerships,[43] the 2016 MPF further consolidates the informalization trend, making explicit that 'the paramount priority is to achieve fast and operational returns, and not necessarily formal readmission agreements'.[44] The preference for informal (and, if possible, confidential) arrangements over EURAs has been expressed unequivocally by the Commission in its fifth progress report on the MPF,[45] and more recently in a 'non-paper' addressed to the Member States.[46]

Then, the lack of success of formal cooperation on readmission, together with low deportation rates, and the increased number of irregular arrivals into the EU after 2015 help explain one of the most salient examples among informal readmission arrangements: the Joint Way Forward (JWF) on migration issues between Afghanistan and the EU—followed upon its expiry (and until the seizure of power by the Taliban) by the 'Joint Declaration on cooperation with Afghanistan'.[47] In the JWF, the EU tacitly categorized Afghanistan as a safe country despite the deteriorating security situation in the country at the time. Albeit in the form of 'soft' law and stating that '[it] is not intended to create legal rights or obligations under international law',[48] these arrangements established specific mechanisms and mutual, comprehensive, and far-reaching commitments to return and readmit in a similar fashion to those of EURAs. Moreover, the EU concluded return and readmission arrangements with Guinea, The Gambia, Ethiopia, and Ivory Coast,[49] and Standard Operating Procedures (SOPs) for the identification and return of irregular migrants with Bangladesh in 2017.[50] The EU has aimed (so far unsuccessfully) at reaching further SOPs with other sub-Saharan

[43] Mobility Partnerships have the status of non-binding political declarations which may, or may not, include the conclusion of an EURA or other instruments.

[44] European Commission, 'Communication on Establishing a New Partnership Framework' (n 21) 7.

[45] European Commission, 'Fifth Progress Report on the Partnership Framework with Third Countries under the European Agenda on Migration', COM(2017) 471 Final, 6 September 2017, 2–3.

[46] European Commission, 'Non-Paper on a Strategic Approach on Readmission Agreements and Arrangements', 8429/22, 29 April 2022, available at: < https://www.statewatch.org/media/3680/eu-com-readmission-strategic-approach-non-paper-8429-22.pdf>.

[47] Contrary to the Joint Way Forward, the text of the 'Joint Declaration' was not made available to the public. However, following public pressure, it was finally published on the website of the European External Action Service some months later (see European External Action Service (EEAS), 'EU–Afghanistan Joint Declaration on Migration Cooperation', 26 April 2021, available at: <https://www.eeas.europa.eu/eeas/eu-afghanistan-joint-declaration-migration-cooperation_en?s=234>).

[48] Ibid, 1.

[49] European Commission, 'Communication on Enhancing Cooperation on Return and Readmission' (n 3) 6.

[50] European Commission, 'Decision of 8 September 2017 on the Signature of the EU-Bangladesh Standard Operating Procedures for the Identification and Return of Persons without an Authorisation to Stay', C(2017) 6137 Final, 8 September 2017.

countries,[51] and also aims at concluding a non-binding readmission instrument with Iraq.[52]

In parallel to readmission instruments, the EU also incorporates readmission commitments in all-encompassing partnerships with third countries (where migration management features prominently). The use of development and trade policies as a bargaining chip in migration negotiations was typical of the EU's foreign policy in the early 2000s,[53] and has experienced a revival since 2015. In its Communication on the MPF, the Commission stressed that '[p]ositive and negative incentives should be integrated in the EU's development policy . . . for those who do not cooperate on readmission and return. The same should be true of trade policy.'[54] This has also been the approach in recent deals concluded with Tunisia,[55] Mauritania,[56] and Egypt,[57] aimed at developing 'comprehensive partnerships' that embed migration into larger discussions including trade, development, and other economic issues.[58] In short, these deals make EU funding and strengthened cooperation in a number of policy areas conditional on migration cooperation with the EU,[59] be it through containment policies or cooperation on return and readmission.

Lastly, it is worth mentioning the EU–Turkey statement. This instrument, adopted with a country with which there was already an EURA in place, is unclear as regards its authorship and legal bindingness. Its *sui generis* nature stems from its ambiguous incorporation of EU institutions into it, as it was formally not adopted by the EU but separately by the Members of the European Council—even though it was adopted by all the members of the European Council one day after a European Council summit, published on its website, and regularly monitored

[51] Santos Vara (n 39) 28.

[52] Council of the European Union, 'A non-binding instrument on return and readmission between the EU and Iraq: Authorisation to negotiate an NBI', 13551/23, 4 October 2023.

[53] Sandra Lavenex and Rahel Kunz, 'The Migration–Development Nexus in EU External Relations' (2008) 30 Journal of European Integration 439.

[54] European Commission, 'Communication on a New Partnership Framework' (n 21) 9.

[55] European Commission, 'Memorandum of Understanding on a Strategic and Global Partnership between the European Union and Tunisia', Press Release IP/23/3887, 16 July 2023, available at: <https://ec.europa.eu/commission/presscorner/detail/en/ip_23_3887.

[56] European Commission, 'EU–Mauritania Joint Declaration', 8 March 2024, available at: <https://home-affairs.ec.europa.eu/eu-mauritania-joint-declaration_en>.

[57] European Commission, 'Joint Declaration on the Strategic and Comprehensive Partnership between the Arab Republic of Egypt and the European Union', News Article, 17 March 2024, available at: <https://neighbourhood-enlargement.ec.europa.eu/news/joint-declaration-strategic-and-comprehensive-partnership-between-arab-republic-egypt-and-european-2024-03-17_en>.

[58] European Commission, 'Commission Takes Stock of Key Achievements on Migration and Asylum', Press Release IP/24/1413, 12 March 2024, available at: <https://ec.europa.eu/commission/presscorner/detail/en/ip_24_1413>.

[59] Tineke Strik and Ruben Robbesom, 'Compliance or Complicity? An Analysis of the EU–Tunisia Deal in the Context of the Externalisation of Migration Control' (2024) 71 Netherlands International Law Review 199. These deals follow a consistent pattern: they are informal, non-transparent, and concluded with non-democratic governments with questionable human rights records.

in its implementation by the Commission.[60] Among other things, the EU–Turkey statement established a 1:1 scheme under which the EU would resettle a Syrian (recognized) refugee for every Syrian returned to Turkey from the Greek islands. The extent to which this readmission scheme has worked in practice is analysed in section 2.3.1.[61]

1.2.3 Complementary tools

Included in formal or informal readmission instruments, in addition to them, or as an incentive for third countries to cooperate in the field, the EU has at its disposal several additional instruments to better enforce its readmission objectives. In addition to the use of trade and development as leverage in readmission negotiations (see above section 1.2.2), the EU has employed visa policies and practical tools, such as the European Travel Document, to implement its readmission agenda.

First, the use of visa policies has had an important role in the conclusion of EURAs for a long time. From 2002 onwards, particularly in the Western Balkans, visa facilitation agreements have been consistently offered as a 'sweetener' to overcome the lack of interest in signing readmission agreements.[62] The use of visa policy as a positive incentive is however combined with its use as a punitive tool to put pressure on those states which are deemed uncooperative. In its 2017 Communication on the delivery of the European Agenda on Migration, the Commission noted that, in case of persistent non-cooperation, taking coordinated visa measures against those states 'may provide additional leverage'.[63] This has materialized in the 2019 Visa Code reform, whose Article 25(a) now punishes nationals of third countries who are 'considered not to be cooperating sufficiently', by requiring of them more documents, higher visa fees, lengthier processing times, and so on.

[60] European Council, 'EU–Turkey Statement', Press Release 144/16, 18 March 2016, available at: <https://www.consilium.europa.eu/en/press/press-releases/2016/03/18/eu-turkey-statement/>. Nevertheless, the General Court, and later the Court of Justice, determined that they lacked jurisdiction to rule on an agreement that was concluded by the Member States and not by the EU (Joined cases C-208/17, *P, NF v European Council*, C-209/17, *P NG v European Council* and C-210/17, *P, NM v European Council* [2018] ECLI:EU:C:2018:705).

[61] As with soft EU arrangements, it is not the purpose of this chapter to analyse the controversies raised by the statement in relation to it circumventing the European Parliament and the CJEU, as well as its impact on the fundamental rights of individuals, but rather to analyse its operability as a readmission tool. On these other issues, see Santos Vara (n 39); Sergio Carrera, Leonard den Hertog, and Marco Stefan, 'The EU–Turkey Deal: Reversing "Lisbonisation" in EU Migration and Asylum Policies' in Sergio Carrera, Juan Santos Vara, and Tineke Strik, *Constitutionalising the External Dimensions of EU Migration Policies in Times of Crisis: Legality, Rule of Law and Fundamental Rights Reconsidered* (Edward Elgar Publishing 2019); Mauro Gatti and Andrea Ott, 'The EU–Turkey Statement: Legal Nature and Compatibility with EU Institutional Law' in Sergio Carrera, Juan Santos Vara, and Tineke Strik, *Constitutionalising the External Dimensions of EU Migration Policies in Times of Crisis: Legality, Rule of Law and Fundamental Rights Reconsidered* (Edward Elgar Publishing 2019).

[62] Florian Trauner and Imke Kruse, 'EC Visa Facilitation and Readmission Agreements: A New Standard EU Foreign Policy Tool' (2008) 10 European Journal of Migration and Law 411, 415.

[63] European Commission, 'Communication on the Delivery of the European Agenda on Migration', COM(2017) 558 Final, 27 September 2017 22.

Second, being aware that the lack of travel documents is one of the main practical obstacles to the deportation of irregular migrants, the European legislator adopted in 2016 a Regulation on a uniform European Travel Document.[64] A few months earlier, the Commission Communication on the MPF had stressed that having third countries accept the EU *laissez-passer* for return operations was one of the five key elements to be prioritized in the context of return and readmission.[65] This new Regulation substitutes the (rather unused) standard travel document established by a Council Recommendation in 1994, and aims at reducing administrative and bureaucratic burdens, as well as obtaining higher acceptance from third countries by establishing a uniform format and enhanced technical and security features. The European Travel Document is envisaged to be used not only in the context of EURAs, but more generally in the context of readmission.[66]

2. Assessing the EU's readmission policy: Challenges and implementation gaps

2.1 Measuring the unmeasurable: Readmission instruments and return rates

If one attempts to grasp the effectiveness of return and readmission policies quantitatively comparing the number of return decisions and 'effective' returns (as the EU Commission does), return rates in the EU have remained strikingly modest and in a decreasing trend—falling as low as 19% in 2023.[67] Thus, if one analyses the EU's readmission system in relation to its stated return objectives, the result is one of clear policy failure.

Whereas these statistics reveal a clear deportation gap, they must be analysed with caution, as return rates offer a reductionist picture of return and readmission 'effectiveness'. In this line, Carrera stresses that assessing readmission exclusively by means of return rates assumes that migrants' legal statuses are something existential, 'fixed in stone', ignoring that irregular migrants can contest the legality of their removal order and transition to lawful residence, or leave by their own means without notifying state authorities.[68] Moreover, it overlooks the technical, diplomacy-related, or other obstacles to deportation in the context of readmission (see sections 2.2 and 2.3 in this chapter). It also ignores that there are a number of

[64] Regulation (EU) 2016/1953 on the establishment of a European travel document for the return of illegally staying third-country nationals [2016] L 311/13.
[65] European Commission, 'Communication on Establishing a New Partnership Framework' (n 21) 7.
[66] Regulation (EU) 2016/1953 (n 64) Recitals 6 and 9.
[67] See Eurostat database (n 1).
[68] Carrera (n 6) 59.

persons who cannot be removed due to human rights safeguards (see Chapter 2, Chapter 3, and section 2.3.3 of this chapter)—hardly an 'obstacle' hindering the effective implementation of EU law, but rather the result of EU (fundamental rights) law in action.

This approach is thus based on an essentially flawed premise: that every irregular migrant that is not returned adds to a gap that can (and should) be closed by means of EU law and policy.[69] This overlooks that return orders are often issued to people in respect of whom there is no reasonable prospect of removal in the first place. Thus, the success or failure of readmission policies should be assessed realistically, not based on what the EU could 'ideally' do, but on what it can do *all things considered.*

Be that as it may, if one looks at readmission instruments, the lack of transparency and available statistics makes the assessment of EURAs (let alone informal agreements) methodologically limited.[70] EURAs have been posited by EU institutions as a central component of return policies that brings significant added value,[71] but with a failure to provide concrete evidence on their practical operability. Indeed, the Commission acknowledged in its Communication on the evaluation of EURAs that the quality of available data on the implementation of these instruments is hindered by incomplete and non-harmonized statistics, as well as by the fact that several Member States did not provide any data to the Commission or did not use EURAs at all.[72] For those who did provide statistics, these did not indicate whether removals had taken place within or outside the framework of EURAs or other bilateral or EU-wide readmission tools. Moreover, Eurostat statistics include the nationality of the returnee but do not specify the requested state and do not distinguish between voluntary and forced returns. These methodological obstacles are worsened by the secrecy surrounding the implementation of EURAs, particularly as regards the functioning of Joint Readmission Committees and the implementing protocols signed bilaterally between Member States and countries of origin.[73]

It is worth noting that for those countries with which the EU has concluded an EURA, return rates are generally higher than for other third countries. In 2023, the return rate of nationals of countries with an EURA in place was 34%—while for

[69] The Commission recently acknowledged that assessing readmission policies solely by way of return rates might fail to provide a comprehensive picture of Member States' experience with readmission cooperation (European Commission, 'Communication on Enhancing Cooperation on Return and Readmission' (n 3) 8).

[70] Paula García Andrade and others, 'EU Cooperation with Third Countries in the Field of Migration', European Parliament, Study requested by the LIBE Committee, 5 October 2015 72, available at: <https://op.europa.eu/en/publication-detail/-/publication/26d712e6-e10a-11e5-8a50-01aa75ed71a1/language-en>.

[71] European Commission, 'Communication on Enhancing Cooperation on Return and Readmission' (n 3) 9.

[72] European Commission, 'Communication on an Evaluation of EU Readmission Agreements', COM(2011) 76 Final, 23 February 2011 3.

[73] Carrera (n 6) 41 and 45.

nationals of countries without an EURA it was as low as 13%.[74] In the same year, nationals of third countries with an EURA accounted for only 27% of the return decisions but 48% of all effective returns. However, the role of EURAs remains ambiguous: first, because the state of nationality and requested state do not necessarily coincide; second, because TCNs might well be returned under bilateral or other arrangements and not under the EURA; third and most importantly, because the overrepresentation of Balkan states and other neighbouring countries among the signatories of EURAs makes it difficult to establish whether this increased efficiency derives from the usage of EURAs alone, or whether other region-specific characteristics, such as the lure of EU Membership or the conclusion of visa facilitation agreements with these countries also play a significant role. Indeed, the high deportation rates for the nationals of these countries contrasts with that of countries such as Sri Lanka and Pakistan, where annual return rates remain consistently below 15% despite the conclusion of EURAs in 2005 and 2010 respectively. In the case of Turkey, out of 20,985 Turkish citizens that were ordered to leave in 2023, only 5,560 were effectively deported.[75] If one tries to analyse the evolution of return rates of nationals of third countries before and after the conclusion of EURAs, the results obtained are inconclusive and vary widely across countries (see Figure 4.1).

The difficulties in informing a proper evaluation of readmission tools are equally present (and might even be exacerbated) in the context of informal arrangements. Indeed, the gross opacity surrounding them prevents a correct evaluation of its implementation challenges. Whereas the SOPs with Bangladesh can be found online (although not in an official EU website), the remaining arrangements with The Gambia, Guinea, Ethiopia, and Ivory Coast remain secret. Against this backdrop, the European Parliament had to rely on a leaked version of the arrangement with Ethiopia in order to be able to put forward parliamentary questions on its implementation.[76] The role and competences of Joint Working Groups (equivalent to Joint Readmission Committees for EURAs) are also unknown.

In the meantime, recent research suggests that the informalization of readmission cooperation has had a small impact on the number of returns.[77] If one

[74] In past years (e.g. in 2019), the return rate to countries with an EURA in place went even beyond 50%. This percentage has been calculated based on data provided by Eurostat (n 1). It has however been calculated excluding Hong Kong and Macao (as Eurostat includes these as returns to China), as well as Belarus (since the EURA with this country only entered into force in July 2020 and was suspended in 2021).

[75] Ibid. These statistics do not show the expulsion of nationals of other third countries and therefore remain limited. In the Turkish case, for instance, Syrian nationals returned to Turkey under the readmission agreement (or the EU–Turkey statement) would not be captured by these statistics.

[76] European Parliament, 'Agreement between the EU and Ethiopia on Return Procedures', Question for Written Answer to the Commission, Judith Sargentini (Verts/ALE), 15 February 2019, available at: <https://www.europarl.europa.eu/doceo/document/E-8-2018-000957_EN.html>.

[77] Victoria Rietig, 'Carrots and Sticks in Migration Cooperation: Three Uncomfortable Truths', *ICMPD*, 17 January 2024 2, available at: <https://www.icmpd.org/blog/2024/carrots-and-sticks-in-migration-cooperation-three-uncomfortable-truths>.

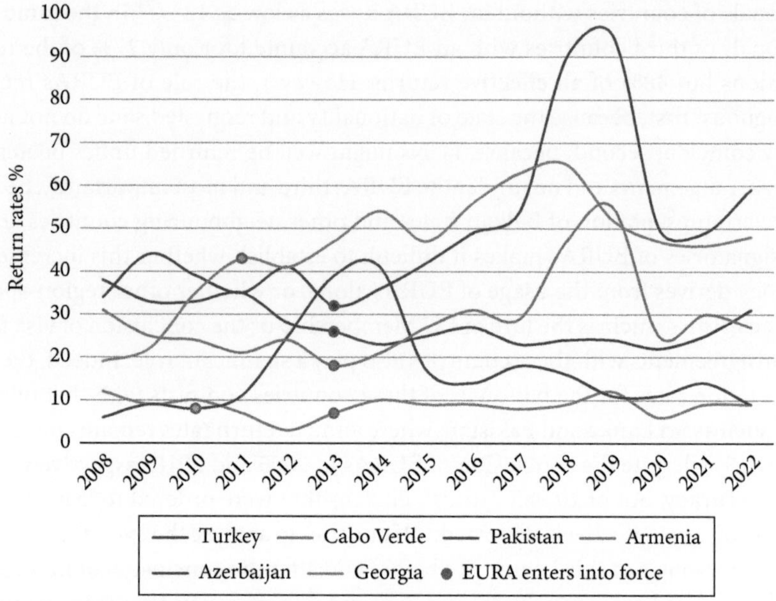

Figure 4.1 Effectiveness of returns for selected third countries[1]

[1]The sample includes those third countries with an EURA signed from 2009 onwards, as Eurostat only gathers data from 2008 onwards, and data after 2020 are not yet available for the EU-27 (as of July 2022). Hence, for those countries with an EURA concluded in 2008 or before, no statistics are available prior to the conclusion of the agreements. Belarus is excluded, since the EURA was concluded in 2020 and suspended in 2021.

undertakes a comparative analysis of return rates before and after the conclusion of readmission arrangements, little to no effects can be observed (see Figure 4.2)—with return rates remaining significantly lower than the average for all third countries (let alone countries with an EURA). For example, the 2016 JWF with Afghanistan resulted in a dramatic increase in deportations in the year of its conclusion (from 1,255 persons removed in 2015 (3.5%) to 8,095 (30%) in 2016), but was followed by an equally sharp decrease in the years that followed (2,260 persons returned in 2019 and 1,120 in 2020, amounting to 7% and 6% of return decisions respectively). In the case of the EU–Turkey statement, whereas the role of the deal in bringing down the number of irregular crossings and lives lost at sea remains disputed,[78] there is consensus on its failure as a deportation tool, with a total

[78] While the statement has been praised by the Commission for its role in reducing sharply the number of irregular arrivals and the lives lost at sea (see: European Commission, 'Second Report on the Progress Made in the Implementation of the EU–Turkey Statement', COM(2016) 349 Final, 15 June 2016, 2), Spijkerboer contends that there was no causal relation between the EU–Turkey statement and the decreased number of irregular arrivals and border deaths, claiming that the downward trend was

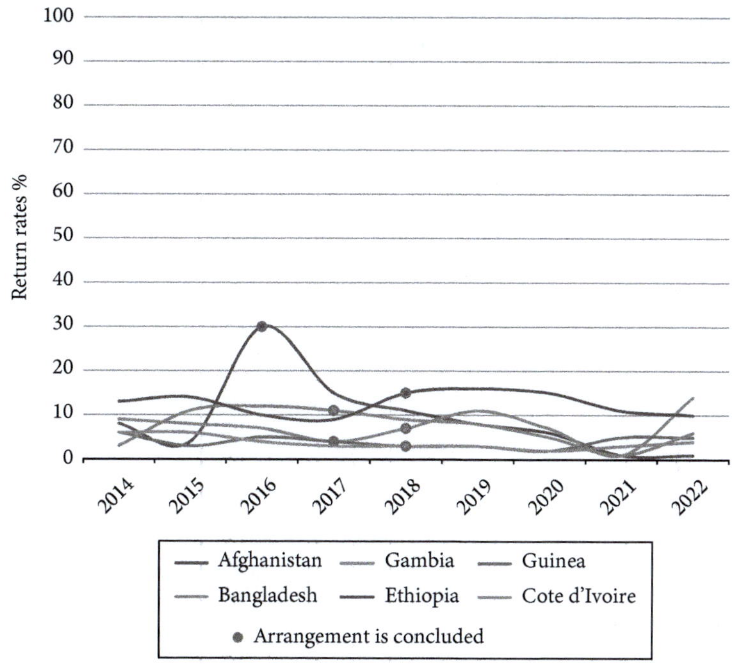

Figure 4.2 Effectiveness of returns for selected third countries[1] (II)

Source: author's compilation based on Eurostat data.

[1]The sample includes those countries with an informal arrangement on readmission. It does not include countries with other arrangements which might include specific mentions to readmission or with arrangements, such as the EU–Turkey statement, where the EU denies its authorship.

of 2,140 persons deported between 2016 and 2020—and no returns since March 2020 due to Turkey's unilateral suspension of the readmission part of the deal.[79]

The caveats highlighted above thus seem to frustrate any attempt to make sweeping statements about the concrete impact of the EU's readmission policies and instruments. This is worsened by the institutional secrecy regarding readmission

prior to and not affected by the agreement (T Spijkerboer, 'Fact Check: Did the EU–Turkey Deal Bring Down the Number of Migrants and of Border Deaths?' *Border Criminologies*, 28 September 2016, available at: <https://blogs.law.ox.ac.uk/research-subject-groups/centre-criminology/centreborder-criminologies/blog/2016/09/fact-check-did-eu>).

[79] European Commission, 'Commission Staff Working Document: Türkiye 2023 Report', SWD(2023) 696 Final, 8 November 2023 53. According to UNHCR, the return trend since 2016 is as follows: 801 (2016), 683 (2017), 322 (2018), 195 (2019), 139 (2020). See: UNHCR, 'Returns from Greece to Turkey (under EU–Turkey statement) as of 31 March 2020', 1 April 2020, available at: <https://data.unhcr.org/en/documents/details/75075>.

tools. It must be noted that the EU's first comprehensive analysis of readmission cooperation, adopted in February 2021, remains a classified document.[80]

Based on this, the remaining part of this chapter will rest on a more modest claim, namely that, regardless of the cooperative framework in place, a significant number of irregular migrants who are targeted by readmission policies cannot be deported. The starting point will be not that EU readmission policies do not have the capacity to influence migratory flows at all, but that they fail to do so in the ways that they claim to strive for. Thus, the following sub-sections zoom in on the real-life conditions that limit the EU's readmission capacity, pointing at the existing limitations in the conclusion of formal or informal cooperation frameworks with third countries (section 2.2). This is followed by an analysis of specific obstacles hindering the removal of TCNs, be it within or outside readmission frameworks (section 2.3).

2.2 When EU law meets international politics: In search of cooperation

The unwillingness of third countries to readmit their own citizens and the need to secure their cooperation are rightly framed by the EU as among the main obstacles precluding deportations. Ultimately, the gap between the EU's agenda and its reception by potential partner countries reveals that the boundaries that the EU faces internally do not necessarily correspond to those faced as an international player. At a deeper level, the lack of progress in bringing third countries on board responds to fundamental North–South interest conflicts,[81] as Europe's readmission agenda is generally unwanted by governments and civil society actors in key countries of origin and transit.[82]

The key question for EU policy-makers remains how to turn readmission into a priority for target countries and make *prima facie* conflicting interests converge. In order to tackle the unbalanced nature of readmission dialogues, the so-called package approach seeks to insert readmission within broader policy discussions, as seen in section 1. Indeed, the interest of third countries might be sparked by the inclusion of visa facilitation, the prospect of EU membership, or preferential trade conditions, among others. A case in point is offered by the EU–Turkey readmission agreement, signed in 2013 after more than ten years of negotiations, linked to a visa

[80] European Commission, 'Return and readmission: improving cooperation within the EU and with external partners', Press Release, 10 February 2021, available at: <https://ec.europa.eu/commission/presscorner/detail/en/ip_21_503>.

[81] Stephen Castles, 'Why Migration Policies Fail' (2004) 27 Ethnic and Racial Studies 205, 221.

[82] See, for example, the analyses of the African civil society representatives published by the European Council on Refugees and Exiles (ECRE) (available at: <https://www.ecre.org/ecre-publications/working-papers/>).

liberalization dialogue, and framed within the multidimensional relation between the EU and Turkey.[83] Moreover, the country-specific circumstances present in the Turkish case (or in the Western Balkans or other neighbouring countries) are often not available in negotiations with most 'migration countries', where EU membership is off the table and Member States are reluctant to offer favourable visa conditions and legal migration channels.[84] In fact, favourable visa conditions are also seen by the EU as opening another door for irregular migration—since visa overstayers already account for the majority of irregular migrants in Europe.[85] In addition, the claim that the EU's role as a trade power can be used to make migration countries comply with the EU's readmission agenda is only partially supported by evidence, and remains strongly dependent on pre-existing institutional relationships among countries (e.g. in the context of EU enlargement and neighbourhood policies).[86] For other countries, the mutually beneficial character of the relationship with the EU is not so clear-cut.

For example, in its relationships with African countries, the EU has framed its rather aggressive diplomatic style as comprehensive and mutually beneficial (e.g. in the context of the EU Trust Fund for Africa), while in practice it is one-sided and subservient to the EU's migration agenda.[87] This has not gone unnoticed by the African Union, which has openly expressed its reservations at the EU's approach in a field (migration) which was never top of the agenda for African policy-makers.[88] Moreover, cooperation on readmission is greatly unpopular in many countries of origin, conditioning their governments' responses—particularly in democratic countries where policy-making is naturally more accountable and responsive to public opinion.[89] This is especially true for EURAs, since their unpopularity among local populations in the countries of origin stands in sharp contrast with the EU's desire to openly publicize them.[90] Intrinsic to this dispute is the fact that readmission agreements establish reciprocal obligations which are nevertheless overwhelmingly applied to deport from (and not to) the EU in what Cassarino

[83] Çiğdem Akın Yavuz, 'Analysis of the EU–Turkey Readmission Agreement: A Unique Case' (2019) 21 European Journal of Migration and Law 486, 497.

[84] Rietig (n 77) 2.

[85] European Commission, 'Irregular Migration and Return', available at: <https://home-affairs.ec.europa.eu/policies/migration-and-asylum/irregular-migration-and-return_en>.

[86] Paula Hoffmeyer-Zlotnik, Sandra Lavenex, and Philipp Lutz, 'The Limits of EU Market Power in Migration Externalization: Explaining Migration Control Provisions in EU Preferential Trade Agreements' (2024) 62 Journal of Common Market Studies 1351.

[87] Mehari Taddele Maru, 'Migration Policy-Making in Africa: Determinants and Implications for Cooperation with Europe' (2021) EUI Working Paper RSC 2021/54 1, 22–23.

[88] Ibid, 6.

[89] Ibid, 10. This also helps explain the EU's tendency to conclude readmission deals with countries with questionable democratic and human rights records such as Tunisia, Mauritania, or Egypt (see section 1.2.2).

[90] Carrera (n 6) 46.

rightly describes as 'unbalanced reciprocities'.[91] The reluctance to sign EURAs is exacerbated by the determination of the EU to include third-country nationals clauses, which require partner countries to readmit nationals of third countries who transited their territory on their way to the EU.[92] Since these countries are not only countries of origin but also (and sometimes mainly) of transit and destination, they can be reluctant to accept third-country national clauses and put at risk their relations with bordering countries by tightening border controls.[93] Connected to this, and leaving aside the irony of the European Union's mistrust towards the development of regional free movement regimes, its demand for stricter border control with its neighbours is at odds with the African Union's increasing drive for regional integration and free movement of people.[94]

These circumstances, together with the fact that positive incentives are often out of the equation for many of these 'migration countries', have led to a situation in which negotiations with key partners such as Morocco or, more recently, Nigeria and Jordan (to name a few) seem to be stalled *sine die*.[95] It is also hardly surprising that that the EU remains unable to sign a readmission agreement with a mainland African country as of today. Indeed, reaching a 'win–win' partnership remains problematic as the 'win' is mostly limited to financial aid, which is nevertheless linked to the EU's migration agenda and not sufficient to compensate for the loss of remittances (which can exceed development aid and foreign investment put together) or the fact that emigration offers these countries a way to relieve pressure on domestic unemployment.[96]

Shifting away from domestic public hostility, third countries might be more inclined to negotiate informal cooperative mechanisms. As a matter of fact, the Commission and the European External Action Service (EEAS) seem to have been more successful in negotiating non-binding agreements.[97] However, several of

[91] Jean-Pierre Cassarino, *Unbalanced Reciprocities: Cooperation on Readmission in the Euro-Mediterranean Area* (Middle East Institute 2010).

[92] Annabelle Roig and Thomas Huddleston, 'EC Readmission Agreements: A Re-Evaluation of the Political Impasse' (2007) 9 European Journal of Migration and Law 363, 363.

[93] Cassarino, *Unbalanced Reciprocities* (n 91) 39.

[94] See African Union, Protocol to the Treaty establishing the African Economic Community relating to free movement of persons, right of residence, and right of establishment, Addis Ababa, 29 January 2018.

[95] European Commission, 'Communication on the State of Play of Implementation of the Priority Actions under the European Agenda on Migration', COM(2016) 85 Final, 10 February 2016 17. This gap is sometimes filed by bilateral readmission agreements. For example, Spain has a bilateral readmission agreement with Morocco, where 21% of its returnees come from. Although sometimes contingent on the state of bilateral relations return rates of Moroccan citizens from Spain in the 2010-2020 period rose up to 63% (see Eurostat (n 1)).

[96] Cassarino, 'Readmission Policy in the European Union' (n 32) 25.; ECRE, 'An Offer You Can't Refuse: The External Dimension', Editorial, 20 November 2020, available at <https://www.ecre.org/editorial-an-offer-you-cant-refuse-the-external-dimension/>.

[97] European Court of Auditors, 'EU Readmission Cooperation with Third Countries: Relevant Action Yielded Limited Results', Special Report 17/2021, 13 September 2021 20, available at: <https://www.eca.europa.eu/en/publications?did=59347>.

the above-mentioned problems persist. For example, the negotiation of SOPs on return and readmission with Sub-Saharan countries seems to last as long as negotiations for EURAs and in most cases continues to stagnate as of today. In the specific case of the SOP agreed between the EU and Mali, both parties agreed on the content of the draft SOP in 2016, but this was not subsequently signed and implemented by Mali.[98] In the event that these agreements are reached, cooperation frameworks do not necessarily lead to an increase in deportation numbers, as seen in section 2.1.

According to research on EU migration policy networks (analysing the frequency of discussions among actors involved in the EU migration policy system), countries of origin and transit occupy a marginal position in practice. This study reveals that, despite persistent talks on the need to increase cooperation with third countries, data 'captured very few interactions between representatives of these countries and European actors, and none with the Ministry of Interior or the [European Commission]'.[99] In addition, foreign ministries did not take a leading role in migration issues despite their external dimension, as this remained dominated by the ministries of interior.[100] It is therefore unsurprising (but still unsettling) that EU institutions put forward negotiation mandates with target countries without first ensuring that these are willing to negotiate an agreement.[101] The New Pact on Migration and Asylum reiterates Eurocentric policies that seek to secure the cooperation of 'migration countries' without taking into account those who will necessarily have to implement it, in what Thym described as 'a bill prepared without the waiter'.[102] In fact, the emphasis of the MPF and the New Pact on returns and increased border controls has already been opposed by the African Union, and runs contrary to the negotiations of the Post-Cotonou Partnership Agreement and the Africa–EU Strategy.[103] As seen in section 1.1, the RAMM maintains the underlying ideas of the MPF, and codifies an obligation to 'promote and build tailor-made and mutually beneficial partnerships' into secondary legislation—as if EU law held transformative power over the state of the Union's relations with third countries.

[98] Santos Vara (n 39) 28.

[99] Leila Hadj Abdou and Andrea Pettrachin, 'Exploring the EU's Status Quo Tendency in the Migration Policy Field: A Network-Centred Perspective' (2022) 30(6) Journal of European Public Policy 1, 11.

[100] Ibid.

[101] Peers and others (n 33) 572.

[102] Daniel Thym, 'European Realpolitik: Legislative Uncertainties and Operational Pitfalls of the "New" Pact on Migration and Asylum', *Immigration and Asylum Law and Policy*, 28 September 2020, available at: <http://eumigrationlawblog.eu/european-realpolitik-legislative-uncertainties-und-operational-pitfalls-of-the-new-pact-on-migration-and-asylum/>.

[103] Strikingly, thirteen out of sixteen priority countries in the MPF are in Africa despite their opposition to it. See Tsion Tadesse Abebe and Mbiyozo, 'The New Pact's Focus on Migrant Returns Threatens Africa–EU Partnership' in Sergio Carrera and Andrew Geddes (eds), *The EU Pact on Migration and Asylum in Light of the United Nations Global Compact on Refugees* (European University Institute 2021).

2.3 What next? Implementing readmission in practice

EU readmission agreements and arrangements are primarily considered 'technical' instruments. While they are not believed to create legal obligations for third countries to readmit their own nationals (though they might impose obligations to readmit nationals from other countries), their main purpose is to align political will with the necessary technical and financial resources to do so more efficiently.

However, Member States still face significant challenges in returning irregular migrants, be it within or outside readmission schemes. Indeed, the establishment of cooperation frameworks may or may not improve returns, but it does not automatically make readmission policies immune to diplomatic tensions or the lack of cooperation from third countries. Moreover, assuming that every non-removable migrant can be made removable by deepened cooperation on return on readmission overlooks the role of migrant agency, as well as the fact that migratory flows are to a great extent self-sustaining processes beyond the reach of partner countries. It also ignores intra-EU legal safeguards, the existence of different interpretations of readmission obligations (by the EU and third countries), and the existence of identity determination challenges. These factors are analysed in turn.

2.3.1 In search of cooperation (II)

As noted by the European Court of Auditors, cooperation on readmission can function without a readmission agreement or arrangement in place and, conversely, such readmission schemes do not guarantee smooth cooperation in practice. In short, readmission depends on the commitment and capacity of partner countries. Sometimes, third countries do not formally contest readmission, but they might introduce new layers of requirements, verifications, or permits that hinder it in practice.[104] The day-to-day enforcement of readmission might be hindered by the very same obstacles that the EU and its Member States find in reaching an agreement or arrangement with a given country, as seen in section 2.2. Moreover, in the absence common rules, third countries might have different normative approaches as to their obligations under international law—and to migration control more generally.[105] In this context, it is common that the embassies of the countries of origin refuse to give documents for ethical reasons or when returnees do not wish to return voluntarily. There are, for example, reported cases of migrants from The Gambia and Afghanistan who became non-removable because their embassies in the host countries refused to accept persons who did not express their wish to return voluntarily, particularly when having little social and

[104] European Court of Auditors (n 97) 11, 38 and 40.

[105] On the existence of different approaches to international law and migration, with a focus on Africa, see Thomas Spijkerboer, '"I Wish There Was a Treaty We Could Sign"' in Sergio Carrera and Andrew Geddes (eds), *The EU Pact on Migration and Asylum in Light of the United Nations Global Compact on Refugees* (European University Institute 2021).

family links to their countries of origin.[106] This was also the case of the applicant before the Court of Justice of the EU (CJEU) in *Mahdi*, as the embassy of Sudan did not issue travel documents for the purpose of forced returns.[107] Also, the outright refusal of deportation flights is a reality that EU Member States do face when enforcing returns, often resulting in 'bouncing' removals, whereby migrants are deported and subsequently sent back to the host state.[108]

Although cooperation, particularly in the form of EURAs, may contribute to increased compliance and operability, the gap between the law on the books and the realities encountered on the ground persists. The signing of both EURAs and soft instruments does not guarantee their effective implementation in the long run, as their conclusion is based on unequally perceived benefits by the parties, and their implementation 'is based on a fragile balance between the concrete benefits and costs attached to it'.[109] Unable to resist the imposition of the EU's agenda, and arguably taking advantage of it, third countries may simply agree to engage in cooperative frameworks with the EU or its Member States, take the funding, and subsequently resist the implementation of the objectives that they are in disagreement with.[110] Moreover, a country's willingness to meet the EU's objectives does not necessarily mean that it has the structural capacity to do so. According to Cassarino, the required costs are not only financial, but also stem from the need to undertake deep institutional and legal reforms and, again, from the unpopularity of these in the societies of origin.[111]

With countless examples outside of readmission frameworks, implementation obstacles linked to insufficient cooperation (e.g. consistent delays in replying to readmission requests or supplying the necessary documentation) are also well documented in the context of EURAs.[112] The case of Pakistan is considered particularly problematic, as Member States reported in 2014 (four years after the entry into force of the EURA) that it regularly took more than a year to get a response from Pakistani authorities to readmission requests—in violation of the EU–Pakistan readmission agreement.[113] In practice, this means that by the time that readmission procedures begin, the maximum detention periods for the purpose of removal in

[106] Maaike Vanderbruggen and others, 'Point of No Return: The Futile Detention of Unreturnable Migrants', *Detention Action*, January 2014, 18 and 23, available at: <https://ecre.org/point-of-no-return-the-futile-detention-of-unreturnable-migrants>. For example, in Belgium, only Afghan men used to be deported, whereas women and children were not issued travel documents and simply remained in the country irregularly.

[107] Case C-146/14 PPU, *Bashir Mohamed Ali Mahdi* [2014] EU:C:2014:1320 para 21.

[108] European Commission, 'Communication on Enhancing Cooperation on Return and Readmission' (n 3) 4.

[109] Cassarino, *Unbalanced Reciprocities* (n 91) 5.

[110] ECRE (n 96).

[111] Cassarino, 'Readmission Policy in the European Union' (n 32) 25.

[112] European Migration Network (EMN), 'Good Practices in the Return and Reintegration of Irregular Migrants', 2014, available at: <https://emnbelgium.be/publication/good-practices-return-and-reintegration-irregular-migrants-belgium-and-eu-emn>.

[113] Ibid, 22.

most Member States, and twelve out of the maximum of eighteen months allowed by the Return Directive, are already exhausted.[114] In a few instances, Member States reported that third countries took more than two years to respond to readmission requests in the context of an EURA.[115] In other cases, however, they reported a sharp increase in the collaboration and effectiveness of returns after the conclusion of an EURA—most notably in the case of Georgia (see Figure 4.2).[116]

Once cooperation is secured, however, its smooth functioning remains extremely fragile and dependent on the existence of willingness and capacity at the other end. A case in point is, again, provided by Turkey, with which the EU has both a formal EURA and a hybrid agreement by means of the EU–Turkey statement. In both cases, the vulnerability of these cooperative schemes has become evident in recent years. Concerning the EURA, the Commission complained in 2019 that Turkey readmits its own nationals inconsistently and that, concerning nationals of third countries, it has simply decided not to implement the (legally binding) provisions until the EU lifts the visa requirement for Turkish nationals travelling to the Schengen area on a short-term basis.[117] As of 2024, Turkey has never applied the third-country national clause of the EU–Turkey readmission agreement.[118] As regards the EU–Turkey statement, readmissions under this framework remain suspended since March 2020.[119] This shows how even in the presence of readmission frameworks, cooperation often collapses in the wake of sudden migratory flows or as soon as the diplomatic balance breaks. The volatility of return rates following the conclusion of readmission frameworks can generally be seen in Figures 4.1 and 4.2.

When positive incentives are either not available or insufficient to secure cooperation, the EU has at its disposal a range of punitive measures against non-cooperative countries—or against their nationals. These can range from simple political pressure for the country of origin to accept deportations[120] to different sanctioning measures. Perhaps the most illustrative example of punitive measures in this context is offered by visa sanctions. After the 2019 Visa Code reform, the EU first made use of Article 25(a) in 2021 in order to apply restrictive visa measures to The Gambia, a country that has been particularly uncooperative despite having

[114] Directive 2008/115/EC on common standards and procedures in Member States for returning illegally staying third-country nationals [2008] OJ L348/98 (Return Directive) art 15(6).

[115] European Migration Network (EMN) (n 112) 23.

[116] Ibid, 22.

[117] European Commission, 'Staff Working Document: Turkey 2019 Report Accompanying the 2019 Communication on EU Enlargement Policy', SWD(2019) 220 Final, 29 May 2019 46–47. Turkey maintains this position as of December 2024.

[118] Gamze Ovacık, Meltem Ineli-Ciger and Orçun Ulusoy, 'Taking Stock of the EU-Turkey Statement in 2024' (2024) 26 European Journal of Migration and Law 154, 166.

[119] European Commission, 'Commission Staff Working Document: Türkiye 2023 Report' (n 79) 53.

[120] Statewatch, 'EU to Pile Pressure on Iraq to Cooperate with Deportations', 9 March 2022, available at: <https://www.statewatch.org/news/2022/march/eu-to-pile-pressure-on-iraq-to-cooperate-with-deportations/>.

an informal readmission arrangement with the EU.[121] Similar measures have been adopted against Ethiopia in April 2024 (which also has an informal readmission arrangement in place with the EU), suspending certain visa facilitations, extending processing times, and restricting multiple entry visas and fee waivers for diplomatic passport holders.[122]

However, these sanctions are unlikely to have far-reaching effects on the policies of countries where remittances represent an important part of their GDP and readmission remains deeply unpopular—although return rates in The Gambia did rise to 14% in 2023 (see Figure 4.2). Furthermore, the pre-existing barriers to obtain visas by nationals of these countries diminishes the EU's ability to exert leverage on this issue. Indeed, African countries are already disproportionately targeted by draconian visa conditions, with one in three Schengen visa applications being turned down in 2022.[123] Ultimately, the use of restrictive visa policies might actually contribute to an increased body of (removable and non-removable) irregular migrants who will decide to come and stay in the EU irrespective of the lack of visa prospects, 'illegalizing' people who would otherwise be coming regularly to the EU. It must also be borne in mind that visa sanctions undertaken in the past by individual Member States increased diplomatic tensions and had little to no effect on readmission numbers.[124]

2.3.2 *Identification and documentation of returnees*

The Commission has pointed at the identification of irregular migrants and the issuance of travel documents as the most common obstacles to effective returns.[125] For obvious reasons, establishing people's identity is a precondition for their deportation. To do so, Member States may use diverse methods, including interviews, DNA tests, language analysis, age assessment, fingerprinting, and so on.[126] However, identity determination processes for the purposes of deportation must

[121] Council of the European Union, 'Council adopts visa measures against the Gambia', Press Release, 7 October 2021, available at: <https://www.consilium.europa.eu/en/press/press-releases/2021/10/07/council-adopts-visa-measures-against-the-gambia/>.

[122] Council of the European Union, 'Ethiopia: Council restricts visa provision', Press Release, 29 April 2024, available at: <https://www.consilium.europa.eu/en/press/press-releases/2024/04/29/ethiopia-council-restricts-visa-provision/>.

[123] In fact, Africa accounted for seven out of the ten countries with the highest rejection rates in the EU (see Mehari Taddele Maru, 'Predetermined Bias: Comparing the Visa Rejection Rate of Africans versus the Rest of the World', *Henley Global*, 5 June 2024, available at: <https://www.henleyglobal.com/publications/africa-wealth-report-2024/comparing-visa-rejection-rate-africans-versus-world>).

[124] Jean-Pierre Cassarino and Luisa Marin, 'The New Pact on Migration and Asylum: Turning European Union Territory into a Non-Territory', *EU Law Analysis*, 30 November 2020, available at: <http://eulawanalysis.blogspot.com/2020/11/the-new-pact-on-migration-and-asylum.html>.

[125] European Commission, 'Communication on Enhancing Cooperation on Return and Readmission' (n 3) 9.

[126] For an overview of the different techniques used across Member States, see: European Migration Network (EMN), 'Establishing Identity for International Protection: Challenges and Practices', February 2013, Table 7, available at: <https://emn.ie/publications/establishing-identity-for-international-protection-challenges-and-practices-emn-synthesis-report/>.

not only establish whether the identity of the person is determined (or presumed) for the expelling state, but also be agreed upon by the requested state. Even if there is an obligation under international law for countries to readmit their own nationals, there are no such customary obligations concerning the legal and practical processes to determine who is a national of which country. Although identification processes are deeply technical and complex, they are also contingent on the laws of third countries. This can lead, again, to diplomatic clashes and inter-state frictions.[127] As a result, it is not uncommon for countries of origin to return charter flights when they consider that the identity has not been established adequately according to domestic standards.[128] Again, the legal challenges relating to identity and nationality determination reveal an issue of legal boundaries. Certainly, the nationality determination norms of the countries of origin are not *local* to EU law (as they are not part of EU law), but they are *adopted* by it, in the sense that they are relevant within it.[129] In other words, foreign laws (as interpreted by foreign tribunals), while certainly not an integral part of EU law, become a *sine qua non* for its effective implementation.

Cooperative frameworks on readmission can (and do) help in this process by setting out rules and principles on what amounts to either proof or *prima facie* evidence of nationality.[130] However, practical obstacles concerning identity and nationality determination are also well documented in the context of readmission frameworks. The case of the EURA with Pakistan stands out again due to its low implementation, particularly concerning expulsions from Greece.[131] It is also one of the few EURAs which explicitly outlaws readmission on the basis of *prima facie* evidence.[132] In 2015 Pakistani authorities unilaterally stopped applying the EURA under the grounds that the nationality determination processes carried out by EU Member States were flawed.[133] Later in 2015, and according to Frontex, in a Joint Return Operation from Greece to Pakistan, only nineteen out of forty-five returnees with valid passports or travel documents were allowed to disembark given that Pakistani authorities began to require supplementary biometric checks.[134]

[127] Maria Gregou, 'Drawing the Geographic Boundaries of Expulsion and Readmission in Greece: The Dynamics of an Elusive Process' (2014) 16 European Journal of Migration and Law 505, 524.

[128] For analysis of these obstacles in the context of deportations from Greece to a variety of countries with and without cooperative mechanisms in place, see: Gregou (n 127).

[129] Adam Perry, 'Law's Boundaries' (2020) 26 Legal Theory 103, 115.

[130] For a comparative analysis of the means of proof for the purposes of identity determination, see Carrera (n 6) 32.

[131] Gregou (n 127) 532.

[132] Agreement between the European Community and the Islamic Republic of Pakistan on the readmission of persons residing without authorisation [2010] OJ L 287 art 4.

[133] Carrera (n 6) 17.

[134] Frontex, 'Joint Return Operation from Greece to Pakistan on 02 December 2015', Evaluation Report, 5 February 2016 2, available at: <https://shorturl.at/TTGeI>.

Closely linked to the identity determination challenges is the lack of valid travel documents for removal purposes. To address this obstacle, the EU has adopted a standard European Travel Document which is meant to facilitate its recognition by third countries through the inclusion of enhanced security and technical features (see section 1.2.3). Most EURAs include a presumption of acceptance of the standard travel document if the partner country does not comply with its obligation to produce travel documents after a given period.

Nevertheless, the adoption of the new standard travel document in 2016 was, again, unwelcomed by the African Union which, through its ambassador to the EU, expressed its strong opposition to it and said that the document was 'unheard of in terms of international law and international practice'.[135] The Malian government was particularly outspoken on this issue. After an attempt by French authorities to return two (supposedly) Malian nationals with the EU travel document, Mali sent these people back and questioned their nationality.[136] In addition, the Malian government issued a public statement questioning the validity of the EU document under international law, and clarifying that Mali would under no circumstances accept the repatriation of persons with documents other than a Malian passport or a *laissez-passer* document validly issued by Mali.[137] Beyond the African context, the European Court of Auditors observed that most countries insist on re-documenting their citizens themselves, opposing the issuance of the EU travel documents.[138] These clashes around the EU travel document signal, again, the impulse of the EU and its Member States to solve, by means of EU law, an issue that is by its very nature contingent on external actors for its effective implementation.

2.3.3 *Readmission and statelessness*

Identification and deportation challenges are also common in the case of stateless persons. Although the 2024 Pact on Migration and Asylum includes sporadic references to statelessness,[139] there is no general obligation for Member States to

[135] Statewatch, 'Observatory on the Refugee Crisis in the Med and inside the EU', 24 November 2015 11, available at: <https://www.europeansources.info/record/statewatch-observatory-the-refugee-crisis-in-the-med-and-inside-the-eu-a-humanitarian-emergency/>.

[136] BBC, 'Mali Sends Back Migrants Deported by France', 30 December 2016, available at: <https://www.bbc.com/news/world-africa-38467244>.

[137] Statement available at: <https://www.allincluded.nl/posts/le-mali-appele-compagnies-aeriennes-barrer-acces-aux-personnes-avec-laissez-passer-europeen/refus-lp-ue-mali/>.

[138] European Court of Auditors (n 97) 23.

[139] The Screening Regulation (2024/1356) (art 2(5)), the Asylum Procedures Regulation (2024/1348) (art 3(15)), and the Regulation on Asylum and Migration Management (2024/1351) (art 2(2)) include a definition of a stateless person that mirrors the definition provided by the 1954 Statelessness Convention, as 'a person who is not considered as a national by any State under the operation of its law' (Convention Relating to the Status of Stateless Persons, 28 September 1954, 360 UNTS 117 art 1). The Screening Regulation (art 12(3)) and the Asylum Procedures Regulation (arts 27(2) and 29(4)(a)) also establish that the Member States should take steps to identify whether the persons concerned are stateless, and the Asylum and Migration Management Regulation includes a reference to the need to respect the 1954 Statelessness Convention in Recital 49.

establish statelessness determination procedures.[140] More importantly, the legal consequences upon the determination that a person is stateless are scant, unless a residence permit or additional rights are granted under national law. Although case law from United Nations Treaty Bodies (UNTBs) and the European Court of Human Rights (ECtHR) has, in particularly extreme cases, clarified aspects of children's right to a nationality,[141] as well as the right of some stateless people to obtain a residence permit,[142] statelessness does not generally grant a right to citizenship or residence. In other words, the Member States are, at least in theory, free to deport stateless (and irregular) migrants—although their deportation often proves impossible in practice.

There are reported cases of persons who, despite being recognized as *de jure stateless* by their host Member State, are still considered as irregular (and removable) migrants even where there are no countries willing to readmit them.[143] In the absence of a country of nationality willing to readmit, the stakes of becoming both stateless and non-removable are high.[144] Thus, in the absence of domestic procedures for the determination of statelessness and the granting of citizenship or a residence permit,[145] the lack of a citizenship remains a 'practical' obstacle to deportation, as stateless people do not have a right to remain under EU law. Therefore, their non-removability stems from states' incapacity to find a third country willing to readmit, rather than from migrants' legal right to remain.

In other cases, the impossibility to deport might stem from their *de facto* statelessness or the lack of recognition of the applicant's statelessness by the host Member State. In the UK case of *Pham*, the applicant was a person who had had his British nationality withdrawn due to criminal convictions, and whose readmission under a bilateral Memorandum of Understanding (MoU) was hampered by the fact that Vietnam questioned his Vietnamese nationality.[146] With British authorities unable to deport the applicant, the UK Supreme Court reached the conclusion that Mr Pham was a Vietnamese citizen and that, by denying him citizenship, Vietnam was acting against its own laws—and hence the legal limbo that followed for Mr. Pham was for Vietnam to blame. As a result, the decision to strip

[140] According to the European Network on Statelessness (ENS), only a minority of EU Member States have comprehensive statelessness determination procedures (see European Network on Statelessness, 'Statelessness determination and status', available at: <https://index.statelessness.eu/themes/statelessness-determination-and-status>.

[141] *D.Z. v the Netherlands*, CCPR/C/130/D/2918/2016 (CCPR 20 January 2021).

[142] *Hoti v Croatia*, App No 63311/14 (ECtHR 26 April 2018); *Sudita Keita v Hungary*, App No 42321/15 (ECtHR 12 August 2020). These cases are analysed in Chapter 6 or this book, on regularization.

[143] Maaike Vanderbruggen (n 106) and others, 25–26.

[144] In *D.Z.* (n 141), the UN Human Rights Committee determined that the Netherlands had violated the rights of a stateless child by registering the applicant as 'nationality unknown' and repeatedly threatening him with deportation.

[145] For a comparative overview of domestic policies on statelessness, see the Statelessness Index provided by the European Network on Statelessness (available at <https://index.statelessness.eu/>).

[146] UK Supreme Court, *Pham v Secretary of State for the Home Department* [2015] UKSC 19.

him of British citizenship did not make him *de jure* (but only *de facto*) stateless.[147] Similarly, in *Kadzoev*, the CJEU observed that there was no 'reasonable prospect' of the applicant being readmitted to any third country because Mr Kadzoev was identified as Russian by Bulgarian authorities but not by Russian ones.[148]

These cases reveal the futility of determining a person's nationality for the purposes of expulsion without the acquiescence of the country which will have to sanction it. It also illustrates the failure of UK and Bulgarian courts to reflect on the impact of foreign norms into local legal systems. In addition, they shed light on the situation of some non-removable migrants which, in the context of nationality determination disputes, might become *de facto* stateless, formally holding a nationality (or at least doing so according to the host state), but in practice unable to avail themselves of the protection of that country.[149]

2.3.4 *The role of migrant agency*

Beyond the complex technical processes of identity determination and inter-state disputes, the lack of cooperation of migrants themselves can also frustrate their removal.[150] Their unwillingness to cooperate in expulsion procedures, be it through the destruction of identity documents or by absconding, reveals the role of migrant agency in watering down the effectiveness of states' deportation attempts. In some cases, migrants may cooperate with state authorities as far as the disclosure of their identity is concerned, and yet they might become non-removable simply because they declare that they do not wish to return voluntarily to their countries of origin (see *Mahdi* case in section 2.3.1)—although this alone should be considered as 'lack of cooperation' in an EU law sense (see Chapter 5 section 2(1)(4)(1)). Regardless of the punitive responses of domestic and EU law to these types of behaviour (in terms of access to rights or otherwise—see Chapter 5), individual conducts can indeed play a role in states' failure to expel undocumented migrants.

2.3.5 *The importance of rights*

Lastly, Member States' readmission practices are limited by migrants' rights and safeguards, which stem directly from the application of higher-ranking norms of EU law that require return practices to be 'ineffective'. These 'obstacles' to

[147] This interpretation is questionable if one considers that the UN Statelessness Convention defines a stateless person as one that 'is not considered as a national by any State under the operation of its law'. For an extensive analysis of the case see Carrera (n 5) Chapter 3.2.

[148] Case C-357/09, *Said Shamilovich Kadzoev* [2009] EU:C:2009:741 paras 18, 22, and 67.

[149] On the distinction between *de jure* and *de facto* statelessness, see Sophie Nonnenmacher and Ryszard Cholewinski, 'The Nexus between Statelessness and Migration' in Alice Edwards and Laura van Waas (eds), *Nationality and Statelessness under International Law* (Cambridge University Press 2014). As a matter of fact, and contrary to what was found by British courts, Mr Pham was *de jure* stateless, as the 1954 Statelessness Convention considers stateless 'a person who is not considered as a national by any State under the operation of its law' (see UN General Assembly, Convention on the Reduction of Statelessness, 30 August 1961, 989 UNTS 171 art 1(1)).

[150] Coleman (n 29) 59.

deportation are thus conceptually different since overcoming them would be not just unrealistic but simply illegal. In any event, although it is not the purpose of this chapter to analyse the legal obstacles to deportation (as this was the subject of study in Chapter 2 and Chapter 3), it is worth mentioning their relevance in limiting the operability of readmission.

The implementation of the EU–Turkey statement again offers an illustrative example. The Commission acknowledged that, by March 2020 (when readmissions were suspended), only 2,735 Syrians had been deported under the 1:1 scheme envisaged by the statement, whereas almost 27,000 had been resettled in Europe.[151] The statement's failure to meet its deportation objectives becomes obvious as the 1:1 target resulted in a 1:10 ratio in practice. In this context, the Commission has noted that '[f]urther actions are still required to address the return processes and cooperation and therefore, increase returns'.[152] The Commission however overlooks that the 1:1 mechanism, initially depicted as the centrepiece of the arrangement with Turkey, could never be operable in practice—and for good reason. Returning migrants from the Greek islands immediately in exchange for resettled refugees would have violated the country's *non-refoulement* obligations. Regardless of the well-known flaws of the Greek asylum system, as Walter-Franke puts it, 'Greece was bound to grant access to asylum and remedies to the 400,000 persons who reached its shores since March 2016. Due to lengthy procedures, high protection needs and the situation in Turkey, returns remained limited'.[153] As a result, there is a clear difference between the rhetoric of the statement, which established that '[a]ll new irregular migrants crossing from Turkey into Greek islands as from 20 March 2016 will be returned to Turkey',[154] and its actual implementation, limited by the respect for basic fundamental rights and safeguards, as well as the right to apply for asylum.

Similarly, the JWF and the 'Joint Declaration on cooperation with Afghanistan' foresaw the systematic return of Afghans to a country that was at the time ranked as the least peaceful in the world.[155] On the ground, however, deportation was regularly challenged by domestic courts due to the precarious situation in the country.[156] Similarly, Denmark decided in 2019 that Syria was a safe country to

[151] By January 2024, there were already 40,254 Syrian refugees resettled in the EU (see Ovacık, Ineli-Ciger and Ulusoy (n 118) 162), but readmission was still suspended.

[152] European Commission, 'EU-Turkey Statement Four Years On', March 2020, available at: <https://home-affairs.ec.europa.eu/system/files/2020-03/20200318_managing-migration-eu-turkey-statement-4-years-on_en.pdf>.

[153] Marie Walter-Franke, 'Two Years into the EU–Turkey "Deal": Impact and Challenges of a Turbulent Partnership', *Jacques Delors Institut*, 15 March 2018 3, available at: <https://www.delorscentre.eu/en/publications/detail/publication/two-years-eu-turkey-deal-impact-and-challenges-of-a-turbulent-partnership/>.

[154] European Council, 'EU–Turkey Statement' (n 60) para 1.

[155] See Global Peace index 2020, available at: <https://www.visionofhumanity.org/maps/#/>.

[156] In the German context, see Statewatch, 'Germany: Opposition to Ongoing Deportations to Afghanistan', 11 February 2021, available at: <https://www.statewatch.org/news/2021/february/germany-opposition-to-ongoing-deportations-to-afghanistan/>.

be deported to, but has refrained from forcibly deporting Syrians in practice (or at least before Al-Assad's fall in December 2024). This puts pressure on them to leave by their own means and leaves those remaining in a situation of irregularity and destitution (and often vulnerable to pre-removal detention).[157] In these cases, however, the fact remains that many times states do not officially announce the suspension of deportations, nor offer a residence permit to persons that cannot return to these countries.

3. Why does policy failure matter? Readmission gaps and non-removability

As discussed in Chapter 1, the issue of whether and why migration policies fail has been extensively theorized and analysed both qualitatively and quantitatively, in the EU context and beyond. It is not my purpose to substantially contribute to the extensive literature on whether and why migration policies generally fail; rather, I seek to analyse how EU migration policies 'fail' in a specific subfield (readmission)—or at least do so in relation to their openly stated aims.[158] The incapacity to achieve increased return rates stems from the fact that, in this field, EU laws and policies have not had the capacity to transform the external realities surrounding them. Albeit more efficiency-oriented, these tools have not led to the massive expulsion from the EU that they claim to strive for.

It is not my contention that the EU's policies have not had an impact at all, nor that the EU has not been successful in achieving other (implicit) policy aims in the context of readmission. In fact, it might well be argued that, in the meantime, the EU has established reasonably well-functioning readmission systems with most of the Western Balkan states, has managed to bring some other third countries on board, and has brought readmission issues to the forefront, and that its policies might have helped (or at least tried) to soothe anti-immigration discourses—while undermining fundamental rights protection along the way. Moreover, the numerous, persistent, and well-documented obstacles faced in the context of readmission are surely well known by policy-makers, and it is not my intention to argue otherwise. Precisely because of this, the notion that the development of a common EU agenda and increased legislative activity will deliver immediate and spectacular increases in return rates must be understood as a legal fiction that

[157] France 24, 'Stuck in Limbo, Syrians in Denmark Suffer Unbearable Wait', 3 December 2021, available at: <https://www.france24.com/en/live-news/20211203-stuck-in-limbo-syrians-in-denmark-suffer-unbearable-wait>; Urooba Jamal, 'With Dozens in Limbo, Denmark Pressured to Reverse Refugee Policy', *Al-Jazeera*, 16 November 2021, available at: <https://www.aljazeera.com/news/2021/11/16/rights-groups-pressure-denmark-to-reverse-syria-refugee-policy>.

[158] For a critical discussion of the concept of migration policy 'failure' in this context, see Chapter 1 of this book.

operates at a symbolic level. With increased visibility and tough immigration discourses, the EU sends a message to third countries and might attempt to bring back the appearance of control, masking the lack of capacity of the Union to control the external world through 'hard' or 'comprehensive' internal laws which are 'too obviously challenged by the actual social practices'.[159] Thus, just like the establishment of 'Fortress Europe',[160] the readmission agenda seems to set symbolic or 'ideal' goals in a non-ideal institutional and social context. However, its consequences for migrants are very real.

For those who cannot be deported, often for periods that exceed the maximum period of detention allowed by the Return Directive,[161] non-deportability is followed by a legal vacuum. Unless the reasons preventing removal stem from states' *non-refoulement* obligations or the judicial or administrative review of a return decision,[162] the person concerned will remain in the territory of that Member State without holding a legal claim to do so. In the absence of domestic laws that recognize the legal significance of non-removability as a source of rights (for instance, via *Duldung* status in Austria and Germany),[163] EU law does not recognise non-removability due to practical reasons as a legally relevant fact, and so states are free to consider these people as removable regardless of the length of their presence in the host state. Moreover, EU law compels states to issue return decisions to these migrants regardless of the feasibility of deportation in practice, although return decisions *may* be postponed if a Member State so wishes.[164] These persons are thus *de facto* non-removable, unable (and/or unwilling) to be deported in practice, but incapable to obtain written confirmation of their non-removability, and unable to benefit from the more favourable framework afforded by the Return Directive to *de jure* non-removable migrants—unless Member States voluntarily decide to postpone their removal (see Chapter 5).[165] By implementing an external agenda that bets exclusively on increasing return rates, the EU in fact contributes to the creation of an increased bulk of irregular migrant population that cannot be deported due to the reasons examined in this chapter.

As Geddes and Ruhs argue, the EU is in need of an 'evidence-based realism [that] seeks a better-informed understanding of what individual member states, and the EU as a whole, can and cannot realistically do to "control" migration and

[159] Didier Bigo, 'Frontier Controls in the European Union: Who Is in Control?' in Elspeth Guild and Didier Bigo (eds), *Controlling Frontiers: Free Movement Into and Within Europe* (Ashgate 2005) 76.

[160] In fact, and as seen in Chapter 1, fortification and *non-entrée* policies seem to have materialized to a greater extent than deportation policies.

[161] For an illustration of the Italian case, see Cassarino, *Unbalanced Reciprocities* (n 91) 31.

[162] Return Directive (n 114), Article 9.

[163] See further in Chapter 5.

[164] Return Directive (n 114) art 6. The Return Directive notes that Member States *may* postpone the removal of those who cannot be expelled due to 'technical' reasons. As this chapter has illustrated, the term used by the legislator is not entirely accurate, as the obstacles referred to in this chapter as 'practical' go well beyond those of a purely technical nature.

[165] Ibid, art 14.

achieve certain policy objectives, and over what time frame . . . what are highly problematic, however, are populist proposals and arguments for unrealistic "unicorn" solutions that are simply not available, at least not in the short to medium term'.[166] In this context, the difficulties in regulating migration *ad intra* contrast with the high degree of consensus when it comes to the external dimension of migration. In projecting this appearance of control, it is easier for EU Member States to agree on what other countries should do than on what the EU can do. As seen in this chapter, however, the question remains 'whether and to what extent non-EU countries are willing to play along'.[167]

A first step in this direction is to acknowledge that return and readmission should not be analysed exclusively in light of return rates. In the absence of an assessment of the Return Directive by the Commission since 2014—despite its obligation to do so every three years under Article 19 of the Directive—the European Parliament has shown some promising signs of contestation. In its December 2020 Resolution on the implementation of the Return Directive, the European Parliament noted that 'the Directive allows for and supports effective returns, but . . . most factors impeding effective return are absent in the current discourse, as the effectiveness is mainly stressed and understood as return rate'.[168] The Parliament further stressed that evaluating the effectiveness of the Directive requires 'a qualitative assessment of the sustainability of returns and the reintegration of the returnee, including effective post-return monitoring', as well as an assessment of its compliance with fundamental rights safeguards.[169] In April 2021, the Commission adopted its first strategy on voluntary return and reintegration. For the first time, the Commission hints at an alternative to forced return which seems to better incorporate the interests of third countries and migrants themselves. This is also in line with the Directive's claim that 'voluntary return should be preferred over forced return'.[170] In the words of the Commission:

> To measure the real success of a return policy, it is nevertheless important to not only consider the return rates but also the situation of the individuals concerned, enabling their return in a dignified manner and taking into account their reintegration prospects once they return to their country of origin . . . [V]oluntary return aims to ensure the humane, effective and sustainable return of irregular

[166] Andrew Geddes and Martin Ruhs, 'Reforming Asylum and Migration Policies in Europe: Attitudes, Realism and Values' (2019) RSCAS Policy Papers 3.

[167] Leila Hadj-Abdou, 'From the Migration Crisis to the New Pact on Migration and Asylum: The Status Quo Problem' (2021) BRIDGE Working Paper 11.

[168] European Parliament, 'Report on the Implementation of the Return Directive', 2019/228(INI), 2 December 2020, 7, available at: <https://www.europarl.europa.eu/doceo/document/A-9-2020-0238_EN.html>.

[169] Ibid.

[170] Return Directive (n 114) Recital 10. It must be noted that under the notion of 'voluntary' return, the Directive refers to compulsory (but not forcible) return.

migrants. Voluntary return, which is usually considered more cost-effective than forced return, gives returnees real opportunities and takes into account their needs, expectations and prospects once returned. In the framework of a comprehensive partnership, countries of return would also be more inclined to participate and take ownership of the process when the returns are voluntary.[171]

Although far from a paradigm shift (and still based on a disproportionate focus on return as *the* tool to manage migration), the strategy on voluntary return is very much welcome. Indeed, it is grounded on more sustainable (incorporating reintegration and economic self-sufficiency in the country of origin) but also cheaper return,[172] and it can have greater chances of realistically making third countries cooperate. However, as long as EU-wide regularization is off the table for those who cannot possibly be returned—and with large-scale regularization programmes seemingly off the table—voluntary return alone cannot possibly cover the whole range of circumstances precluding the return of irregular migrants.

4. Conclusions

For more than twenty years now, the EU has sought to communitarize its readmission policy, looking outwards and seeking to develop 'comprehensive' and 'mutually beneficial' partnerships with countries of origin and transit. As a matter of fact, readmission is a task that necessarily needs the involvement of third countries. After analysing the most relevant legal and policy developments in this area, this chapter has sought to analyse the ways in which these policies 'fail' in relation to their stated aims.[173]

As much as the external dimension of migration is projected as an example of 'Realpolitik',[174] readmission is a field in which the alleged goals quite evidently do not correspond with real-life constraints. In short, the emergence of 'practical' non-removable migrants is the direct consequence of an EU legal framework that fails to acknowledge its limited capacity to transform the legal, political, and social

[171] European Commission, 'Communication on the EU Strategy on Voluntary Return and Reintegration', COM(2021) 120 Final, 27 April 2021, 1.

[172] Ibid, 5. According to the Commission, voluntary return, including in-cash and in-kind assistance to the returnee, the flight, and the reintegration package, is still around six times cheaper than forced return. For a more recent evaluation of the strategy, see European Commission, 'Towards an operational strategy for more effective returns', COM(2023) 45 Final, 24 January 2023 3.

[173] The aim of this chapter, due to the scope of the book, has been to elaborate on EU readmission policies. However, similar dynamics, as well as cooperation and diplomatic hurdles can be found when analysing bilateral readmission between individual Member States and third countries (see Jean-Pierre Cassarino, 'Informalising Readmission Agreements in the EU Neighbourhood' (2007) 42 The International Spectator 179 9; Coleman (n 29) 59; Cassarino, *Unbalanced Reciprocities* (n 91) 33).

[174] Thym (n 102); Sandra Lavenex, 'Migration and the EU's New Eastern Border: Between Realism and Liberalism' (2001) 8 Journal of European Public Policy 24.

realities around it. As Sassen noted as early as 1996, the fact that immigration is mistakenly treated as a bounded and closed event does not guarantee state (or in this case EU) insularity.[175] Indeed, migration responds to complex patterns, networks, and postcolonial relations which cannot possibly be erased by EU norms. In this context, despite increased political emphasis and resource expenditure (as well as human rights and rule of law violations), deportation rates are unimpressive.

First, EU laws and policies fail to incorporate the needs of those countries whose cooperation is needed to implement the EU agenda. The correlation between readmission policies and the EU's internal migration agenda and, with it, its ever-increasing detachment from the interests of 'migration countries' make it difficult to persuade them to cooperate. These countries are many times influenced by the unpopularity of readmissions within their electorates, the very high contribution of remittances to their GDP, the problems that deportees may face in integrating upon deportation, the lack of capacity of their labour markets to absorb them, and their desire to establish regional free movement regimes and soften border controls. Most of these issues are structural and unlikely to be deeply affected by the agendas of interior ministries in Europe. Whereas the 'carrot-and-stick approach' might appear fruitful with closer neighbours that hold a deeper and multidimensional relationship with the EU, it too often falls apart when the 'carrots' of EU membership or visa liberalization are off the table. Even when a reasonably well-functioning diplomatic balance is found, this has proved to still be fragile and contingent on inter-state relations and migratory flows.

Second, readmission remains a deeply technical endeavour, making it subject to lengthy identity and nationality determination practices, which are exacerbated in the context of statelessness. These challenges also reveal an issue of legal boundaries, as the countries that will necessarily have to interpret and implement nationality laws do so under distinct legal frameworks and normative outlooks. These obstacles can be worsened by the lack of cooperation of third countries or of migrants themselves, be it within or outside readmission schemes.

Third, return and readmission agendas overlook the importance of rights as a factor that limits states' deportation capacities. While legal barriers to expulsion are covered extensively in Chapters 2 and 3, the impossibility for the EU to live up to its readmission goals due to fundamental rights and legal safeguards cannot be underestimated. The clear failure of the EU–Turkey statement to exchange irregular migrants for resettled refugees under the 1:1 scheme or the legal challenges to the implementation of the EU–Afghanistan arrangement show that, regardless of what is agreed internationally, its eventual clash with norms of a higher hierarchy can render these arrangements limited as deportation tools. More generally,

[175] Saskia Sassen, *Losing Control? Sovereignty in the Age of Globalization* (Columbia University Press 1996) 91.

this evidences that human rights safeguards are not 'obstacles', but rather fundamental norms that require deportation policies to be 'ineffective'.

The lack of realism embedded in the migration policies of the EU (and Western states more generally) has been extensively theorized elsewhere—and provides a valid framework from which to assess EU readmission policies. The aim of this chapter has not been to flesh out new theoretical insights in this regard, but rather to illustrate specific ways in which EU readmission policies fail to live up to their own standards, and to put forward the view that, for migrants, this is a policy failure that matters.

EU law fails to address the reality that readmission is not always feasible, leaving a legal limbo for 'practical' non-removable migrants. In the meantime, states are bound to issue return decisions to irregular migrants, even when enforcement is virtually impossible (unless they voluntarily opt for regularization). Moreover, they are under no obligation to formally postpone removal unless non-removability derives from *non-refoulement* obligations or from the judicial or administrative review of return decisions. In most cases, non-removability comes with a legal void until they again become deportable—if at all. The implications of this, and the disparities in rights afforded to different categories of non-removable migrants, will be examined in Chapter 5.

PART III

THE RIGHTS OF NON-REMOVABLE MIGRANTS AND THE SEARCH FOR A REGULAR STATUS

5
Status Formation and Non-Removable Migrants—A Subtle But Far-Reaching Role for EU Law?

Despite the constant and arguably obsessive focus on return and readmission, this book has shown that the EU not only fails to deliver in relation to its stated aims on returns, but also plays an active role in the manufacturing of non-removability—in spite of non-removability being in itself a challenge to EU legality. This chapter explores the limited yet potentially far-reaching role of EU law in regulating non-removable migrants' status and access to rights, finding that Directive 2008/115 (hereinafter Return Directive or simply RD), as interpreted by the Court of Justice of the EU (CJEU), contributes significantly to the stratification of non-removable migrants into different sub-categories.

The presence of irregular migrants who cannot be deported naturally raises questions about how to deal with their enduring residence in the host Member State. Should they be granted more social rights than other irregular migrants? Can they be subject to pre-removal detention? Can they be criminalized and imprisoned for irregular stay? In other words, does non-removability generate spaces of inclusion over and above the rest of the irregular migrant population? As this chapter shows, it depends.

Section 2 begins with an overview of the EU framework on irregular migration. EU law does not offer non-removable migrants a *sui generis* status nor a route to lawful residence, despite the distinctive nature of their situation (i.e. the violation of domestic conditions of entry, stay, or residence, coupled with an impossibility to return to one's country of origin). As a 'non-category', non-removable migrants fall victim to a 'categorical fetishism' characterized by binary understandings of migrant status,[1] being simply subsumed within the irregular migrant population—and hence targeted by laws and policies of exclusion. But the concept of 'illegality' seems to be used far too often, while in fact hiding many different statuses of legal in-betweenness or 'semi-legality'.[2] Whereas there is consensus that being

[1] Heaven Crawley and Dimitris Skleparis, 'Refugees, Migrants, Neither, Both: Categorical Fetishism and the Politics of Bounding in Europe's "Migration Crisis"' (2018) 44 Journal of Ethnic and Migration Studies 48.

[2] Agnieszka Kubal, 'Conceptualizing Semi-Legality in Migration Research' (2013) 47 Law & Society Review 555, 562; Michael Bommes and Giuseppe Sciortino (eds), 'In Lieu of a Conclusion: Steps towards

When Deportation Fails. Diego Ginés Martín, Oxford University Press. © Diego Ginés Martín 2025.
DOI: 10.1093/9780198941231.003.0005

'irregularized'[3] has a defining impact on the rights and safeguards to which people are entitled in law and in practice, section 1.2 reflects on the various ways in which the inability to return to one's country of origin is acknowledged, nationally and municipally, as a valid source of rights. At times, these approaches challenge binary understandings of migrant irregularity by offering non-removable migrants tailored responses and *ad hoc* statuses with varying degrees of formalization. These practices have been framed in the literature as offering responses to a regulatory vacuum left by EU law. This chapter however contends that Member State practice is directly and indirectly constrained by an EU framework that, via the Return Directive, actively participates in the creation of sub-statuses and spaces of 'semi-legality' for non-removable migrants.

In doing so, section 2.1 zooms in on selected provisions of the Return Directive to analyse the ways in which these specifically target (some) non-removable migrants and grant them additional rights compared to other irregular migrants. By delimiting who comes within the Directive's scope, who has a right to formal postponement of return and the safeguards attached to it, who can be administratively detained, or who can be imprisoned due to irregular residence, EU law frames non-removability as more or less legally 'justified'. This will depend on the reasons precluding deportation and on migrants' actual or perceived behaviour. Based on this, section 2.2 identifies a threefold categorization of non-removable migrants, namely: (1) *de jure* non-removables, whose return is formally postponed following the Return Directive; (2) *de facto* non-removables, whose return is not formally postponed in accordance with the Return Directive; and (3) criminally convicted non-removables, who may fall entirely outside of EU law. This categorization, I argue, unveils a hierarchy of deservingness whereby only those with a more 'valid' reason to remain in the host state before the eyes of EU law will obtain a comparatively favourable framework under both EU and domestic law.

1. Non-removable migrants: A 'non-category' under EU law—domestic and municipal approaches

1.1 The Return Directive and non-removable migrants

In the Return Directive, non-removability is regulated through a rather minimalist set of rules. While the relevant norms are discussed at length in section 2,

a Conceptual Framework for the Study of Irregular Migration' in *Foggy Social Structures: Irregular Migration, European Labour Markets and the Welfare State* (Amsterdam University Press 2011) 217–21.

[3] Marieke van Houte, Zeynep Kaşlı and Arjen Leerkes, 'Introduction: Irregularized Humanitarian Migrants—Policies, Rationales, and the Search for More Durable Solutions' (2023) 36 Journal of Refugee Studies 315.

it is worth mentioning that the impossibility to return irregular migrants is foreseen in Article 9 RD. This provision rules that Member States *shall* postpone the removal of irregular migrants when deportation would result in a violation of Member States' *non-refoulement* obligations (Article 9(1) RD), but that they *may* also do so whenever return is not feasible, in particular if technical reasons preclude states' removal attempts (Article 9(2) RD). For those who do see their return order formally postponed, either directly by Article 9(1) or due to Member States' voluntary use of the *may* clause of Article 9(2), Article 14 RD provides a list of principles to be 'taken into account as far as possible' pending return (these being family unity, emergency health care, education for children, and the protection of the special needs of vulnerable people), as well as a right to written confirmation of their situation.[4]

According to most of the literature, the Return Directive offers little added value insofar as the status of non-removable migrants is concerned, as this is mainly regulated at the national level.[5] Indeed, the Directive provides a very shallow regulation of the situation of non-removable migrants, limited to vague principles which, in any event, fall short of states' already existing international commitments.[6] While acknowledging that the issue is mainly addressed domestically, Queiroz argues that EU law grants an 'atypical' migration status to (presumably all) non-removable migrants. The author considers that, however shallow, their status of 'semi-legality' derives from the intersection of the legal and illegal spheres, since their stay is acknowledged and (formally or informally) tolerated by domestic authorities.[7] On the contrary, I will argue (see section 2) that 'semi-legality' under EU law can be increasingly meaningful but only available for a few, and that EU law is responsible for the stratification of non-removable migrants into different classes.

Be that as it may, the Directive's meagre text as concerns non-removable migrants can be understood as the logical consequence of a framework that is generally exclusionary towards irregular migration (deportable or otherwise). This is built on seemingly fixed legal boundaries and dichotomous understandings of migrant (il)legality. Similar to the migrant/refugee binary, the legal/illegal one must be understood as a legal construct that distorts the complexities of human mobility. Whereas the former is based on a crystal-clear distinction between two groups of people—'needy, yet rare refugees and masses of less vulnerable, less

[4] Directive 2008/115/EC on common standards and procedures in Member States for returning illegally staying third-country nationals [2008] OJ L348/98 (Return Directive) arts 9 and 14.

[5] Fabian Lutz, 'Non-Removable Returnees under Union Law: Status Quo and Possible Developments' (2018) 20 European Journal of Migration and Law 28, 49, and 52; Paul Schoukens and Siemen Buttiens, 'Social Protection of Non-Removable Rejected Asylum-Seekers in the EU: A Legal Assessment' (2017) 19 European Journal of Social Security 313; Izabella Majcher, *The European Union Returns Directive and Its Compatibility with International Human Rights Law: Analysis of Return Decision, Entry Ban, Detention, and Removal* (Brill Nijhoff 2019) 198–228.

[6] Majcher (n 5) 199.

[7] Benedita Menezes Queiroz, 'Non-Removable Migrants in Europe: An Atypical Migration Status?' (2018) 24 European Public Law 29, 291.

needy migrants',[8] in the latter case the Treaty on the Functioning of the European Union (TFEU) distinguishes between legally residing third-country nationals (TCNs), to whom the EU owes 'fair treatment', and irregular migration, which is to be 'combatted' by EU laws and policies.[9]

With EU-wide regularization (a legitimate tool to 'combat' irregular stay) off the table, EU policies have focused on the deterrence of irregular stay by limiting access to rights and criminalizing the employment of irregular migrants, leaving regularization programmes and mechanisms to the Member States[10]—while actively discouraging Member States from implementing large-scale regularization programmes, in particular since 2008.[11] In sum, besides seeking to establish a 'fortress' at its external borders, the EU and its Member States have also undergone a process of internal fortification, not only through deportation, but also by creating exhausting living conditions that make irregular migrants (deportable or not) leave by their own means.[12] This is achieved by limiting access to rights to a bare minimum, or even through the criminalization of irregular stays themselves.[13]

Despite the Commission's timid and unsuccessful attempts to adopt *ad hoc* solutions for non-removable migrants,[14] these are still part of the irregular migrant

[8] Rebecca Hamlin, *Crossing: How We Label and React to People on the Move* (Stanford University Press 2021) 155; Lamis Abdelaaty and Rebecca Hamlin, 'Introduction: The Politics of the Migrant/Refugee Binary' (2022) 20 Journal of Immigrant & Refugee Studies 233. In recent years, it has been a commonplace for EU policy-makers to insist on the need to curve irregular migration as a *sine qua non* to be able to provide refuge to those who *really deserve* international protection (see, for example, European Commission, '2021 State of the Union Address by President von der Leyen', 15 September 2021, available at: <https://state-of-the-union.ec.europa.eu/state-union-2021_en>).

[9] Consolidated version of the Treaty on the Functioning of the European Union (TFEU), [2012] OJ C 326 art 79. This provision, which comprises the legal basis for a common migration policy, reads in its paragraph 1 that 'The Union shall develop a common immigration policy aimed at ensuring, at all stages, the efficient management of migration flows, fair treatment of third-country nationals residing legally in Member States, and the prevention of, and enhanced measures to combat, illegal immigration and trafficking in human beings'.

[10] Regularisation is analysed extensively in Chapter 6. For a comprehensive (albeit somewhat outdated) overview of regularisation practices across the EU, see Martin Baldwin-Edwards and Albert Kraler (eds), *REGINE—Regularisations in Europe* (Amsterdam University Press 2009).

[11] See Council of the European Union, 'European Pact on Immigration and Asylum', 13440/08, 24 September 2008, 7.

[12] On the notion of the 'politics of exhaustion' as a tool of migration governance and control, see Leonie Ansems de Vries and Marta Welander, 'Politics of Exhaustion: Reflecting on an Emerging Concept in the Study of Human Mobility and Control', *Border Criminologies*, 15 January 2021, available at: <https://www.law.ox.ac.uk/research-subject-groups/centre-criminology/centreborder-criminologies/blog/2021/01/politics>.

[13] Nicola Delvino, 'European Union and National Responses to Migrants with Irregular Status: Is the Fortress Slowly Crumbling?' in Sarah Spencer and Anna Triandafyllidou (eds), *Migrants with Irregular Status in Europe: Evolving Conceptual and Policy Challenges* (Springer International Publishing 2020) 73–75.

[14] See among others European Commission, 'DG Home Contact Group "Return Directive" (2008/115/EC): Brainstorming on Best Practices in Relation to "Non-Removable Returnees"', 21 March 2013; European Commission, 'Communication on EU Return Policy', COM(2014) 199 Final, 28 March 2014. On the contrary, none of its most recent Communications, nor the 2018 proposal for a recast Return Directive, nor the 2024 Pact on Migration and Asylum include any reference to the situation of non-removable migrants.

population and are as such targeted by policies of exclusion. As discussed in Chapter 1 (section 2.3), punitive approaches to irregular migration are based on the notion that irregularity is a liminal, temporary state that precedes full exclusion from Europe's territory (via deportation) or formal inclusion (via residence or citizenship), rather than a chronic condition. The existence of non-removable migrants thus runs contrary to the logic of the Return Directive that irregular migrants should be either returned or regularized under Article 6(4) RD (see Chapter 1 section 2). In a way, the legal recognition of non-removable migrants as a category of people with a distinctive legal status and a defined set of rights might have been seen by EU institutions and Member States as a premature acknowledgement that return policies are bound to fail. Non-removable migrants are, after all, a group of people that 'should not exist',[15] as their very existence is a challenge to a legal framework that gravitates around the achievement of increased return rates. This can help explain the legislator's neglect of their status, rendering non-removable migrants a 'non-category' under EU law. In a policy field deeply marked by 'categorical fetishism' and binary categorizations,[16] non-removable migrants are simply subsumed within the irregular migrant population, even though they do not share one of the key attributes of irregularity (i.e. deportability). In other words, non-removable migrants are persons whose distinctiveness is not recognized by EU law as worthy of a *sui generis* migration status,[17] nor of regularization prospects, regardless of the length of residence.[18]

And yet, non-removable migrants do exist, to the extent that Member States' low records on return enforcement are consistently perceived as one of the largest and most structural challenges to the EU's migration policy. Moreover, as seen in Chapters 2, 3, and 4, non-removability often derives, directly or indirectly, from the workings of European laws and policies. As argued in Chapter 4, the Union's overambitious goals in the field of return must be understood to operate at a symbolic level, setting 'ideal' policy aims in a non-ideal institutional and social setting.

[15] Mathilde Heegaard Bausager, Johanne Köpfli Moller, and Solon Ardittis, 'Study on the Situation of Third-Country Nationals Pending Return/Removal in the EU Member States and the Schengen Associated Countries', Ramboll and Eurasylum—European Commission, 11 March 2013, 4, available at: <https://home-affairs.ec.europa.eu/system/files/2020-09/11032013_sudy_report_on_immigration_return-removal_en.pdf>.

[16] Crawley and Skleparis (n 1).

[17] At the domestic level, the *sui generis* nature of non-removability is recognized in some Member States via toleration certificates, most notably *Duldung* in Germany and Austria (see Theresa Schütze, 'The (Non-)Status of "Duldung": Non-Deportability in Germany and the Politics of Limitless Temporariness' (2023) 36 Journal of Refugee Studies 409).

[18] As seen in Chapter 1, the CJEU ruled in *Mahdi* that Member States have no regularization obligations, even when they have exhausted return procedures and there is still no reasonable prospect of removal (Case C-146/14 PPU, *Bashir Mohamed Ali Mahdi* [2014] EU:C:2014:1320 para 89). Moreover, as analysed in Chapter 3, the ECtHR has also been reluctant to grant independent normative value to the passage of time as a tool to regularize migration status or access citizenship (see, among others, Başak Çalı, 'All You Need Is Time? Discrepancies between the European Court of Human Rights Case Law and Liberal Normative Theory on Long-Term Migrants' (2017) 50 Israel Law Review 447).

However, the consequences for those persons who remain irregularly in the EU are very real, as migration statuses are significant 'stratifiers' of rights.[19] Migrants' categorizations as regular or irregular entitle and disentitle them to basic rights and safeguards, and also make their exclusion from society look ethically acceptable to the public.[20] As a result, not being able to access a regular status is hugely significant for the lives of migrants—with empirical evidence even showing significantly higher death rates among irregular migrants resulting from health care exclusion.[21] As Menjívar puts it:

> An undocumented status can affect anything from the immigrants' health risks, their vulnerability in the streets, and their ability to combat domestic violence, to their health-seeking behavior, their chances in the labor market, their wages, and their identities. Indeed, legal statuses create a class of immigrants with rights and privileges distinct from those holding temporary work visas, and it can be said that documented and undocumented immigrants have such different experiences that they can be regarded as two different social classes.[22]

Non-removable persons, as irregular migrants, are no doubt vulnerable to laws and policies of exclusion, as lawful residence and access to rights go hand in hand. The contrast between universalist accounts of fundamental rights and the dilution of their application to irregular migrants (in Europe and beyond) have been analysed extensively and falls beyond the scope of this chapter.[23] In the same vein, existing studies point to the fact that non-removable migrants in Europe often live under deplorable conditions, facing constant threats of detention and deportation, as

[19] Albert Kraler, 'Regularization of Irregular Migrants and Social Policies: Comparative Perspectives' (2019) 17 Journal of Immigrant & Refugee Studies 94, 96.

[20] Gonzalez argues that immigration status, and in particular irregularity, works as a 'master status', ie as the overriding identity marker that shapes almost every aspect of one's life and social interactions (see Roberto G Gonzales, 'Chapter 8. Adulthood: How Immigration Status Becomes a Master Status' in *Lives in Limbo: Undocumented and Coming of Age in America* (University of California Press 2016)). In later work, the author acknowledges that understanding irregularity as 'master status' is compatible with exhibiting further layers of stratification (see Roberto G Gonzales and Edelina M Burciaga, 'Segmented Pathways of Illegality: Reconciling the Coexistence of Master and Auxiliary Statuses in the Experiences of 1.5-Generation Undocumented Young Adults' (2018) 18 Ethnicities 178).

[21] Lorenzo Piccoli and Philippe Wanner, 'The Political Determinants of the Health of Undocumented Immigrants: A Comparative Analysis of Mortality Patterns in Switzerland' (2022) 22 BMC Public Health 804.

[22] Cecilia Menjívar, 'Liminal Legality: Salvadoran and Guatemalan Immigrants' Lives in the United States' (2006) 111 American Journal of Sociology 999, 1000.

[23] See, among others: Marie-Bénédicte Dembour, *When Humans Become Migrants: Study of the European Court of Human Rights with an Inter-American Counterpoint* (Oxford University Press 2015); Colm O'Cinneide, 'The Human Rights of Migrants with Irregular Status: Giving Substance to Aspirations of Universalism' in Sarah Spencer and Anna Triandafyllidou (eds), *Migrants with Irregular Status in Europe: Evolving Conceptual and Policy Challenges* (Springer International Publishing 2020); European Agency for Fundamental Rights (FRA), 'Fundamental Rights of Migrants in an Irregular Situation in the European Union', 21 November 2011, available at: <https://fra.europa.eu/en/publication/2012/fundamental-rights-migrants-irregular-situation-european-union>.

well as difficulties to access basic social rights such as education, health, or housing (let alone work or social benefits).[24]

Is there then, any difference between those migrants who cannot possibly be deported and the rest of the irregular migrant population? As illustrated above, the dichotomy between regular and irregular migrants constitutes a 'hard', 'primary', and seemingly fixed legal boundary that is constitutionalized in Article 79 TFEU. It is also one that shapes media, policy, and, to a certain extent, academic debates. Yet sociologists have for some time reflected on the limitations of 'hard' legal boundaries in defining migrants' statuses and lived experiences. Acknowledging the pervasiveness of 'hard' boundaries, Robertson refers to complex processes of 'status-making' that result from multiple and intersectional forms of classification and categorisation, and are also key to determining migrants' statuses.[25] Similarly, Lydia Morris observes that, while irregular migrants represent the clearest example of exclusion in terms of civic stratification, even within irregular migration there are internal distinctions and further processes of stratification.[26] While being labelled as regular or irregular, migrants are also legally and socially categorized as children or adults, skilled or unskilled, more or less vulnerable, newly arrived, long-term or second generation, and so on.[27]

Moreover, legal and socio-legal scholars have also reflected on the limitations of binary understandings of migration statuses.[28] As noted by Kubal, the notion of illegality has become 'dangerously broad', bringing legally ambiguous situations of 'semi-legality' under the all-encompassing umbrella of irregular migration.[29] Not being able to return to one's country of origin, too, *may* give rise to grey areas and have an impact on the rights to which irregular migrants are entitled in law and in practice.

In this context, however, it remains true that the legal frameworks on the rights of non-removable migrants differ greatly across EU Member States, and hence their 'status-making' processes often take place domestically. The absence of regularization obligations under EU law, as well as states' broad margin of discretion concerning the granting of postponed removal under the optional clause of Article 9(2) RD, have led to highly diverse legal frameworks. As a result, most studies have revolved around domestic and municipal responses to non-removability. Behind

[24] Maaike Vanderbruggen and others, 'Point of No Return: The Futile Detention of Unreturnable Migrants', *Detention Action*, January 2014, 50, available at: <https://ecre.org/point-of-no-return-the-futile-detention-of-unreturnable-migrants>.

[25] Shanthi Robertson, 'Status-Making: Rethinking Migrant Categorization' (2019) 55 Journal of Sociology 219, 220.

[26] Lydia Morris, 'Managing Contradiction: Civic Stratification and Migrants' Rights' (2003) 37 The International Migration Review 74, 89.

[27] Ibid.

[28] The rejection of dichotomous understandings of migration status does not necessarily lead to the rejection of legal boundaries and categories altogether, as part of sociological scholarship seems to suggest. From the perspective of law and legal research, this does not seem feasible nor desirable.

[29] Kubal (n 2) 556.

restrictive narratives, it remains the case that national and municipal policies have to deal with a growing population of irregular migrants whose presence cannot be eradicated in the medium term.[30] Exclusionary discourses therefore hide more nuanced policy practices that necessarily have to tackle (albeit in very diverse ways) the social needs derived from this phenomenon, both for the benefit of migrants and the wider population.[31]

Building on existing literature, section 1.2 will briefly reflect on the plurality of domestic and municipal approaches to non-removability, stressing how these at times challenge binary understandings of migrant (il)legality and recognise the impossibility of deportation, *per se*, as a source of rights. This analysis paves the way for section 2, where I re-direct the focus to the EU framework. Here, I will argue that, contrary to common assumptions that domestic rules emerge in response to an EU law vacuum, these are subtly yet fundamentally shaped by the pre-defined categories of non-removable migrants established under the Return Directive.

1.2 Domestic and local responses to non-removability along the illegality continuum

Whereas in a few EU countries there is no specific legislation recognizing non-removable migrants as such,[32] domestic laws in a majority of Member States do acknowledge that deportation gaps respond to a variety of reasons beyond the control of both the state and migrants themselves. They also recognize that these can lead to prolonged irregular stays and foresee a wide range of sub-statuses with different rights attached.[33]

Even if the stay of the vast majority of non-removable migrants is characterized by socio-economic marginalization and uncertainty over future removal or regularization, Member States do address some of their basic needs. Behind what has been described as an EU 'legal vacuum',[34] Member States adopt a wide range of policy responses that are partially inclusive of non-removable migrants. Albeit in a fragmented way, Member States complement policies aimed at preventing

[30] Delvino, 'European Union and National Responses to Migrants with Irregular Status' (n 13) 74.

[31] Ibid, 93.

[32] According to the European Migration Network, these are Belgium, Cyprus, Greece, Hungary, Italy, Malta, and Portugal. In these countries, all irregular migrants are merely defined by the fact that they do not fulfil the conditions of entry, stay, or residence. See European Migration Network (EMN), 'Responses to Long-term Irregularly Staying Migrants: Practices and Challenges in the EU and Norway', July 2021, 12, available at: <https://www.emnspain.gob.es/en/-/responses-to-long-term-irregular-staying-migrants-practices-and-challenges-in-the-eu-and-norway>.

[33] Ibid, 12.

[34] Jean-Baptiste Farcy, 'Chapter 19. Unremovability under the Return Directive: An Empty Protection?' in Galina Cornelisse and Philippe de Bruycker (eds), *Law and Judicial Dialogue on the Return of Irregular Migrants from the European Union* (Hart 2020) 445.

irregular arrivals and stays with others that address the situation of irregular migrants within the host country. Indeed, ignoring the needs of the irregular migrant population is not only legally, socially and morally questionable, but their complete marginalization also raises concerns of public health, public order, or public security,[35] particularly as regards long-term non-removable persons. This became particularly obvious in the context of Covid-19 due to the importance of ensuring universal access to medical care and to the vaccination campaign,[36] as well as the need to fill labour shortages in essential occupations. In a few Member States, these policy aims were achieved by means of large-scale regularization programmes, a policy taboo among EU countries since the 2008 Pact on Immigration and Asylum.[37] Beyond the exceptional circumstances raised by the Covid-19 pandemic, Member States mitigate their exclusionary approach towards non-removable migrants in diverse ways. Depending on the obstacle halting deportation (be it legal, practical, or policy-based), the behaviour of the returnee, and the legal framework applicable under domestic law, states have developed a 'plethora of temporary and ad hoc statuses',[38] ranging from the non-recognition of non-removability under circumstances equivalent to those of other irregular migrants, to the availability of routes to regularization—ceasing to be included under the category of study of this book.

Several EU-wide studies have attempted to systematize the different legal statuses offered to non-removable migrants under domestic law; that is, to trace domestic processes of legal 'status-making' for those who cannot be removed. In a 2011 report on the rights of migrants in an irregular situation, the EU Agency for Fundamental Rights (FRA) noted that the domestic solutions differed greatly across Member States and could often not be subsumed within the concept of irregularity or full regular status. Based on this, and placing the status of non-removable migrants on an ascending scale, the FRA suggested a fourfold distinction between 'non-recognition of non-removability', 'de facto toleration', 'formal toleration', and 'temporary residence permit'.[39] Moreover, a European Commission study on the situation of TCNs pending return distinguished between 'official postponement or toleration status', 'official or de facto postponement', and 'no postponement and no distinct rights granted' as the most relevant analytical groups to

[35] Delvino, 'European Union and National Responses to Migrants with Irregular Status' (n 13) 75.

[36] For an overview of domestic vaccination campaigns and irregular migrants, see PICUM, 'The COVID-19 Vaccines and Undocumented Migrants: What Are European Countries Doing?' July 2021, available at: <https://picum.org/covid-19-vaccines-undocumented-migrants-europe/>.

[37] PICUM, 'Regularising Undocumented People in Response to the Covid-19 Pandemic', 1 July 2020, available at <https://picum.org/blog/regularising-undocumented-people-in-response-to-the-covid-19-pandemic/>. See Chapter 6 for an in-depth analysis of regularization in the EU.

[38] Noora Lori, 'Statelessness, "In-Between" Statuses, and Precarious Citizenship' in Ayelet Shachar, Rainer Bauböck, Irene Bloemraad, and Maarten Vink (eds), *The Oxford Handbook of Citizenship* (Oxford University Press 2017) 758.

[39] European Union Agency for Fundamental Rights (FRA), 'Fundamental Rights of Migrants in an Irregular Situation in the European Union' (n 23) 34.

study non-removable migrants from a comparative perspective.[40] More recently, the European Migration Network (EMN) produced a report on national responses to long-term irregularly staying migrants, distinguishing between '(1) issuance of a temporary authorisation or permit to stay [including "tolerated stay"];[41] (2) issuance of a certificate or other written confirmation to postpone return or extend the period for voluntary departure, and; (3) *de facto* suspension of return without any certification issued'.[42] Setting aside the first sub-category of non-removable people (which is granted a status that goes beyond EU law obligations), the second and third categories reflect EU law's distinction between (*de jure*) postponed returnees and those whose (*de facto*) non-removability is not recognized, and will therefore be discussed in section 2 in light of the EU framework.

Beyond national frameworks, municipalities—and cities in particular (where most irregular migrants reside in Europe)—have to come to terms with the practical consequences brought about by the presence of a community that is still largely excluded from national provisions on access to rights and public services.[43] In short, municipalities must navigate the everyday reality of migrant exclusion, facing concrete challenges that affect not only the rights of irregular migrants, but also their own policy objectives. Thus, municipalities have to reconcile different (and at times contradictory) goals regarding irregular migration, balancing local priorities with restrictive national and EU policies.[44] It must be borne in mind that the integration of irregular residents helps achieve a number of policy aims, *inter alia* addressing homelessness and the underreporting of crime, child protection and welfare, public health, community cohesion, avoiding exploitation in housing and employment, and so on.[45]

It is therefore at the local level that more specific dilemmas come to the fore and processes of semi-legality become more prevalent.[46] These are, of course, constrained by cities' obligations under EU and domestic law, which are too often intended to frustrate daily life so that irregular migrants self-deport.[47] And yet, cities

[40] Mathilde Heegaard Bausager, Johanne Köpfli Moller, and Solon Ardittis (n 15) 2.

[41] By 'tolerated stay', the study refers to the use of certificates which are specific to non-removable migrants (most notably *Duldung* in Austria and Germany) and go beyond the mere postponement of removal in terms of institutional formalization and access to rights. The widespread use of this certificates in Germany has led some scholars to wonder whether *Duldung* is a 'residence title on its own' even if they are still considered to be irregularly staying (see Jürgen Bast, 'The Legal Position of Migrants—German Report' in Eibe Riedel and Rüdiger Wolfrum (eds), *Recent Trends in German and European Constitutional Law* (Springer 2006) 89).

[42] European Migration Network (EMN) (n 32) 6.

[43] Nicola Delvino, 'European Cities and Migrants with Irregular Status: Municipal Initiatives for the Inclusion of Irregular Migrants in the Provision of Services' (2017) COMPAS—University of Oxford 202.

[44] Ibid, 5.

[45] Nicola Delvino, Sarah Spencer, and Myriam Cherti, 'Migrants with Irregular Status in Europe: Guidance for Municipalities' (2024) C-MISE/COMPAS 23.

[46] Sébastien Chauvin and Blanca Garcés-Mascareñas, 'Contradictions in the Moral Economy of Migrant Irregularity' in Sarah Spencer and Anna Triandafyllidou (eds), *Migrants with Irregular Status in Europe: Evolving Conceptual and Policy Challenges* (Springer International Publishing 2020).

[47] Ibid, 33.

manage to provide access to services such as medical care, education, housing, or legal counselling on regularization prospects.[48] This shows, again, the extent to which migrants' statuses are produced by 'intersecting (and often contesting) legal, discursive and social processes',[49] as well as how black-and-white interpretations of migration statuses can be contested at different levels.

2. Non-removable migrants in the Return Directive: Subcategories and access to rights

As noted by Delvino, the Return Directive is 'at the same time the main foundation at the EU level of Fortress Europe and, paradoxically, also the main recognition of safeguards and protections for irregular migrants in the EU immigration *acquis*',[50] becoming the main instrument to determine the entitlements of irregular migrants under EU law. Concerning non-removable migrants, Recital 12 establishes that the situation of TCNs who cannot be removed 'should be addressed', and that '[t]heir basic conditions of subsistence should be defined according to national legislation'.[51] As this chapter has illustrated so far, this issue is insufficiently regulated at the EU level and largely left to Member States—and it is not my intention to argue otherwise.

It is however my claim that, whereas the Return Directive does not seem to regulate the rights of non-removable migrants extensively, it legally constructs their deservingness and the legitimacy of their claims in specific ways. Beyond dichotomous understandings of (il)legality (although still greatly conditioned by them), I argue that the Return Directive also participates in more informal processes of 'status-making' through law. Based on the typology of obstacles to deportation (as analysed in Chapters 2, 3, and 4) and the behaviour of the returnee, the following sections will show how the Return Directive frames the presence of non-removable migrants as more or less worthy of protection, pre-defining spaces of inclusion and exclusion which are then developed at the domestic level.

[48] Delvino, 'European Union and National Responses to Migrants with Irregular Status' (n 13) 16–35; Delvino, Spencer, and Cherti (n 45). For a concrete example of the contrast between national policies and their local implementation in the context of the Netherlands, see Joanne Van Der Leun, 'Excluding Illegal Migrants in The Netherlands: Between National Policies and Local Implementation' (2006) 29 West European Politics 310.

[49] Robertson (n 25) 225.

[50] Delvino, 'European Union and National Responses to Migrants with Irregular Status' (n 13) 82. However, one can also find scattered references to the rights of some irregular migrants across other instruments of the EU *acquis*. For example, the Employers Sanctions Directive (2009/52/EC) includes, among others, the right to remuneration as well as the facilitation of the issuance of complaints for undocumented migrants engaged in irregular employment. For victims of trafficking, Directive 2004/81/EC foresees further rights including a residence permit for as long as they cooperate with domestic proceedings.

[51] Return Directive (n 4) Recital 12.

2.1 The Return Directive and non-removable migrants: Spaces of inclusion and exclusion

2.1.1 Scope

Article 2 RD defines its scope of application and allows Member States to disapply the Directive to persons who are apprehended and refused entry at border areas and, most importantly for our purposes, to those who 'are subject to return as a criminal law sanction or as a consequence of a criminal law sanction, according to national law, or who are the subject of extradition procedures'.[52] Interestingly, the original proposal was intended to be applicable to all irregular migrants regardless of the reason leading to irregularity.[53] During negotiations, the Commission sought to explain that a difference should be made between the 'ending of legal stay' (determined strictly by domestic law) and the procedures applicable to return once irregular residence has been established (to be regulated by the Directive), but several Member States requested the inclusion of this derogation, which finally made its way into the final version of the Directive.[54]

It appears obvious that the criminal convictions referred to in Article 2(2)(b) cannot derive from the criminalization of irregular stay. As the CJEU held in *El Dridi* and *Achughbabian*, if Member States could place irregular migrants outside of the reach of EU law simply by criminalizing their stay, they would be effectively depriving the Directive of its purpose and binding effect.[55] Still, for those TCNs whose return decision derives from a criminal conviction (unrelated to irregular residence), Member States are free to derogate from the Directive's application. By making use of this provision, Member States can exclude any third-country national from the application of the Directive upon the commission of a criminal offence—no matter the legal status prior to its commission or the level of attachment to the host society.

2.1.2 Postponed removal, safeguards pending return and written notification

For non-removable migrants who fall within the scope of application of the Return Directive, Article 9 makes a distinction between persons whose removal *shall* be formally postponed by the Member States, and those whose removal *may* be postponed 'taking into account the specific circumstances of the individual case'.

[52] Ibid, art 2(2)(b).

[53] European Commission, 'Proposal for a Directive on common standards and procedures in Member States for returning illegally staying third-country nationals', COM(2005) 391 Final, 1 September 2005 art 2.

[54] Fabian Lutz, *The Negotiations on the Return Directive: Comments and Materials* (WLP 2010) 32. The same derogation is maintained in the Commission's 2018 proposal for a recast of the Return Directive.

[55] Case C-329/11, *Alexandre Achughbabian v Préfet du Val-de-Marne* [2011] EU:C:2011:807 para 41; Case C-61/11 PPU, *Hassen El Dridi, alias Karim Souf* [2011] EU:C:2011:268 para 49.

Under Article 9 RD, postponement of removal is only mandatory for as long as suspensory effect is granted during an appeal procedure, and when it would violate the principle of *non-refoulement*.[56] Conversely, states *may* postpone removal for any other reasons, particularly when this cannot be enforced due to 'technical reasons, such as lack of transport capacity, or failure of the removal due to lack of identification'.[57]

This distinction contrasts, again, with the Commission's 2005 proposal, which required Member States to refrain from issuing a return decision when doing so would be at odds with states' fundamental rights obligations (in particular *non-refoulement* and respect for family and private life under the European Convention on Human Rights (ECHR)), and also compelled Member States to formally postpone removal in instances of non-removability due to technical reasons.[58] In fact, the Parliament went as far as proposing a duty for Member States to regularize seriously ill migrants with no appropriate medical treatment in the country of origin.[59] As seen in Chapter 2, these medical cases now largely fall under the non-removal jurisprudence of the European Court of Human Rights (ECtHR), but beyond the reach of subsidiary protection as interpreted by the CJEU.

In the Return Directive's current version, however, the category of 'more deserving' non-removable TCNs is watered down, as it now excludes all the 'practical' as well as legal non-removables if their obstacle to deportation stems from family and/or private life reasons rather than from states' *non-refoulement* obligations. In these cases, the postponement of their removal is regulated by a *may* clause which indicates that there is no more obligation to formally postpone their removal than there is to grant them a residence permit under Article 6(4) RD. These people are thus only *de facto* (and not *de jure*) non-removable until or unless Member States voluntarily choose to formally postpone their removal under Article 9 RD. It is particularly striking that the Return Directive makes no reference to family and/or private life as an obstacle to expulsion, since this allows for the possibility to have a legal right not to be deported while being simultaneously denied the formal postponement of the return decision. The decision made by the legislator to keep these people out of postponed removal is not a trivial formality but can greatly affect their status and access to rights under EU and domestic law, as the following sections show.

[56] Return Directive (n 4) art 9(1). In recent jurisprudence, the CJEU has made clear that, where return would be contrary to the principle of *non-refoulement*, return decisions cannot be issued in the first place (Case C-69/21, *X v Staatssecretaris van Justitie en Veiligheid* [2022] EU:C:2022:913 para 58).

[57] Ibid, art 9(2)(b).

[58] European Commission, 'Proposal for a Directive on Common Standards and Procedures in Member States for Returning Illegally Staying Third-country Nationals' (n 53) arts 6(4) and 8(2)(b).

[59] Lutz, *The Negotiations on the Return Directive* (n 54) 40.

2.1.2.1 Safeguards pending return under Article 14 RD

The Return Directive provides, in its Article 14, for a list of safeguards pending return, yet only for TCNs whose removal has been formally postponed in accordance with Article 9 RD. Again, the Commission had proposed a more favourable framework with rights explicitly inspired by the Reception Conditions Directive (although still more limited than those of asylum seekers and without a right to work).[60] In the end, a 'self-standing' set of safeguards was established,[61] framed as 'principles' to be taken into account 'as far as possible' by Member States, rather than as enforceable rights.[62] In short, these include family unity, emergency health care and essential treatment of illness, access to education for children, and the need to respect the special needs of vulnerable persons.[63]

Article 14 RD safeguards seem to merely reflect (and as a matter of fact fall short of) states' already existing obligations under international and European human rights law.[64] Indeed, prior to the adoption of the Return Directive, emergency health care or basic education for children were not offered by Member States on the basis of charity, but to abide by their international obligations.[65] And yet, more than a decade after the adoption of the Return Directive, its Article 14 has proved a useful tool to defend the rights of (some) undocumented migrants.

First, because, despite the letter of the Directive referring to these safeguards as 'principles' to be 'taken into account as far as possible', the CJEU has interpreted them as imposing specific duties on the Member States. In *Abdida*, the CJEU referred to '[t]he *requirement* to provide emergency health care and essential treatment of illness under Article 14(1)(b) of Directive 2008/115' (emphasis added).[66] Moreover, the Court interpreted the provision in light of Recital 12 RD to argue that the right to health care would be rendered meaningless 'if there were not also a concomitant requirement to make provision for the basic needs of the third country national concerned'.[67] Whatever the term 'basic needs' actually means, the CJEU seems to make clear that the right to health care in the Return Directive is not a mere guideline but a concrete right that has to be supplemented by addressing the 'basic needs' of the person concerned—developing what Peers labelled at the time of the ruling as an 'alternative protection' under the Return Directive.[68]

[60] European Commission, 'Proposal for a Directive on Common Standards and Procedures in Member States for Returning Illegally Staying Third-country Nationals' (n 53) art 13(1).

[61] Lutz, *The Negotiations on the Return Directive* (n 54) 64.

[62] Return Directive (n 4) art 14(1).

[63] Ibid.

[64] Majcher (n 5) 199; European Union Agency for Fundamental Rights (FRA), 'Fundamental Rights of Migrants in an Irregular Situation in the European Union' (n 23) 29.

[65] Majcher (n 5) 199.

[66] Case C-562/13, *Centre public d'action sociale d'Ottignies-Louvain-la-Neuve v Moussa Abdida* [2014] EU:C:2014:2453 para 60.

[67] Ibid.

[68] Steve Peers, 'Could EU Law Save Paddington Bear? The CJEU Develops a New Type of Protection', *EU Law Analysis*, 21 December 2014, available at: <http://eulawanalysis.blogspot.com/2014/12/could-eu-law-save-paddington-bear-cjeu.htm>.

This rationale has been interpreted by scholars and the European Commission to extend to all the paragraphs of Article 14(1) RD, which are to be understood as enforceable rights that also give rise to a concomitant obligation to provide for the basic needs of postponed returnees.[69] In addition, the Commission's Return Handbook (intended to be the Directive's basic interpretative instrument) clarified that the right to emergency health care is a basic minimum right and that, for those with postponed removal, it must not be made dependent on the payment of fees.[70] As regards the right to education, the Return Handbook states that the conditions to exercise this right must be drawn from the asylum *acquis*, in particular Article 14 of the Reception Conditions Directive.[71] Therefore, with the passage of time and thanks to CJEU jurisprudence, Article 14 RD safeguards have shifted from guidelines to concrete and enforceable rights under EU law—and therefore subject to judicial review by the CJEU. Nonetheless, these rights are reserved to those persons who have a 'better' reason for not being deported under Article 9(1) RD (or whose removal has been facultatively postponed by Member States under Article 9(2)).

Second, the distinction between *de jure* and *de facto* non-removable persons found in the Return Directive not only gives autonomous rights under EU law to some undocumented migrants over others, but also sends the message that non-removable returnees become more or less worthy of protection depending on whether they have a better or worse justification for non-removal under Article 9 RD. While it might be argued that the shallow rights granted under Article 14 RD are insufficient, create little added value, and can thus hardly be understood as creating a more privileged category of irregular migrants, the notion of formally postponed (*de jure*) as opposed to non-postponed (*de facto*) returnees has permeated into domestic laws. Whereas nothing impedes Member States from applying these safeguards strictly, research conducted by the EMN in 2021 shows that obtaining a formal postponement of removal in line with Article 9 RD positively affects access to fundamental rights within and beyond Article 14 RD—although these are still kept well below those provided to regular migrants and are often discretionary and difficult to access.[72] In deciding who comes to qualify as a 'postponed returnee', Member States apply the *may* clause of Article 9 RD differently. In around half

[69] European Commission, 'Recommendation (EU) 2017/2338 of 16 November 2017 Establishing a Common "Return Handbook" to Be Used by Member States' Competent Authorities When Carrying out Return-Related Tasks' [2017] OJ L 339 (Return Handbook) 64; Majcher (n 5) 207; Lutz, 'Non-removable Returnees under Union Law' (n 5) 32. In his Opinion in *Abdida*, AG Bot argued that all the mentioned safeguards were 'guaranteed' by Article 14 RD, and went as far as claiming that this provision, interpreted in light of Recital 12, included an obligation for the state to secure accommodation taking into account the special needs of the applicant (see Opinion of AG Bot in *Abdida* (n 66) paras 128 and 157).

[70] Return Handbook (n 69) 64.

[71] Ibid. This provision establishes that 'Member States shall grant to minor children of applicants and to applicants who are minors access to the education system under similar conditions as their own nationals for so long as an expulsion measure against them or their parents is not actually enforced'.

[72] European Migration Network (EMN) (n 32) 5.

of the Member States, postponement of removal is offered, also, to persons who cannot be removed due to practical reasons,[73] while others make a distinction between 'practical' and 'legal' non-removables,[74] postponing return decisions for the latter category only.

Whatever their use of Article 9 RD might be, in an overwhelming majority of EU Member States irregular migrants whose return is not postponed in accordance with Article 9 RD generally access the same rights and services as undocumented migrants whose presence is unknown to the authorities (i.e. compulsory education and emergency health care as stemming from international human rights standards) and face greater challenges in accessing the rights and services to which they are entitled.[75] On the contrary, the postponement of removal in accordance with the Return Directive usually comes with greater rights attached. For instance, access to emergency and basic health care is made available for postponed returnees in every Member State, with the exception of Bulgaria and Slovenia (which only grant emergency health care). Compulsory education is granted to postponed returnees on a mandatory basis and in equal conditions with regular residents and nationals in all Member States except Bulgaria. Moreover, ten Member States additionally foresee educational and professional programmes for adults.[76] Beyond the rights covered under Article 14 RD, Member States frequently offer additional rights to postponed returnees which are unavailable for *de facto* non-removables. For example, accommodation (thirteen Member States) and social assistance (fourteen Member States) are often granted, although to a lesser extent than for lawful residents and many times on a discretionary basis. Moreover, access to legal services is generally granted on a more favourable manner than for *de facto* non-removables.[77]

2.1.2.2 Written notification

The possession of written notification is a key tool for non-removable migrants to show (e.g. in case of a police control) that their removal has been formally postponed or cannot be enforced.[78] This is the case not only for formally postponed returnees to be able to prove their status and have access to the rights they are entitled to under EU or domestic law (see section 2.1.2.1), but also for every non-deportable person to avoid futile pre-removal detention (or re-detention) (see section 2.1.4).

[73] Ibid, 13. These are Austria, Belgium, Bulgaria, Cyprus, Germany, Estonia, Greece, Spain, Finland, France, Croatia, Luxembourg, Latvia, Malta, Slovenia, and Slovakia.

[74] Ibid. These are Cyprus, Czech Republic, Hungary, Ireland, Italy, Lithuania, Latvia, the Netherlands, Portugal, Poland, and Sweden.

[75] Ibid, 7 and 19.

[76] Ibid, 20–21.

[77] Ibid.

[78] Lutz, 'Non-Removable Returnees under Union Law' (n 5) 35.

With that in mind, we can find, again, a position of relative privilege for *de jure* non-removable migrants. While the Return Directive's Preamble establishes that 'third-country nationals who are staying illegally but who cannot yet be removed' (i.e. all non-removable migrants) should be provided with a written notification so that they can demonstrate their situation in the event of police or administrative checks, it is certainly worrying that this right only arises in the operative part of the Directive for *de jure* non-removable migrants.[79] Article 14(2) RD establishes that Member States *shall* provide non-removable migrants with a written confirmation of their decision, but this obligation arises only in the context of a formally postponed return decision under the circumstances foreseen in Article 9 RD.

In *Mahdi*, the CJEU interpreted the Return Directive as including a right to written notification for irregular migrants who have exhausted the maximum period of pre-removal detention and upon whom there is no reasonable prospect of removal.[80] However, the right of other irregular migrants whose return cannot be enforced to such written notification remains unclear. As Peers puts it, 'the Court was not asked as such in *Mahdi* whether two such categories exist, and so perhaps was not intending to create such a distinction. But it ought to clarify in future that there are not two such categories.'[81] In the meantime, many Member States undertake a restrictive interpretation of the Return Directive according to which only the formal postponement of return decisions gives rise to written certification of non-removal. In around half of EU Member States, 'practical' non-removables (particularly those deemed uncooperative) have their return decision informally suspended and are not issued any written confirmation of their status.[82]

2.1.3 A right to work?

It goes without saying that the Return Directive does not include a right to work for irregular migrants. Quite the opposite: EU law is built to dissuade employers from recruiting irregular migrants through Directive 2009/52 (Employers Sanctions Directive or simply ESD). This Directive not only mandates that Member States impose sanctions on employers who recruit irregular migrants, but also establishes (as an inevitable consequence of the above) a general ban on their employment.[83]

[79] Return Directive (n 4) Recital 12. On the ambiguous role and the (lack of) legal bindingness of recitals under EU law, see Case C-136/04, *Deutsches Milch-Kontor v Hauptzollamt Hamburg-Jonas* [2005] EU:C:2005:716 para 32; Case C-134/08, *Hauptzollamt Bremen v J. E. Tyson Parketthandel* [2009] EU:C:2009:229 paras 16 and 19.

[80] *Mahdi* (n 18) para 89.

[81] Steve Peers, *EU Justice and Home Affairs Law: Volume I: EU Immigration and Asylum Law* (4th edn, Oxford University Press 2016) 516.

[82] European Migration Network (EMN) (n 32) 14. For example, in the Netherlands, written notification outside Article 9(1) RD cases is only granted due to medical reasons or when authorities qualify the person as 'cooperative'.

[83] Directive 2009/52/EC providing for minimum standards on sanctions and measures against employers of illegally staying third-country nationals [2009] OJ L 168 (Employers Sanctions Directive) art 3.

However, according to Article 3(3) ESD, Member States *may* decide not to apply such prohibition to irregular migrants 'whose removal has been postponed and who are allowed to work in accordance with national law'.[84] While the Employers Sanctions Directive does not make an explicit reference to the Return Directive (adopted six months before), this provision appears to be a veiled reference to it, meaning that only those who have their return postponed under Article 9 RD can be granted a right to work under domestic legislation. A more generous interpretation of Article 3(3) would alternatively mean that any return decision that cannot (*de jure* or *de facto*) be enforced for any reasons would trigger the possibility for Member States to authorize the employment of non-removable migrants.[85]

In practice, Member States have undertaken a rather strict interpretation of undocumented migrants' right to work whereby it is very limited and generally reserved to those with 'tolerated stay'—namely postponed returnees with a distinctive (and more formalized) status as non-removable persons.[86] The right to work for the rest of the body of postponed returnees (with no 'tolerated stay') is only available in Bulgaria and Luxembourg, whereas non-removables with no formal postponement of removal do not enjoy a right to work in any Member State.[87] Even though state practice shows that the derogation of Article 3(3) ESD is rarely used in practice, it is again very revealing that one of the very rare exceptions to the prohibition of employment of irregular migrants in the EU *acquis* seems to be precisely applicable to postponed returnees, stressing again their relative worthiness *vis-à-vis* other irregular migrants.

2.1.4 Detention, cooperation obligations, and criminalization

2.1.4.1 Pre-removal detention: Article 15 RD

The Return Directive provides, if certain conditions are met, for a maximum period of administrative detention of up to eighteen months, which must have the sole aim of preparing removal. The prolonged periods of detention foreseen were one of the most criticized elements of the Directive, labelled at the time of its adoption as a 'Directive of shame'.[88] As it has been pointed out in the literature, however, the legal developments that have followed since its adoption suggest that Member States have significantly reduced the use of pre-removal detention,[89] shifting the

[84] Ibid, art 3(3).

[85] Peers, *EU Justice and Home Affairs Law* (n 81) 515.

[86] Even if the conditions of 'tolerated stay' are more beneficial than those of postponed return, their residence is considered irregular and therefore their right to work under national law stems from Article 3(3) of the Employers Sanctions Directive (as it would otherwise be contrary to EU law).

[87] European Migration Network (EMN) (n 32) 21.

[88] Diego Acosta Arcarazo, 'The Good, the Bad and the Ugly in EU Migration Law: Is the European Parliament Becoming Bad and Ugly? (The Adoption of Directive 2008/15: The Returns Directive)' (2009) 11 European Journal of Migration and Law 19; Lutz, *The Negotiations on the Return Directive* (n 54) 73–80.

[89] Delvino, 'European Union and National Responses to Migrants with Irregular Status' (n 13) 84.

Return Directive into a 'positive normative example for legal orders around the globe' thanks to judicial dialogue between European and domestic courts.[90] Be that as it may, this section seeks to unravel how the EU framework on detention applies to non-removable migrants and identify which categories within this group are more likely to be targeted by pre-removal detention.

First of all, the Return Directive requires the existence of a 'reasonable prospect of removal' for pre-removal detention to take place.[91] This is nothing but the logical consequence of a detention system whose sole objective is to prepare deportation if other less coercive means are not available.[92] This provision is (or should be) a key safeguard for non-removable migrants because, as soon as a person is deemed non-removable, detention ceases to be legally justified.[93] As a result, pre-removal detention must not be applied to meet public order, public policy, or public security concerns,[94] although it is worrying that the Commission's proposal for a recast Return Directive envisages such possibility of 'light imprisonment' in its proposed Article 18(1)(c), even if this should arguably be addressed by means of criminal law only.[95] Such amendments would in practice increase the likelihood of non-removable migrants being administratively detained on public order grounds despite there being no evidence of a reasonable prospect of removal.

So far, however, it remains the case that all irregular migrants have a right not to be detained if there is no 'reasonable prospect of removal' and, in any case, after the maximum period of pre-removal detention envisaged under domestic legislation (up to a maximum of eighteen months). In *Kadzoev*, concerning a stateless non-removable migrant, the CJEU clarified that, when the maximum period of detention has been reached, the question of whether there is a reasonable prospect of

[90] Galina Cornelisse and Madalina Moraru, 'Judicial Dialogue about the Return Directive: Which Role for Courts in an Era of Executive Governance?' *EU Immigration and Asylum Law and Policy*, 1 September 2020, available at: <https://eumigrationlawblog.eu/judicial-dialogue-about-the-return-directive-which-role-for-courts-in-an-era-of-executive-governance/>. Nevertheless, the proposed recast of the Directive proposes an enhanced use of pre-removal detention, and includes a wider definition of 'risk of absconding' that, according to the European Parliament would affect at least 60% of migrants with return orders, who would subsequently become more likely to be administratively detained (see European Parliament, 'The Proposed Return Directive (Recast): Substitute Impact Assessment', PE 631.727, 12 February 2019 9, available at: <https://www.europarl.europa.eu/thinktank/en/document/EPRS_STU(2019)631727>).

[91] Return Directive (n 4) art 15(4). The CJEU has confirmed that the lawfulness of detention must be reviewed *ex officio* (see Joined cases C-704/20 and C-39/21, *Staatssecretaris van Justitie en Veiligheid v C, B, and X* [2022] EU:C:2022:858 para 83).

[92] Ibid, art 15(1). The Commission's proposal for a recast Return Directive however deletes the word 'only' from paragraph 1 of Article 18 (currently 15), opening the door to pre-removal detention for reasons other than executing removal (in itself an oxymoron and potentially contrary to the jurisprudence of the ECtHR which requires a 'realistic prospect of removal'—see section 2.2.3).

[93] Lutz, 'Non-Removable Returnees under Union Law' (n 5) 37.

[94] Case C-357/09, *Said Shamilovich Kadzoev* [2009] EU:C:2009:741 para 70; Return Handbook (n 69) 67.

[95] European Union Agency For Fundamental Rights (FRA), 'The Recast Return Directive and Its Fundamental Rights Implications', 10 January 2019, available at: <https://fra.europa.eu/en/publication/2019/recast-return-directive-and-its-fundamental-rights-implications>.

removal no longer arises and the person must be released immediately.[96] Although there is evidence that the maximum detention periods are often not respected in practice,[97] every irregular migrant for whom there is no reasonable prospect of successful removal (considering the maximum detention periods) should be free from detention.[98] Yet, in the field of detention, we can find again a distinction between *de jure* and *de facto* non-removable migrants.

This is first because those in the first category hold written certification that allows them to better prove the absence of a reasonable prospect of removal before police or administrative authorities. For the rest, it certainly becomes more difficult unless the state legally recognizes its inability to deport by means of a formal postponement of removal. In fact, in the absence of documentation that substantiates the lack of a reasonable prospect of removal,[99] detention and re-detention of non-removable migrants notwithstanding the unfeasibility of their deportation is well documented in practice.[100]

Moreover, 'practical' non-removables become the targets of detention under Article 15(6)(b) RD, which foresees the existence of 'delays in obtaining the necessary documentation from third countries' as one of the two valid reasons to prolong detention for an additional twelve months (up to the maximum of eighteen).[101] While the European Parliament rightly suggested that such extension should be applied only when the delays could be attributed to returnees and not to other reasons beyond their reach,[102] the final text did not incorporate this amendment. As the Return Directive stands, it seems that the 'practical' non-removables (or at least some of them) are under EU law more vulnerable to detention regardless of their cooperation during return processes, as the very reason precluding their removal conforms states' legal basis for lengthier detention.

[96] *Kadzoev* (n 94) para 60. This was confirmed in *Országos* (see Case C-924/19 PPU, *Országos* [2020] EU:C:2020:367 para 281).

[97] European Parliament, 'Prolongation of Detention by Member States of Illegally Staying Third-Country Nationals Beyond the 18-month Time Limit in Violation of the Return Directive', Debate 2014/2701 RSP, 17 April 2014, available at: <https://www.europarl.europa.eu/doceo/document/PV-7-2014-04-17_EN.pdf?redirect>.

[98] Whereas the CJEU has not made this point explicit (because in *Kadzoev* the maximum period of detention under domestic law was the same as that provided by EU law), the Commission has interpreted that the maximum period of detention to be considered with views to establishing a 'reasonable prospect of removal' is the one provided for in domestic law (Return Handbook (n 69) 72).

[99] In the case of persons whose non-removal derives from family and/or private life considerations, even if their return is not always formally postponed, the administrative or judicial decision halting their removal should suffice to prove that deportation is not feasible. It is therefore reasonable to assume that, since their obstacle to removal is one of a legal nature, they are less vulnerable to pre-removal detention.

[100] Maaike Vanderbruggen and others (n 24) 50–61.

[101] Return Directive (n 4) art 15(6)(b). The CJEU has however interpreted this provision narrowly and made clear that the lack of identity documents is not in itself a valid reason to justify prolonged detention (see *Mahdi* (n 18) para 68).

[102] Lutz, *The Negotiations on the Return Directive* (n 54) 68.

A further distinction made by the legislator in Article 15 RD is the one between cooperative and uncooperative migrants. In addition to the delays in obtaining documentation from third countries, Member States may extend pre-removal detention if (and only if) persons do not cooperate.[103] This provision is the Return Directive's only reference to cooperation in return proceedings. The concept of (lack of) cooperation is however a contentious and easily malleable one, and so the CJEU has attempted to clarify its content. In *Mahdi*, a Sudanese national who had initially agreed to his deportation subsequently stated that he did not wish to return voluntarily. As a result, the Embassy of Sudan refused to issue the necessary travel documents for readmission, as the country only supported voluntary returns. Asked about whether the conduct of the applicant could be categorized as a lack of cooperation within the meaning of Article 15(6)(a) RD, the CJEU noted that it was for the host Member State to determine 'whether the lack of identity documents can be attributed solely to the fact that Mr Mahdi withdrew the statement concerning his voluntary return',[104] and that the authorities of the host country needed to demonstrate that it was likely that the return proceedings would last longer because of the conduct of the person concerned.[105] The CJEU further explained that '[i]f the removal of the third-country national is taking, or has taken, longer than anticipated for another reason, no causal link may be established between the latter's conduct and the duration of the operation in question and therefore no lack of cooperation on his part can be established'.[106] In short, the CJEU made clear in *Mahdi* that for Member States to categorize an irregular migrant as non-cooperative for the purposes of prolonged detention, they must prove the existence of a causal link between the attitude of the person concerned and the return's procedure duration.

2.1.4.2 An obligation to cooperate under EU law? Criminalization practices

At the domestic level, the cooperation of migrants in their return proceedings is often a *sine qua non* for accessing rights pending removal. Those who are deemed uncooperative struggle to see their rights recognized, and the lack of cooperation is many times used by Member States as a reason to not postpone removal and to deny written notification pending removal.[107]

At the EU level, the notion of a 'duty to cooperate' in return proceedings seems to be slowly crystallizing into EU law. The Commission's proposal for a recast Return Directive introduces an abstract 'obligation to cooperate' in its Article 7, accompanied by a non-exhaustive list of what this entails for the returnee. According to the European Parliament, this 'codifies an obligation that was already implicit

[103] Return Directive (n 4) art 15(6)(a).
[104] *Mahdi* (n 18) paras 77 and 80.
[105] Ibid, para 82.
[106] Ibid.
[107] European Migration Network (EMN) (n 32) 14.

in the current Return Directive'.[108] However, the proposed provision is not clear on the consequences attached to the lack of cooperation (other than the exclusion from voluntary return programmes), and it does not grant any positive incentives to cooperation, arguably making it difficult to obtain returnee collaboration in practice.

Under the current framework, returnee cooperation has been addressed by the CJEU in the context of states' criminalization practices. For decades, states have been attaching criminal sanctions for irregular stays,[109] to the extent that, by 2014, the FRA reported that in almost all Member States irregular entry and stay were criminal offences, many times punished with custodial sentences.[110] However, the criminalization of irregular stay, particularly by means of imprisonment, has been contested by national judges before the CJEU, greatly limiting states' 'crimmigration' powers in the widely analysed cases of *El Dridi* and *Achughbabian*.[111]

In *El Dridi*, concerning an applicant who had been sentenced to prison for staying irregularly without 'valid grounds' and contrary to a removal order issued against him, the CJEU was asked whether a sentence of imprisonment could be imposed on an irregular migrant 'on the sole ground that he remains, without valid grounds, on the territory of that state, contrary to an order to leave that territory within a given period'.[112] The CJEU noted that while Member States are free to adopt criminal law measures to dissuade TCNs from staying irregularly in their territory, they must not do so in a way that undermines the effectiveness of the Return Directive (i.e. expelling irregular migrants). As a result, the CJEU ruled that Member States cannot issue custodial sentences solely on the basis of irregular stay, as this is likely to delay in practice the enforcement of return decisions, thereby frustrating the main goal pursued by the Return Directive.[113] However, the CJEU further established that this does not limit Member States' capacity to regulate, via criminal law, 'the situation in which coercive measures have not resulted in the removal of a third-country national staying illegally on their territory'.[114] This point was further clarified in *Achughbabian*, under similar circumstances—namely an undocumented migrant sentenced to imprisonment for irregular stay. In this case,

[108] European Parliament, 'The Proposed Return Directive (Recast)' (n 90) 61.

[109] Joanna Parkin, 'The Criminalisation of Migration in Europe: A State-of-the-Art of the Academic Literature and Research' (2013) CEPS Papers in Liberty and Security in Europe.

[110] European Union Agency for Fundamental Rights (FRA), 'Criminalisation of Migrants in an Irregular Situation and of Persons Engaging with Them', 27 March 2014 3, available at: <https://fra.europa.eu/en/publication/2014/criminalisation-migrants-irregular-situation-and-persons-engaging-them>.

[111] On the protective nature of these rulings, see Valsamis Mitsilegas, *The Criminalisation of Migration in Europe: Challenges for Human Rights and the Rule of Law* (Springer 2015) 109–10.

[112] *El Dridi* (n 55) para 29.

[113] Ibid, paras 52, 55, and 59. This view has been confirmed in *Affum* (Case C-47/15, *Sélina Affum v Préfet du Pas-de-Calais* [2016] EU:C:2016:408).

[114] *El Dridi* (n 55) para 60.

the CJEU left the door open to prison sentences being imposed 'on third-country nationals to whom the return procedure . . . has been applied and who are illegally staying in the territory of a Member State without there being any *justified ground for non-return*' (emphasis added).[115]

In these rulings, the CJEU limits states' imprisonment practices to those irregular migrants who have exhausted their return proceedings and who are considered to have a 'non-justified' ground for non-return. This *residual* category of non-removable migrants is referred to by Gosme as 'non-cooperative exhausted returnees'.[116] Indeed, Member States have to exhaust domestic return proceedings (reaching the maximum period of administrative detention) and establish that persons do not have a 'justified reason' for not returning to their countries of origin or transit before resorting to imprisonment due to irregular stay. In determining what a 'justified' ground for non-return is, the concept of cooperation again comes to the fore. According to the Commission's Return Handbook, 'justified' reasons for non-removal are those which are either 'outside of the scope of influence of the returnee' or 'are recognised as legitimate or justified by Union or national law'.[117] Here, the CJEU seems to offer greater protection to legal non-removables. This protects those with compulsory postponed return under Article 9 RD (due to *non-refoulement*), but also those who cannot be returned under private and/or family life considerations, as they too have a legitimate reason (under Article 8 ECHR—i.e. Article 7 of the EU Charter of Fundamental Rights) not to be returned regardless of their access to postponed removal. Those who are non-removable due to practical reasons and are categorized as uncooperative will on the contrary form the least deserving category among non-removable migrants and the only possible targets of imprisonment under the Return Directive.

2.2 EU law categories

As highlighted in section 1, the situation of non-removable migrants has been described as an 'atypical status' between legality and illegality. While this seems to be true for a number of them, others remain untouched by the Return Directive's processes of protection and inclusion. The present section identifies a threefold categorization of non-removable migrants under EU law, out of which only one can be said to occupy a space of 'semi-legality' in EU law. The three categories of

[115] *Achughbabian* (n 55) para 48. The Court further interpreted in *JZ* that the notion of a 'non-justified' ground for non-return includes the situation of a TCN with a return decision and an entry ban, with a prior (although unrelated) criminal conviction, and who has not left the territory of the Union after the exhaustion of the return procedures (Case C-806/18, *JZ* [2020] EU:C:2020:724).

[116] Charles Gosme, 'Trapped Between Administrative Detention, Imprisonment, and Freedom-in-Limbo' in Maria João Guia, Robert Koulish, and Valsamis Mitsilegas (eds), *Immigration Detention, Risk and Human Rights: Studies on Immigration and Crime* (Springer International Publishing 2016) 92.

[117] Return Handbook (n 69) 19.

irregular migrants pending removal under EU law are: (1) *de jure* non-removable migrants (formally postponed returnees); (2) *de facto* non-removable migrants (non-postponed returnees); (3) criminally convicted migrants—outside of the scope of the Directive.

2.2.1 De jure *non-removable migrants (postponed returnees)*

First, one can find *de jure* non-removable migrants, namely those who have their return decisions formally postponed under Article 9 RD. By default, this category is formed by those persons whose removal would be contrary to the principle of *non-refoulement*. Moreover, if states voluntarily opt for the postponement of removal of other persons under Article 9(2) RD, these will also become *de jure* non-removable. In the latter case, however, this status will not be granted directly by EU law but discretionarily by Member States, being in many cases unstable and contingent on cooperation with removal procedures.[118] Paradoxically, legal non-removables (i.e. those who have a legal reason for non-removal) do not necessarily see their non-removability recognized *de jure*, as the legislator intentionally excluded family and private life cases from Article 9(1) RD. On the contrary, those who are not expelled due to practical reasons can become *de jure* non-removable migrants if Member States acknowledge their inability to deport by making use of Article 9(2) RD.

Non-removable migrants with a formally postponed return decision are by no means considered to be regularly staying, but they often see themselves in a wealth of in-between statuses. Their reasons for non-return are, to use the Court's language in *Achughbabian*, more 'justified' than those of other irregular migrants, either under EU law (*must* cases—Article 9(1) RD) or domestic legislation (*may* cases—Article 9(2) RD).

Behind a seemingly insignificant distinction between *de jure* and *de facto* non-removable migrants, this chapter has shown how formally postponed returnees actually enjoy enforceable rights (rather than soft guidelines) under Article 14 RD in more favourable conditions than the rest of irregular migrants. These are followed by a 'concomitant requirement to make provision for the basic needs of the third country national concerned' and subject to CJEU review.[119] Moreover, while EU law, *per se*, does not grant additional rights, those with postponed removal in line with the Return Directive generally enjoy greater access to social rights across most Member States, as recent research from the EMN shows. Likewise, postponed returnees seem to be the among the few irregular migrants whose employment is not banned by EU law, as the Employers Sanctions Directive foresees a rare exception to the blanket ban on irregular employment for irregular residents 'whose removal has been postponed'.[120]

[118] European Migration Network (EMN) (n 32) 14.
[119] *Abdida* (n 66) para 60.
[120] Employers Sanctions Directive (n 83) art 3.

Postponed returnees are also awarded written notification of their situation under Article 14(2) RD, giving them a higher degree of formalization which, according to some authors, 'contributes to providing a status even if atypical to non-removable migrants'.[121] Postponed returnees are therefore more likely to avoid pre-removal detention because, having their non-removability legally recognized (and certified with written documentation), it certainly becomes easier to show that there is no 'reasonable prospect of removal' as required by the Return Directive.

Lastly, this sub-group is less vulnerable to criminal imprisonment, as they have 'justified' (and legally recognized) reasons for non-return.

2.2.2 De facto non-removable migrants (non-postponed returnees)

Second, we can find *de facto* non-removable migrants, that is, those who do not see the obstacle to their removal legally recognized by EU law or by the Member State in question. This group is formed by those who are not protected from expulsion by a *non-refoulement* clause, unless Member States trigger Article 9(2) RD beyond these. Yet again, this means that some people may find themselves in this group despite holding a legal claim to non-removal.

The reality of undocumented migrants whose return is not formally postponed seems to be on a par with the rest of the irregular migrants. *De facto* non-removable migrants do not have access to Article 14 RD safeguards pending return as interpreted by the CJEU, since their *sui generis* situation is not recognized by the law. This results in lesser entitlements to rights, but also in greater difficulties in enjoying effective access to the rights to which they are entitled in practice, partly due to migrants' concerns about their detection and apprehension by state authorities.[122]

Similarly, their right to written confirmation of their situation remains ambiguous, as it is present only in the Directive's Preamble and it has been interpreted restrictively by Member States. In this context, the lack of written notification, together with the Directive's provisions on pre-removal detention (see section 2.1.4), make *de facto* non-removables substantially more vulnerable to pre-removal detention, notwithstanding the feasibility of deportation in practice. Lastly, *de facto* non-removables can be criminally imprisoned if they do not have a 'justified' ground for non-removal. However, further distinctions must be made within this category.

First is between 'practical' non-removables (analysed in Chapter 4) and those whose non-removal responds to private and/or family life considerations (analysed in Chapter 3). In the former case, prolonged pre-removal detention becomes more likely as Article 15(6) RD foresees the delays in obtaining documents from

[121] Menezes Queiroz (n 7) 299.
[122] European Migration Network (EMN) (n 32) 5.

third countries as a valid ground to detain returnees for up to eighteen months. In the latter case, the grounds for prolonged detention do not apply and so the lack of a 'reasonable prospect of removal' should be more easily established. Moreover, in cases of non-removal related to family and/or private life, it is a domestic (administrative or judicial) body that bars the removal of the person concerned, and hence returnees should be able to demonstrate the lack of a reasonable prospect of removal with a copy of such decision, avoiding pre-removal detention.[123] In addition, persons who are non-removable on legal grounds have, in some Member States, access to postponed return (or even regularization) under better conditions than 'practical' non-removable migrants.[124] Lastly, Article 8 ECHR non-removables should never be criminally convicted on the grounds of a 'non-justified' ground for non-return.

Second, we can find 'exhausted returnees',[125] that is, those who have exhausted the maximum period of pre-removal detention without being returned. For this sub-group, the CJEU has guaranteed access to written confirmation on their situation (avoiding re-detention) in *Mahdi*,[126] but they can also be targeted by criminal imprisonment if they do not have a 'valid' ground for non-return.

2.2.3 'Undesirable and unreturnable': Criminally convicted returnees

At the very bottom of the spectrum, migrants whose return decision is the result of a criminal law sanction can be entirely excluded from the application of the Return Directive under its Article 2. Clearly, those whose 'criminal behaviour' is limited to their irregular residence cannot form part of this group, as the contrary would deprive the Directive of its purpose and binding effect.[127]

This sub-category is potentially made up of any (regular or irregular) migrant who commits a criminal offence and cannot be expelled, regardless of the reason precluding deportation. This includes, among others, former refugees and beneficiaries of subsidiary protection (see Chapter 2), as well as long-term residents and second-generation migrants (see Chapter 3). It must be recalled that these are people with strong claims to non-removal under Articles 3 and 8 ECHR, regardless of their irregularity or the return proceedings initiated against them. For these people, criminality may not only lead to the withdrawal of lawful residence, but can place them outside the protection of the EU return *acquis* altogether.

Concerning their access to rights, the positive impact that the Return Directive has had in the decade that has followed its implementation should not be

[123] There are, however, reported cases of pre-removal detention where applicants could not be deported on private and/or family life grounds, for example, because removal would separate a mother from her lawfully residing child in violation of states' obligations under Article 8 ECHR (See Vanderbruggen and others (n 2) 40–44).

[124] European Migration Network (EMN) (n 32) 13.

[125] Gosme (n 116) 96.

[126] *Mahdi* (n 18) para 89.

[127] *Achughbabian* (n 55) para 41.

underestimated, as there now seems to be consensus that the Return Directive (or rather the resulting dialogue between domestic courts and the CJEU) has overall ensured that undocumented people are treated better than before.[128] Whereas some of these positive developments are targeted specifically at postponed returnees (see section 2.2.1), the CJEU has clarified a series of key aspects that have had a positive impact on all irregular migrants under the Return Directive's scope. Among other topics, the CJEU has ruled on the maximum periods of pre-removal detention,[129] detention conditions,[130] the criminalisation of irregular stay,[131] the right to an effective remedy,[132] the right to be heard before the issuance of a return decision,[133] and the right to be heard before prolonging detention.[134] More generally, it can well be argued that the Return Directive has brought the field of irregular migration and deportation, traditionally characterized by executive discretion, within judicial scrutiny and the rule of law.[135] Regrettably, all of this can be revoked as soon as a TCN descends into criminality, regardless of how compelling the reasons precluding their deportation might be.

Beneath the safety net provided by the Return Directive, excluded non-removable migrants derive their rights solely from states' international obligations. As noted by Majcher, bodies such as the Committee on Economic, Social and Cultural Rights (CESCR) and the European Committee of Social Rights (ECSR) at times undertake rather progressive interpretations of migrants' (regular or irregular) entitlements, including their access to health care, education, or housing, but they suffer from an obvious enforcement deficit when it comes to undocumented migrants.[136] More importantly, the ECtHR has ruled on pre-removal detention, coining the concept of a 'realistic prospect' of expulsion (in line with EU law's 'reasonable prospect of removal') as a necessary condition for pre-removal detention to be in line with Article 5 ECHR. However, the Strasbourg Court has done so without fixing specific time limits and often in the context of a blatant lack

[128] Madalina Moraru and Galina Cornelisse, 'Introduction: Judicial Dialogue on the Return Directive—Catalyst for Changing Migration Governance?' in Philippe de Bruycker, Galina Cornelisse and Madalina Moraru (eds), *Law and Judicial Dialogue on the Return of Irregular Migrants from the European Union* (Hart 2020); Peers, 'Could EU Law Save the Paddington Bear?' (n 68).

[129] *Mahdi* (n 18); *Kadzoev* (n 94).

[130] Case C-473/13, *Adala Bero v Regierungspräsidium Kassel* [2014] EU:C:2014:2095; Case C-474/13, *Thi Ly Pham v Stadt Schweinfurt, Amt für Meldewesen und Statistik* [2014] EU:C:2014:2096; Case C-514/13, *Bouzalmate* [2014] EU:C:2014:2095.

[131] *El Dridi* (n 55); *Achughbabian* (n 55); Case C-430/11, *Md Sagor* [2012] EU:C:2012:777; *JZ* (n 115).

[132] Case C-181/16, *Sadikou Gnandi v État belge* [2018] EU:C:2018:465; Case C-269/18 PPU, *Staatssecretaris van Veiligheid en Justitie v C and others* [2018] EU:C:2018:544.

[133] Case C-166/13, *Sophie Mukarubega v Préfet de police and Préfet de la Seine-Saint-Denis* [2014] EU:C:2014:2336; Case C-249/13, *Khaled Boudjlida v Préfet des Pyrénées-Atlantiques* [2014] EU:C:2014:2431.

[134] Case C-383/13 PPU, *M. G., N. R. v Staatssecretaris van Veiligheid en Justitie.* [2013] EU:C:2013:533.

[135] Moraru and Cornelisse (n 128) 17.

[136] Majcher (n 5) 199.

of deportation prospects linked to statelessness or *non-refoulement*.[137] As regards health care, the ECtHR has made clear that the Convention does not grant a general right to health care, as it only provides for positive obligations if the denial of health care would 'put an individual's life at risk through the denial of health care which they have undertaken to make available to the population generally'.[138] Concerning children's right to education, enshrined in Article 2 of Protocol 1 to the ECHR, the ECtHR has held that this compels states to guarantee the enjoyment of this right to 'anyone within their jurisdiction' and cannot be made conditional on residency requirements.[139] Needless to say, these rights also apply to migrants who are not excluded from the Return Directive.

2.2.4 Conclusions: Constructing deservingness

The three categories identified in this section are neither homogenous nor static. Firstly, they are not homogenous inasmuch as EU law provides for further distinctions that might additionally penalize, for example, the situation of persons who do not cooperate with their return. Moreover, domestic and municipal laws and policies remain key to define access to rights and safeguards in practice. Also, beyond legal analyses, migrants' cumulative identities determine their reception by the local community and associated life experiences in multiple ways—although this goes well beyond the scope of this chapter and legal scholarship more generally.[140] Second, the categories proposed, as any form of migrant categorization, are not static but fluid, since migrants regularly transition across different legal statuses, going up and down hierarchies of desirability.[141] Indeed, there is nothing natural, existential, or fixed about these categories, as persons can 'jump' from one category to the other, be regularized, or ultimately be deported if the reasons precluding removal cease to exist. For instance, Member States can decide to trigger the *may* clause under Article 9 RD and formally postpone the return decision of a 'practical' non-removable, or may bring a criminally convicted migrant within the Directive's scope if they so wish. Similarly, *any* TCN, no matter how settled in the host country, may suddenly fall into the abyss of Article 2 RD and belong to the 'least deserving' group among irregular migrants upon the commission of a criminal offence.

And yet, depending on the obstacles precluding deportation and on returnees' behaviour, EU law seems to consider the stay of some people as less 'disapproved

[137] See *A. and others v UK* [GC], App No 3455/05 (ECtHR 19 February 2009) para 167; *MD and others v Russia*, App No 71321/17 (ECtHR 14 September 2021) para 126; *Mainov v Russia*, App No 11556/17 (ECtHR 15 May 2018) paras 24–26; *Kim v Russia*, App No 44260/13 (ECtHR 17 July 2014) paras 52, 53, and 56; *Ali Reza v Bulgaria*, App No 35422/16 (ECtHR 17 May 2022).

[138] *Cyprus v. Turkey* [GC], App No 25871/94 (ECtHR 10 May 2001) para 219.

[139] *Timishev v Russia*, Apps No 55762/00 and 55974/00 (ECtHR 13 December 2005) paras 63–67.

[140] See, for example: Natalie Domaas, 'More than a Migration Status: Examining Intersectionality and Its Effect on the Experiences of Migrant Women in France' (2021) 21 Journal of Immigrant & Refugee Studies 249; Robertson (n 25).

[141] Robertson (n 25) 226.

of', and hence legitimate enough to be awarded more favourable conditions. As this chapter has shown, the Return Directive's superficial regulation has in practice led to the creation of differentiated groups, in a way in which belonging to one or another has far-reaching consequences. For example, the decision to keep 'practical' non-removables (who actually make up the majority of non-removable persons) out of formally postponed return in Article 9 RD is far from irrelevant as it deeply (and negatively) affects their access to social rights, written notification, and their protection from detention and criminalization—unless Member States voluntarily decide otherwise. The different 'statuses' provided for by EU law, ranging from those who have 'better' reasons for not being deported (most deserving) to those who have committed a criminal offence (least deserving), are key to understanding their access to rights under both EU and domestic law.

While previous EU law scholarship has referred to the situation of non-removable migrants generally as an *atypical* migration status of 'semi-legality', this chapter has illustrated how, under the current framework, the legal acknowledgement of their distinctive situation via formal postponement of return is very narrowly constructed and only available under EU law for a few. The decision of the legislator to limit such obligation to cases of *non-refoulement* means that these are conceptualized as having more valid grounds for non-return. In contrast, the rest of the body of non-removable migrants are left at the mercy of Member States, regardless of whether their non-removability is due to reasons completely beyond their control. However, if Member States voluntarily decide to apply the *may* clause of Article 9(2) RD, they will be bound to offer the more favourable conditions foreseen for *de jure* non-removable migrants. On the contrary, if return decisions are not formally postponed, access to rights will be most likely on a par with the rest of the irregular migrant population. For the least deserving category, formed by those who are subjected to return as a criminal law sanction, their (unworkable) return decision comes with an EU legal void.

3. Conclusions

Neither the Return Directive nor the 2018 Commission proposal for a recasting of the Directive foresee a specific migration status for non-removable migrants, as the Commission is well aware of the reluctance of a majority of the Member States in the Council to pursue further integration on this matter.[142] The applicable

[142] In fact, the text of the proposed recast would likely make the situation of non-removable migrants worse off, as it includes more grounds for detention (with no requirement for a reasonable prospect of removal—Article 18), a wider definition of a 'risk of absconding' (Article 6), and an obligation for returnees to cooperate in return procedures (Article 7).

legal framework therefore does not seem likely to change substantially in the near future.

Even if their presence in the EU can in some cases last for decades, non-removable migrants remain classified as irregular migrants and are not offered legal routes to regularization under EU law *as non-removable persons*.[143] The prevalence of 'hard' and dichotomous boundaries between regular and irregular migration means that their stay is, according to the TFEU, to be 'combatted', and is therefore intrinsically characterized by rightlessness and exclusion. And yet, as important as these formal boundaries might be, scholars increasingly point at the relevance of diverging legal, policy, and social processes of 'status-making' beyond binary understandings of migrant categories. Based on this, and on the perceived legal vacuum existing at the EU level, the existing studies on non-removable migrants have largely focused on national and municipal responses to the protracted stay of irregular migrants pending return. These responses have been rightly understood to often go well beyond EU law obligations.

It has been my contention, however, that non-removability falls between the cracks, but not completely beyond the reach of EU law. Whereas the Return Directive only offers a very shallow, seemingly non-binding, and incomplete list of safeguards to be taken into account 'as far as possible' (and only to postponed returnees), these have been considered by the CJEU as enforceable rights in *Abdida*, where the Court additionally establishes a concomitant obligation to provide for returnees' basic needs. More importantly, comparative research shows that those with postponed return under the Return Directive generally enjoy greater access to social rights in an overwhelming majority of Member States. In addition, postponed returnees have a right to the written certification of their situation which makes them less vulnerable to pre-removal detention, and also hold a 'justified ground' for non-return which impedes their imprisonment due to irregular stay. The EU framework thus produces different categories of non-removable migrants which, depending on the obstacle precluding removal and the perceived behaviour of the returnee, and in interaction with domestic frameworks, create sub-statuses of relative privilege or disadvantage. Those who engage into criminal behaviour are the least deserving among irregular migrants, as the return *acquis* ceases to apply to them regardless of the obstacle precluding expulsion.

The spaces of inclusion generated by EU law are not only insufficient in terms of rights, but are also constructed very narrowly, as they seem to only impose tangible obligations on states insofar as the most 'privileged' category of non-removable migrants is concerned—and leave Member States a wide margin of discretion to decide who these people are. At the EU level, this category is formed only by those

[143] The lack of legal residence available due to non-removability as such is without prejudice to the routes to lawful residence available (to removable and non-removable persons alike) under EU law as refugees or beneficiaries of subsidiary protection, as family members of EU citizens or TCNs, and so on.

whose non-removal derives from *non-refoulement*, although Member States do often grant postponed removal to other returnees under the *may* clause of Article 9 RD. For the rest, there is no such thing as an 'atypical' or 'semi-legal' status under EU law, as the applicable framework is no more favourable than that generally applied to the irregular migrant population.

While EU law constructs deservingness in a given way, domestic policy-makers often have more beneficial (and shifting) interpretations of who deserves to have their removal formally postponed. The categories identified are therefore neither homogenous nor static, and the solutions adopted at the national level are hugely diverse. Indeed, under the current framework, a person who is unreturnable due to 'practical' obstacles may be regularized after a period of two to five years of irregular residence in Spain, be issued a toleration certificate (*Duldung*) in Germany, be offered postponed return in Belgium, or remain fully clandestinely in Italy.[144] Regardless of the blatant fundamental rights concerns raised by situations of protracted irregularity (together with the public policy challenges derived from migrant exclusion), the different approaches to this question have also raised concerns about secondary movements, as they could be considered as an incentive for undocumented migrants to move across EU Member States in search of better conditions.[145] Chapter 6 will hint at possible regularization options to tackle some of these issues.

144 European Migration Network (EMN) (n 32) 13 and 32.

145 European Commission, 'Staff Working Document, Fitness Check on EU Legislation on Legal Migration' SWD(2019) 1055 Final, 29 March 2019, 85.

6
In Search of Legal Status—Non-Removability and Paths to Regularization

This book has examined the persistent gaps between return agendas and discourses, on the one hand, and the complexities of their real-life implementation, on the other. It has also examined the consequences of these gaps, inquiring into the legal status of non-removable migrants and emphasizing the role of EU law in constructing their status and pre-defining their access to rights. Considering that the great majority of irregular migrants are not deported, as well as the precarity and liminality of those who inevitably stay in Europe, important questions arise: Are there limits as to how long persons can reside irregularly? What are their possibilities to transition to regularity? Does European law have a say on their right to regularize their status? The aim of this chapter is to examine regularization pathways for irregular migrants (and in particular non-removable migrants).

Despite the daily resort to regularization across EU Member States, these lack common standards and do not generally offer a legal definition of the term.[1] In fact, scholars working on irregular migration and regularization often provide different definitions, stemming from the varied typologies of regularizations in place.[2] There are however common elements in these definitions. Regularization, broadly conceived, is an umbrella term that includes any state procedure (be it through an administrative or a judicial decision) by which irregular migrants are granted a lawful status.[3] Indeed, all regularization definitions agree on their core element being about the *transition* of third-country nationals (TCNs),[4] who are already present in a given state, from irregular to regular residence.[5] From a legal

[1] Kevin Fredy Hinterberger, *Regularisations of Irregularly Staying Migrants in the EU: A Comparative Legal Analysis of Austria, Germany and Spain* (Nomos 2023) 56.

[2] Martin Baldwin-Edwards and Albert Kraler (eds), *REGINE—Regularisations in Europe* (Amsterdam University Press 2009) 9; Hinterberger (n 1) 26 and 55; Gabriella Lazaridis, *International Migration into Europe: From Subjects to Abjects* (Palgrave Macmillan UK 2015) 132; Joseph Apap, Philippe De Bruycker, and Philippe Schmitter, 'Regularisation of Illegal Aliens in the European Union. Summary Report of a Comparative Study' (2000) 2 European Journal of Migration and Law 263.

[3] Hinterberger (n 1) 59.

[4] While EU citizens can also reside unlawfully (i.e. in breach of residence conditions set out in Directive 2004/38), this chapter focuses on the regularization of third-country nationals only, as the former generally falls beyond the scope of analysis of this book (with the exception of section 4.2 in Chapter 3) and their stay is regulated under a different legal framework.

[5] As set out in Chapter 1 of this book, irregular TCNs are, according to the Return Directive, those who do not fulfil, or no longer fulfil, the (domestic) conditions of entry, stay, or residence in a given Member State.

When Deportation Fails. Diego Ginés Martín, Oxford University Press. © Diego Ginés Martín 2025.
DOI: 10.1093/9780198941231.003.0006

standpoint, regularized migrants are no longer in breach of national immigration legislation, that is, their stay in the country is no longer legally disapproved of.[6] Based on these preliminary considerations, this chapter is structured as follows.

Section 1 elaborates briefly on the EU legal framework on return and regularization under Directive 2008/115 (hereinafter Return Directive or simply RD) as well as on the shifting policy responses to regularization in recent decades. Ultimately, despite the underlying rationale of the Return Directive being that states should either return or regularize irregular migrants, the return *acquis* is based on a political (but also legal) emphasis on return that incorporates states' obligations to return, but in no way compels states to regularize—nor foresees common rules if Member States opt for regularization.

Considering that the remainder of the chapter is based on the normative assumptions that regularization should be a privileged tool for irregular migration management, and *the* tool to address situations of non-removability, section 2 proposes four arguments in favour of regularization, with a focus on non-removability. The arguments are based on the effectiveness of EU law, human rights, state welfare, and the rule of law.

Although this book is EU-wide in scope, section 3 scrutinizes domestic frameworks, as regularization is almost entirely left to the Member States. It examines national regularization practices, structuring its analysis along two key dimensions. First, based on the method of regularization, it distinguishes between regularization programmes and regularization mechanisms. Second, it categorizes regularizations based on their underlying purpose, differentiating between market-driven and rights-based regularizations—zooming in on existing regularization prospects for non-removable migrants.

Section 4 hints at possible regularization options for non-removable migrants under European law. It first analyses the possibilities for both the Court of Justice of the European Union (CJEU) and the European Court of Human Rights (ECtHR) to interpret the Return Directive and the European Convention on Human Rights

[6] Regularizations, as understood in this chapter, do not include 'toleration' statuses such as *Duldung* (see Chapter 5 of this book), since 'tolerated' migrants are still considered to be in breach of domestic immigration legislation and they still hold a valid (albeit non-enforceable) return decision. They also exclude the granting of asylum. Even if refugee status or subsidiary protection can *de facto* regularize a person who was previously residing irregularly, this is regulated by asylum (and not immigration) law. It however includes the regularization through migration law of non-recognized refugees who, in the context of dysfunctional asylum systems, are not recognized as such. This study also omits regularization through marriage (pertaining to civil law and, in a way, derivative from the spouse's right), regularization through operation of the law (e.g. after the accession of a country to the EU), or regularization through change of personal circumstances (e.g. acquisition of nationality). While these lead in practice to 'irregular migration outflows', they are not analysed here as regularization practices because they are not specifically aimed at the regularization of irregular migrants (see Maegan Hendow and Ayesha Qaisrani, 'Pathways and Policy Evolution: Comparing National Laws and Policies Addressing Irregular Migrants' (2024) MIRREM Working Paper 6/2024 55–74).

(ECHR) in ways that explicitly address non-removability. It then goes on to explore potential legal and policy responses to non-removability at the EU level.

1. Return, regularization, and EU law

As mentioned in Chapter 1 of this book, the EU *acquis* on irregular migration is deeply asymmetric. With the EU's constitutional mandate being to 'combat' irregular migration,[7] both return and regularization provide for irregular migration 'outflows' and, as such, are valid tools to put an end to irregular stays. However, secondary EU law addresses deportation in the Return Directive, but leaves regularization measures up to the Member States. And yet, Article 6(4) RD notes that Member States *may*, alternatively, afford irregular migrants a residence permit under domestic law at any time due to 'compassionate, humanitarian, or other reasons'.[8] In other words, Member States are obliged to return unless they (freely) decide to regularize irregular migrants, with both measures being in compliance with the Return Directive. One must also bear in mind that the Directive's Chapter II is entitled 'Termination of Illegal Stay'.[9] Thus, even though the Return Directive's main aim is to establish an 'effective return policy',[10] the underlying logic of the Directive is to provide greater certainty by compelling Member States to either return or regularize irregular migrants (particularly if there is no reasonable prospect of removal). Then, there seems to be consensus that the Directive must be interpreted broadly as an instrument aimed at the 'termination of illegal stay'—be it through return, in line with the Directive's rules, or regularization, in accordance with domestic procedures.[11]

However, the Return Directive's underlying aims, on the one hand, and the resulting policy outcomes, on the other, have followed increasingly divergent paths. In practice, regularizations have always been contested in the EU, and policy efforts have overwhelmingly focused on 'combatting' irregular migration by resorting to

[7] Consolidated version of the Treaty on the Functioning of the European Union (TFEU) [2012] OJ C 326 art 79.

[8] Directive 2008/115/EC of the European Parliament and of the Council of 16 December 2008 on common standards and procedures in Member States for returning illegally staying third-country nationals [2008] OJ L348/98 (Return Directive) art 6(4).

[9] Ibid, Chapter II.

[10] Case C-38/14, *Subdelegación del Gobierno en Gipuzkoa v Zaizoune* [2015] EU:C:2015:260 para 30; Case C-329/11, *Alexandre Achughbabian v Préfet du Val-de-Marne* [2011] EU:C:2011:807 para 45; Case C-61/11 PPU, *Hassen El Dridi, alias Karim Soufi* [2011] EU:C:2011:268 paras 35 and 59.

[11] European Commission, 'Commission Recommendation (EU) 2017/2338 of 16 November 2017 Establishing a Common "Return Handbook" to be used by Member States' Competent Authorities when Carrying Out Return-Related Tasks' [2017] OJ L 339 (Return Handbook) 20; Fabian Lutz, *The Negotiations on the Return Directive: Comments and Materials* (WLP 2010) 42; Hinterberger (n 1) 79; Alan Desmond, 'The Return Directive: Clarifying the Scope and Substance of the Rights of Migrants Facing Expulsion from the EU' in Russell King and Katie Kuschminder (eds), *Handbook of Return Migration* (Edward Elgar Publishing 2022) 146.

return, while discouraging regularization measures. As early as 2001, prior to the adoption of the Return Directive, the Commission expressed that '[i]llegal entry or residence should not lead to the desired stable form of residence' and that 'illegal residents cannot be considered as a pool to meet labour shortages . . . [since] the possibility to have access to undeclared work might be perceived as the most important "pull factor" for potential migrants'.[12] It remains true that at the time the EU followed a changing and at times ambivalent discourse towards regularization, in a context in which large-scale regularization programmes were routinely adopted by a significant number of Member States (see further section 3 of this chapter). The 2000s however culminated with the adoption of the 2008 Pact on Immigration and Asylum, where EU Member States committed to abandon large-scale regularization programmes (then widely used, particularly by Mediterranean Member States) and use case-by-case regularization only.[13] The Pact's political guidelines deeply influenced the Commission's approach in the years that followed and installed a policy taboo around the issue of regularization, becoming deeply unpopular in EU policy circles.[14]

The 2015 refugee crisis only increased the hostility towards irregular migration. In this context, external fortification and policies of *non-entrée* (see section 1.1 in Chapter 1 of this book) have been coupled with increasingly hostile approaches towards irregular migrants already within the Member States, with scant access to rights and criminalization aimed at creating exhausting living conditions that lead migrants to leave by their own means.[15] In the field of regularization, the refugee crisis seemed to decisively shift the debate against it, positing return as the only desirable policy option—and the one capable of avoiding the much-feared 'pull-effect'.[16]

Externalization policies designed to prevent migrants from entering Europe seem more popular now than ever before.[17] For irregular residents already in

[12] European Commission, 'Communication regarding a common policy in the "fight" against illegal immigration and human trafficking', COM(2001) 672 Final 6.

[13] Council of the European Union, European Pact on Immigration and Asylum, 13440/08, 24 September 2008 7.

[14] Cathryn Costello, *The Human Rights of Migrants and Refugees in European Law* (Oxford University Press 2015) 100; Hinterberger (n 1) 43.

[15] Nicola Delvino, 'European Union and National Responses to Migrants with Irregular Status: Is the Fortress Slowly Crumbling?' in Sarah Spencer and Anna Triandafyllidou (eds), *Migrants with Irregular Status in Europe: Evolving Conceptual and Policy Challenges* (Springer International Publishing 2020) 73–75.

[16] Albert Kraler, 'Regularization of Irregular Migrants and Social Policies: Comparative Perspectives' (2019) 17 Journal of Immigrant & Refugee Studies 94, 94.

[17] Perhaps the clearest and most recent example is provided by Italy's deal with Albania for the processing of asylum claims outside of the EU's borders (see Andreina de Leo, 'On the incompatibility of the Italy–Albania Protocol with EU asylum law', *SIDIBlog*, 15 November 2023, available at: <http://www.sidiblog.org/2023/11/15/on-the-incompatibility-of-the-italy-albania-protocol-with-eu-asylum-law/>). In this context, and after the conclusion of migration deals with Tunisia, Mauritania, and Egypt, Commission president Ursula von der Leyen praised, in a letter addressed to EU leaders, the 'innovative strategies to prevent irregular migration by tackling asylum applications further from the EU external border', and for the first time opened the way for such policies to be adopted at the EU level

Europe, the adoption of an EU regularization framework is still a no-go for the European legislator. In this scenario, institutional frustration with low return rates will remain so long as the meaning attached to the concept of 'effectiveness' is tied to return rates rather than to the 'termination of illegal stay' (including regularization), as the former often depend on external factors beyond the reach of the Member States, as repeatedly seen in this book.[18] However, while the mainstream approach remains one of exclusion, marginalization, and criminalization,[19] national developments in the aftermath of Covid-19 suggest regularization is gaining ground in at least some Member States—both discursively and in practice. These signal that tougher approaches on migration *externally* might be at times accompanied by an increased resort to regularizations *internally*. As a matter of fact, all Member States implement regularization measures, although the type and frequency of these measures vary widely. Prior to their analysis, and given the chapter's normative stance *for* regularization, the next section develops four arguments in its favour. Some of these have already been addressed, explicitly or implicitly, in earlier chapters of this book, but here they will be systematically organized and presented.

2. The case for regularization

This chapter is based on the normative assumption that regularization ought to be the preferred policy option to address non-removability. Based on this, it assesses and advocates for regularization at the national and EU levels and evaluates whether there might be legal obligations to regularize under existing norms of European law.

As noted above, non-removable migrants emerge in the context of a legislative gap. In fact, the EU not only lacks legal instruments on regularization, but has often used its political influence to advocate against its use by Member States. Yet, why should one resort to regularization? After all, legislative and enforcement gaps in EU law are nothing out of the ordinary. There are some matters on which EU institutions come together to produce legislation, and others on which inter-institutional agreement is neither possible nor desirable. It is thus only normal that legislation is produced on issues where Member States converge (i.e. deportation),

(Ursula von der Leyen, 'Letter to the EU leaders', 25 June 2024, available at: <https://www.eunews.it/wp-content/uploads/2024/06/Letter-from-President-von-der-Leyen-to-EU-leaders-on-migration-EUCO-June-2024.pdf>).

[18] European Commission, 'Communication on a more effective return policy in the European Union', COM(2017) 200 Final, 2 March 2017; European Commission, 'Communication on a European agenda on migration', COM(2015) 240 Final, 13 May 2015, 9.

[19] Maurizio Ambrosini and Minke HJ Hajer, *Irregular Migration: IMISCOE Short Reader* (Springer International Publishing 2023) 74.

but not on more sensitive fields that Member States may legitimately wish to address domestically (i.e. regularization). On the other hand, while return enforcement deficits are certainly more troubling, one could well argue that gaps in the enforcement of legislation are also widespread and well documented across every field of EU law.[20] But given the magnitude of this enforcement deficit, with the majority of irregular migrants in the EU becoming non-removable either legally or *de facto*, relevant questions arise as to the length of their stay, as well as the consequences of protracted non-removal for both migrants and Member States. There are, in this context, important arguments that point to regularization as a safety valve for irregular migration stocks in Europe.

2.1 Regularization and EU law effectiveness

First, regularization is in line with the Return Directive's aim to end 'illegal stay' and, more generally, a valid tool to 'combat' irregular migration in line with Article 79 of the Treaty on the Functioning of the European Union (TFEU). Regularization is surely a subsidiary policy option under the Return Directive, which intentionally leaves it up to the Member States. This is particularly obvious considering that the legislator consciously created legal obligations to return, consolidating it, in law and in practice, as the preferred option. And yet, under certain circumstances, it seems that regularization might be the most effective (and in practice only) way to put an end to irregularity.

This argument, already hinted at in section 1 of this chapter and in Chapter 1 of this book, can be labelled as the 'effectiveness' argument. In essence, the reasoning goes that, where return is not legally or factually possible, regularization seems to be the only option that ensures the 'termination of illegal stay', in line with the Return Directive and primary law.[21] This is also consistent with the fact that Member States are obliged to return or regularize irregular migrants, not being allowed to simply tolerate them.[22] The extent to which this could generate a legal obligation to regularize under EU law is dealt with in section 4 of this chapter. In the meantime, one can make the more modest assumption that, for non-removable migrants, regularization emerges as the most effective way to reduce grey areas and ensure an effective application of the EU *acquis*. It could also, over time, put a remedy to the gross divergence between return decisions and 'effective' returns,

[20] In the field of asylum the clearest example is perhaps found in the movement of asylum seekers beyond the country of first entry ('secondary movements') contrary to the principles set up in the Dublin III Regulation (after the 2024 Pact regulated by the Regulation on Asylum and Migration Management (RAMM)).

[21] Return Handbook (n 11) 20; Lutz (n 11) 42; Hinterberger (n 1) 79; Desmond (n 11) 146.

[22] Return Handbook (n 11) 19 and 45; Case C-546/19, *BZ v Westerwaldkreis* [2021] EU:C:2021:432 para 57.

since part of this gap precisely responds to the issuance of unenforceable return decisions.[23] Overall, a greater focus on regularization would increase legal and policy effectiveness in a field where unrealistic deportation agendas and chronic enforcement deficits have fuelled anti-immigration rhetorics for years.[24]

2.2 Regularization and human rights

Despite universalistic aspirations, it is widely recognized that migration statuses, and in particular transitions in and out of irregularity, function as a gate to access fundamental rights.[25] Even if irregular migrants' access to rights may depend on further processes of stratification and 'status-making' (which might distinguish between children and adults, removables and non-removables, and so on),[26] irregularity forms a structural constraint on their agency and a crucial determinant of their vulnerability and exclusion.[27] Therefore, from a human rights perspective, regularization is not only key for migrants to gain entitlement to a wide range of fundamental rights and freedoms, such as the right to work,[28] but also has material effects on their ability to access those rights to which they are already entitled—leading to a double-layered exclusion.[29] Thus, it is generally only with regularization that migrants are able to emerge from their 'invisible' life, 'integrate', and access both civil and social rights.[30]

[23] Desmond (n 11) 147.

[24] To be sure, greater 'effectiveness' is not here achieved by increasing return numbers, but by adopting in practice a holistic notion of 'effectiveness' that truly places an emphasis on the termination of irregularity (as suggested by EU legislation) instead of betting exclusively on return.

[25] See, among others, Colm O'Cinneide, 'The Human Rights of Migrants with Irregular Status: Giving Substance to Aspirations of Universalism' in Sarah Spencer and Anna Triandafyllidou (eds), *Migrants with Irregular Status in Europe: Evolving Conceptual and Policy Challenges* (Springer International Publishing 2020); Marie-Bénédicte Dembour, *When Humans Become Migrants: Study of the European Court of Human Rights with an Inter-American Counterpoint* (Oxford University Press 2015); European Agency for Fundamental Rights (FRA), 'Fundamental rights of migrants in an irregular situation in the European Union', 21 November 2011, available at: <https://fra.europa.eu/en/publication/2012/fundamental-rights-migrants-irregular-situation-european-union>. For a deeper analysis of the impact of migration statuses on fundamental rights, refer to Chapter 5 of this book.

[26] Shanthi Robertson, 'Status-Making: Rethinking Migrant Categorization' (2019) 55 Journal of Sociology 219, 220.

[27] Kraler, 'Regularization of Irregular Migrants and Social Policies' (n 16) 3.

[28] Ambrosini and Hajer (n 19) 74. Irregular migrants not only work in the informal economy but generally hold the worst paid and more physically exhausting jobs, and are more vulnerable to non-payment of wages and other violations of their employment rights (see Albert Kraler, 'Regularisations—An Instrument to Reduce Vulnerability, Social Exclusion and Exploitation of Migrants in an Irregular Situation in Employment?' (2012) ICMPD, FRA Working Paper 20).

[29] O'Cinneide (n 25) 53. In practice, irregular status can even lead to higher mortality rates due to practical barriers to health-care access (see Lorenzo Piccoli and Philippe Wanner, 'The Political Determinants of the Health of Undocumented Immigrants: A Comparative Analysis of Mortality Patterns in Switzerland' (2022) 22 BMC Public Health 804).

[30] Claudia Finotelli, 'Regularisation of Immigrants in Southern Europe: What Can Be Learned from Spain?' in Michael Bommes and Giuseppe Sciortino (eds), *Foggy Social Structures: Irregular Migration, European Labour Markets and the Welfare State* (Amsterdam University Press 2011) 189. It remains

Moreover, there are humanitarian and human rights-based arguments for regularization. Indeed, human rights can be relevant for irregular migrants as they might impose a positive duty on states to regularize their status. Then, migrants might be allowed to stay on the basis of their human rights entitlements, when this is the only way to ensure respect to their most basic rights, or when applicants are in particularly vulnerable situations. Domestic mechanisms awarding residence due to humanitarian and human rights-related reasons are analysed in section 3 of this chapter, while human rights-based regularization mechanisms under European law will be analysed in section 4.

2.3 Regularization and state welfare: Utilitarian arguments

There are also more pragmatic arguments that can support regularization from the host state's perspective. Despite extended myths of Western states being flooded with low-skilled immigrants fleeing war and poverty, evidence shows that labour demand is a pivotal 'root cause' of migration, and that migration largely responds to a long-standing demand for foreign workers.[31] While foreign workers alone cannot address all the problems of Europe's ageing population,[32] there are a number of economic and labour market-oriented arguments for regularization. These can be referred to as 'utilitarian' arguments. Indeed, regularization not only protects migrants' rights and decreases the likelihood of them being exploited, but can also help further diverse policy aims. Here, regularization is not an end in itself, but an instrument to respond to the specific needs of receiving states.

First, regularizations allow for better population management, with host states holding a clearer picture of their overall population.[33]

Second, from a law-enforcement perspective, regularizations help enforce labour and social standards and can contribute to reducing vulnerability and exclusion, and generally to achieving greater social cohesion.[34]

Third and most importantly, regularizations are often posited as tools to (re) regulate and fill shortages in the labour market, fight the underground economy,

true that access to lawful status via regularization is normally provided by means of temporary, precarious, and reversible residence permits, in an example of what Chauvin and Garcés Mascareñas call 'probationary citizenship' (see Sébastien Chauvin and Blanca Garcés-Mascareñas, 'Beyond Informal Citizenship: The New Moral Economy of Migrant Illegality' (2012) 6 International Political Sociology 241, 253).

[31] Hein de Haas, *How Migration Really Works: A Factful Guide to the Most Divisive Issue in Politics* (Viking 2023) 110–17.

[32] Ibid, 234.

[33] European Commission, 'Communication on a study on the links between legal and illegal migration', COM(2004) 412 final, 4 June 2004 10.

[34] Albert Kraler, 'Regularisation: A Misguided Option or Part and Parcel of a Comprehensive Policy Response to Irregular Migration?' (2009) IMISCOE Working Papers 17.

increase revenue by means of taxation and social security payments, and pursue other labour and economic aims.[35] With their employment being barred under EU and domestic legislation, irregular migrants work in the informal economy. Moreover, they do so in low-skilled jobs, often not owing to their lack of skills, but rather to their inability to obtain a work permit.[36] Then, regularization can function as an instrument to regain control over the labour market and its economy, enabling workers to emerge into the regular job market. This type of employment-based regularization has been prominent in Mediterranean Member States, and is subsequently analysed in section 3. In the meantime, it suffices to note that 'utilitarian' regularizations do not necessarily work equally for all non-removable migrants, as their personal situation, skills, and potential contribution to the labour market diverge. Though compelling arguments for regularization can be offered, these should be complemented with humanitarian and human rights-based regularizations.

2.4 Regularization and the rule of law

A fourth argument, largely neglected by immigration legislation yet recently suggested in scholarly circles, approaches the issue of regularization from a rule of law lens.

Political theorists working on immigration have long advocated for a moral right to regularize status and access citizenship. With some differences, social membership theories claim that irregular migrants, with the passage of time, acquire moral claims to belong in the societies in which they reside. In the legal realm, this should translate into a right to regularize their stay.[37]

In response to these views, rule of law arguments have traditionally been used to pursue a 'law and order' immigration agenda, as regularization is often considered to undermine the rule of law by rewarding law-breaking behaviour. According to proponents of this view, regularization favours 'queue jumping' and is unfair towards law-abiding migrants—as if legal migration routes were generally available for migrants from the Global South.[38] Much of this controversy is spurred by the *ex*

[35] European Commission, 'Communication on a study on the links between legal and illegal migration' (n 33) 10; Ibid, 2; Kraler, 'Regularisations—An Instrument to Reduce Vulnerability, Social Exclusion and Exploitation of Migrants in an Irregular Situation in Employment?' (n 28) 23; Lazaridis (n 2) 132; Aspasia Papadopoulou, 'Regularization Programmes: An Effective Instrument of Migration Policy?' (2005) 33 Global Migration Perspectives 1, 14–15.

[36] European Commission, 'Communication on a study on the links between legal and illegal migration' (n 33) 11; Kraler, 'Regularisations—An Instrument to Reduce Vulnerability, Social Exclusion and Exploitation of Migrants in an Irregular Situation in Employment?' (n 28) 19.

[37] Joseph H Carens, *The Ethics of Immigration* (Oxford University Press 2013) 151; Thomas Nagel, 'The Problem of Global Justice' (2005) 33 Philosophy & Public Affairs 113, 133; Ayelet Shachar, *The Birthright Lottery: Citizenship and Global Inequality* (Harvard University Press 2009) 184–88.

[38] David Miller, *Strangers in Our Midst: The Political Philosophy of Immigration* (Harvard University Press 2016) 117 and 126.

post character of regularizations, that is, the fact that regular status is granted when people already reside in the country.[39] Another related argument, often put forward by EU institutions, goes that regularization incentivizes further irregular migration, creating a 'pull-effect' for would-be migrants.[40] But the rule of law should also function as a limit to state sovereignty and migration control.

This is the case first because, as noted above, regularization brings migrants into legality, increasing compliance with labour laws, combatting the underground economy, and reducing abuse and criminality.

Second and most importantly, the regularization of long-term migrants is consistent with the principle of legal certainty, acknowledging that, after some time, persons have a right to move on with their lives and make long-term plans in the countries where they live. According to Ellerman, the applicable rationale for regularization should be that of statutes of limitation, according to which most civil and criminal proceedings have time limits beyond which persons can no longer be prosecuted.[41] While immigration systems often attach some value to the passage of time,[42] the general immunity of immigration law breaches from this legal pardon seems difficult to justify. Then, legal certainty would require individuals to be able to reasonably predict the legal consequences of their behaviour. In the immigration field, situations of irregularity and rightlessness, together with low but unpredictable probability of expulsion, often extend for decades, limiting migrants' chances to pursue basic life plans without the fear that states might deport them. Seen in this light, the rule of law would 'demand that the state cut its losses and accept the consequences of its failure to act in a timely manner'.[43] The situation of non-removable migrants is particularly at odds with the principle of legal certainty, as their presence is known of by state authorities and their removal depends on an eventual but uncertain change of circumstances.

Third, large-scale regularizations can, in some cases, promote compliance with the rule of law by providing a 'fresh start' for immigration systems, resolving a backlog of cases where states have failed to exert their deportation prerogatives and offering a realistic response to law-enforcement failure.[44]

[39] Papadopoulou (n 35) 2.

[40] Empirical evidence in Europe and the US however suggests that regularizations have very limited to no effects on migration flows (see Tom K Wong and Hillary Kosnac, 'Does The Legalization of Undocumented Immigrants in the US Encourage Unauthorized Immigration from Mexico? An Empirical Analysis of the Moral Hazard of Legalization' (2017) 55 International Migration 159; Frank Wehinger, 'Do Amnesties Pull in Illegal Immigrants? An Analysis of European Apprehension Data' (2014) 1 International Journal of Migration and Border Studies 231).

[41] Antje Ellermann, 'The Rule of Law and the Right to Stay: The Moral Claims of Undocumented Migrants' (2014) 42 Politics & Society 293.

[42] As it is analysed in sections 2 and 3 of this chapter, time is only one in multiple considerations to grant regularization. This is the case in domestic legislation (section 2) and in supranational jurisprudence (section 3).

[43] Ellermann (n 41) 293 and 299.

[44] Sarah Song and Irene Bloemraad, 'Immigrant Legalization: A Dilemma between Inclusion and the Rule of Law?' (2021) EUI Working Paper, RSC 2021/61 5.

2.5 Interim conclusion

The arguments developed in this section do not suggest that the moral and legal entitlements of all irregular migrants are, or should be, equally robust. Moral and legal claims to regularization change over time and depend on individual circumstances. As regards non-removable migrants, these are a highly heterogenous category of people whose claims to regularization vary greatly. Thus, regularization claims will be greater with the passage of time, where persons are particularly vulnerable, or where they can show a greater attachment to the host society, among other reasons.

Despite the absence of an EU framework on regularization, it remains a daily tool of migration management across Member States. As a matter of fact, the arguments developed above are often among the reasons set forth by regularizing Member States under their domestic legislation. While an exhaustive comparative analysis of domestic regularization practices across all EU Member States goes well beyond the aims of this study, the following section reflects on the different typologies of regularization available across EU Member States, offering an overview of when, how, and why they are used, as well as of their advantages and shortcomings.

3. Regularization in EU Member States

Regularizations, as defined in this chapter,[45] cover state procedures that aim to grant lawful status to irregular migrants. They can however respond to different underlying motivations and rationales, and, as such, do not follow a single logic. As this section illustrates, Member States regularize by making use of different measures. They also regularize following different motivations and, depending on the Member State, they may choose to do so frequently or only exceptionally. In this context, regularizations can be categorized along various dimensions. This chapter identifies two main axes along which regularizations in the EU can be categorized.[46] First, regularizations can be categorized by their format or method of implementation. Second, regularizations can be categorized on the basis of their purpose, namely, by the interests they serve. Both analyses are not mutually exclusive, since a regularization measure can pursue different aims regardless of its method of implementation, and vice versa. Thus, the different dimensions analysed must not be examined in isolation as they are intrinsically intertwined, and

[45] Please refer to the introduction to this chapter.

[46] These are the main dimensions identified, but there are potentially many more criteria along which regularization could be categorized. For example, regularizations can be categorized according to the type of permit issued (i.e. whether it is a short-term or long-term permit, the conditions under it can be lost, maintained. or renewed, etc). This will be sporadically touched upon throughout this chapter.

together they offer a more comprehensive overview of regularization practices in the EU.

3.1 Regularization methods: Programmes and mechanisms

When thinking about regularization, public imaginaries picture mass regularizations, with states regularizing thousands of immigrants at once.[47] These programmes are, indeed, those that lead to greater political and media turmoil. However, immigration scholarship traditionally distinguishes between two different types of regularizations: on the one hand, there are the above-mentioned 'amnesties', where states use one-off collective schemes, limited in time and generally involving a large number of applicants (generally referred to as *regularization programmes*);[48] on the other hand, and contrary to common belief, it is far more common for states to regularize by means of permanent and legally established procedures that pre-define the conditions to regularize. There are commonly referred to as *regularization mechanisms*.[49] These mechanisms are more low-key and generally allow states wider leeway to manoeuvre, adjusting regularizations to pre-defined conditions and specific policy aims.[50]

3.1.1 Regularization programmes

The use of regularization programmes by EU Member States has varied widely over the past decades. Albeit with different frequency and policy goals in mind, most Member States resorted to regularization programmes in the 1990s and in the early 2000s.[51]

The largest and more frequent regularization programmes took place in Italy and Spain. In the Spanish case, the country, which by the 1980s was still an emigration country,[52] saw regularizations as a way to deal with a large and unexpected number of arrivals and integrate migrants into the labour market.[53] Regularization programmes already took place in 1985 and 1991,[54] but by the 2000s they were taking place almost annually, with the single largest programme regularizing

47 Ambrosini and Hajer (n 19) 74.

48 Baldwin-Edwards and Kraler (n 2) 10; Lazaridis (n 2) 132; Organization for Security and Co-operation in Europe (OSCE), 'Regularization of migrants in an irregular situation in the OSCE region: Recent developments, points for discussion and recommendations', 2 August 2021, available at: <https://www.osce.org/odihr/494251>.

49 Ibid.

50 Ambrosini and Hajer (n 19) 75.

51 Kraler, 'Regularisation: A Misguided Option or Part and Parcel of a Comprehensive Policy Response to Irregular Migration?' (n 34) 7.

52 Ruben Andersson, *Illegality, Inc.: Clandestine Migration and the Business of Bordering Europe* (University of California Press 2014) 21.

53 Carmen González-Enríquez, 'Spain, the Cheap Model. Irregularity and Regularisation as Immigration Management Policies' (2009) 11 European Journal of Migration and Law 139, 139.

54 Hinterberger (n 1) 195.

around 578,000 persons in 2005.[55] A similar pattern was followed in Italy, where the largest regularization programme, in 2002, led to the regularization of around 650,000 persons.[56] Despite the rather indiscriminate character of some of the regularizations and the fact that they were relatively easy to access for their beneficiaries, regularization programmes in both countries followed a labour market-oriented rationale.[57] Similar dynamics (but with smaller numbers) could be observed in Portugal and Greece.[58]

However, regularization programmes were notlimited to Mediterranean Member States. Countries such as Denmark, France, Germany, and Luxembourg resorted to regularization programmes, although in smaller numbers and largely to respond to non-removability and asylum backlogs.[59] The Netherlands and Sweden used them very rarely, again following a humanitarian (rather than job market) perspective and, in the Swedish case, targeting non-removable migrants in particular.[60] Poland adopted very flexible regularization programmes in 2003, 2007, and 2012, with the only substantial criterion being prolonged irregular residence.[61] Moreover, Belgium conducted a large-scale regularization programme in 2000, with eligibility being based on asylum backlogs, non-removability, serious illness, or long-lasting ties in the country.[62]

However, as noted above, in the second half of the 2000s regularization programmes grew in unpopularity, in a process that culminated in the 2008 Pact on Immigration and Asylum, where, at the initiative of countries such as Germany, France, Denmark, Austria, and Ireland, EU leaders committed to use only case-by-case regularization.[63] Despite the Pact containing no binding legal obligations, the common position agreed upon in it deeply influenced the attitude of the EU and its

[55] González-Enríquez (n 53) 149.

[56] Martin Baldwin-Edwards and Francesca Zampagni, 'Regularisations and Employment in Italy' (2014) ICMPD REGANE Assessment Report 13.

[57] Baldwin-Edwards and Zampagni (n 56); Julio Gómez Díaz, 'Seguridad social de los extranjeros. Inmigración y Seguridad Social, una gestión integrada' in Manuel Balado Ruiz-Gallegos (ed), *Inmigración, Estado y Derecho: perspectivas desde el siglo XXI* (Bosch 2008). In Italy, 'indiscriminate' regularizations were accompanied by more selective ones addressed to domestic workers (see Kraler, 'Regularization of Irregular Migrants and Social Policies' (n 16) 9). In Spain, employment contracts were sometimes required and applications were many times carried out by potential employers, and not by migrants themselves (see Gómez Díaz 887).

[58] Martin Baldwin-Edwards and Albert Kraler (eds), 'Appendix B: Country Profiles of 22 EU Member States and the USA', in *REGINE—Regularisations in Europe* (Amsterdam University Press 2009) 115.

[59] Kraler, 'Regularisation: A Misguided Option or Part and Parcel of a Comprehensive Policy Response to Irregular Migration?' (n 34) 7.

[60] Kraler, 'Regularization of Irregular Migrants and Social Policies' (n 16) 9–10.

[61] Ibid, 10.

[62] Baldwin-Edwards and Kraler (n 58) 18.

[63] Council of the European Union, 'European Pact on Immigration and Asylum' (n 13) 7. The original intention of proponent Member States was to ban regularization programmes, but the opposition of Mediterranean Member States led to a compromise in the Council's recommendation and a political commitment by the Member States.

Member States towards regularization programmes in the decade that followed.[64] Indeed, Member States largely refrained from using this tool in the 2010s,[65] with the most notable exception being Poland's 2012 programme.[66]

However, the political landscape might have changed during and after Covid-19. The pandemic raised questions as to the vulnerability and precariousness of (irregular) migrant workers in essential sectors,[67] and ultimately led to bottom-up initiatives advocating for collective regularizations in countries such as Belgium, France, Italy, Portugal, and Spain.[68] Only Italy and Portugal adopted such programmes, with Italy focusing on migrant workers in specific sectors facing labour shortages during Covid-19[69] and Portugal offering permits to those with an ongoing regularization process.[70] In the meantime, other Member States strengthened regularization mechanisms and adopted other measures to avoid people falling into irregularity by extending permits.[71]

The emergency context in which these measures were adopted makes it difficult to establish premature conclusions as to whether the policy taboo around regularization programmes remains in place. Indeed, countries such as Spain seem to have definitely shifted from a collective regularization paradigm to one based on robust regularization mechanisms, as the following section will show. In the meantime, however, important regularization programmes have been adopted in Greece and Ireland. In Greece, a regularization programme has been adopted

64 On the Commission's anti-regularization position, see Costello (n 14) 100.

65 This is particularly the case for Spain and Italy. In the former case, the Spanish minister of migrations expressed in the Spanish Parliament that no 'indiscriminate' regularization programmes were foreseen in the context of Covid-19 because all EU Member States committed not to do so in the 2008 Pact (see Agencia EFE, 'Escrivá descarta una regularización "indiscriminada" de inmigrantes', 22 June 2022, available at: <https://www.efe.com/efe/espana/politica/escriva-descarta-una-regularizacion-indiscriminada-de-inmi-grantes/10002-4836753>). In the case of the latter, Italy did implement a regularization programme in 2012, but this was limited to irregular migrants working in specific sectors (see Hendow and Qaisrani (n 6) 63).

66 Organization for Security and Co-operation in Europe (OSCE) (n 48) 9.

67 Anna Triandafyllidou and Brenda SA Yeoh, 'Sustainability and Resilience in Migration Governance for a Post-Pandemic World' (2023) 21 Journal of Immigrant & Refugee Studies 1.

68 Roberta Perna and María Puig Batalla, 'Immigrant Regularisation Politics during COVID-19: Advocacy Coalitions and Governments' Incentives in Italy and Spain' (2023) 28 South European Society and Politics 415, 416.

69 European Commission, 'Italian government adopts targeted regularisation for migrant workers', 18 May 2020, available at: <https://migrant-integration.ec.europa.eu/news/italian-government-adopts-targeted-regularisation-migrant-workers_en>.

70 European Commission, 'Portugal: More than 356,000 immigrants provisionally legalised during COVID-19 pandemic', 16 January 2021, available at: <https://migrant-integration.ec.europa.eu/news/portugal-more-356-000-immigrants-provisionally-legalised-during-covid-19-pandemic_en>. However, this programme was criticized for its restrictive requirements and the temporary and unstable character of the permits (see Caterina Mazzilli, 'Regularising migrants: Portugal's missed chance', *Social Europe*, 6 December 2021, available at: <https://socialeurope.eu/regularising-migrants-portugals-missed-chance).

71 PICUM, 'Regularising undocumented people in response to the COVID-19 pandemic', 1 July 2020, available at: <https://picum.org/blog/regularising-undocumented-people-in-response-to-the-covid-19-pandemic/>; Organization for Security and Co-operation in Europe (OSCE) (n 48) 8.

based on an existing mechanism, pursuing a labour market rationale.[72] More interestingly, Ireland, a country that had held an anti-regularization position in the negotiations leading to the 2008 Pact, implemented in 2022 a regularization programme available for every irregular migrant proving four years of irregular residence by January 2022.[73] Interestingly, this programme was based on factual residence only, it was detached from labour market considerations, and it was very flexible in its requirements, achieving a very high success rate in practice.[74]

3.1.2 Regularization mechanisms

The problems accompanying regularization programmes are clear. In a policy context too often dominated by anti-immigration narratives, regularization programmes can be deeply unpopular among the electorate and lead to media uproar. Moreover, while regularization programmes are a useful tool to offer a 'fresh start' to immigration systems and deal with accumulated irregular migration stocks (and non-removable migrants in particular),[75] they do not seem an adequate tool for everyday migration management. Even if regularization programmes may seek to address specific policy aims and tailor access requirements accordingly, these conditions change from programme to programme and are, by definition, more indiscriminate than regularization mechanisms, where legally pre-determined requirements regulate who can access which type of permit. Then, regularization mechanisms can more accurately pursue specific aims—be it fighting the underground economy, filling labour shortages, or protecting vulnerable people. Lastly, regularization programmes generally offer short-term, precarious permits, with evidence showing that migrants often fall back into irregularity.[76] While this is often also the case with regularization mechanisms, the latter offer states (at least in theory) the possibility to tailor residence permits to the specific needs of applicants. This does not call into question the usefulness (or actual necessity) of regularization programmes in certain contexts, as programmes and mechanisms are not mutually exclusive. It seems evident, however, that predictable and legally predetermined mechanisms should form the day-to-day basis of states' regularization practices, with programmes periodically resetting migration systems.

[72] Hendow and Qaisrani (n 6) 61. This meant that an existing mechanism was amended, activated, and proactively put into place, leading to a one-off regularization (even if based on an existing mechanism) targeting approximately 30,000 irregular migrants.

[73] Ibid. The time required was lower in the case of families.

[74] Irish Department of Justice, 'Policy Paper on the scheme to regularise long-term undocumented migrants in Ireland', 2022, available at: <chrome-extension://efaidnbmnnnibpcajpcglclefindmkaj/https://www.irishimmigration.ie/wp-content/uploads/2022/01/Undocumented-Policy-Scheme-January-2022.pdf>. The programme did not require former legal residence or an employment record, it permitted temporary absences from the country, and it did not require any proof of integration. Moreover, those with a deportation order were equally entitled to apply.

[75] Song and Bloemraad (n 44) 11.

[76] Hendow and Qaisrani (n 6) 63.

As noted above, the 2008 Pact on Immigration and Asylum established a clear preference for 'case-by-case' regularizations, leading to a paradigm change. This was particularly the case in Mediterranean Member States, where programmes were a daily tool of migration management at the time. While the negative consequence arising from the 2008 Pact, that is, the increasing 'anti-regularization ethos' in Europe (and the subsequent accumulation of irregular migration stocks), has been analysed elsewhere in the literature,[77] some Member States have seized the opportunity to develop increasingly effective and sophisticated regularization mechanisms. In Spain, the Foreigners' Decree foresees regularization based on four overarching schemes, namely *arraigo*,[78] humanitarian grounds, cooperation with public authorities or national security or public interest reasons, and 'other exceptional circumstances'.[79] These regularization mechanisms are legally defined as 'temporary residence due to exceptional circumstances',[80] but their usage is far from exceptional. According to the Spanish Ministry of Inclusion, Social Security and Migration, 357,422 residence permits due to 'exceptional circumstances' were granted in 2023, accounting for 42% of all 848,988 residence permits issued.[81] Most residence permits are granted under one of the four 'settlement' mechanisms (*arraigo*), that is, labour, social, family, or education.[82] By the end of 2023, there were 210,334 persons with an *arraigo* residence permit, with migrants spending an average of 2.9 years in irregularity prior to regularization.[83] Thus, even though Spain only introduced its first regularization mechanisms in 2005,[84] it now offers a strong regularization framework that generally avoids long-term irregularity in the country.

Nevertheless, regularization mechanisms diverge greatly across Member States, with some, such as Germany, Austria, and the Netherlands, adopting an anti-regularization stance—yet still having some regularization mechanisms in place.[85] In some Member States regularization follows automatically upon the fulfilment of legally defined conditions,[86] while in others administrative discretion

[77] Costello (n 14) 98–102.

[78] The Spanish word *arraigo* translates to 'rootedness' or 'settlement'.

[79] Real Decreto 557/2011, de 20 de abril, por el que se aprueba el Reglamento de la Ley Orgánica 4/2000, sobre derechos y libertades de los extranjeros en España y su integración social, tras su reforma por Ley Orgánica 2/2009 arts 123–30.

[80] Ibid, Title V.

[81] Permanent Observatory on Migration (OPI), 'Flujo de Autorizaciones de Residencia Concedidas a Extranjeros. Año 2023', available at: <https://www.inclusion.gob.es/web/opi/estadisticas/catalogo/flujo_autorizaciones>.

[82] These are further elaborated upon in the following section.

[83] Permanent Observatory on Migration (OPI), 'Estadística de personas con autorización inicial de residencia por arraigo: Datos semestrales desde el 30 de junio de 2013 al 31 de diciembre de 2023' 7, available at: <https://www.inclusion.gob.es/web/opi/estadisticas/catalogo/arraigo>.

[84] Hinterberger (n 1) 224.

[85] Hendow and Qaisrani (n 6) 61. In the case of Austria, there are a number of regularization mechanisms in place, but these are rarely used in practice (Hinterberger (n 1) 248).

[86] This is the case in Spain across all its permits due to 'exceptional circumstances' (Esteban de la Rosa, 'Art 31 LODYLE' in José Luis Monereo Pérez, José Antonio Fernández Avilés and Luis Ángel

prevails.[87] Still, the current regulatory landscape is one in which most regularizations now take place through mechanisms. But the analytical distinction between regularization programmes and mechanisms tells us little about their underlying logics. A second, and perhaps more interesting, distinction studies regularization measures looking at their motivations, inquiring into who is regularized, why, and under what conditions.

3.2 Regularization purposes: From labour market to human rights

Regularization programmes and mechanisms can follow different purposes. A large-scale regularization programme can aim to fight the underground economy, as well as 'reset' the system in line with the rule of law arguments developed above, or pursue humanitarian aims. Nevertheless, regularization programmes, by their very nature, tend to have broader requirements, as they aim for the sudden regularization of a larger group of persons. It is with mechanisms that Member States can more accurately achieve specific policy aims, allowing them to clearly define the profile of individuals qualifying for a residence permit under each specific mechanism.

Be that as it may, regularization programmes and mechanisms can follow different approaches, each requiring the target population to fulfil specific conditions for eligibility. While there are many possible ways to categorize regularization practices based on their aims, this chapter identifies two major normative approaches: one driven by an economic, labour market logic; and a rights-based (or rights-inspired) one.[88] While the former puts the focus on the host state and its own policy objectives, the latter focuses on the needs of migrants. Both categories are immensely diverse in the population and the specific aims they target, and they are not mutually exclusive. Indeed, states may resort to both types, and a single regularization measure may follow both rationales simultaneously.

Triguero Martínez (eds), *Comentario a la Ley y al Reglamento de Extranjería, Inmigración e Integración Social (LO 4/2000 y RD 557/2011)* (Dykinson 2013) 448). Other examples include Luxembourg's mechanisms for irregular children, Italy's autonomous permit for children of regular parents, or Finland's permits for victims of labour exploitation (PICUM, 'Regularisation mechanisms and programmes: Why they matter and how to design them', 2022 55,56, and 61, available at: <https://picum.org/work-area/regularisation/>).

[87] This is the case of the Netherlands and France (Hendow and Qaisrani (n 6) 64). Some regularization mechanisms in Belgium are also fully discretionary in their design (PICUM, 'Regularisation mechanisms and programmes' (n 86) 28).

[88] In the US context, these two ways to earn regularization have been labelled as 'sweat' and 'tears' by Lakhani (Sarah Morando Lakhani, 'Producing Immigrant Victims' "Right" to Legal Status and the Management of Legal Uncertainty' (2013) 38 Law & Social Inquiry 442, 442). Similar categorizations have been made in the EU context (see Lazaridis (n 2) 132; Kraler, 'Regularization of Irregular Migrants and Social Policies' (n 16) 6). Ambrosini and Hajer speak about five different avenues for regularization, while Hinerberger suggests a sixfold distinction. However, all of them can be subsumed within the two categories suggested in this chapter (see Ambrosini and Hajer (n 19) 76–78; Hinterberger (n 1) 73).

3.2.1 Labour market regularizations

Following a 'utilitarian' logic (see section 2.3), labour market-oriented regularizations have traditionally been implemented in Mediterranean Member States.[89] These regularizations generally focus on the integration of migrants into the labour market and aim at selecting 'good citizens',[90] although the specific forms and conditions vary. As noted above, these were at first implemented mainly by means of regularization programmes that, despite their more indiscriminate character, maintained a link to the labour market.[91] As noted above, however, state practice has shifted in recent years towards the use of regularization mechanisms. Countries such as Belgium, France, Greece, Italy, Portugal, or Spain all have regularization mechanisms based on education and employment, with Italy and Spain again standing out in this regard.[92] Interestingly, Germany, a country traditionally following a humanitarian approach to regularization, increasingly takes into account labour market considerations in its mechanisms, adopting a mixed approach. For instance, recent legislative reforms in the country have led to the possibility of obtaining a 'residence permit for the purpose of employment for qualified foreigners whose deportation has been suspended',[93] mixing a rights-based approach (regularizing non-removable migrants) with labour market demands.[94]

Perhaps the most paradigmatic example of such mechanisms is provided by Spain's extensive regularization under the institution of *arraigo*. Included in Spanish legislation as a temporary residence permit due to 'exceptional circumstances',[95] in practice it serves as a permanent, day-to-day regularization mechanism. Regulated in Article 124 of Spain's Foreigners Decree, it establishes four different paths to lawful residence. First, under labour *arraigo*, applicants must prove two years of (regular or irregular) residence and show proof of having already worked (regularly or irregularly) for at least six months.[96] Second, under social *arraigo*, applicants must show three years of residence, a signed employment contract, and either family links with other TCNs in the country or a report issued by public authorities attesting to their social integration.[97] Third, family

[89] Sébastien Chauvin, Blanca Garcés-Mascareñas, and Albert Kraler, 'Working for Legality: Employment and Migrant Regularization in Europe' (2013) 51 International Migration 118, 118.

[90] Kraler, 'Regularization of Irregular Migrants and Social Policies' (n 16) 3.

[91] In Spain, regularization programmes often required an employment contract, and applications were many times filed by prospective employers (Gómez Díaz (n 57) 887). This was also the case with most regularization programmes in Italy, including its 2020 programme in the context of Covid-19 (Hendow and Qaisrani (n 6) 63).

[92] Organization for Security and Co-operation in Europe (OSCE) (n 48) 11; Hendow and Qaisrani (n 6) 64.

[93] For an analysis of this permit, see Hinterberger (n 1) 329–37.

[94] On Germany's shifting approach towards the labour market, see Christian Joppke, 'From Asylum to Labour: Track Change in German Migration Policy' (2023) 47 West European Politics 813.

[95] Real Decreto 557/2011 (n 79) Título V.

[96] Real Decreto 557/2011 (n 79) art 124(1).

[97] Ibid, art 124(2).

arraigo applies to parents or tutors of Spanish children, TCNs overseeing and living with a Spanish national with disabilities, spouses or registered partners of Spanish nationals,[98] and TCNs whose mother or father were originally Spanish.[99] Lastly, education *arraigo*, introduced following a 2022 legal reform, offers residence permits to TCNs who can show two years of residence and agree to complete an educational programme that leads to a professional certification in designated sectors.[100] All mechanisms require a clean criminal record and, with the exception of family *arraigo* (which, by its nature, would belong to the following section), they are linked to the labour market. Quantitatively, *arraigo* represents the most important regularization tool in Spain, with hundreds of thousands of permits granted every year.[101] Despite being primarily a labour market-oriented tool, *arraigo* regularizations are highly accessible and, in practice, they also work as a tool to handle rejected asylum seekers and non-removable migrants.[102]

3.2.2 Rights-based regularizations

Most Member States have regularization mechanisms that follow a rights-based approach. Though they have often been labelled as 'humanitarian' regularizations,[103] these go beyond purely humanitarian cases and include all sorts of regularization measures based on applicants' rights and needs (and not on state interests). Regularizing grounds under this category include, among others, family and private life, the best interests of the child, prolonged irregular residence, and non-removability, as well as strictly 'humanitarian' permits based on serious illness, human trafficking, gender violence, or labour exploitation.[104] These regularizations are generally based on (but not mandated by) previous commitments under international and European law. For instance, states might regularize those who have already become non-removable under European standards, but who would otherwise remain in a situation of indefinite irregularity. Again, labour market and rights-based aims are not mutually exclusive, inasmuch as Member

[98] Ibid, art 124(3). This also applies to ascendants over 65 years (under 65 if dependent), as well as descendants under 21 (over 21 if dependent) of Spanish nationals or their spouses or registered partners.

[99] Ibid.

[100] Ibid, 124(4). The sectors vary depending on the changing needs of the Spanish labour market. The residence permit can be extended to complete the educational programme and, once this is completed, a two-year residence permit is granted by submitting a signed contract in the same field.

[101] In 2023 alone, 203,969 permits were granted under *arraigo* (Permanent Observatory on Migration (OPI) (n 81)).

[102] Laura García-Juan and Javier Alonso Calderón, 'El arraigo social como alternativa legal para los solicitantes de asilo de larga duración en la Unión Europea' (2023) 14 Migraciones Internacionales 1. In Spain, *arraigo*, together with other rights-based mechanisms (analysed in section 3.2.2) serves to solve some issues derived from a highly dysfunctional asylum system with very low recognition rates and difficulties in filing asylum applications (see Spanish Ombudsman, 'Informe annual 2022: Volumen I', 2022 170, available at: <https://www.defensordelpueblo.es/informe-anual/informe-anual-2022/>).

[103] Organization for Security and Co-operation in Europe (OSCE) (n 48) 11.

[104] Permits based on labour exploitation can simultaneously follow a labour market logic, encouraging victims to report, tackling irregular employment, and bringing them into the formal economy.

States may use both types of regularizations, and might even mix economic and humanitarian aims within the very same mechanism.

Rights-based regularization programmes and mechanisms were largely incorporated by European countries in the 1990s, when the collapse of the USSR and later Yugoslavia led to mixed migration flows with large numbers of persons in need of protection, but often with claims that did not fit traditional refugee definitions.[105] At the same time, regularization programmes and mechanisms were established to recognize migrants' existing ties to the host Member State, thereby following a family and private life logic.[106]

Rights-based regularizations have traditionally been more prominent than labour market ones in 'northern' Member States.[107] For example, and despite resorting to regularization only scarcely, the Netherlands and Sweden do so following a humanitarian logic only.[108] This was implemented via regularization programmes in the early 2000s, and later through mechanisms, focusing in particular on seriously ill persons and, in the case of the Netherlands, on family life claims.[109] However, permits based on rights-based logics are adopted in most Member States.[110] For example, Spain, a country that largely follows a labour market approach in its regularization practices, has regularization mechanisms under a range of 'humanitarian grounds',[111] as well as for irregular migrants that cooperate with labour authorities or against organized crime[112] and for victims of gender-based violence and human trafficking.[113] In Italy, state authorities must examine whether failed asylum seekers meet the criteria for special protection permits, which are granted on the basis of fundamental rights and the principle of *non-refoulement*.[114] In Greece, regularization can also be obtained for various humanitarian reasons.[115]

105 Kraler, 'Regularisation: A Misguided Option or Part and Parcel of a Comprehensive Policy Response to Irregular Migration?' (n 34) 7. This was the strategy of states such as Denmark, France, Germany, Luxembourg, and the UK.

106 Ibid, 8.

107 Kraler, 'Regularization of Irregular Migrants and Social Policies' (n 16) 15.

108 Ibid, 9–10.

109 Ibid. Medical reasons and serious illness can also lead to residence permits in Belgium, Croatia, Greece, Italy, Luxembourg, Slovenia, and Spain (Organization for Security and Co-operation in Europe (OSCE) (n 48) 12).

110 European Migration Network (EMN), 'Comparative overview of national protection statuses in the EU and Norway', May 2020 11, available at: <https://home-affairs.ec.europa.eu/whats-new/publications/comparative-overview-national-protection-statuses-eu-and-norway_en>.

111 Real Decreto 557/2011 (n 79) art 126. These include victims of certain crimes or of crimes aggravated by racism, antisemitism, or other forms of discrimination; victims of crimes that have taken place in the family environment; individuals with severe health conditions that cannot be treated in their home country; and those who meet the requirements for a temporary residence permit in Spain but cannot return to their home country to initiate the visa application process due to safety concerns for themselves or their families.

112 Ibid, arts 127 and 137.

113 Ibid, arts 131–34 and 140–46.

114 PICUM, 'Regularisation mechanisms and programmes' (n 86) 25.

115 Ibid, 5. These include being a victim of human trafficking, domestic violence, or domestic abuse, or the impossibility to return to a safe country, among other reasons.

3.2.2.1 Regularization and non-removability

One of the single most important reasons for many Member States to regularize is precisely found in non-removability, with many mechanisms based on or conditioned upon the applicant being non-removable. In this way, domestic legislation can avoid limbo situations by complementing an EU framework that precludes deportation without any subsequent regularization obligations, or simply respond to backlogs in deportation orders due to practical implementation obstacles. For example, an important number of Member States grant residence permits based on private and family life reasons, inspired by Article 8 ECHR. In some cases, there is a direct link with non-removability, as the law requires applicants to be non-removable on Article 8 ECHR grounds. This is the case with the Netherlands, where irregular migrants can qualify for a residence permit if, following a balancing exercise between state interests and migrants' claims, their removal would be contrary to Article 8 ECHR.[116] Moreover, in Austria, the 'right to remain' might be granted if administrative authorities conclude that removal is not possible due to family and/or private life reasons.[117] In other cases, however, residence permits might be granted upon the fulfilment of some family and/or social integration criteria regardless of whether the person would have a self-standing legal right not to be removed.[118] Moreover, non-removability based on *non-refoulement* obligations can also provide lawful statuses beyond asylum law.[119]

In Germany and Austria, non-removability (be it due to legal or practical reasons) in principle only leads to 'tolerated' (but still irregular) status via *Duldung*,[120] although it is possible to 'jump' from *Duldung* status to a residence permit. In fact, most of the regularization routes in both countries are available only for non-removable migrants with *Duldung* status. As noted above, Austria's most significant regularization mechanisms are contingent on public authorities determining that removal is 'permanently inadmissible' due to family and/or private reasons, while 'special protection' residence permits require applicants to be non-removable for at least one year.[121] In Germany, regularization mechanisms are addressed, almost exclusively, to non-removable migrants, that is, those whose

[116] This however takes place in a process characterized by administrative discretion and the gap between non-removal and regularization persists (see PICUM, 'Regularisation mechanisms and programmes' (n 86) 32).

[117] Hinterberger (n 1) 141.

[118] This is the case with Spain's family *arraigo* (see section 3.2.1). Also, the existence of family ties with legal residents and other indicators of social integration are key elements of social *arraigo* (see section 3.2.1). This is also the case in France following the 'Valls Circular', although in this case regularization processes are characterized by administrative discretion (Hendow and Qaisrani (n 6) 66).

[119] This applies in Finland, Greece, Ireland, Lithuania, Poland, and Sweden (European Migration Network (EMN) (n 110) 18).

[120] For an in-depth analysis of *Duldung* status, see Theresa Schütze, 'The (Non-)Status of "Duldung": Non-Deportability in Germany and the Politics of Limitless Temporariness' (2023) 36 Journal of Refugee Studies 409.

[121] Hinterberger (n 1) 141 and 248–49.

return has been suspended and who have obtained *Duldung* status.[122] Then, the basic requirement to obtain a 'right to remain' is to have lived in Germany for several years with a *Duldung* status,[123] although additional conditions vary. These can be linked to rights-based considerations (e.g. 'permanent integration', serious illness, or the existence of a deportation ban or other legal barriers to deportation), or follow economic objectives by aiming at workers with specific skills.[124]

In the majority of Member States, however, non-removability, *per se*, is not contemplated as a stand-alone ground for regularization. This does not entail that non-removable migrants cannot benefit from regularization. For example, by regularizing those suffering from serious illnesses, states offer a route to regularization to a group of people that would be difficult to deport anyway. Moreover, refugeehood and non-removability are often intertwined, with some of the reasons precluding deportation being connected to asylum law—and non-removable migrants often being failed asylum seekers. Then, irrespective of regularization mechanisms specifically addressed to non-removable migrants, other mechanisms can be made available to persons who, unwelcomed by asylum systems, still have important protection needs. Even when driven by a labour market rationale, regularization becomes a useful tool to avoid long-term irregularity and non-removability. For instance, in Spain, regularizations under *arraigo* are an effective and inclusive tool that generally helps avoid long-term irregularity in the country.[125] One must bear in mind that, regardless of the purpose of regularizations being *prima facie* 'utilitarian', countries such as Spain and Italy use regularization much more extensively than other countries,[126] ultimately benefiting a wide range of people, including non-removable migrants, vulnerable persons, and failed asylum seekers, among others.

3.3 Interim conclusion

The classification of regularization practices provided in this section is no doubt oversimplified, as Member States resort to different types and may simultaneously mix labour market and rights-based aims in a single regularization measure. For example, a regularization mechanism might require applicants to simultaneously show prolonged residence, social ties, non-removability, and hold a job offer.

122 Kraler, 'Regularization of Irregular Migrants and Social Policies' (n 16) 9.
123 Hinterberger (n 1) 170.
124 Ibid, 170, 171, 249, 250, and 259.
125 Permanent Observatory on Migration (OPI) (n 83) 7.
126 Around 75% of all regularizations conducted in the period between 1973 and 2008 in the EU took place in Spain, Italy, and Greece (Lazaridis (n 2) 134). The lowest regularization statistics take place in the Netherlands, Sweden, and Poland (Kraler, 'Regularization of Irregular Migrants and Social Policies' (n 16) 6).

Bearing this in mind, this section has offered an overview of regularization practices in the EU.

Despite anti-regularization discourses, Member States routinely turn to regularization as a migration management tool. But the lack of an EU framework on the issue is not without consequences. Member States regularize following different formats and purposes, they do so with greater or lesser frequency, and they give migrants widely divergent permits. Some Member States see themselves as pro-regularization, while some openly adopt an anti-regularization approach and do so only sporadically. Where one Member State provides flexible and easily accessible permits, another might impose draconian requirements, or uncertain conditions in processes characterized by administrative discretion. Some countries might demand prolonged irregular residence from applicants, where others will ask them to be economically self-sufficient or have a job offer. Where one grants a precarious permit that might be revoked at any time, another might provide a long-term, easily renewable permit. One Member State might require twenty years of residence where another requires two. In short, some frameworks will make it easier for (some) migrants to navigate their lives, where others will not. Then, irrespective of the evident human rights concerns raised by long-term irregularity and non-removability, and the challenges posed from an EU law 'effectiveness' perspective, the lack of harmonization in this field also has raised concerns in EU institutions as regards secondary movements in a context of internal open borders.[127]

4. European solutions to a European problem? The way forward

As seen in section 3, EU Member States have differing interpretations as to who is worthy of a residence permit. Depending on the Member State of residence, the same non-removable migrant can be offered a residence permit, 'tolerated stay', or remain fully irregularly. In this context, and considering the strikingly low return rates in the EU, it would be key for European law to acknowledge that, where individuals cannot be removed, prolonged irregularity and non-removability are beneficial neither for the migrants nor for the host state, and to offer some minimum regularization standards. While radical legislative changes in the field of regularization appear unlikely in the short term, this section hints at possible ways in which non-removability could be addressed—be it by the European Courts or the European legislator.

[127] European Commission, 'Staff Working Document, Fitness Check on EU Legislation on Legal Migration', SWD(2019) 1055 Final, 29 March 2019 51; Council of the European Union, 'Presidency paper on addressing challenges relating to migrants in a situation of prolonged illegal stay', 7560/20, 27 April 2020.

4.1 European Courts to the rescue? Regularization prospects

This book has dealt with the role of the CJEU and the ECtHR in the creation of non-removable migrants (Chapter 2 and 3). It has also suggested that the CJEU could have undertaken a different interpretation of EU asylum law to avoid non-removable migrants falling into irregularity in the first place (Chapter 2). The following paragraphs however anticipate possible regularization prospects before the CJEU and the ECtHR.

4.1.1 The CJEU: Regularization under the Return Directive?

Section 2 has emphasized that regularization is not only in line with the Return Directive's underlying objective to terminate 'illegal stay' but, in the case of non-removability, becomes the only way to do so. Then, despite the privileged position of return in the EU *acquis*, regularization might become the most effective way to ensure the effective implementation of EU law—in what I have labelled as the 'effectiveness argument'. However, the legislator created legal obligations for Member States to return, while it intentionally kept regularization under an optional provision in Article 6(4) RD. This raises doubts as to whether regularization might in some scenarios become a legal obligation, or remain simply a valid (but non-enforceable) policy option. In other words, the question remains whether an effectiveness-based interpretation of the EU law might generate concrete and enforceable legal obligations to regularize.

On the one hand, scholars have contended that the only way to interpret Article 6(4) RD in light of the principle of effectiveness and the EU Charter of Fundamental Rights (the Charter) is by granting, under certain circumstances, a right to regularize for non-removable migrants. Acosta has suggested that the CJEU should interpret Article 6(4) RD as affording, under certain circumstances, a residence permit to non-removable migrants by turning the provision's *may* clause into a binding obligation. According to him, such interpretation would follow by reading the provision in light of the Charter, taking into account the vulnerability of long-term irregular migrants, states' inaction, the lack of deportation prospects, and the principle of effectiveness of EU law (widely used by the CJEU in other strands of its jurisprudence—and which here would require the 'termination of illegal stay').[128] A similar interpretation is provided by Desmond.[129] According

[128] Diego Acosta Arcarazo, 'The Charter, Detention and Possible Regularization of Migrants in an Irregular Situation under the Returns Directive: *Mahdi*' (2015) 52 Common Market Law Review 1361. Similarly, Majcher interprets that for the Return Directive to be interpreted in full respect of fundamental rights and the right of people to leave with dignity, non-removable migrants should be offered a right to regularize (Izabella Majcher, *The European Union Returns Directive and Its Compatibility with International Human Rights Law: Analysis of Return Decision, Entry Ban, Detention, and Removal* (Brill Nijhoff 2019) 225).

[129] Desmond (n 11) 146–48.

to Hinterberger, the Return Directive provides for an obligation to regularize in two circumstances: first, when there are 'permanent obstacles' to deportation, following a similar interpretation of the Return Directive put forward by Acosta and Desmond on the termination of irregular stay in accordance with the Directive's aims; second, when deportation would violate the principle of *non-refoulement*.[130] In less ambitious terms, the European Parliament 'suggests' that Member States expand the use of the *may* clause of Article 6(4) RD to regularize when return proves to be impossible.[131]

However, CJEU jurisprudence has been clear on the lack of binding force of the regularizing clause of Article 6(4) RD. Even though the CJEU has relied extensively on the effectiveness of EU law in other cases concerning the interpretation of the Return Directive,[132] it ruled in *Mahdi* that the Return Directive did not require Bulgaria to issue a permit to a non-removable migrant, even though he could not receive identity documents from his country of origin, he had exhausted the maximum period of detention, and there was no reasonable prospect of removal.[133] In *X*, the CJEU held that the Return Directive, read in line with the Charter, requires Member States to refrain from issuing a return decision or a removal order if there are substantial grounds to believe that return would expose the applicant to a serious risk of torture or inhuman or degrading treatment or punishment (i.e. if it would be contrary to *non-refoulement*).[134] This prohibits states from adopting unenforceable return decisions which are contrary to the principle of *non-refoulement* in order to subsequently postpone them following Article 9 RD. However, the CJEU again makes clear that, with or without a return decision, non-removable migrants do not acquire a right to regularize their status under Article 6(4) RD.[135] Thus, regardless of the reasons precluding removal or the length of irregular stay, the Return Directive's *may* clause under Article 6(4) RD has never been interpreted as containing binding legal obligations to regularize.

[130] Hinterberger (n 1) 103–06.

[131] European Parliament, 'Report on the Implementation of the Return Directive', 2019/2208(INI), 17 December 2020 para 23, available at: <https://www.europarl.europa.eu/doceo/document/A-9-2020-0238_EN.html>.

[132] *El Dridi* (n 10) para 49; *Achughbabian* (n 10) para 41; Case C-181/16, *Sadikou Gnandi v État Belge* [2018] EU:C:2018:465 para. 50; Case C-383/13 PPU, M. G., N. R. v Staatssecretaris van Veiligheid en Justitie [2013] EU:C:2013:533 para 36; Case C-441/19, *TQ v Staatssecretaris van Justitie en Veiligheid* [2021] EU:C:2021:9 para 80.

[133] Case C-146/14 PPU, *Bashir Mohamed Ali Mahdi* [2014] EU:C:2014:1320 para 89.

[134] Case C-69/21, *X v Staatssecretaris van Justitie en Veiligheid* [2022] EU:C:2022:913 para 80. This seems to be incompatible with the CJEU's prior ruling in *BZ*, where the Court held that the mere toleration of irregular migrants, without a residence permit and with no return decision being adopted, is incompatible with the Directive (even in *non-refoulement* cases) (*BZ* (n 22) paras 57–58).

[135] *X* (n 134) para 103.

4.1.2 The ECtHR: Regularization under Articles 3 and 8 ECHR?

Together with negative non-removal obligations, the ECHR can also include positive obligations for states to provide a residence permit to non-removable migrants. While Articles 3 and 8 ECHR have been mainly analysed in this book as a barrier to expulsion, these provisions also can also be used to regularize the stay of otherwise irregular migrants.

First, the presence of non-removable migrants raises the question of whether prolonged situations of destitution resulting from irregular status can, in themselves, amount to inhuman or degrading treatment in the sense of Article 3 ECHR. As early as 1991, Antonio Cassese wondered whether the notion of inhuman and degrading treatment could be applied to socio-economic conditions.[136] With its landmark judgment in *M.S.S.*, the ECtHR finally addressed this issue in respect of an asylum-seeker in Greece. In this case, the Court found that the situation of extreme poverty and destitution of the applicant, together with his insecurity and vulnerability, the indifference of state authorities, and the 'total lack of any likelihood of his situation improving', reached the level of severity needed to trigger Article 3 ECHR.[137] However, the ECtHR has so far been unwilling to apply the same rationale in the context of irregular migration, despite the fact that Article 3 ECHR is an absolute and non-derogable provision. This means that its protection should not be balanced against state interests and should apply regardless of the applicant's migration status. In a series of inadmissibility decisions prior and subsequent to *M.S.S.*, the ECtHR has consistently denied Article 3 ECHR protection in cases of long-term (legal) non-removable migrants who were denied the possibility to regularize their status and hence were unable to live in dignity, often for decades (see Chapter 2).[138] In this context, legal scholars have already advocated for the expansion of the *M.S.S.* rationale to cases of protracted irregular residence and statelessness,[139] as there seems to be no reason why the effects of *M.S.S.* should

[136] Antonio Cassese, 'Can the Notion of Inhuman and Degrading Treatment Be Applied to Socio-Economic Conditions?' (1991) 2 European Journal of International Law 141.

[137] *M.S.S. v Belgium and Greece*, App No 30696/09 (ECtHR 21 January 2011) paras 253, 254, 259, and 263.

[138] *Teshome Goraga Bonger v the Netherlands*, App No 10154/04 (ECtHR, Decision of 15 September 2005); *I v the Netherlands*, App No 24147/11 (ECtHR, Decision of 10 July 2012); *K v the Netherlands*, App No 33403/11 (ECtHR, Decision of 25 September 2012); *Mohammad Rafiq Naibzay v the Netherlands*, App No 68564/12 (ECtHR, Decision of 25 October 2012). This case law is analysed and referred to by Dembour as the '*Bonger* case law' or 'destitution case law' (see Marie-Bénédicte Dembour, 'The Darkest Case Law: Condoning Rightlessness (Bonger et Alia)', *When Humans Become Migrants: Study of the European Court of Human Rights with an Inter-American Counterpoint* (Oxford University Press 2015) 442–81).

[139] Laurens Lavrysen, 'M.S.S. v Belgium and Greece (2): The impact on EU asylum law', *Strasbourg Observers*, 24 February 2011, available at: <https://strasbourgobservers.com/2011/02/24/m-s-s-v-belgium-and-greece-2-the-impact-on-eu-asylum-law/>; Majcher (n 128) 223. Michelle Foster and Hélène Lambert, 'Statelessness as a Human Rights Issue: A Concept Whose Time Has Come' (2016) 28 International Journal of Refugee Law 564; Hélène Lambert, 'Nationality and statelessness before the European Court of Human Rights: A landmark judgment but what about Article 3 ECHR?', *Strasbourg Observers*, 16 May 2018, available at: <https://strasbourgobservers.com/2018/05/16/nationality-and-statelessness-before-the-european-court-of-human-rights-a-landmark-judgment-but-what-about-article-3-echr/>.

be unavailable for these persons—who often share with the applicant in *M.S.S.* many characteristics, such as vulnerability, precarious residence, state inaction, lack of prospects of leaving the country, and lack of prospects of circumstances changing.

Second, as seen in Chapter 3, obtaining protection from removal or regularization under Article 8 ECHR will depend on a 'lottery-like' and highly casuistic jurisprudence. For those who are already protected from removal and who remain in a situation of precarious residence, the same balancing criteria apply, but an even higher threshold will be required to obtain a residence permit under the ECHR. Contrary to Article 3 ECHR jurisprudence, Article 8 ECHR case law has included a right to regularize stay for quite a number of years. However, the ECtHR has traditionally held that a failure to issue a residence permit will only reach the Convention under exceptional circumstances,[140] in such a way that a right to regularization can hardly be inferred from Article 8 ECHR.[141] Yet this position is not necessarily static, and the ECtHR has recently shown some promising developments.

First, in *Pormes* the Court stressed that the 'exceptional circumstances' test for regularization under Article 8 ECHR was only meant to apply in cases where the person concerned was aware from the outset that his or her immigration status was precarious.[142] In the rest of the cases, the assessment of whether a person has a human right to regularize 'has to be carried out from a neutral starting point'.[143] Regardless of the fact that *Pormes* ended with a non-violation verdict due to the applicant's criminal convictions, the fact that the ECtHR began its reasoning from a 'neutral starting point' is very much welcome and could potentially lead to a more tangible human right to regularization.

Second, the ECtHR has produced landmark rulings concerning the regularization of stateless (and non-removable) persons. In *Hoti* and in *Sudita Keita*, the ECtHR considered that the applicants' statelessness was not merely an additional source of vulnerability to be considered in balancing the interests at stake, but rather a pivotal issue that justified states' obligation to provide a residence permit.[144] This reasoning allows the ECtHR to expand regularization opportunities for non-removable migrants. Indeed, non-removable migrants are often, if not *de jure* (like

[140] *Slivenko v Latvia*, App No 48321/99 (ECtHR 9 October 2003); *Rodrigues da Silva and Hoogkamer v the Netherlands*, App No 50435/99 (ECtHR 31 January 2006); *Aristimuño Mendizabal v France*, App No 51431/99 (ECtHR 17 January 2006); *Sisojeva and others v Latvia*, App No 60654/00 (ECtHR 16 June 2005); *Jeunesse v the Netherlands* [GC], App No 12738/10 (ECtHR 3 October 2014).

[141] Jean-Baptiste Farcy, 'Unremovability under the Return Directive: An Empty Protection?' in Galina Cornelisse and Philippe de Bruycker (eds), *Law and Judicial Dialogue on the Return of Irregular Migrants from the European Union* (Hart 2020) 449.

[142] *Pormes v the Netherlands*, App No 25402/14 (ECtHR 14 December 2020) para 58.

[143] Ibid, para 61.

[144] *Hoti v Croatia*, App No 63311/14 (ECtHR 26 April 2018) paras 110, 117, 126, 128, and 136–38; *Sudita Keita v Hungary*, App No 42321/15 (ECtHR 12 August 2020) paras 35–40.

the applicants in *Hoti* and *Sudita Keita*), *de facto* stateless, inasmuch as they may be both stateless and irregular, or simply hold the nationality of a country to which they are unable to return. In *Jeunesse*, concerning a non-removable migrant from Suriname, a relevant factor for the ECtHR to find a violation in the denial of a residence permit was the fact that the applicant's presence in the host country had been 'tolerated' for sixteen years, during which the state had failed to deport or refrained from deporting Ms Jeunesse.[145] Contrary to statelessness, non-removability was here one in many cumulative factors taken into account by the Court. However, these rulings open up a space for the ECtHR to take more seriously into account the impossibility to return to one's country of origin in its regularization case law. As a matter of fact, these cases take place in a context where there is not a real conflict between states' sovereign prerogatives and migrants' rights, as states have failed to exercise the former in a timely manner and migrants are unable to enjoy their rights elsewhere.

4.2 Legal responses to non-removability

Beyond judicial action, there are a wide range of solutions to be adopted to tackle non-removability at the EU level. Hinterberger has suggested the adoption of an 'EU Regularization Directive', which would complement the Return Directive and address the inconsistencies of domestic regularization procedures.[146] In his proposal, an initial phase would establish binding regularization obligations in a limited number of cases, including where removal would be contrary to Articles 3 and 8 ECHR, or where persons are permanently non-removable.[147] Other solutions suggested include the adoption of a 'temporary corrective protection status' in the context of the Return Directive in order to tackle the Union's flagrant return deficit.[148] Again, the specific features of a potential *sui generis* status for non-removable migrants under EU law (comparable to the issuance of *Duldung* status in Germany and Austria) would be up to the legislator to decide upon.

In a context where migrants' rights activism seems more focused on resistance and avoiding the further erosion of existing rights, the prospect of a Regularization Directive seems chimerical. However, in recent years the Commission and (surprisingly) the Council (via its Croatian presidency) have expressed the need for further integration on the rights of non-removable persons:

[145] *Jeunesse* (n 140) para 116.

[146] Kevin Fredy Hinterberger, 'An EU Regularization Directive. An Effective Solution to the Enforcement Deficit in Returning Irregularly Staying Migrants' (2019) 26 Maastricht Journal of European and Comparative Law 736; Hinterberger (n 1) 355–68.

[147] Hinterberger (n 146) 764. In a second phase, the remaining regularizations would be harmonized, although Member States would be granted some discretion (ibid, 765).

[148] Benedita Menezes Queiroz, 'Non-Removable Migrants in Europe: An Atypical Migration Status?' (2018) 24 European Public Law 29, 306–08.

> The variety of differing Member State approaches for dealing with non-removable returnees may constitute an incentive for secondary movements since this category of migrants may try to move to those Member States which offer the best conditions of stay. A 'common discipline' amongst Member States concerning the treatment of non-removable persons could prevent . . . In addition, it has been argued that the existence of large numbers of 'non-removables' with few rights and limited possibility to work in order to come up for their own living contributes to a negative public perception of migration and undermines the public acceptance of a sustainable EU migration policy as a whole. Common standards which would allow at least certain categories of 'non-removables' to work may contribute to alleviate this phenomenon.[149]

With record lows in the number of people that EU Member States are able to deport, it is high time the legislator recognizes that, as long as people remain in EU territory due to reasons beyond their control, Member States should not be able to act as if the obstacle to deportation did not exist, but must offer some form of harmonized protection. While radical changes in the current framework do not seem likely in the short term, the trilogue negotiations for a recast Return Directive open up a space to tackle at least some of the most pressing issues affecting non-removable migrants.

5. Conclusions

In a context where migration irregularity often operates as a 'master status',[150] negatively affecting every aspect of migrants' lives and denying access to fundamental rights, regularization becomes the only viable option for non-removable migrants to come back from invisibility. Section I of this book inquired into the processes that lead to an increasing population of irregular yet non-deportable people in Europe. Their precarious situation as regards status and access to rights (Chapter 5), together with the denial of their 'right to have rights' elsewhere,[151] creates strong claims for regularization.

[149] European Commission, 'Staff Working Document, Fitness Check on EU Legislation on Legal Migration' (n 128) 85. This passage was paraphrased by the presidency of the Council who strongly advocated for further harmonization on the issue at the EU level in a 2020 presidency paper leaked by Statewatch (See Council of the European Union, 'Presidency paper on addressing challenges relating to migrants in a situation of prolonged illegal stay' (n 127)).

[150] Roberto G Gonzales, 'Chapter 8. Adulthood: How Immigration Status Becomes a Master Status', *Lives in Limbo: Undocumented and Coming of Age in America* (1st edn, University of California Press 2016).

[151] For a contemporary application of Hannah Arendt's notion, see Noora Lori, 'Statelessness, "In-Between" Statuses, and Precarious Citizenship', *The Oxford Handbook of Citizenship* (Oxford University Press 2017) 755.

EU law leaves Member States the choice to return or regularize irregular migrants. Even though the Return Directive's underlying logic is the termination of illegal stay (be it through return or regularization), the existence of comprehensive return obligations, together with the lack of explicit regularization obligations in the Return Directive, denotes that EU norms on irregular migration are built to deport—but are very often incapable of doing so. This overwhelming focus on return by the legislator, Member States, and EU policy-makers helps explain the CJEU's questionable interpretation that the Return Directive does in no circumstances offer a right of residence, even when this seems to be the only interpretation that guarantees the effectiveness of EU law. This has led to paradoxical interpretations of EU law where the CJEU reinforces the very same situations of legal limbo it seeks to combat. In *X*, the Court notes that Member States not only must postpone, but should refrain from issuing a return decision if its execution would be contrary to Article 4 of the Charter.[152] In the very same judgment, the CJEU reiterates that no right of residence is required.[153] One wonders how the resulting situation of legal limbo is compatible with the CJEU's own claim that 'it would be contrary . . . to the purpose of Directive 2008/115 . . . to tolerate the existence of an intermediate status of third-country nationals who are in the territory of a Member State without a right to stay or a residence permit'.[154]

This chapter has taken a normative stance in favour of the regularization of non-removable migrants, not only from the perspective of EU law effectiveness, but also taking into account human rights, rule of law, and state welfare arguments. Based on these, and after an analysis of domestic regularization frameworks and their underlying methods and purposes, it has advocated for regularization opportunities under EU law. However, when undocumented migrants are finally able to access lawful residence (if at all), it is often through temporary, precarious, and reversible permits.[155] As will be discussed in this book's Conclusions, regularization might only be the beginning of yet another struggle for permanent residence and, eventually, citizenship.

[152] *X* (n 134) para 76.
[153] Ibid, para 103.
[154] *BZ* (n 22) para 57.
[155] Chauvin, Garcés-Mascareñas, and Kraler (n 89).

PART IV
CONCLUSIONS

7
Conclusions
Between Deportation and Belonging

In February 2021, around 200 migrants in an irregular situation demonstrated in a church in Brussels to grab the government's attention. Most had lived and worked irregularly in Belgium for years (many for decades) but had little prospect of their situation improving. Their demand was clear: after years of residence, they wanted 'papers'.[1] Some years before, in 2014, a group of European NGOs had released the report 'Point of No Return: The Futile Detention of Unreturnable Migrants', based on the experiences of migrants who had been detained for the purposes of deportation in Belgium, France, Hungary, and the United Kingdom, but who ultimately could not be deported to their countries of origin. On average, interviewees had spent eight years in the country where they resided irregularly. Some of their personal stories are as follows:

> Michel left his country [Burundi] at the age of 15 . . . Since 2002, Michel has been detained four times, spending a total of three months in detention. The last time, he was released by the authorities after being diagnosed with hepatitis, which cannot be treated in Burundi. As Michel does not have any identity documents, however, France would not be able to send him back anyway . . . Kambale, 44, fled during the civil war in Angola. After the war he could not return because the authorities did not recognise him as an Angolan citizen. Now he is unreturnable, because the Angolan embassy does not permit his return . . . Tareq left Iraq due to the danger in his region. His asylum claim was dismissed, because the situation in that region of Iraq was not considered sufficiently dangerous. Tareq was detained twice, but, as he does not have a valid passport, repatriation to Iraq is impossible . . . Rehan fled from Afghanistan, leaving his wife and child behind. His first asylum application was refused; he was detained for eleven months. As the Afghan embassy accepts and assists only voluntary returns, he cannot be expelled from Hungary . . . Abdul is a Rohingya from Burma. He is stateless, so cannot return to Burma or Bangladesh. Despite this, when he claimed asylum he was placed on the Detained Fast Track . . . Tidiane had left his country [Mali] one

[1] Camille Gijs, '"Why are we forgotten?": Undocumented Immigrants Make Stand in Brussels Church', *POLITICO*, 23 February 2021, available at: <https://www.politico.eu/article/belgium-brussels-undocumented-immigrants-church-beguinage-protest/>.

When Deportation Fails. Diego Ginés Martín, Oxford University Press. © Diego Ginés Martín 2025.
DOI: 10.1093/9780198941231.003.0007

year previously, in October 2012, after he escaped an attack on his house by rebels . . . Arrested by the French police, he spent five days in detention before being released by the administrative judge because of the war in his country . . . One year in France . . . [He is still] undocumented and unreturnable because of risk of inhuman and degrading treatment . . . Marie was living with her two-year-old son and his father when she was arrested and detained. Two weeks later Marie was released, due to the fact that the mother of a child with a residence permit cannot be expelled . . . [After] twelve years in Belgium, [she is] still undocumented and unreturnable due to family ties . . . Betty arrived in France twenty years ago. She is the mother of four children who have only lived in France. She was sentenced by a criminal court to five years in prison and a legal ban from France. This means that, as long as the legal ban is not deleted, she cannot apply for a residence permit . . . She does not have a passport, and the Ghanaian consulate refused to give her a travel document . . . David, 33, fled from Sierra Leone in 2000. As his personal data cannot be found in the registration system of Sierra Leone, he is unreturnable. He has been detained for more than 11 months.[2]

These stories account for the everyday reality of many people in Europe. In a context where deportation is increasingly normalized, both legally and discursively, the fact remains that, year after year, only a small fraction of those ordered to leave the territory of the EU are actually deported.[3] Often in-between the regular and the irregular migrant, between the migrant and the refugee, the very existence of non-removable migrants poses a challenge to long-established binary constructions of legal migration categories. This book has explored the mechanisms that, at the European level, help explain the creation of situations of non-removability, and elaborated on non-removable migrants' legal status and regularization prospects. By focusing on European law, this book scratches only the surface of an issue that necessarily materializes at the domestic level.[4] However, the book has

[2] Maaike Vanderbruggen and others, 'Point of No Return: The Futile Detention of Unreturnable Migrants', *Detention Action*, 17 January 2014, 13, 15, 19, 21, 29, 39, 41, 63, and 67, available at: <https://ecre.org/point-of-no-return-the-futile-detention-of-unreturnable-migrants>.

[3] Eurostat statistics on the number of third-country nationals (TCNs) found to be irregularly present, ordered to leave, and returned following an order to leave since 2008 are available at: <https://ec.europa.eu/eurostat/statistics-explained/index.php?title=Returns_of_irregular_migrants_-_quarterly_statistics>.

[4] References to domestic legislation and their relevance to the issue have been incorporated throughout the book. A deeper analysis of domestic practices on non-removability would have been neither feasible nor desirable, as there are already comparative studies of domestic practices on non-removability. See Mathilde Heegaard Bausager, Johanne Köpfli Moller, and Solon Ardittis, 'Study on the Situation of Third-Country Nationals Pending Return/Removal in the EU Member States and the Schengen Associated Countries', Ramboll and Eurasylum—European Commission, 11 March 2013, available at: <https://home-affairs.ec.europa.eu/system/files/2020-09/11032013_sudy_report_on_immigration_return-removal_en.pdf>; European Migration Network (EMN), 'Comparative Overview of National Protection Statuses in the EU and Norway', May 2020, available at: <https://home-affairs.ec.europa.eu/whats-new/publications/comparative-overview-national-protection-statuses-eu-and-norway_en>; European Migration Network (EMN), 'Responses to Long-term Irregularly Staying Migrants: Practices and Challenges in the EU and Norway', July 2021, available at: <https://

also shown that non-removability is not only an EU-wide problem, but it is often at the European level that these situations originate. For those who become non-removable, EU law can become both a trap into or an escape from precarious residence, statuslessness, and destitution.

1. Manufacturing non-removability

Part I of this book unravelled the intricate combination of factors precluding deportation in Europe, as well as the legal and policy processes that, at the European level, often lead to situations of legal limbo. First, non-removability derives from an asymmetrical relationship between asylum law and states' international obligations under the principle of *non-refoulement*. Chapter 2 systematically exposed this gap, zooming in on states' *non-refoulement* obligations under Article 3 of the European Convention on Human Rights (ECHR). If compared with refugee status and subsidiary protection under EU asylum law, the ECHR offers not only a wider substantive scope, but also absolute and non-derogable obligations. These stand in sharp contrast with refugee status and subsidiary protection, which are subject to exclusion and withdrawal under EU law, normally in the context of criminal convictions. Second, non-removability can derive from membership-based challenges to deportation. Chapter 3 has analysed legal manifestations of belonging under European law. In the context of the ECHR, the right to belong in the host society gravitates around Article 8 ECHR, on the right to respect for one's family and private life. A closer look at this provision shows that it can often function as a legal safeguard against deportation while offering no legal status. I have argued that, even for those with strong claims to belong under long-term residence (for third-country nationals (TCNs)) or EU citizenship (for EU citizens), precarious residence and non-removability can become a reality upon the materialization of diverse life events such as the loss of a job, descent into poverty, criminality, and the like. Third, non-removability can (and in the majority of cases does) emerge due to 'practical' obstacles to deportation. These take place in all those cases where TCNs do not have a legal claim to challenge deportation, and yet this proves materially impossible. Chapter 4 has focused on these challenges to deportation, which have been analysed in the context of the EU's readmission policies—since the practical implementation of deportation necessarily requires the participation of third countries. Exposing the lack of coherence between the EU's internal policy aims and their external implementation, Chapter 4 has revealed its operability gaps—from identity determination challenges to the lack of cooperation of countries of origin, statelessness, or the role of migrant agency, among others.

www.emnspain.gob.es/en/-/responses-to-long-term-irregular-staying-migrants-practices-and-challenges-in-the-eu-and-norway>.

In short, non-removability illustrates the reality of states being unable to enforce their own deportation aims, while also being unwilling to let go of their migration control impulses. Then, non-removability is as much an example of 'policy failure' as it is a tool of migration control.

This book speaks to a long-lasting literature questioning the divergence between policy aims and results as regards migration control—in what it commonly known as the 'liberal paradox'.[5] Instead of making a substantial theoretical contribution as to whether and why migration policies generally 'fail', Part I of this book has focused on the specific mechanisms that make the EU fall short of its openly stated aims on deportation. Indeed, the impact of deportation on fundamental rights and the dependence on third countries for its effective implementation are at odds with the obsessive reliance on return rates as primary indicators of policy effectiveness. However, the paradigm of migration policy 'failures' fails to give an accurate picture of the processes that lead no non-removability.

This is first because existing debates on migration policy effectiveness are overly simplistic and often fail to define what migration policy effectiveness means in the first place.[6] These definitions also disregard that, while there are some practical obstacles to the deportation of immigrants, in some other cases non-removability derives from the prevalence of human rights norms. This is hardly an example of policy failure, but rather an example of the application of norms of a higher hierarchical value. As such, return policies in the EU require a gradual shift in predominant notions of effectiveness, still assessed in quantitative terms as a comparison between the return decisions issued by the Member States and the number of effective deportations. Assuming that a well-functioning system is one that deports massively and evaluating return policies solely in relation to the number of deportations will hardly provide a realistic picture of their effectiveness. This requires zooming in not only on the numbers, but also the sustainability and the adequacy of returns; that is, inquiring whether too many return decisions are issued to persons in respect of whom there is no realistic prospect of removal, promoting voluntary (truly voluntary) return programmes, and so on. As the European Parliament stressed in its Resolution on the implementation of Directive 2008/115 (Return Directive), 'most factors impeding effective return are absent in the current discourse, as the effectiveness is mainly stressed and understood as return rate'.[7]

Second, the concept of migration policy failure fails to capture that non-removability is as much an example of failure as it is a manifestation of migration

[5] James Frank Hollifield, Philip L Martin, and Pia M Orrenius, *Controlling Immigration: A Global Perspective* (3rd edn, Stanford University Press 2014); Gary P Freeman, 'Modes of Immigration Politics in Liberal Democratic States' (1995) 29 The International Migration Review 881.

[6] Mathias Czaika and Hein de Haas, 'The Effectiveness of Immigration Policies' (2013) 39 Population and Development Review 487.

[7] European Parliament, 'Report on the Implementation of the Return Directive' 2019/2208(INI), 2 December 2020 7, available at: <https://www.europarl.europa.eu/doceo/document/A-9-2020-0238_EN.html>.

control. This book has shown that the European legal and policy framework often favours the manufacturing of non-removability. Nevertheless, it is states that ultimately choose to keep migrants in a limbo state of non-deportability. Indeed, migration control is associated with border control and deportation, but it begins at an earlier stage with persons' classification—be it as citizens or migrants, as migrants or refugees, or as regular or irregular migrants.[8] In other words, migration control begins by defining who is the subject of migration control in the first place.[9] Along these lines, De Genova points at the concepts of 'migrant illegality' and 'deportability' as central mechanisms of migration control. As he puts it, '[m]igrant "illegality" is lived through a palpable sense of deportability, which is to say, the possibility of deportation'.[10] In these cases, it is the omnipresent threat of deportation, rather than actual deportation, that serves as a tool of migration control.[11] Then, while states might not normally be successful in deporting irregular migrants, they might be fully effective in excluding them from membership and access to rights. In this context, EU Member States have different (non-)deportability regimes with varying levels of enforcement interests and capacities.[12] While non-removability will always derive from a policy choice of states not to regularize when deportation proves impossible (and, as such, is a manifestation of migration control), some Member States will even have weak interests in deportation, given the dependence of their labour markets on the informal sector.[13] Then, the *chronification* of irregular residence for non-removable migrants can thus be understood as a policy failure, an exercise of migration control, or a combination of both.

2. Navigating non-removability

After determining the processes that manufacture non-removability, Part II focused on the legal status of non-removable persons. Though targeted by policies of exclusion as irregular migrants—with irregularity often functioning as the 'master status' for undocumented migrants—non-removable migrants experience further processes of social stratification. Chapter 5 has argued that, behind the seemingly shallow regulation of non-removable migrants' status under the Return Directive,

[8] Chandran Kukathas, 'Immigration', in *Immigration and Freedom* (Princeton University Press 2021) 10.
[9] Ibid.
[10] Nicholas P De Genova, 'Migrant "Illegality" and Deportability in Everyday Life' (2002) 31 Annual Review of Anthropology 419, 439.
[11] Ibid, 438.
[12] Arjen Leerkes and Marieke Van Houte, 'Beyond the Deportation Regime: Differential State Interests and Capacities in Dealing with (Non-) Deportability in Europe' (2020) 24 Citizenship Studies 319.
[13] Ibid, 333.

one can find further processes of inclusion and exclusion, depending on removal obstacles and returnee behaviour.

The issue will surely remain relevant in the coming years. Although the normalization of deportation remains, and will remain uncontested at the policy level, the EU should focus on what is within its scope of influence and be better equipped when expulsion fails, acknowledging the structural limitations of deportation. In this context, the so far stagnated process of a recasting of the Return Directive offers an opportunity to propose more adequate solutions. As it stands, however, the proposal maintains the status quo, including an abstract obligation for returnees to cooperate in return procedures, but without attaching incentives for those who do cooperate and cannot be returned. Be that as it may, regularization remains the only option for non-removable migrants to come out of invisibility and be able to access fundamental rights and participate fully in the social fabric of host countries without fear of deportation or exploitation. Chapter 6 advocated for regularization, provided an overview of domestic regularization practices, and reflected on non-removable migrants' possibilities to regularize their stay under European law.

In the meantime, it is worth noting that a holistic response to irregularity and non-removability should not only provide for regularization when return proves impossible (in particular when deportation does not materialize after exhausting pre-removal detention), but it should protect people from falling into irregularity in the first place. While this book has mainly focused on obstacles to expulsion, non-removability begins with the 'illegalization' of people. Thus, a comprehensive response to the issue must also look at the different processes that 'illegalize' people in the first place, since every migrant that is pushed out of asylum or legal migration will become an irregular (and potentially non-removable) migrant. At a judicial level, this book has argued that the Court of Justice of the European Union (CJEU) could offer more expansive interpretations of EU asylum law so that persons who are already non-deportable have access to subsidiary protection. More generally, when courts decide on the acquisition and loss of asylum or any other type of permits, they rule on the potential illegalization of people who might eventually become non-removable. In the legislative and policy realm, the adoption of narrow definitions of asylum, the existence of lottery-like asylum decision-making, the adoption of restrictive visa policies, or the lack of legal pathways to protection and legal migration routes are all key in the 'illegalization' of people that often have strong claims to non-removal. In this context, domestic practices that facilitate the acquisition and renewal of residence permits avoid the need to resort to regularization, a process which is often deeply contested and politicized.[14]

[14] For example, in 2022 Spain undertook a legislative reform of its Foreigners Decree that includes legal channels to facilitate students remaining in Spain after the completion of studies, that extends the validity of temporary work permits to four years, that adopts easier renewal conditions for work permits, and makes it easier for unaccompanied children to obtain a permit when transitioning into adulthood (see Real Decreto 557/2011, de 20 de abril, por el que se aprueba el Reglamento de la Ley

3. Life after non-removability

This book has illustrated the complex journey of many migrants, from irregular entry or lawful residence into irregularity, from there to a (non-enforceable) return decision, and then into a limbo-like state of non-removability. The fate of non-removable migrants who ultimately obtain a residence permit generally falls beyond the scope of this book. However, regularization might not be the end of precarity and exclusion.

Residence permits can be short-term, long-term, or permanent; they can have more or less stringent conditions for their renewal; and they might come with more or less rights attached—from free movement in the EU to family reunification or equal treatment. Moreover, migration statuses are not fixed in stone but are intrinsically fluid. Then, in the same way that migrants can transition from non-removability to lawful residence, they can fall back into irregularity. After all, temporary and fragile residence permits are also tools of migration control.

Migration statuses are increasingly dynamic and precarious, with immigrants experiencing multiple transitions in and out of (il)legality.[15] The increased precarity and reversibility of residence permits leads to forms of 'probationary citizenship'.[16] In short, states offer regularization to those TCNs whom they consider worthy of a permit, asking desirable candidates to fulfil certain requirements. However, just like irregularity, lawful residence is part of a 'probationary period during which migrants are scrutinized and policed'.[17] In these periods, states will generally grant temporary permits, which will only be renewed where applicants demonstrate continuous fulfilment of a number of conditions.[18] These will not only require applicants to be law-abiding citizens with clean criminal records, but might imply a continuous assessment of their employment situation, income levels, and so on.[19] Of course, state practice varies. In particular, labour market-oriented regularizations are generally marked by greater insecurity of residence,

Orgánica 4/2000, sobre derechos y libertades de los extranjeros en España y su integración social, tras su reforma por Ley Orgánica 2/2009 arts 71, 72, 198, and 199).

[15] Sébastien Chauvin, Blanca Garcés-Mascareñas, and Albert Kraler, 'Working for Legality: Employment and Migrant Regularization in Europe' (2013) 51 International Migration 118, 127. For example, in Spain, offered in Chapter 6 as an example of good practice in the field of regularization, 86% of the residence permits in force in 2023 were of a temporary nature (Permanent Observatory on Migration (OPI), 'Flujo de Autorizaciones de Residencia Concedidas a Extranjeros. Año 2023' 11, available at: <https://www.inclusion.gob.es/web/opi/estadisticas/catalogo/flujo_autorizaciones>.

[16] Sébastien Chauvin and Blanca Garcés-Mascareñas, 'Beyond Informal Citizenship: The New Moral Economy of Migrant Illegality' (2012) 6 International Political Sociology 241, 253.

[17] David Moffette, 'Governing Immigration through Probation: The Displacement of Borderwork and the Assessment of Desirability in Spain' (2014) 45 Security Dialogue 262, 263.

[18] Ibid, 270.

[19] Ibid; Albert Kraler, 'Regularization of Irregular Migrants and Social Policies: Comparative Perspectives' (2019) 17 Journal of Immigrant & Refugee Studies 94, 3.

with migrants having to continuously earn their residency rights.[20] On the contrary, humanitarian regularizations often offer greater security of residence.[21]

Therefore, regularizations, while offering an essential tool for inclusion, might be only the first step in an arduous process to obtain fuller modes of memberships up until national citizenship. These processes of membership consolidation will be conditional on their continuous performance as 'good' citizens.[22] Then, statuses of liminality may extend beyond irregular residence, to other forms of lawful yet precarious residence.[23] For many, regularization brings partial inclusion and visibility, but secure residence remains elusive.

[20] Kraler (n 19) 11.
[21] Ibid.
[22] Ibid, 3.
[23] Moffette (n 17) 275.

Bibliography

BOOKS AND BOOK CHAPTERS

Acosta Arcarazo D, *The Long-Term Residence Status as a Subsidiary Form of EU Citizenship: An Analysis of Directive 2003/109* (Brill Nijhoff 2011).

Acosta Arcarazo D, *The National versus the Foreigner in South America* (Cambridge Core 2018).

Ambrosini M and Hajer MHJ, *Irregular Migration: IMISCOE Short Reader* (Springer International Publishing 2023).

Andersson R, *Illegality, Inc.: Clandestine Migration and the Business of Bordering Europe* (University of California Press 2014).

Baldwin-Edwards M and Kraler A (eds), *REGINE—Regularisations in Europe* (Amsterdam University Press 2009).

Basilien-Gainche M-L, 'European States Returning European Citizens: France and the Roma Populations' in Elspeth Guild, Paul Minderhoud, and Sandra Mantu (eds), *EU Citizenship and Free Movement Rights Taking Supranational Citizenship Seriously* (Brill 2020).

Bast J, 'The Legal Position of Migrants—German Report' in Eibe Riedel and Rüdiger Wolfrum (eds), *Recent Trends in German and European Constitutional Law* (Springer 2006).

Battjes H, *European Asylum Law and International Law* (M Nijhoff 2006).

Bauböck R, 'Whose Bad Guys Are Terrorists?' in Rainer Bauböck (ed), *Debating Transformations of National Citizenship* (Springer International Publishing 2018).

Benhabib S, *The Rights of Others: Aliens, Residents and Citizens* (Cambridge University Press 2004).

Bigo D, 'Frontier Controls in the European Union: Who Is in Control?' in Elspeth Guild and Didier Bigo (eds), *Controlling Frontiers: Free Movement Into and Within Europe* (Ashgate 2005).

Bommes M and Sciortino G (eds), 'In Lieu of a Conclusion: Steps towards a Conceptual Framework for the Study of Irregular Migration' in Michael Bommes and Giuseppe Sciortino (eds), *Foggy Social Structures: Irregular Migration, European Labour Markets and the Welfare State* (Amsterdam University Press 2011).

Bosniak L, *The Citizen and the Alien: Dilemmas of Contemporary Membership* (Princeton University Press 2006).

Çalı B and Cunningham S, 'The European Court of Human Rights and Removal of Long-Term Migrants: Entrenched Statism with a Human Voice?' in Başak Çalı, Ledi Bianku, and Iulia Motoc (eds), *Migration and the European Convention on Human Rights* (Oxford University Press 2021).

Carens JH, *Immigrants and the Right to Stay* (MIT Press 2010).

Carens JH, *The Ethics of Immigration* (Oxford University Press 2013).

Carrera S, *Implementation of EU Readmission Agreements: Identity Determination Dilemmas and the Blurring of Rights* (Springer International Publishing 2016).

Carrera S and Allsopp J, 'The Irregular Immigration Policy Conundrum: Problematizing "Effectiveness" as a Frame for EU Criminalization and Expulsion Policies' in Ariadna Ripoll Servent and Florian Trauner (eds), *The Routledge Handbook of Justice and Home Affairs Research* (Routledge 2018).

Carrera S, Santos Vara J, and Strik T, *Constitutionalising the External Dimensions of EU Migration Policies in Times of Crisis: Legality, Rule of Law and Fundamental Rights Reconsidered* (Edward Elgar Publishing 2019).

Cassarino J-P, *Unbalanced Reciprocities: Cooperation on Readmission in the Euro-Mediterranean Area* (Middle East Institute 2010).

Chalmers D, Davies G, and Monti G, *European Union Law: Cases and Materials* (Cambridge University Press 2010).

Chauvin S and Garcés-Mascareñas B, 'Contradictions in the Moral Economy of Migrant Irregularity' in Sarah Spencer and Anna Triandafyllidou (eds), *Migrants with Irregular Status in Europe: Evolving Conceptual and Policy Challenges* (Springer International Publishing 2020).

Chavez LR, *Shadowed Lives: Undocumented Immigrants in American Society* (Harcourt Brace College Publishers 1992).

Chomsky A, *Undocumented: How Immigration Became Illegal* (Beacon Press 2014).

Coleman NP, *European Readmission Policy: Third Country Interests and Refugee Rights* (Brill Nijhoff 2008).

Costello C, *The Human Rights of Migrants and Refugees in European Law* (Oxford University Press 2015).

Costello C, 'On Refugeehood and Citizenship' in Ayelet Shachar and others (eds), *The Oxford Handbook of Citizenship* (Oxford University Press 2017).

Coutts S, 'A Contingent Citizenship—Union Citizenship and Expulsion' in Elspeth Guild, Paul Minderhoud, and Sandra Mantu (eds), *EU Citizenship and Free Movement Rights Taking Supranational Citizenship Seriously* (Brill 2020).

Czaika M and de Haas H, 'Evaluating Migration Policy Effectiveness' in Alina Triandafyllidou (ed), *Routledge Handbook of Immigration and Refugee Studies* (Routledge 2016).

Dauvergne C, *Making People Illegal: What Globalization Means for Migration and Law* (Cambridge University Press 2008).

De Genova N and Peutz NM, *The Deportation Regime: Sovereignty, Space, and the Freedom of Movement* (Duke University Press 2010).

De Haas H, *How Migration Really Works: A Factful Guide to the Most Divisive Issue in Politics* (Viking 2023).

De la Rosa E, 'Art 31 LODYLE' in José Luis Monereo Pérez, José Antonio Fernández Avilés, and Luis Ángel Triguero Martínez (eds), *Comentario a la Ley y al Reglamento de Extranjería, Inmigración e Integración Social (LO 4/2000 y RD 557/2011)* (Dykinson 2013).

De Witte B and Martinelli T, 'Treaties between EU Member States as Quasi-Instruments of EU Law' in Marise Cremona and Claire Kilpatrick (eds), *EU Legal Acts: Challenges and Transformations* (Oxford University Press 2018).

Delvino N, 'European Union and National Responses to Migrants with Irregular Status: Is the Fortress Slowly Crumbling?' in Sarah Spencer and Anna Triandafyllidou (eds), *Migrants with Irregular Status in Europe: Evolving Conceptual and Policy Challenges* (Springer International Publishing 2020).

Dembour M-B, *When Humans Become Migrants: Study of the European Court of Human Rights with an Inter-American Counterpoint* (Oxford University Press 2015).

Dembour M-B, 'The Migrant Case Law of the European Court of Human Rights: Critique and Way Forward' in Başak Çalı, Ledi Bianku, and Iulia Motoc (eds), *Migration and the European Convention on Human Rights* (Oxford University Press 2021).

Desmond A, 'The Return Directive: Clarifying the Scope and Substance of the Rights of Migrants Facing Expulsion from the EU' in Russell King and Katie Kuschminder (eds), *Handbook of Return Migration* (Edward Elgar Publishing 2022).

Dzehtsiarou K (ed), 'Legitimacy of the Court and Legitimacy of Its Judgments', *European Consensus and the Legitimacy of the European Court of Human Rights* (Cambridge University Press 2015).

Eisele K, 'The EU's Readmission Policy: Of Agreements and Arrangements' in Sergio Carrera, Juan Santos Vara, and Tineke Strik (eds), *Constitutionalising the External Dimensions of EU Migration Policies in Times of Crisis: Legality, Rule of Law and Fundamental Rights Reconsidered* (Edward Elgar Publishing 2019).

Evans M, 'Abusing or Misusing the Right of Free Movement? The UK's Policy towards EU Nationals Sleeping Rough' in Elspeth Guild, Paul Minderhoud, and Sandra Mantu (eds), *EU Citizenship and Free Movement Rights: Taking Supranational Citizenship Seriously* (Brill 2020).
Evans PB, Rueschemeyer D, and Skocpol T (eds), *Bringing the State Back In* (Cambridge University Press 1985).
Farcy J-B, 'Chapter 19. Unremovability under the Return Directive: An Empty Protection?' in Galina Cornelisse and Philippe de Bruycker (eds), *Law and Judicial Dialogue on the Return of Irregular Migrants from the European Union* (Hart 2020).
Ferrera M, *The Boundaries of Welfare: European Integration and the New Spatial Politics of Social Protection* (Oxford University Press 2005).
Finotelli C, 'Regularisation of Immigrants in Southern Europe: What Can Be Learned from Spain?' in Michael Bommes and Giuseppe Sciortino (eds), *Foggy Social Structures: Irregular Migration, European Labour Markets and the Welfare State* (Amsterdam University Press 2011).
García Andrade P, 'The Role of the European Parliament in the Adoption of Non-Legally Binding Agreements with Third Countries' in Juan Santos Vara and Sánchez-Tabernero Soledad R (eds), *The Democratization of EU International Relations Through EU Law* (Routledge 2018).
Gatti M and Ott A, 'The EU–Turkey Statement: Legal Nature and Compatibility with EU Institutional Law' in Sergio Carrera, Juan Santos Vara, and Tineke Strik (eds), *Constitutionalising the External Dimensions of EU Migration Policies in Times of Crisis: Legality, Rule of Law and Fundamental Rights Reconsidered* (Edward Elgar Publishing 2019).
Gennep A, *Les rites de passage* (A et J Picard 1981).
Gómez Díaz J, 'Seguridad social de los extranjeros. Inmigración y Seguridad Social, una gestión integrada' in Manuel Balado Ruiz-Gallegos (ed), *Inmigración, Estado y Derecho: perspectivas desde el siglo XXI* (Bosch 2008).
Gonzales RG, 'Chapter 8. Adulthood: How Immigration Status Becomes a Master Status', *Lives in Limbo: Undocumented and Coming of Age in America* (University of California Press 2016).
Gosme C, 'Trapped Between Administrative Detention, Imprisonment, and Freedom-in-Limbo' in Maria João Guia, Robert Koulish, and Valsamis Mitsilegas (eds), *Immigration Detention, Risk and Human Rights: Studies on Immigration and Crime* (Springer International Publishing 2016).
Hamlin R, *Crossing: How We Label and React to People on the Move* (Stanford University Press 2021).
Harvey C, 'Promoting Insecurity: Public Order, Expulsion and the European Convention on Human Rights' in Elspeth Guild and Paul Minderbound (eds), *Security of Residence and Expulsion: Protection of Aliens in Europe* (Kluwer Law International 2001).
Hathaway JC and Foster M, *The Law of Refugee Status* (Cambridge Core 2014).
Hinterberger KF, *Regularisations of Irregularly Staying Migrants in the EU: A Comparative Legal Analysis of Austria, Germany and Spain* (Nomos 2023).
Hollifield JF, Martin PL, and Orrenius PM, *Controlling Immigration: A Global Perspective* (3rd edn, Stanford University Press 2014).
Ippolito F and Trevisanut S (eds), *Migration in the Mediterranean: Mechanisms of International Cooperation* (Cambridge University Press 2016).
Ippolito F and Velluti S, 'The Relationship between the ECJ and the ECtHR: The Case of Asylum' in Kanstantsin Dzehtsiarou and others (eds), *Human Rights Law in Europe: The Influence, Overlaps and Contradictions of the EU and ECHR* (Routledge 2014).
Joppke C, 'Immigration Challenges the Nation-State' in *Challenge to the Nation-State* (Oxford University Press 1998).
Kukathas C, 'Immigration' in *Immigration and Freedom* (Princeton University Press 2021).
Lazaridis G, *International Migration into Europe: From Subjects to Abjects* (Palgrave Macmillan UK 2015).
Lori N, 'Statelessness, "In-Between" Statuses, and Precarious Citizenship' in Ayelet Shachar and others (eds), *The Oxford Handbook of Citizenship* (Oxford University Press 2017).

Lutz F, *The Negotiations on the Return Directive: Comments and Materials* (WLP 2010).

Majcher I, *The European Union Returns Directive and Its Compatibility with International Human Rights Law: Analysis of Return Decision, Entry Ban, Detention, and Removal* (Brill Nijhoff 2019).

Menezes Queiroz B, *Illegally Staying in the EU: An Analysis of Illegality in EU Migration Law* (Bloomsbury 2018).

Micinski NR, *Delegating Responsibility: International Cooperation on Migration in the European Union* (University of Michigan Press 2022).

Miller D, *Strangers in Our Midst: The Political Philosophy of Immigration* (Harvard University Press 2016).

Mindus P, 'The Status of European Citizenship: An Overview' in Patricia Mindus (ed), *European Citizenship after Brexit: Freedom of Movement and Rights of Residence* (Springer International Publishing 2017).

Mitsilegas V, *The Criminalisation of Migration in Europe: Challenges for Human Rights and the Rule of Law* (Springer 2015).

Mitsilegas V, *EU Criminal Law after Lisbon: Rights, Trust and the Transformation of Justice in Europe* (Hart Publishing 2016).

Mole N, *Asylum and the European Convention on Human Rights* (Council of Europe Publishing 2010).

Morano-Foadi S, Vickers L, and Velluti S (eds), 'Who Has the Right to Have Rights?', *Fundamental Rights in the EU: A Matter for Two Courts* (Hart Publishing 2015).

Moraru M and Cornelisse G, 'Introduction: Judicial Dialogue on the Return Directive—Catalyst for Changing Migration Governance?' in Philippe de Bruycker, Galina Cornelisse, and Madalina Moraru (eds), *Law and Judicial Dialogue on the Return of Irregular Migrants from the European Union* (Hart 2020).

Moraru M, Cornelisse G, and Bruycker P de, *Law and Judicial Dialogue on the Return of Irregular Migrants from the European Union* (Hart 2020).

Moreno-Lax V, *Accessing Asylum in Europe: Extraterritorial Border Controls and Refugee Rights under EU Law* (Oxford University Press 2017).

Moreno-Lax V and Costello C, 'The Extraterritorial Application of the EU Charter of Fundamental Rights: From Territoriality to Facticity, the Effectiveness Model' in Steve Peers and others (eds), *The EU Charter of Fundamental Rights: A Commentary* (Hart Publishing 2014).

Motomura H, *Immigration Outside the Law* (Oxford University Press 2014).

Murphy C, *Immigration, Integration and the Law: The Intersection of Domestic, EU and International Legal Regimes* (Routledge 2016).

Natter K, 'Beyond the Dichotomomy of Liberal and Illiberal Migration Governance' in Emma Carmel, Katharina Lenner, and Regine Paul (eds), *Handbook on the Governance and Politics of Migration* (Edward Elgar Publishing 2021).

Nonnenmacher S and Cholewinski R, 'The Nexus between Statelessness and Migration' in Alice Edwards and Laura van Waas (eds), *Nationality and Statelessness under International Law* (Cambridge University Press 2014).

Oberman K, 'Immigration as a Human Right' in Sarah Fine and Lea Ypi (eds), *Migration in Political Theory: The Ethics of Movement and Membership* (Oxford University Press 2016).

O'Cinneide C, 'The Human Rights of Migrants with Irregular Status: Giving Substance to Aspirations of Universalism' in Sarah Spencer and Anna Triandafyllidou (eds), *Migrants with Irregular Status in Europe: Evolving Conceptual and Policy Challenges* (Springer International Publishing 2020).

Peers S, *EU Justice and Home Affairs Law: Volume I: EU Immigration and Asylum Law* (4th edn, Oxford University Press 2016).

Peers S and others (eds), *EU Immigration and Asylum Law (Text and Commentary): Second Revised Edition: Volume 2: EU Immigration Law* (Brill Nijhoff 2012).

Pollack MA, 'The Legitimacy of the European Court of Justice: Normative Debates and Empirical Evidence' in Andreas Follesdal and others (eds), *Legitimacy and International Courts* (Cambridge University Press 2018).
Popelier P, 'The Court as Regulatory Watchdog: The Procedural Approach in the Case Law of the European Court of Human Rights' in Patricia Popelier, Armen Mazmanyan, and Werner Vandenbruwaene (eds), *The Role of Constitutional Courts in Multilevel Governance* (Intersentia 2012).
Rubio-Marín R, 'Introduction: Human Rights and the Citizen/Non-Citizen Distinction Revisited' in *Human Rights and Immigration* (Oxford University Press 2014).
Sangiovanni A, '"Feed Them First, Then Ask Virtue of Them": Broadening and Deepening Freedom of Movement' in Rainer Bauböck (ed), *Debating European Citizenship* (Springer 2019).
Santos Vara J, 'Soft International Agreements on Migration Cooperation with Third Countries: A Challenge to Democratic and Judicial Controls in the EU' in Sergio Carrera, Juan Santos Vara, and Tineke Strik (eds), *Constitutionalising the External Dimensions of EU Migration Policies in Times of Crisis: Legality, Rule of Law and fundamental rights reconsidered* (Edward Elgar Publishing 2019).
Sassen S, *Losing Control? Sovereignty in the Age of Globalization* (Columbia University Press 1996).
Sawyer C and Blitz BK, *Statelessness in the European Union: Displaced, Undocumented, Unwanted* (Cambridge University Press 2011).
Shachar A, *The Birthright Lottery: Citizenship and Global Inequality* (Harvard University Press 2009).
Sharma NR, *Home Rule: National Sovereignty and the Separation of Natives and Migrants* (Duke University Press 2020).
Shaw J, 'EU Citizenship: Still a Fundamental Status?' in Rainer Bauböck (ed), *Debating European Citizenship* (Springer 2019).
Shaw J and Nic Shuibhne N, 'General Report: Union Citizenship: Development, Impact and Challenges' in Ulla Neergaard, Catherine Jacqueson, and Nina Holst-Christensen (eds), *Union Citizenship: Development, Impact and Challenges* (DJØF Publishing 2014).
Soysal YN, *Limits of Citizenship: Migrants and Postnational Membership in Europe* (University of Chicago 1994).
Spaventa E, *Free Movement of Persons in the EU: Barriers to Movement in Their Constitutional Context* (Kluwer Law International 2008).
Spaventa E, 'Striving for Equality: Who "Deserves" to Be a Union Citizen?' *Scritti in onore di Giuseppe Tesauro.*, vol 3 (Editoriale Scientifica 2014).
Spaventa E, 'Once a Foreigner, Always a Foreigner: Who Does Not Belong Here Anymore? Expulsion Measures' in Hendrik Verschueren (ed), *Residence, Employment and Social Rights of Mobile Persons* (Intersentia 2016).
Spaventa E, 'What Role for Fundamental Rights in Expulsion Cases?' in Sandra Mantu (ed), *Expulsion and EU Citizenship* (Nijmegen Migration Law Series 2017).
Spijkerboer T, '"I Wish There Was a Treaty We Could Sign"' in Sergio Carrera and Andrew Geddes (eds), *The EU Pact on Migration and Asylum in Light of the United Nations Global Compact on Refugees* (European University Institute 2021).
Squire V, 'The Construction and Contestation of Illegality' in Emma Carmel, Katharina Lenner and Regine Paul (eds), *Handbook on the Governance and Politics of Migration* (Edward Elgar Publishing 2021).
Tadesse Abebe T and Mbiyozo A-N, 'The New Pact's Focus on Migrant Returns Threatens Africa–EU Partnership' in Sergio Carrera and Andrew Geddes (eds), *The EU Pact on Migration and Asylum in Light of the United Nations Global Compact on Refugees* (European University Institute 2021).
Torpey J, *The Invention of the Passport: Surveillance, Citizenship and the State* (Cambridge University Press 1999).
Triandafyllidou A, *Irregular Migration in Europe: Myths and Realities* (Ashgate Pub 2010).

Tsourdi L, 'What Protection for Persons Fleeing Indiscriminate Violence? The Impact of the European Courts on the EU Subsidiary Protection Regime' in David Cantor and Jean-François Durieux (eds), *Refuge from Inhumanity? War Refugees and International Humanitarian Law* (Brill Nijhoff 2014).

Turner VW, 'Liminality and Communitas', in *The Ritual Process: Structure and Anti-structure* (Aldine de Gruyter 1995).

Valcke A, 'Expulsion from the "Heart of Europe": The Belgian Law and Practice Relating to the Termination of EU Residence Rights' in Elspeth Guild, Paul Minderhoud, and Sandra Mantu (eds), *EU Citizenship and Free Movement Rights: Taking Supranational Citizenship Seriously* (Brill 2020).

Villiger ME, 'Expulsion and the Right to Respect for Private and Family Life (Article 8 of the Convention)—An Introduction to the Commission's Case Law' in Franz Matscher and Herbert Petzold (eds), *Protecting Human Rights: The European Dimension* (Heymans 1988).

Walzer M, *Spheres of Justice: A Defense of Pluralism and Equality* (Basic Books 1983).

JOURNAL ARTICLES

Abdelaaty L and Hamlin R, 'Introduction: The Politics of the Migrant/Refugee Binary' (2022) 20 Journal of Immigrant & Refugee Studies 233.

Achiume ET, 'Migration as Decolonization' (2019) 71 Stanford Law Review 1509.

Acosta Arcarazo D, 'The Good, the Bad and the Ugly in EU Migration Law: Is the European Parliament Becoming Bad and Ugly? (The Adoption of Directive 2008/15: The Returns Directive)' (2009) 11 European Journal of Migration and Law 19.

Acosta Arcarazo D, 'The Charter, Detention and Possible Regularization of Migrants in an Irregular Situation under the Returns Directive: Mahdi' (2015) 52 Common Market Law Review 1361.

Acosta Arcarazo D, 'Civic Citizenship Reintroduced: The Long-Term Residence Directive as a Post-National Form of Membership' (2015) 21 European Law Journal 200.

Anderson B, Gibney MJ, and Paoletti E, 'Citizenship, Deportation and the Boundaries of Belonging' (2011) 15 Citizenship Studies 547.

Apap J, De Bruycker P, and Schmitter P, 'Regularisation of Illegal Aliens in the European Union. Summary Report of a Comparative Study' (2000) 2 European Journal of Migration and Law 263.

Arnardóttir OM, 'The "Procedural Turn" under the European Convention on Human Rights and Presumptions of Convention Compliance' (2017) 15 International Journal of Constitutional Law 9.

Azoulai L and Coutts S, 'Restricting Union Citizens' Residence Rights on Grounds of Public Security. Where Union Citizenship and the AFSJ Meet: P.I.' (2013) 50 Common Market Law Review 553.

Bauloz C, 'Foreigners: Wanted Dead or Alive: Medical Cases before European Courts and the Need for an Integrated Approach to Non-Refoulement' (2016) 18 European Journal of Migration and Law 409.

Belavusau U and Kochenov D, 'Kirchberg Dispensing the Punishment: Inflicting "Civil Death" on Prisoners in Onuekwere (C-378/12) and MG (C-400/12)' (2016) 41 European Law Review 557.

Bellamy R, 'Evaluating Union Citizenship: Belonging, Rights and Participation within the EU' (2008) 12 Citizenship Studies 597.

Bendixsen S and Näre L, 'Welfare State Bordering as a Form of Mobility and Migration Control' (2024) 50 Journal of Ethnic and Migration Studies 2689.

Benhabib S, 'The End of the 1951 Refugee Convention? Dilemmas of Sovereignty, Territoriality, and Human Rights' (2020) 2 Jus Cogens 75.

Çalı B, 'All You Need Is Time? Discrepancies between the European Court of Human Rights Case Law and Liberal Normative Theory on Long-Term Migrants' (2017) 50 Israel Law Review 447.
Cardwell PJ, 'New Modes of Governance in the External Dimension of EU Migration Policy' (2013) 51 International Migration 54.
Carens JH, 'Aliens and Citizens: The Case for Open Borders' (1987) 49 The Review of Politics 251.
Carling J, 'Migration in the Age of Involuntary Immobility: Theoretical Reflections and Cape Verdean Experiences' (2002) 28 Journal of Ethnic and Migration Studies 5.
Cassarino J-P, 'Informalising Readmission Agreements in the EU Neighbourhood' (2007) 42 The International Spectator 179.
Cassese A, 'Can the Notion of Inhuman and Degrading Treatment Be Applied to Socio-Economic Conditions?' (1991) 2 European Journal of International Law 141.
Castles S, 'Why Migration Policies Fail' (2004) 27 Ethnic and Racial Studies 205.
Chacon J, 'Producing Liminal Legality' (2015) 92 Denver Law Review 709.
Chauvin S and Garcés-Mascareñas B, 'Beyond Informal Citizenship: The New Moral Economy of Migrant Illegality' (2012) 6 International Political Sociology 241.
Chauvin S, Garcés-Mascareñas B, and Kraler A, 'Working for Legality: Employment and Migrant Regularization in Europe' (2013) 51 International Migration 118.
Chimni BS, 'The Geopolitics of Refugee Studies: A View from the South' (1998) 11 Journal of Refugee Studies 350.
Cholewinski R, 'Strasbourg's Hidden Agenda: The Protection of Second-Generation Migrants from Expulsion under Article 8 of the European Convention on Human Rights Part A' (1994) 12 Netherlands Quarterly of Human Rights 287.
Cohen JL, 'Whose Sovereignty? Empire Versus International Law' (2004) 18 Ethics & International Affairs 1.
Costello C, 'Metock: Free Movement and "Normal Family Life" in the Union' (2009) 46(2) Common Market Law Review 587.
Costello C and Mann I, 'Border Justice: Migration and Accountability for Human Rights Violations' (2020) 21 German Law Journal 311.
Coutin SB and others, 'Deferred Action and the Discretionary State: Migration, Precarity and Resistance' (2017) 21 Citizenship Studies 951.
Crawley H and Skleparis D, 'Refugees, Migrants, Neither, Both: Categorical Fetishism and the Politics of Bounding in Europe's "Migration Crisis"' (2018) 44 Journal of Ethnic and Migration Studies 48.
Czaika M and de Haas H, 'The Effectiveness of Immigration Policies' (2013) 39 Population and Development Review 487.
Davies G, 'Has the Court Changed, or Have the Cases? The Deservingness of Litigants as an Element in Court of Justice Citizenship Adjudication' (2018) 25 Journal of European Public Policy 1442.
De Genova NP, 'Migrant "Illegality" and Deportability in Everyday Life' (2002) 31 Annual Review of Anthropology 419.
De Vries K and Spijkerboer T, 'Race and the Regulation of International Migration. The Ongoing Impact of Colonialism in the Case Law of The European Court of Human Rights' (2021) 39 Netherlands Quarterly of Human Rights 291.
Dembour M-B, 'Human Rights Law and National Sovereignty in Collusion: The Plight of Quasi-Nationals at Strasbourg Part A' (2003) 21 Netherlands Quarterly of Human Rights 63.
Domaas N, 'More than a Migration Status: Examining Intersectionality and Its Effect on the Experiences of Migrant Women in France' (2021) 21 Journal of Immigrant & Refugee Studies 249.
Ellermann A, 'The Rule of Law and the Right to Stay: The Moral Claims of Undocumented Migrants' (2014) 42(3) Politics & Society 293.
Errera R, 'The CJEU and Subsidiary Protection: Reflections on Elgafaji - and After' (2011) 23 International Journal of Refugee Law 93.

Farahat A, 'The Exclusiveness of Inclusion: On the Boundaries of Human Rights in Protecting Transnational and Second Generation Migrants Special Issue: The European Court of Human Rights and Immigration: Limits and Possibilities' (2009) 11 European Journal of Migration and Law 253.

Faraldo-Cabana P, 'One Step Forward, Two Steps Back? Social Rehabilitation of Foreign Offenders under Framework Decisions 2008/909/JHA and 2008/947/JHA' (2019) 10 New Journal of European Criminal Law 151.

Fikfak V, 'Changing State Behaviour: Damages before the European Court of Human Rights' (2018) 29 European Journal of International Law 1091.

Foster M and Lambert H, 'Statelessness as a Human Rights Issue: A Concept Whose Time Has Come' (2016) 28 International Journal of Refugee Law 564.

Frasca E and Roman E, 'The Informalisation of EU Readmission Policy: Eclipsing Human Rights Protection Under the Shadow of Informality and Conditionality' (2023) 8 European Papers—A Journal on Law and Integration 931.

Freeman GP, 'Modes of Immigration Politics in Liberal Democratic States' (1995) 29 The International Migration Review 881.

Frelick B, Kysel IM, and Podkul J, 'The Impact of Externalization of Migration Controls on the Rights of Asylum Seekers and Other Migrants' (2016) 4 Journal on Migration and Human Security 190.

Gammeltoft-Hansen T and Hathaway JC, 'Non-Refoulement in a World of Cooperative Deterrence' (2015) 53 Columbia Journal of Transnational Law 235.

García Andrade P, 'The Distribution of Powers between EU Institutions for Conducting External Affairs through Non-Binding Instruments' (2016) 1 European Papers 115.

García Andrade P, 'EU External Competences in the Field of Migration: How to Act Externally When Thinking Internally' (2018) 55 Common Market Law Review 157.

García Andrade P, 'The External Dimension of the EU Immigration and Asylum Policies Before the Court of Justice' (2022) 7 European Papers 109.

García-Juan L and Calderón JA, 'El arraigo social como alternativa legal para los solicitantes de asilo de larga duración en la Unión Europea' (2023) 14 Migraciones Internacionales 1.

Gelazis NM, 'The European Union and the Statelessness Problem in the Baltic States' (2004) 6 European Journal of Migration and Law 225.

Ghezelbash D and others, 'Securitization of Search and Rescue at Sea: The Response to Boat Migration in the Mediterranean and Offshore Australia' (2018) 67 International & Comparative Law Quarterly 315.

Gibney MJ, 'Asylum and the Expansion of Deportation in the United Kingdom' (2008) 43 Government and Opposition 146.

Ginés Martín D, 'Citizens or Migrants? Precarious Residence in the Context of EU Citizenship' (2021) 25 Revista de Derecho Comunitario Europeo 653.

Ginés Martín D, 'In Limbo: Divergent Conceptualisations of Ill-Treatment by European Courts and the Creation of Non-Removable Migrants' (2021) 6 European Papers—A Journal on Law and Integration 1173.

Gonzales RG and Burciaga EM, 'Segmented Pathways of Illegality: Reconciling the Coexistence of Master and Auxiliary Statuses in the Experiences of 1.5-Generation Undocumented Young Adults' (2018) 18 Ethnicities 178.

González-Enríquez C, 'Spain, the Cheap Model. Irregularity and Regularisation as Immigration Management Policies' (2009) 11 European Journal of Migration and Law 139.

Greenman K, 'A Castle Built on Sand: Article 3 ECHR and the Source of Risk in Non-Refoulement Obligations in International Law' (2015) 27 International Journal of Refugee Law 264.

Gregou M, 'Drawing the Geographic Boundaries of Expulsion and Readmission in Greece: The Dynamics of an Elusive Process' (2014) 16 European Journal of Migration and Law 505.

Hadj Abdou L and Pettrachin A, 'Exploring the EU's Status Quo Tendency in the Migration Policy Field: A Network-Centred Perspective' (2022) 30 Journal of European Public Policy 1.

Hailbronner K, 'Readmission Agreements and the Obligation of States under Public International Law to Readmit Their Own and Foreign Nationals' (1997) 57 Zeitschrift für ausländisches öffentliches Recht und Völkerrecht 1.
Hanson JK and Sigman R, 'Leviathan's Latent Dimensions: Measuring State Capacity for Comparative Political Research' (2021) 83 The Journal of Politics 1495.
Heindlmaier A and Blauberger M, 'Enter at Your Own Risk: Free Movement of EU Citizens in Practice' (2017) 40 West European Politics 1198.
Hinterberger KF, 'An EU Regularization Directive. An Effective Solution to the Enforcement Deficit in Returning Irregularly Staying Migrants' (2019) 26 Maastricht Journal of European and Comparative Law 736.
Hoffmeyer-Zlotnik P, Lavenex S, and Lutz P, 'The Limits of EU Market Power in Migration Externalization: Explaining Migration Control Provisions in EU Preferential Trade Agreements' (2024) 62 JCMS: Journal of Common Market Studies 1351.
James Cantor D and others, 'The Emperor's New Clothing: National Responses to "Undesirable and Unreturnable" Aliens under Asylum and Immigration Law' (2017) 36 Refugee Survey Quarterly 1.
Joppke C, 'Why Liberal States Accept Unwanted Immigration' (1998) 50 World Politics 266.
Joppke C, 'From Asylum to Labour: Track Change in German Migration Policy' (2023) 47 West European Politics 813.
Klaassen M, 'Between Facts and Norms: Testing Compliance with Article 8 ECHR in Immigration Cases' (2019) 37 Netherlands Quarterly of Human Rights 157.
Kleinlein T, 'The Procedural Approach of the European Court of Human Rights: Between Subsidiarity and Dynamic Evolution' (2019) 68 International and Comparative Law Quarterly 91.
Kochenov D and Pirker B, 'Deporting the Citizens within the European Union: A Counter-Intuitive Trend in Case C-348/09, P.I. v. Overbürgemeisterin Der Stadt Remscheid' (2013) 19 Columbia Journal of European Law 369.
Kostakopoulou D, 'Scala Civium: Citizenship Templates Post-Brexit and the European Union's Duty to Protect EU Citizens' (2018) 56 Journal of Common Market Studies 854.
Kraler A, 'Regularization of Irregular Migrants and Social Policies: Comparative Perspectives' (2019) 17 Journal of Immigrant & Refugee Studies 94.
Kubal A, 'Conceptualizing Semi-Legality in Migration Research' (2013) 47 Law & Society Review 555.
Lakhani SM, 'Producing Immigrant Victims' "Right" to Legal Status and the Management of Legal Uncertainty' (2013) 38 Law & Social Inquiry 442.
Lambert L, 'Extraterritorial Asylum Processing: The Libya-Niger Emergency Transit Mechanism' (2021) 68 Forced Migration Review 18.
Lafleur J-M and Mescoli E, 'Creating Undocumented EU Migrants through Welfare: A Conceptualization of Undeserving and Precarious Citizenship' (2018) 52 Sociology 480.
Lavenex S, 'Migration and the EU's New Eastern Border: Between Realism and Liberalism' (2001) 8 Journal of European Public Policy 24.
Lavenex S, 'Shifting up and out: The Foreign Policy of European Immigration Control' (2006) 29 West European Politics 329.
Lavenex S and Kunz R, 'The Migration–Development Nexus in EU External Relations' (2008) 30 Journal of European Integration 439.
Leerkes A and Van Houte M, 'Beyond the Deportation Regime: Differential State Interests and Capacities in Dealing with (Non-) Deportability in Europe' (2020) 24 Citizenship Studies 319.
Luo S, 'Human Rights Paradox: Explaining the Undeportability of Irregular Chinese Migrants in the UK' (2024) 29 Theoretical Criminology 25.
Lutz F, 'Non-Removable Returnees under Union Law: Status Quo and Possible Developments' (2018) 20 European Journal of Migration and Law 28.
Majcher I and Strik T, 'Legislating without Evidence: The Recast of the EU Return Directive' (2021) 23 European Journal of Migration & Law 103.

Maslowski S, 'The Expulsion of European Union Citizens from the Host Member State: Legal Grounds and Practice' (2015) 4 Central and Eastern European Migration Review 61.

McAdam J, 'The European Union Qualification Directive: The Creation of a Subsidiary Protection Regime' (2005) 17 International Journal of Refugee Law 461.

McHarg A, 'Reconciling Human Rights and the Public Interest: Conceptual Problems and Doctrinal Uncertainty in the Jurisprudence of the European Court of Human Rights' (1999) 62 The Modern Law Review 671.

Menezes Queiroz B, 'Non-Removable Migrants in Europe: An Atypical Migration Status?' (2018) 24 European Public Law 29.

Menjívar C, 'Liminal Legality: Salvadoran and Guatemalan Immigrants' Lives in the United States' (2006) 111 American Journal of Sociology 999.

Miller D, 'Immigrants, Nations, and Citizenship' (2008) 16 Journal of Political Philosophy 371.

Moffette D, 'Governing Immigration through Probation: The Displacement of Borderwork and the Assessment of Desirability in Spain' (2014) 45 Security Dialogue 262.

Montaldo S, 'Offenders' Rehabilitation: Towards a New Paradigm for EU Criminal Law?' (2018) 8 European Criminal Law Review 223.

Morris L, 'Managing Contradiction: Civic Stratification and Migrants' Rights' (2003) 37 The International Migration Review 74.

Nagel T, 'The Problem of Global Justice' (2005) 33 Philosophy & Public Affairs 113.

Nic Shuibhne N, 'Derogating from the Free Movement of Persons: When Can EU Citizens Be Deported?' (2006) 8 Cambridge Yearbook of European Legal Studies 187.

Nic Shuibhne N, 'Limits Rising, Duties Ascending: The Changing Legal Shape of Union Citizenship' (2015) 52 Common Market Law Review 889.

Nimführ S and Sesay B, 'Lost in Limbo? Navigating (Im)Mobilities and Practices of Appropriation of Non-Deportable Refugees in the Mediterranean Area' (2019) 7 Comparative Migration Studies 26.

Oette L and Babiker MA, 'Migration Control à La Khartoum: EU External Engagement and Human Rights Protection in the Horn of Africa' (2017) 36 Refugee Survey Quarterly 64.

O'Leary S, 'Putting Flesh on the Bones of European Union Citizenship' (1999) 24 European Law Review 68.

Ortega F and Peri G, 'The Effect of Income and Immigration Policies on International Migration' (2013) 1 Migration Studies 47.

Ott A, 'Informalization of EU Bilateral Instruments: Categorization, Contestation, and Challenges' (2020) 39 Yearbook of European Law 569.

Ovacık G, Ineli-Ciger M, and Ulusoy O, 'Taking Stock of the EU-Turkey Statement in 2024' (2024) 26 European Journal of Migration and Law 154.

Panizzon M, 'Readmission Agreements of EU Member States: A Case for EU Subsidiarity or Dualism?' (2012) 31 Refugee Survey Quarterly 101.

Papadopoulou A, 'Regularization Programmes: An Effective Instrument of Migration Policy?' (2005) 33 Global Migration Perspectives 1.

Parker O, 'Roma and the Politics of EU Citizenship in France: Everyday Security and Resistance' (2012) 50 JCMS: Journal of Common Market Studies 475.

Perna R and Puig Batalla M, 'Immigrant Regularisation Politics during COVID-19: Advocacy Coalitions and Governments' Incentives in Italy and Spain' (2023) 28 South European Society and Politics 415.

Perry A, 'Law's Boundaries' (2020) 26 Legal Theory 103.

Phuong C, 'Persecution by Third Parties and European Harmonization of Asylum Policies' (2001) 16 Georgetown Immigration Law Journal 81.

Piccoli L and Wanner P, 'The Political Determinants of the Health of Undocumented Immigrants: A Comparative Analysis of Mortality Patterns in Switzerland' (2022) 22 BMC Public Health 804.

Poli S, 'The Integration of Migration Concerns into EU External Policies: Instruments, Techniques and Legal Problems' (2020) 5 European Papers 71.

Rijpma J, 'External Migration and Asylum Management: Accountability for Executive Action Outside EU-Territory' (2017) 2 European Papers 571.
Robertson S, 'Status-Making: Rethinking Migrant Categorization' (2019) 55 Journal of Sociology 219.
Roig A and Huddleston T, 'EC Readmission Agreements: A Re-Evaluation of the Political Impasse' (2007) 9 European Journal of Migration and Law 363.
Schmid L, 'Saving Migrants' Basic Human Rights from Sovereign Rule' (2022) 116 American Political Science Review 1.
Schoukens P and Buttiens S, 'Social Protection of Non-Removable Rejected Asylum-Seekers in the EU: A Legal Assessment' (2017) 19 European Journal of Social Security 313.
Schütze T, 'The (Non-)Status of "Duldung": Non-Deportability in Germany and the Politics of Limitless Temporariness' (2023) 36 Journal of Refugee Studies 409.
Sherlock A, 'Deportation of Aliens and Article 8 ECHR' (1998) 23 European Law Review 62.
Slominski P and Trauner F, 'Reforming Me Softly—How Soft Law Has Changed EU Return Policy since the Migration Crisis' (2021) 44 West European Politics 93.
Soomro A, 'People, Paper and Power: The Birth of the Passport in International Law' (2023) 14 Asian Journal of International Law 1.
Steinorth C, 'Uner v The Netherlands: Expulsion of Long-Term Immigrants and the Right to Respect for Private and Family Life' (2008) 8 Human Rights Law Review 185.
Stoyanova V, 'How Exceptional Must "Very Exceptional" Be? Non-Refoulement, Socio-Economic Deprivation, and Paposhvili v Belgium' (2017) 29 International Journal of Refugee Law 580.
Strik T, 'The Global Approach to Migration and Mobility' (2017) 5 Groningen Journal of International Law 310.
Strik T and Robbesom R, 'Compliance or Complicity? An Analysis of the EU–Tunisia Deal in the Context of the Externalisation of Migration Control' (2024) 71 Netherlands International Law Review 199.
Thym D, 'Respect for Private and Family Life under Article 8 ECHR in Immigration Cases: A Human Right to Regularize Illegal Stay' (2008) 57 International and Comparative Law Quarterly 87.
Thym D, 'When Union Citizens Turn into Illegal Migrants: The Dano Case' (2015) 40 European Law Review 249.
Thym D, 'The Elusive Limits of Solidarity: Residence Rights of and Social Benefits for Economically Inactive Union Citizens' (2015) 52 Common Market Law Review 17.
Trauner F and Kruse I, 'EC Visa Facilitation and Readmission Agreements: A New Standard EU Foreign Policy Tool' (2008) 10 European Journal of Migration and Law 411.
Triandafyllidou A and Yeoh BSA, 'Sustainability and Resilience in Migration Governance for a Post-Pandemic World' (2023) 21 Journal of Immigrant & Refugee Studies 1.
Van Der Leun J, 'Excluding Illegal Migrants in The Netherlands: Between National Policies and Local Implementation' (2006) 29 West European Politics 310.
Van Houte M, Kaşlı Z, and Leerkes A, 'Introduction: Irregularized Humanitarian Migrants—Policies, Rationales, and the Search for More Durable Solutions' (2023) 36 Journal of Refugee Studies 315.
Verschueren H, 'Preventing "Benefit Tourism" in the EU: A Narrow or Broad Interpretation of the Possibilities Offered by the ECJ in Dano?' (2015) 52 Common Market Law Review 363.
Vogel D, Kovacheva V, and Prescott H, 'The Size of the Irregular Migrant Population in the European Union—Counting the Uncountable?' (2011) 49(5) International Migration 78.
Vrbek S, 'Reasons for EU Double Standards: Comparative Overview of the Cases of the Erased and the Non-Citizens' (2015) 43 Nationalities Papers 302.
Warbrick C, 'The Structure of Article 8' (1998) 1 European Human Rights Law Review 32.
Weatherhead KT, 'Removing "Non-Removables"' (2016) 51 Forced Migration Review 2.
Wehinger F, 'Do Amnesties Pull in Illegal Immigrants? An Analysis of European Apprehension Data' (2014) 1 International Journal of Migration and Border Studies 231.

Wong TK and Kosnac H, 'Does the Legalization of Undocumented Immigrants in the US Encourage Unauthorized Immigration from Mexico? An Empirical Analysis of the Moral Hazard of Legalization' (2017) 55 International Migration 159.

Yavuz ÇA, 'Analysis of the EU–Turkey Readmission Agreement: A Unique Case' (2019) 21 European Journal of Migration and Law 486.

Zomignani Barboza J, 'International Protection for Criminals: To Grant or Not to Grant? Lessons from Australia, Belgium, and Canada' (2024) 36 International Journal of Refugee Law 223.

WORKING PAPERS

Baldwin-Edwards M and Zampagni F, 'Regularisations and Employment in Italy' (2014) ICMPD REGANE Assessment Report.

Carrera S, 'The Strasbourg Court Judgement N.D. and N.T. v. Spain. A Carte Blanche to Push Backs at EU External Borders?' (2020) EUI Working Paper RSCAS 2020/21.

Carrera S and Merlino M, 'Assessing EU Policy on Irregular Immigration Under the Stockholm Programme' (2010) Centre for European Policy Studies (CEPS).

Czaika M and de Haas H, 'The Effect of Visa Policies on International Migration Dynamics' (2014) International Migration Institute Working Paper 89.

Delvino N, 'European Cities and Migrants with Irregular Status: Municipal Initiatives for the Inclusion of Irregular Migrants in the Provision of Services' (2017) COMPAS—University of Oxford.

Delvino N, 'The European Union and Migrants with Irregular Status: Opportunities and Limitations in EU Law and Policy for European Local Authorities Providing Assistance to Irregular Migrants' (2018) COMPAS—University of Oxford.

Delvino N, Spencer S, and Cherti M, 'Migrants with Irregular Status in Europe: Guidance for Municipalities' (2024) C-MISE/COMPAS.

Geddes A and Ruhs M, 'Reforming Asylum and Migration Policies in Europe: Attitudes, Realism and Values' (2019) RSCAS Policy Paper 2019/13.

Gibney MJ and Hansen R, 'Deportation and the Liberal State: The Forcible Return of Asylum Seekers and Unlawful Migrants in Canada, Germany and the United Kingdom' (2003) UNHCR New Issues in Refugee Research Working Paper 77.

Hadj-Abdou L, 'From the Migration Crisis to the New Pact on Migration and Asylum: The Status Quo Problem' (2021) BRIDGE Network Working Paper 11.

Hendow M and Qaisrani A, 'Pathways and Policy Evolution: Comparing National Laws and Policies Addressing Irregular Migrants' (2024) MIRREM Working Paper 6/2024.

Kraler A, 'Regularisation: A Misguided Option or Part and Parcel of a Comprehensive Policy Response to Irregular Migration?' (2009) IMISCOE Working Papers.

Kraler A, 'Regularisations—An Instrument to Reduce Vulnerability, Social Exclusion and Exploitation of Migrants in an Irregular Situation in Employment?' (2012) ICMPD, FRA Working Paper.

Limam M and Del Sarto RA, 'Periphery under Pressure: Morocco, Tunisia and the European Union's Mobility Partnership on Migration' (2015) EUI Working Paper RSCAS 2015/75.

Maru MT, 'Migration Policy-Making in Africa: Determinants and Implications for Cooperation with Europe' (2021) EUI Working Paper RSC 2021/54.

Noll G, 'Fixed Definitions or Framework Legislation? The Delimitation of Subsidiary Protection Ratione Personae' (2002) UNHCR New Issues in Refugee Research, Working Paper 55.

Paoletti E, 'Deportation, Non-Deportability and Ideas of Membership' (2010) Refugee Studies Centre Working Paper Series 1.

Parkin J, 'The Criminalisation of Migration in Europe: A State-of-the-Art of the Academic Literature and Research' (2013) CEPS Papers in Liberty and Security in Europe.

Song S and Bloemraad I, 'Immigrant Legalization: A Dilemma between Inclusion and the Rule of Law?' (2021) EUI Working Paper RSC 2021/61.

Vermeulen B and others, 'Persecution by Third Parties' (1998) Nijmegen University Centre for Migration Law 75.

REPORTS AND OTHER ONLINE SOURCES (last accessed 10 February 2025)

Amnesty International, 'A Blueprint for Despair, Human Rights Impact of the EU–Turkey Deal', 14 February 2017, available at: <https://www.amnesty.org/en/documents/eur25/5664/2017/en/>.

Ansems de Vries L and Marta Welander M, 'Politics of Exhaustion: Reflecting on an Emerging Concept in the Study of Human Mobility and Control', *Border Criminologies*, 15 January 2021, available at: <https://www.law.ox.ac.uk/research-subject-groups/centre-criminology/centreborder-criminologies/blog/2021/01/politics>.

Ballesteros M and others, 'Obstacles to the Right of Free Movement and Residence for EU Citizens and Their Families', European Parliament, Study for the LIBE and PETI Committees, September 2016, available at: <https://www.europarl.europa.eu/thinktank/en/document/IPOL_STU(2016)571375>.

Bausager MH, Köpfli Moller J, and Ardittis S, 'Study on the Situation of Third-Country Nationals Pending Return/Removal in the EU Member States and the Schengen Associated Countries', Ramboll and Eurasylum (European Commission), 11 March 2013, HOME/2010/RFXX/PR/1001, available at: <11032013_sudy_report_on_immigration_return-removal_en.pdf>.

BBC, 'Mali Sends Back Migrants Deported by France', 30 December 2016, available at: <https://www.bbc.com/news/world-africa-38467244>.

BBC, 'Turkey Says Millions of Migrants May Head to EU', 2 March 2020, available at: <https://www.bbc.com/news/world-europe-51707958>.

Border Violence Monitoring Network, 'Black Book of Pushbacks', 18 December 2020, available at: <https://borderviolence.eu/black-book-of-pushbacks-2020/>.

Brick K, 'Regularizations in the European Union: The Contentious Policy Tool', *Migration Policy Institute Insight*, December 2011, available at: <https://www.migrationpolicy.org/pubs/EURegularization-Insight.pdf>.

Brunello S and Perego A, 'Obstacles to the Right of Free Movement and Residence for EU Citizens and Their Families: Country Report for Italy', European Parliament, Study for the LIBE and PETI Committees, June 2016, available at: <https://www.europarl.europa.eu/thinktank/en/document/IPOL_STU(2016)556970>.

Cassarino J-P, 'Readmission Policy in the European Union', European Parliament, Study for the LIBE Committee, September 2010, available at: <https://www.europarl.europa.eu/RegData/etudes/etudes/join/2010/425632/IPOL-LIBE_ET%282010%29425632_EN.pdf>.

Cassarino J-P and Marin L, 'The New Pact on Migration and Asylum: Turning European Union Territory into a Non-Territory', *EU Law Analysis*, 30 November 2020, <http://eulawanalysis.blogspot.com/2020/11/the-new-pact-on-migration-and-asylum.html>.

Connor P and Passel JS, 'Europe's Unauthorized Immigrant Population Peaks in 2016, Then Levels Off', Pew Research Centre, 13 November 2019, available at: <https://www.pewresearch.org/global/2019/11/13/europes-unauthorized-immigrant-population-peaks-in-2016-then-levels-off/>.

Cornelisse G and Moraru M, 'Judicial Dialogue about the Return Directive: Which Role for Courts in an Era of Executive Governance?', *EU Immigration and Asylum Law and Policy*, 1 September 2020, available at: <https://eumigrationlawblog.eu/judicial-dialogue-about-the-return-directive-which-role-for-courts-in-an-era-of-executive-governance/>.

Costantini L, 'Madrid crea un "DNI municipal" para los inmigrantes irregulares', *El País*, 28 October 2016, available at: <https://elpais.com/ccaa/2016/10/28/madrid/1477636316_204766.html>.

Costantini L, 'Un año sin 'DNI municipal' para inmigrantes', *El País*, 21 March 2018, available at: <https://elpais.com/ccaa/2018/03/20/madrid/1521565616_452838.html>.

Council of Europe Commissioner for Human Rights, 'Migrants in Limbo in Europe Have the Right to Live in Dignity', Human Rights Comment, Strasbourg, 15 November 2016, available at: <https://www.coe.int/en/web/commissioner/-/migrants-in-limbo-in-europe-have-the-right-to-live-in-dignity?desktop=true>.

Council of the EU, 'Council Adopts Visa Measures against the Gambia', Press Release , 7 October 2021, available at: <https://www.consilium.europa.eu/en/press/press-releases/2021/10/07/council-adopts-visa-measures-against-the-gambia/>.

De Leo A, 'Managing Migration the Italian Way: The "Innovative" Italy–Albania Deal under Scrutiny', Verfassungsblog, 29 October 2024, available at: <https://verfassungsblog.de/managing-migration-the-italian-way/>.

De Leo A, 'On the Incompatibility of the Italy–Albania Protocol with EU Asylum Law', *SIDIBlog*, 15 November 2023, available at: <http://www.sidiblog.org/2023/11/15/on-the-incompatibility-of-the-italy-albania-protocol-with-eu-asylum-law/>.

Dennison J and Geddes A, 'The Fragility of EU Border and Migration Politics', *EUIdeas*, 23 November 2021, available at: <https://euideas.eui.eu/2021/11/23/the-fragility-of-eu-border-and-migration-politics/>.

El País, 'Así se expulsa a un europeo de la UE', 12 January 2014, available at: <https://elpais.com/internacional/2014/01/12/actualidad/1389559237_314818.html>.

Enria N and Gerwens S, 'Greek–Turkish Border Crisis: Refugees Are Paying the Price for the EU's Failure to Reform Its Asylum System', *LSE Blog*, 25 March 2020, available at: <https://blogs.lse.ac.uk/europpblog/2020/03/25/greek-turkish-border-crisis-refugees-are-paying-the-price-for-the-eus-failure-to-reform-its-asylum-system/>.

European Commission, 'EU Turkey Statement Four Years On', March 2020, available at: <https://home-affairs.ec.europa.eu/system/files/2020-03/20200318_managing-migration-eu-turkey-statement-4-years-on_en.pdf#:~:text=Agreed%20on%2018%20March%202016,channels%20to%20Europe%20for%20them>.

European Commission,'Italian Government Adopts Targeted Regularisation for Migrant Workers', 18 May 2020, available at: <https://migrant-integration.ec.europa.eu/news/italian-government-adopts-targeted-regularisation-migrant-workers_en>.

European Commission,'Portugal: More than 356,000 Immigrants Provisionally Legalised during COVID-19 Pandemic', 16 January 2021, available at: <https://migrant-integration.ec.europa.eu/news/portugal-more-356-000-immigrants-provisionally-legalised-during-covid-19-pandemic_en>.

European Commission, 2021 State of the Union Address by President von der Leyen, Strasbourg, 15 September 2021, available at: <https://state-of-the-union.ec.europa.eu/state-union-2021_en>.

European Commission, 'Return and Readmission: Improving Cooperation within the EU and with External Partners', Press Release, Brussels, 10 February 2021, available at: <https://ec.europa.eu/commission/presscorner/detail/en/ip_21_503>.

European Commission, 'Memorandum of Understanding on a Strategic and Global Partnership between the European Union and Tunisia', Press Release, 16 July 2023, available at: <https://ec.europa.eu/commission/presscorner/detail/en/ip_23_3887>.

European Commission, 'Press Statement by President von der Leyen following the Meeting with Spanish Prime Minister Sánchez and Mauritanian President Mohamed Ould El-Ghazouani', 8 February 2024, available at: <https://ec.europa.eu/commission/presscorner/detail/en/statement_24_703>.

European Commission, 'EU–Mauritania Joint Declaration', 8 March 2024, available at: <https://home-affairs.ec.europa.eu/eu-mauritania-joint-declaration_en>.

European Commission, 'Commission Takes Stock of Key Achievements on Migration and Asylum', Press Release, 12 March 2024, available at: <https://ec.europa.eu/commission/presscorner/detail/en/ip_24_1413>.

European Commission, 'Press Statement by President von der Leyen with Austrian Chancellor Nehammer, Belgian Prime Minister De Croo, Cypriot President Christodoulides, Greek Prime Minister Mitsotakis, Italian Prime Minister Meloni and Egyptian President El-Sisi', 17 March 2024, available at: <https://ec.europa.eu/commission/presscorner/detail/en/STATEMENT_24_1521>.

European Commission,'Joint Declaration on the Strategic and Comprehensive Partnership between The Arab Republic Of Egypt and the European Union', News Article, 17 March 2024, available at: <https://neighbourhood-enlargement.ec.europa.eu/news/joint-declaration-strategic-and-comprehensive-partnership-between-arab-republic-egypt-and-european-2024-03-17_en>.

European Commission, 'President von der Leyen Reaffirms EU's Strong Support for Lebanon and Its People and Announces a €1 Billion Package of EU Funding', 2 May 2024, available at: <https://neighbourhood-enlargement.ec.europa.eu/news/president-von-der-leyen-reaffirms-eus-strong-support-lebanon-and-its-people-and-announces-eu1-2024-05-02_en>.

European Commission, 'Pact on Migration and Asylum', 21 May 2024, available at: <https://home-affairs.ec.europa.eu/policies/migration-and-asylum/pact-migration-and-asylum_en>.

European Commission, 'Irregular Migration and Return', 21 March 2024, available at: <https://home-affairs.ec.europa.eu/policies/migration-and-asylum/irregular-migration-and-return_en>.

European Council on Refugees and Exiles (ECRE), 'An Offer You Can't Refuse: The External Dimension', Editorial, 20 November 2020, available at: <https://www.ecre.org/editorial-an-offer-you-cant-refuse-the-external-dimension/>.

European Council on Refugees and Exiles (ECRE), 'A Seamless Link? ECRE's Analysis of Human Rights Risks and Broader Implications Linking Asylum and Return Procedures', Policy Note, 8 November 2021, available at: <https://ecre.org/ecre-policy-note-a-seamless-link/>.

European Council on Refugees and Exiles (ECRE), 'Migration Control Conditionality, a Flawed Model', Policy Note, 9 January 2020, available at: <https://ecre.org/ecre-policy-note-migration-control-conditionality-a-flawed-model/>.

European Council on Refugees and Exiles (ECRE), Weekly Bulletin, 2 March 2021, available at: <https://mailchi.mp/ecre/ecre-weekly-bulletin-02032021?e=989a4aebdd>.

European Court of Auditors, 'EU Readmission Cooperation with Third Countries: Relevant Actions Yielded Limited Results, Special Report 17/2021', 13 September 2021, available at: <https://www.eca.europa.eu/en/Pages/DocItem.aspx?did=59347>.

European Court of Auditors, 'Frontex, Audit Preview', January 2020, available at: <https://www.eca.europa.eu/lists/ecadocuments/ap20_02/ap_frontex_en.pdf>:

European Court of Human Rights, 'Guide on Article 8 of the European Convention on Human Rights', 31 August 2021, available at: <https://www.echr.coe.int/documents/guide_art_8_eng.pdf>.

European Court of Human Rights, 'Guide on the Case Law of the European Convention on Human Rights: Immigration', 31 December 2021, available at: <https://first.vaks.gov.ua/wp-content/uploads/sites/2/2022/02/Guide_Art_8_ENG.pdf>.

European External Action Service (EEAS), 'EU–Afghanistan Joint Declaration on Migration Cooperation', 26 April 2021, available at: <https://www.eeas.europa.eu/eeas/eu-afghanistan-joint-declaration-migration-cooperation_en?s=234>.

European Migration Network (EMN), 'Establishing Identity for International Protection: Challenges and Practices', February 2013, available at: <https://emn.ie/publications/establishing-identity-for-international-protection-challenges-and-practices-emn-synthesis-report/>.

European Migration Network (EMN), 'Good Practices in the Return and Reintegration of Irregular Migrants', Synthesis Report for the EMN Focus Study, 2014, available at: <https://www.emn.at/en/emn-informs-test-en-2-2-2-2-2-2-2-2-2-2-2-2-2/>.

European Migration Network (EMN), 'Responses to Long-Term Irregularly Staying Migrants: Practices and Challenges in the EU and Norway', July 2021, available at: <https://www.emnspain.gob.es/en/-/responses-to-long-term-irregular-staying-migrants-practices-and-challenges-in-the-eu-and-norway>.

European Migration Network (EMN), 'The Different National Practices Concerning Granting of Non-EU Harmonised Protection Statuses', December 2010, available at: <https://emn.ie/publications/the-different-national-practices-concerning-granting-of-non-eu-harmonised-protection-statuses-emn-synthesis-report-2/>.

European Network on Statelessness, 'Statelessness Determination and Status', available at: <https://index.statelessness.eu/themes/statelessness-determination-and-status>.

European Parliament, 'The Proposed Return Directive (Recast) Substitute Impact Assessment', 12 February 2019, available at: <https://www.europarl.europa.eu/thinktank/en/document.html?reference=EPRS_STU(2019)631727>.

European Parliament, 'Agreement between the EU and Ethiopia on Return Procedures, Question for Written Answer to the Commission', Judith Sargentini (Verts/ALE), 15 February 2019, available at: <https://www.europarl.europa.eu/doceo/document/E-8-2018-000957_EN.html>.

European Parliament, 'Prolongation of Detention by Member States of illegally Staying Third-Country Nationals Beyond the 18-month Time Limit in Violation of the Return Directive', Debate 2014/2701 RSP, 17 April 2014, available at: <PV-7-2014-04-17_EN.pdf>.

European Parliament, 'Walls and fences at EU borders', Briefing, 13 December 2022, available at: <https://www.europarl.europa.eu/thinktank/en/document/EPRS_BRI(2022)733692>.

European Parliament, 'Report on the Implementation of the Return Directive' (2019/2208(INI)), 2 December 2020, available at: <https://www.europarl.europa.eu/doceo/document/TA-9-2020-0362_EN.html>.

European Union Agency for Fundamental Rights (FRA), 'Fundamental Rights of Migrants in an Irregular Situation in the European Union', 21 November 2011, available at: <https://fra.europa.eu/en/publication/2012/fundamental-rights-migrants-irregular-situation-european-union>.

European Union Agency for Fundamental Rights (FRA), 'Criminalisation of Migrants in an Irregular Situation and of Persons Engaging with Them', 27 March 2014, available at: <https://fra.europa.eu/en/publication/2014/criminalisation-migrants-irregular-situation-and-persons-engaging-them>.

European Union Agency for Fundamental Rights (FRA), 'The Recast Return Directive and Its Fundamental Rights Implications, Opinion', 10 January 2019, available at: <https://fra.europa.eu/en/publication/2019/recast-return-directive-and-its-fundamental-rights-implications>.

Eurostat, 'Enforcement of Immigration Legislation Statistics', available at: <https://ec.europa.eu/eurostat/statistics-explained/index.php?title=Enforcement_of_immigration_legislation_statistics>.

France 24, 'Stuck in Limbo, Syrians in Denmark Suffer Unbearable Wait', 3 December 2021, available at: <https://www.france24.com/en/live-news/20211203-stuck-in-limbo-syrians-in-denmark-suffer-unbearable-wait>.

Frontex, 'Evaluation Report, Joint Return Operation from Greece to Pakistan on 02 December 2015', Warsaw, 5 February 2016, available at: <https://shorturl.at/TTGeI>.

Frontex, 'Significant Rise in Irregular Border Crossings in 2023, Highest since 2016', News Release, 26 January 2024, available at: <https://www.frontex.europa.eu/media-centre/news/news-release/significant-rise-in-irregular-border-crossings-in-2023-highest-since-2016-C0gGpm>.

García Andrade P, 'EU Cooperation on Migration with Partner Countries within the New Pact: New Instruments for a New Paradigm?', *Immigration and Asylum Law and Policy*, 8 December 2020, available at: <https://eumigrationlawblog.eu/eu-cooperation-on-migration-with-partner-countries-within-the-new-pact-new-instruments-for-a-new-paradigm/>.

García Andrade P, 'Cooperation with Third Countries within the EU Legislative Reform on Migration and Asylum', *EU Immigration and Asylum Law and Policy*, 09 September 2024, available at: <https://eumigrationlawblog.eu/cooperation-with-third-countries-within-the-eu-legislative-reform-on-migration-and-asylum/>.

García Andrade P, Martín I, and Mananashvili S, 'EU Cooperation with Third Countries in the Field of Migration', European Parliament, Study for the LIBE Committee, October 2015, available at: <https://op.europa.eu/en/publication-detail/-/publication/26d712e6-e10a-11e5-8a50-01aa75ed71a1/language-en>.

Gijs C, '"Why are we forgotten?": Undocumented Immigrants Make Stand in Brussels Church', *POLITICO*, 23 February 2021, available at: <https://www.politico.eu/article/belgium-brussels-undocumented-immigrants-church-beguinage-protest/>.

Gil AR, 'Regularisation of Migrants' Status in Portugal: Immigration or Public Health Policy?' *EU Immigration and Asylum Law and Policy*, 4 October 2021, available at: <https://eumigrationlawblog.eu/regularisation-of-migrants-status-in-portugal-immigration-or-public-health-policy/>.

Internation Organisation for Migration (IOM), Missing Migrants Project, available at: <https://missingmigrants.iom.int/>.

International Rescue Committee, 'What Is the EU Turkey Deal?', 18 March 2022, available at: <https://eu.rescue.org/article/what-eu-turkey-deal#:~:text=The%20'EU%2DTurkey%20deal'%20is%20the%20term%20often%20used,Turkey%20to%20the%20Greek%20islands>.

Irish Times, 'New Scheme Will Allow Undocumented Migrants to "Come Out of the Shadow"', 3 December 2021, available at: <https://www.irishtimes.com/news/ireland/irish-news/new-scheme-will-allow-undocumented-migrants-to-come-out-from-the-shadows-1.4745896>.

Kassam A, 'Spain Accuses Morocco of "Show of Disrespect" for EU in Migrant Row', *The Guardian*, 19 May 2021, available at: <https://www.theguardian.com/world/2021/may/19/spain-accused-of-summary-deportations-as-thousands-sent-back-to-morocco>.

Lambert H, 'Nationality and Statelessness before the European Court of Human Rights: A Landmark Judgment But What about Article 3 ECHR?' *Strasbourg Observers*, 16 May 2018, available at: <https://strasbourgobservers.com/2018/05/16/nationality-and-statelessness-before-the-european-court-of-human-rights-a-landmark-judgment-but-what-about-article-3-echr/>.

Lavrysen L, 'M.S.S. v Belgium and Greece (2): The Impact on EU Asylum Law', *Strasbourg Observers*, 24 February 2011, available at: <https://strasbourgobservers.com/2011/02/24/m-s-s-v-belgium-and-greece-2-the-impact-on-eu-asylum-law/>.

Lighthouse Reports, 'Unmasking Europe's Shadow Armies', 6 October 2021, available at: <https://www.lighthousereports.nl/investigation/unmasking-europes-shadow-armies/>.

Lighthouse Reports, 'Desert Dumps', 21 May 2024, available at: <https://www.lighthousereports.com/investigation/desert-dumps/>.

Maru MT, 'Predetermined Bias: Comparing the Visa Rejection Rate of Africans versus the Rest of the World', *Henley Global*, 5 June 2024, available at: <https://www.henleyglobal.com/publications/africa-wealth-report-2024/comparing-visa-rejection-rate-africans-versus-world>.

Mazzilli C, 'Regularising Migrants: Portugal's Missed Chance', *Social Europe*, 6 December 2021, available at: <https://socialeurope.eu/regularising-migrants-portugals-missed-chance>.

Moreno-Lax V and others, 'The EU Approach on Migration in the Mediterranean', European Parliament, Study requested by the LIBE Committee, June 2021, available at: <https://www.europarl.europa.eu/thinktank/en/document/IPOL_STU(2021)694413>.

Naranjo J and Kadner M, 'Gambia paga su rechazo a repatriar a sus nacionales', *El País*, 25 October 2021, available at: <https://elpais.com/internacional/2021-10-25/gambia-paga-su-rechazo-a-repatriar-a-sus-nacionales.html>.

Organization for Security and Cooperation in Europe (OSCE), 'Regularization of Migrants in an Irregular Situation in the OSCE Region: Recent Developments, Points for Discussion and Recommendations', 2 August 2021, available at: <https://www.osce.org/odihr/494251>.

Parkes R and McQuay M, 'Ending the EU's Ambivalence to Free Movement in Africa', *IAI Commentaries*, 13 November 2020, available at: >https://www.iai.it/en/pubblicazioni/ending-eus-ambivalence-free-movement-africa>.

Peers S, ‘Could EU Law Save Paddington Bear? The CJEU Develops a New Type of Protection’, *EU Law Analysis*, 21 December 2014, available at: <http://eulawanalysis.blogspot.com/2014/12/could-eu-law-save-paddington-bear-cjeu.html>.

Peers S, ‘Torture Victims and EU Law’, *EU Law Analysis*, 28 April 2018, available at: <http://eulawanalysis.blogspot.com/2018/04/torture-victims-and-eu-law.html>.

Permanent Observatory on Migration (OPI), ‘Flujo de Autorizaciones de Residencia Concedidas a Extranjeros. Año 2023’, 4 December 2024, available at: <https://www.inclusion.gob.es/web/opi/estadisticas/catalogo/flujo_autorizaciones>.

Permanent Observatory on Migration (OPI), ‘Estadística de personas con autorización inicial de residencia por arraigo: Datos semestrales desde el 30 de junio de 2013 al 31 de diciembre de 2023’ 7, available at: <https://www.inclusion.gob.es/web/opi/estadisticas/catalogo/arraigo>.

PICUM, ‘Regularising Undocumented People in Response to the Covid-19 Pandemic’, 1 July 2020, available at: <https://picum.org/regularising-undocumented-people-in-response-to-the-covid-19-pandemic/>.

PICUM, ‘The COVID-19 Vaccines and Undocumented Migrants: What Are European Countries Doing?’, July 2021 (last updated), available at: <https://picum.org/covid-19-vaccines-undocumented-migrants-europe/>.

PICUM, ‘Regularisation Mechanisms and Programmes: Why They Matter and How to Design Them’, 2022, available at: <https://picum.org/work-area/regularisation/>.

Rietig V, ‘Carrots and Sticks in Migration Cooperation: Three Uncomfortable Truths’, *ICMPD*, 17 January 2024 2, available at: <https://www.icmpd.org/blog/2024/carrots-and-sticks-in-migration-cooperation-three-uncomfortable-truths>.

Rigby J and Crisp J, ‘Fortress Europe’, *The Telegraph*, 20 December 2021, available at: <https://www.telegraph.co.uk/global-health/fortress-europe-borders-wall-fence-controls-eu-countries-migrants-crisis/>.

Shmalz D, ‘Enlarging the Hole in the Fence of Migrants’ Rights, A.A. and others v. North Macedonia’, *Verfassungsblog*, 6 April 2022, available at: <https://verfassungsblog.de/enlarging-the-hole-in-the-fence-of-migrants-rights/>.

Spanish Ombudsman, ‘Informe annual 2022: Volumen I’, 2022 170, available at: <https://www.defensordelpueblo.es/informe-anual/informe-anual-2022/>.

Spielman D, ‘The Judicial Dialogue between the European Court of Justice and the European Court of Human Rights or How to Remain Good Neighbours after the Opinion 2/13’, 27 March 2017, available at: <ECHRCJUEdialog.BRUSSELS.final_.pdf>.

Spijkerboer T, ‘Fact Check: Did the EU–Turkey Deal Bring Down the Number of Migrants and of Border Deaths?’, *Border Criminologies*, 28 September 2016, available at: <https://blogs.law.ox.ac.uk/research-subject-groups/centre-criminology/centreborder-criminologies/blog/2016/09/fact-check-did-eu>

Statewatch, ‘Deportation Union: Rights, Accountability and the EU’s Push to Increase Forced Removals’, 19 August 2020, available at: <https://www.statewatch.org/deportation-union-rights-accountability-and-the-eu-s-push-to-increase-forced-removals/>.

Statewatch, ‘EU Deportations: Overview of Readmission Cooperation in Key Countries’, 9 March 2022, available at: <https://www.statewatch.org/news/2022/march/eu-deportations-overview-of-readmission-cooperation-in-key-countries/>.

Statewatch, ‘EU to Pile Pressure on Iraq to Cooperate with Deportations’, 9 March 2022, available at: <https://www.statewatch.org/news/2022/march/eu-to-pile-pressure-on-iraq-to-cooperate-with-deportations/>.

Statewatch, ‘Germany: Opposition to Ongoing Deportations to Afghanistan’, 11 February 2021, available at: <https://www.statewatch.org/news/2021/february/germany-opposition-to-ongoing-deportations-to-afghanistan/>.

Statewatch, ‘Observatory on the Refugee Crisis in the Med and inside the EU’, 24 November 2015, available at: <https://www.statewatch.org/media/documents/news/2015/nov/eu-med-docs.pdf>.

Thym D, ‘European Realpolitik: Legislative Uncertainties and Operational Pitfalls of the “New” Pact on Migration and Asylum’, *Immigration and Asylum Law and Policy*, 28 September 2020, available at: <http://eumigrationlawblog.eu/european-realpolitik-legislative-uncertainties-und-operational-pitfalls-of-the-new-pact-on-migration-and-asylum/>.

Thym D, 'Secondary Movements: Overcoming the Lack of Trust among the Member States?', *EU Immigration and Asylum Law and Policy*, 29 October 2020, available at: <https://eumigrationlawblog.eu/secondary-movements-overcoming-the-lack-of-trust-among-the-member-states/>.

UNHCR, 'Statement on Subsidiary Protection Under the EC Qualification Directive for People Threatened by Indiscriminate Violence' January 2008, available at: <https://www.unhcr.org/protection/operations/479df9532/unhcr-statement-subsidiary-protection-under-ec-qualification-directive.html>.

UNHCR, 'Public Statement in Relation to Cases Bundesrepublik Deutschland v. B and D pending before the Court of Justice of the European Union', July 2009, available at: <https://www.refworld.org/type,AMICUS,UNHCR,4a5de2992,0.html>.

UNHCR, 'Mapping Statelessness in the Netherlands', November 2011, available at: <https://index.statelessness.eu/resources/mapping-statelessness-netherlands>.

UNHCR, 'Returns from Greece to Turkey (under EU–Turkey statement) as of 31 March 2020', Geneva, 1 April 2020, available at: <https://data2.unhcr.org/en/documents/details/75075>.

Urooba Jamal, 'With Dozens in Limbo, Denmark Pressured to Reverse Refugee Policy', *Al-Jazeera*, 16 November 2021, available at: <https://www.aljazeera.com/news/2021/11/16/rights-groups-pressure-denmark-to-reverse-syria-refugee-policy>.

Valina Hoset R and Roman Vaca C, 'Obstacles to the Right of Free Movement and Residence for EU Citizens and Their Families: Country Report for Spain', European Parliament, Study for the LIBE and PETI Committees, December 2016, available at: <https://op.europa.eu/en/publication-detail/-/publication/fc3b3d49-9a84-11e6-9bca-01aa75ed71a1>.

Van Liempt I and others, 'Evidence-Based Assessment of Migration Deals: The Case of the EU–Turkey Statement', Utrecht University, December 2017, available at: <https://www.kpsrl.org/sites/default/files/2018-08/Van%20Liempt%20Final%20Report.pdf>.

Vanderbruggen M and others, 'Point of No Return: The Futile Detention of Unreturnable Migrants', *Detention Action*, 17 January 2014, available at: <https://ecre.org/point-of-no-return-the-futile-detention-of-unreturnable-migrants/>.

Walter-Franke M, 'Two Years into the EU–Turkey "Deal": Impact and Challenges of a Turbulent Partnership', *Jacques Delors Institut, Berlin*, 15 March 2018, available at: <https://www.delorscentre.eu/en/publications/detail/publication/two-years-eu-turkey-deal-impact-and-challenges-of-a-turbulent-partnership/>.

Wibault T, 'Is There a Space for Humanitarian Protection within Subsidiary Protection? A Reading of M'Bodj', *European Database of Asylum Law*, 5 February 2015, available at: <https://www.asylumlawdatabase.eu/en/journal/there-space-humanitarian-protection-within-subsidiary-protection-reading-m%E2%80%99bodj>.

Index

For the benefit of digital users, indexed terms that span two pages (e.g., 52–53) may, on occasion, appear on only one of those pages.

Figures are indicated by an italic *f*